Ancestors in the Attic:
James Atwater Barrett
Chronicles of a Civil War Union Soldier

James Atwater Barrett
(carte de visite taken October 23, 1863)
and signature (Barrett Collection)

Cover Photo: James Atwater Barrett (seated) and "the Cuffe" [Cuffy/Cuffee] standing behind. This is an original photo from 1863 that was found in our Barrett family collection. Unfortunately, the young man was not identified on the back of the photo. However, this photo was referenced to in the letter written on November 7, 1863 by James' father, George M. Barrett. In doing research, it was found that Cuffe/Cuffy/Cuffee was a traditional Creole name, based on African customs, given to a male child born on Friday.

A compilation of Civil War experiences using
diary entries, letters and documents
This was a Collaborative Effort
By His Direct Descendants:

Leslie James Peterson – Linda J. Peterson
Meliscent Peterson Gill — Patricia Louise Peterson

"Lest We Forget
And for future descendants
I gathered these apples off
The family tree"

© Cousins 2016
ISBN-13: 978-1544240961
ISBN-10: 1544240961
LCCN: 2017900406
www.ancestorsintheattic.net

We dedicate this book in Great Aunt Emma Jane's memory.

Emma Jane Barrett Lothrop [Daughter of James A. Barrett]
Aunt, Artist, Poet, Teacher (Barrett Collection)

It is because of her loving devotion, vision
and collection of family memorabilia
that this book is possible.

Table of Contents

Notes

Abbreviated Barrett Genealogy

(1592-1906)

Humphrey Barrett Sr.
b. 1592 England
Arrived in Concord, MA
d. 7 Nov. 1662
Concord, MA

Humphrey Barrett Jr.
b. 1630 England
d. 3 Jan. 1715
Concord, MA

Benjamin Barrett
b. 7 May 1681
Concord, MA
d. 23 Oct. 1728
Concord, MA

Col. James Barrett
b. 31 July 1710
Concord, MA
d. 11 Apr. 1779
Concord. MA

James Barrett Jr.
b. 4 Jan. 1732
Concord, MA
d. 30 Oct. 1799
Concord, MA

Major James Barrett III
b. 8 Aug. 1761
Concord, MA
d. 12 Sept. 1850
Concord, MA

George Minot Barrett
b. 23 Dec. 1794
Concord, MA
d. 14 July 1873
Concord, MA

Married
Elizabeth
Prescott

Their Six
Children

Married
Isabella K.
Green

#1 George
Prescott Barrett
b. 15 Oct. 1822
Concord, MA
d. 7 Mar. 1827
Concord, MA

#2 Rebecca
Minot Barrett
b. 12 Sept. 1825
Concord, MA
d. 25 June 1879

#6 George
Henry Barrett
b. 17 Aug. 1836
Concord, MA
d. 28 June 1897
Watertown, MA

#5 **James Atwater
Barrett
b. 7 May 1832
Concord, MA
d. 14 Dec. 1885
Brooklyn, NY

#3 Mary
Prescott Barrett
b. 21 Dec. 1827
Concord, MA
d. 7 June 1878
Concord, MA

#4 Emily
Augusta Barrett
b. 14 May 1829
Concord, MA
d. 1906

Married
Nathan Henry
Warren

Married
Charles
Thompson

Married
Jane Farmer

Abbreviated Barrett Genealogy

(1832-Current)

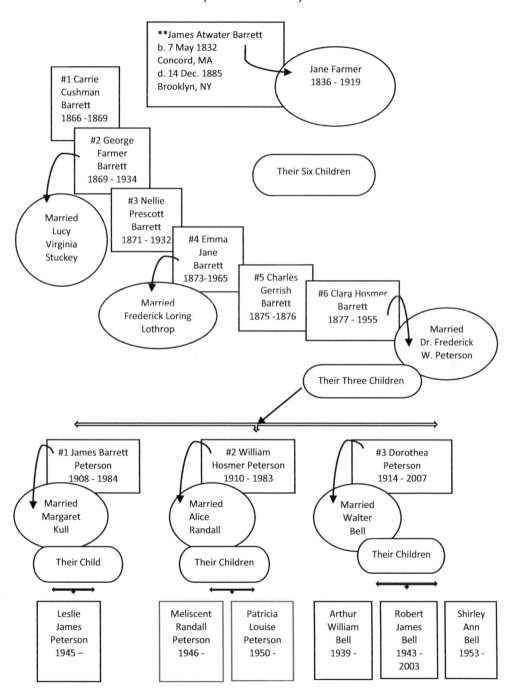

**James Atwater Barrett
b. 7 May 1832
Concord, MA
d. 14 Dec. 1885
Brooklyn, NY

Jane Farmer
1836 - 1919

#1 Carrie Cushman Barrett
1866 -1869

#2 George Farmer Barrett
1869 - 1934

#3 Nellie Prescott Barrett
1871 - 1932

#4 Emma Jane Barrett
1873-1965

#5 Charles Gerrish Barrett
1875 -1876

#6 Clara Hosmer Barrett
1877 - 1955

Their Six Children

Married Lucy Virginia Stuckey

Married Frederick Loring Lothrop

Married Dr. Frederick W. Peterson

Their Three Children

#1 James Barrett Peterson
1908 - 1984

#2 William Hosmer Peterson
1910 - 1983

#3 Dorothea Peterson
1914 - 2007

Married Margaret Kull

Married Alice Randall

Married Walter Bell

Their Child

Their Children

Their Children

Leslie James Peterson
1945 –

Meliscent Randall Peterson
1946 -

Patricia Louise Peterson
1950 -

Arthur William Bell
1939 -

Robert James Bell
1943 - 2003

Shirley Ann Bell
1953 -

Foreword

The beginning of our book, *Ancestors in The Attic* was conceived when the cousins began to explore the letters, papers, scrapbooks and memorabilia (the Barrett Collection) in their attics. From our birth, the Barrett name was prized in our family. The names of James, Meliscent and Barrett were passed down from generation to generation. Members of the family valued the written work, the character of the individual, family history and the village of Concord, Massachusetts. It was felt that each succeeding generation would and should exhibit the characteristics of "loyalty, nobility, worth, honesty and the industry of the ancestors."

Our attics revealed the following: In 1640 nine times Great Grandfather Humphrey Barrett Sr. arrived in Concord, Massachusetts. Fast forward to six times Great Grandfather Colonel James Barrett. He was born in 1710 in Concord, Massachusetts. Farming was his profession. In 1775, he commanded the Concord Militia at the Old North Bridge defeating the English (the first American resistance to the British).

We now move forward to our hero, Great Grandfather, James Atwater Barrett. He was born May 7, 1832 in Concord, Massachusetts. He moved from Concord to Brooklyn, New York in the 1850s. James enlisted in the Union Army in 1861 as a Sergeant.

James A. Barrett's birthplace in Concord, MA (Barrett Collection)

James Atwater Barrett kept diaries with entries from 1864 to 1865. It is unknown if he kept diaries or journals of the earlier years. They are yet to be found. James used his correspondence and diaries (dated from 1861 to 1865) as references, as well as his own personal recollections when he completed the original draft of the narrative account of his Civil War experiences as his contribution to *The Prescott Memorial: Or A Genealogical Memoir of the Prescott Families in America. In Two Parts*[i] written by William Prescott, M.D. It was published in 1870. The Prescott transcription of James' final submission, in its entirety, may be found in the Endnotes.

The collection of James' Civil War correspondence to and from his family members and friends, Emily's (one of James' sisters) journal entries, as well as various communications, original documents, original narrative and photographs were safely secured, treasured and stored by Jane "Jennie" Farmer Barrett. The original letters were distributed among family members after being "transcribed" by his daughter Emma Jane and later distributed to two nephews and a niece (pictured below) to be cherished and for safekeeping.

William, James and Dottie
Peterson (L to R)
(Barrett Collection)

The family truly appreciates their Great Aunt Emma Jane's painstaking labor of love. This was done in a time before the modern conveniences of copying machines and computers. Some of the copies are handwritten, typed and others are carbon paper[1] duplicates.

Emma Jane's father had died suddenly when she was about twelve years old. The memories of her father were the recollections that she had as a child and the precious memorabilia that had been lovingly kept in trunks, boxes and scrapbooks. At times, it must have been bittersweet; as well as a blessing for her to reread her father's letters and diaries. Emma Jane wanted her young nephews and niece as well as their descendants to

---

[1] A thin piece of paper that has a dark waxy substance on one side. It is placed between two pieces of paper when using a typewriter to make duplicate documents and letters.

come to know the Grandfather that had long passed before their births. Emma Jane possessed tender memories of her father that she has shared with the family.

The cousins found a note written to Emma Jane when she was a little girl. It is implied that Emma Jane must have been ill with a high fever when her father left this note for her. The "girls" could easily be interpreted as her dolls that she sought for comfort.

"Dear Daughter

Good morning. Here I am so near and yet so far. <u>Near</u> because I stand close beside you, and <u>far</u> because you do not perceive me with your material eyes, hence there seems that absence, that remoteness. But I rejoice that I can be with you, and though you do not see me, you can see my written message and that reassures you that I am still alive and conscious. Do not forget me or that I ever forget you.

Tell the girls I came.   Father

James A. Barrett"

[A postscript was added by her sister]

"You may feel me touch your forehead…Nelly"

Emma Jane included the following cherished recollection at the beginning of one of the copies of her father's narrative. She remembered "quietly combing the Isthmus of Panama across a bald spot on his head, while he, as quietly, read his paper." Not the usual observation between a father and child that one would expect in the 1880's. She wrote that "he was our beloved companion, and tired as he was, he would lie down on our hair cloth sofa in the parlor, and close his eyes. Meanwhile, we [George F, Nell P., Clara H and I] would quietly wait over and around him, for the story to begin with, "Once upon a time…""

Barrett children as young adults, L to R:
George; Nell (middle-top); Clara (middle-lower);
Emma Jane (Barrett Collection)

As James' original narrative account was copied and recopied; Emma Jane also included small embellishments to illustrate her transcriptions. We have included several of her pen and ink drawings. These do not diminish the work but enhance it. Some of the sketches were inspired by the 1885 edition of the *48th Regt. N.Y.S.Vols.* (48th Regiment New York State Volunteers). We have also included several Carte de visite portraits from our collection. These small affordable photos were very popular during that time period.

We doubt seriously that James thought that his diaries, letters or the original draft of his narrative would ever be published. One should not read the following pages expecting a scholarly work, but very personal observations.

The terminology, grammar, punctuation and "turn of the phrase" had not been changed or corrected or so we thought. As the cousins read what was thought as the original narrative, diaries and letters; we found that Emma Jane had done some editing and added a few of her own flourishes. As an example, please see the first page of Chapter 1. Did she feel at times that it wasn't appropriate, uninteresting or too personal? Unfortunately, those questions go unanswered.

We found that James' uncorrected documents had a certain charm when reading them in their original form. It was decided that adding extra spacing did help with clarity and readability. James used various symbols: "@" to mean "a"; "&" to mean "and"; "&c" to mean "etcetera" throughout his letters. He always signed his letters using a complete signature. It was also thought that it was a convenience to the reader to change the style of font to help differentiate between the various diary entries (James' and Emily's), letters (to and from family and friends), and James' narration.

We have discovered that Emma Jane had access to letters that are as yet to be in our personal possession. A letter was found in the Gerrish Papers in the Special Collections of The Concord Free Library at Concord, Massachusetts. Another letter was found in an old trunk that was owned by George F. Barrett (James' son) in an abandoned outbuilding in Nebraska. Unfortunately, the trunk and its contents is a lost treasure.

Another discovery was the original handwritten register for Company "H" 48th New York State Volunteers that the family has kept in its collection. Utilizing a variety of resources[2]; it was thought that first and last names of the soldiers (if discernible) should be included in the index and hopefully prove helpful to those interested parties undertaking research. It was felt that it also honors those individuals who experienced such turbulent and at times horrific conditions. The index has been constructed to

---

[2] Adjutant General's Office, S.O. (1864). *Record of the Commissioned Officers, Non-Commissioned Officers, and Privates in the Civil War Volumes 1 and 2.* Comstock & Cassidy. Adjutant General's Office, S.O. (1866). *Annual Report of the Adjutant General of the State of New York.* C. Wendell. Adjutant General's Office. S.O. (1893). *48th New York Infantry Soldier Roster-Annual Report of the Adjutant General of the State of New York For the Year 1893*, Volume 24 New York State Archives. (ca.1861-1900). *Civil War Muster Roll Abstracts of New York State Volunteers, United States Sharpshooters, and United States Colored Troops.*

identify individual soldiers by military rank. The individuals may be listed in more than one category.

James A. Barrett exhibits strong feelings about the abolition of slavery. The intensity of his attitude may have been influenced by family members. One of his brother-in-laws, Nathan Henry Warren, was a "conductor" for the Underground Railroad. His terminology becomes perplexing when reading the references that James makes regarding his own servants and people of color. It is a complex contradiction which should be viewed in terms of the time and what might then be considered acceptable.

He worked, in the last few years of his life, to actively contribute to the publication of *The History of the Forty-Eighth Regiment New York State Volunteers* written in 1885 by Abraham J. Palmer, D.D. Dr. Palmer attributed the publication of the history of the regiment to Major James A. Barrett. Unfortunately, James died on December 14, 1885 and never saw the finished manuscript. However, it was published just in time for a copy to be placed upon his coffin.

We have included a brief and simplistic Barrett genealogy and endnotes. This was done with our children in mind to help them to begin to understand the complexity of their family history and relationships. James courted and married his third cousin, Jane Farmer. This was not an unusual occurrence in the Barrett and related family genealogy. Similar circumstances were fairly common for families of that era. The family tree is an intricate intertwinement. Family members enjoyed close bonds and at times, it offered career opportunities. James noted in his narrative that he worked for J.P. Swain, Inc. in New York. The owners of the company were his uncle and cousin.

The footnotes found in this book may at times seem simplistic and naïve. James used terminology including military terms, references to political events, regional idioms and reflections of social subtleties that were unfamiliar to us. The footnotes have helped us to broaden our understanding about the Civil War era and gave us glimpses into social interactions of that time. We found items of forgotten information scattered throughout the letters. Some items were found to be entertaining pieces of trivia (i.e. a baseball game or gingerine) and others were sobering reminders of reality (i.e. finding women on the battlefield or meeting survivors of Andersonville.)

The endeavor that we have been led to accomplish would not have been possible without the guidance and good counsel that we have received during the entire process. Our many thanks to:

Jim Cunningham (Col. James Barrett Farm Project Manager and Barrett Family
	Genealogy)
Karen Cumins Freeburg (Retired Attorney at Law, good friend and persevering
	volunteer proofreader and editor)
William Dietrick, M.D. (Surgeon)
Luis M. Evans (Author of *So Rudely Sepulchered: The 48th New York Volunteer Infantry
	Regiment During the Campaign for Charleston, July 1863* and member of the
	48th New York Volunteer Infantry Reenactors)

Michael Gill (Husband, cousin, friend and gourmet chef who lovingly prepared meals for us that encouraged, fortified and sustained us to complete this huge task)

Peter Glyer (Retired from the Army Corps of Engineers, Volunteer Docent at Fredricksburg, Virginia)

Justin Johnson (Book Conservator, Huntington Library, San Marino, California)

Alan Jutzi (Retired Curator, Rare Books, Huntington Library, San Marino, California)

Sean Barrett Peterson (Son, cousin, computer technical advisor and social webmaster)

Gloria Swift (Retired Park Ranger/Curator, Fort Pulaski, Georgia)

Glenn Togawa (Retired Architect from Togawa Smith Martin, Inc., Los Angeles, California)

Leslie Wilson (Curator of the Library Special Collections, Concord Free Public Library, Concord, Massachusetts),

Mike Weinstein (Park Ranger, Fort Pulaski, Georgia).

The family collection (the Barrett Collection, named in honor of our ancestors) containing original documents, letters, photos and memorabilia will be donated, following publication of this book, to the Concord Free Public Library, Special Collections at Concord, Massachusetts to help continue the family story and to assist further research.

Chapter 1

Every Story Has a Beginning

> Spring of 1861-October 26, 1861—James works at JP Swain & Co.,
> New York—Enlists in the 48th Regiment New York State Volunteers[ii]--
> Receives marching orders--Ends up at Ft. Monroe waiting to sail for
> the South

[Note that all the following transcriptions have been faithfully copied from the original documents, as written by James, except where noted.]

First page of Emma's "transcription" of James' narrative (Barrett Collection).
This is a great example of Emma Jane's interpretation of her father's documents.
To the reader: please note the differences between her edited version
and James' original narration.

[*James' first draft of narrative]
    When the War broke out in the spring of 1861   I was a clerk in the employ of JP
Swain & Co Front St N.Y.   A Republican in politics I looked upon Slavery as the vital
cause of all our troubles: the cancer eating at the very root of our Nation's life & I felt a

conviction that in some way unknown to any except Him who holdeth the destinies of nations in his power this war was destined to remove this blot from our National honor

Of course I was not indifferent to the stirring scenes which aroused our militia & sent them to the defense of the Capitol but I did not at first enter into the military spirit further than to join a company for the purpose of drilling & preparing for what might happen We drilled 2 hours every night

[*Letter]
Excuse this paper I did not notice the stains until after I had written one page

Brooklyn April 21 1861
Dear Father
Yours of 16th came to hand yesterday I am very glad to hear that you are so much better &[3] hope pray that you may soon be entirely well. & Now the spring has so far advanced I presume we have received her severest blasts & may look for milde & settled weather & with   I trust your rheumatism will leave you. I am glad you are so well provided with good help so that you can feel that affairs outside are not going to rack & ruin in your absence. Please remember me to Martin & tell him to keep his tools sharp & his Musket clean.These are exciting times I never saw New York in such @[4] tumult. War seems to be the Motto of the day We hear it in thunder tones from the cannon's mouth The electric wire sends it to distant points The press takes it up & circulates it in every town & hamlet in the Nation It is discussed at every fireside & is the all absorbing topic of conversation on the street the counting room & the places of public resort The Pulpit adds its testimony to this universal outburst of patriotism & If Prayers are of any avail (& I truly believe they are) The Patriots who have gone forth in their countries cause may rest assured that they are the objects of special remembrance from thousands & tens of thousands sincere hearts at that Bar where justice & mercy are rendered without stint or measure. Flags without number displaying the Stars & Stripes unfurl their ample folds to the winds of Heaven. So that the very air we breathe seems charged & recharged with Patriotism In fact the spirit of 75 has returned & judging from present appearances It has not lost @ whit of vigor from its four score years of slumber Every new dispatch is received with eager interest by all classes of our people Men Women & children all alike seem thoroughly aroused in this hour of need. The firm determination of our people is to stand by the Constitution & the union & when the late dispatches brought accounts of blood spilt

Wild excitement settled down into honest Indignation.   & Our recruiting list told the result Merchants are generally giving their clerks who wish to go Their time free & their salaries continued   J Frye & Co's Bookkeeper goes today Clark is talking of going & even I have got my sluggish blood so aroused that I am ready to go when my Country needs me But at present while better men than I are offering so freely I think I perhaps can serve my countries cause as well here as anywhere. Some must stay at home But I must say when I see some men with families

---

[3] Throughout his letters, James uses the symbol "&" instead of writing the word "and".

[4] James uses the symbol "@" to mean the word "a" throughout his letters.

<u>too</u> going so freely I do feel as if I ought to go who have no family & no one depending upon me for support. Gerrish feels much the same But thinks his health hardly equal to the task We are both going to join @ company this week "The home guard" for the purpose of drilling & becoming somewhat acquainted with Military tactics   So in case our services should be needed they would be all the more usefull & we would trust to Providence to give us the necessary strength to endure the trials & hardships of the Camp. I see by the paper that 64 men have gone from Concord Is this so & who have gone that I know Mrs Nayes hailed me at Church this morning & asked me if I had heard & wanted me to let her know when I heard about it. We raised over $80. this morning at church to make under garments & flannels for volunteers. When I think of the Company from Concord I almost wish myself among them have they gone yet if not when are they going I would like to see them & give them God's speed when they pass through here

Now don't you be anxious on my account I don't suppose it is at all probable that I shall go. I am @ Coward   I may as well as confess it Altho if I know my own heart I would go if duty called & if I did not think that there are plenty better or hardier men thanI who are ready & anxious to go Mother alludes to Charley & Gorge as liable to go I suppose she left me out on account of my deaf ear   But I was ashamed to give that as an excuse for not doing jury duty & I certainly should not offer it as an excuse for not bearing arms in my Countries defence. I trust & hope that Our country will come out of the troubles that now assail us purer & stronger than before   That the accursed dross[5] of slavery will be purged from among us & that we may in future be in fact what we have long been in theory @ free people respecting the rights & interests of all high or low rich or poor black or white   Then indeed shall we be able to realize that although this cup seemed bitter Yet it was only so to our imperfect perception & that God in his administration of human affairs often "Behind @ frowning providence hides @ shining Face" I have full confidence in our Administration. I feel as if they were inspired with more than earthly wisdom & that the God of nations has raised them up for the special purpose of saving this Country the progress & prosperity of which has never been equaled in the history of the world from the danger which threatens it.

I think this will do for now my paper is giving out & so am I   please write soon. with much love to all I remain as ever Your son, Jas. A. Barrett

---

[5] Meaning the remains, dregs or refuse. dross. (n.d.) COLLINS ENGLISH DICTIONARY – COMPLETE AND UNABRIDGED. (1991, 1994, 1998, 2000, 2003). Retrieved November 1, 2015, from http://www.thefreedictionary.com/dross

Carte de visite of James' sister, Emily Augusta Barrett Thompson
(Barrett Collection)

[Emma Jane's transcription of Emily Augusta Barrett's first journal entry]
Sat. May 18, 1861
Brother James walked in very unexpectedly and glad we were to see him. He is only going to stay a short time.

[*Letter]

New York   May 25 1861

Dear Father
I suppose you want to hear how the folks here received the news I brought. I arrived safely thursday morning. & have waited til now before writing hoping to get @ letter from home advising me of further news. I enclose 20 Dolls which I borrowed of you. Charley[6] had not rec^d my letter & did not get it till after I saw him. He thinks he should have been taken rather by surprise if he had rec^d it in due time He & the Bates's[iii] are opposed to my enlisting I told Mr Swain[iv] & I think he is much pleased with the idea of my going to washington I knew well enough he would.

I am drilling hard every night. & hope to be soon qualified to do good service when My Country calls It is rather strange how things get round But I find it is already quite current here that I am bound for the <u>South</u> Our Company here are talking strongly of organizing under the State Militia laws & increasing our number to 150 & then send off @ company of those who feel like going But I would prefer to go from home & hail from old Concord & I am therefore anxiously

---

[6] James is referring to his cousin, Charles Pickering Gerrish. In 1860, they were both listed in the Federal Census as living in the same household as the Bates in Brooklyn, New York. *United States Census Office. 8th Census, 1860*. (1860). U.S. Census, 1860. Washington, D.C.: Govt. Print. Office (See endnotes)

waiting to hear further news   What has been heard from Our Company at the Seat of war? I don't know why it is   I cannot explain to myself But I sort of feel as if my fate was bound up & identified with that company & I am prepared to accept the issue. I presume you think it strange that I who always rather shrank from danger should be so anxious to join the Army. But there is @ higher power that tunes our hearts & gives us courage to perform the duties that are required of us & face the dangers with which those duties are attended. Believe me it is no love for war which urges me on   Nor am I attracted by that love for adventure which is so strong with many. I deserve no credit for being willing to go. It would be @ discredit to do otherwise Our Country is in danger   It must & shall be sustained. & I should be unworthy of my Country under whose free institutions I have grown & been prospered. unworthy of my Ancestry whose untarnished name I bear (@ God forbid that I be first to disgrace it) unworthy of the liberty I love & False to my God if I were unwillingly to devote my energies & my life if need be to the defence & maintenance of those principles which I have been taught to love & without which life itself is not worth the asking But It may be said I am not needed there are plenty others who are ready & willing to go   It may be so   There may be those who are willing to do my duty for me. But what earthly right have I to ask another to do duties which belong to me & entrench myself in some ark of safety vanily hoping that the storm that beats so harshly on some may fail to reach & trouble me. I should be worse than those people of Old who when bidden to the feast or wedding "All of one accord began to make excuse" If there is excuse for any one it is for those who have cares & responsibilities to keep them at home or who are disabled by sickness or infirmity. Neither of which will include me. I am therefore waiting anxiously to get my summons   I would prefer to go on & start from home But can join @ company when they get here if necessary. I was pleased to witness the spirit (which possessed nearly everyone at the east.) of willingness to sacrifice money & friends for the common cause This is as it should be. The courage of those who go must be supported by the courage of those who remain. We must waste no time with idle words or soft sentimentalities The time for action has come. The Campaign is fairly opened   The Battle is waging   The excitement here is intense   The assassination of Col Elsworth[v] excited the sympathy of all   He was @ Noble fellow & will be greatly missed   But his brave followers spurred on by the memory of his fall will soon give their enemies cause to know that they are not men to be trifled with. But enough of this   I fear I have already dwelt too long on this subject   Mr Dakin is here   I expect to meet him at Mr Leete's tomorrow afternoon. You will probably see him so I need not say much about him here suffice to say the Pike's Peak affair[7] is @ joint % & until it is tested an experiment They have some Butter on the way here which I am going to sell for them or JPS & Co will sell it if I am not here.

   I hope you will not try to do any hard work
   You must take life easy & not overtax your strength   I have not time to write more now

---

[7] Gold was discovered in the area of present-day Denver in 1858, and newspapers referred to the gold-mining area as "Pike's Peak."

Please write soon or get some of the others to write all the news   With much love to all I remain as ever

Yours affectionately

Jas. A. Barrett

Mrs. Bates was much pleased with the seeds Rebecca sent. The weather is fine here & things are looking finely

Carte de visite of Mrs. Mary Holbrook Covington Bates
(Barrett Collection)

[Emma Jane's transcription of Emily's journal entry]
Sat. June 1, 1861
Brother James visit gave us much joy but it was mingled with sadness when we learned his mission home; it was to enroll his name among the volunteers for the war and although I would not utter a word to discourage his going when his conscience so dictated, I began to realize as never before the bitterness of that parting when a dear friend or brother goes forth to meet the hardships and privations of the camp and the dangers of the battlefield leaving fond and anxious hearts waiting with hope and fear for the issue. Poor James seems to be baffled in all his efforts to serve his country. He returned last week on Wed. to New York.

[*Narrative]
Then came the news of Bull Run[8] which sounded through the land & the President's call for 75000 came home to all who loved their Country & bade them do their best to defend it   I always had a great horror of war & it seemed as if nothing could tempt me to join in its bloody scenes   But now it seemed as if all who could   should go   I was just in my prime of life 29 & had no responsibilities to keep me at home   I gave up my situation & enlisted in the 48th Regt N. Y. S. Vols[9]   Co H. with Col Jas H. Perry

Col. James H. Perry
(*48th Regt. N.Y.S.Vols.*, A.J. Palmer, D.D., 1885)

[Emma Jane's transcription of Emily's journal entry]
　　　Sat. July 13, 1861
　　　Had a letter from James this week. He continues wishing to go to the war and thinks of joining a company forming there unless he can join one from Concord. It is dreadful to think of a dear friend being shot down or wounded by a cruel and heartless foe with no dear one to care for him. War is a terrible evil. I hope that the cause of it, slavery, will be rooted out of existence never more to pollute our land, demoralizing its people and making human beings barbarians.

---

[8] The First Battle of Bull Run was fought on July 21, 1861, in Prince William County, Virginia.
[9] The 48th was organized at Brooklyn, N.Y., on September 10, 1861. The Regiment became known as "Perry's Saints" or "The Continental Guard".

[*Narrative]
We went into Camp near Fort Hamilton N Y Harbor on July 27/ 61 about 100 men in all Capt D W Strickland my old drill master was my Capt[n] & He appointed me 1st or Orderly Serg[t] of my co   We remained there recruiting drilling &c[10] until our Reg[t] was large enough to be mustered[11] when we went to Annapolis   Here we commenced to draw our rations & cook them by companies & I found my position not an enviable one   The prescribed ration is ample such as it is if properly economized   But it sometimes would happen if a Soldier had a day's supply given him he would eat it all at one meal & then think it hard that he could get no more till the next day The pork was too fat or the Beef too salt   In fact I found myself surrounded by grumblers & I was expected to satisfy them I found it useless to argue with them

But I happily hit on another plan   I selected a good man for head cook & whenI found an inveterate grumbler put him in to assist for a week & see if he could make things hold out better   This answered the purpose   I found as a general thing those who found most fault had had the poorest bringing up   My Capt was an excellent drillmaster & all my officers were very popular with the company & our Co soon came to be one of the best drilled in the Reg[t]

We all felt a Co pride & I always tried to encourage this feeling While at annapolis we were ordered to equalize companies   There were 2 companies only about half full & others had more than the regular number   This seemed very hard as most of the men enlisted in their respective companies from choice. One Co was all raised In one town & vicinity & bound together by ties of friendship & they had to select out 15 & send to other companies Our Company had to give away 11 & the unpleasant duty of selecting them fell on me   Of course I selected as a general thing the poorest soldiers & it was not a pleasant task. Altho the improved military appearance of the company somewhat compensated for it We were brigaded[12] here under Gen[l] Vielie & rec[d] our Flag

---

[10] James uses the symbol "&c" to mean "etcetera".

[11] To call (troops) together, as for inspection. /To cause to come together; gather/To call forth; summon up/To assemble. (n.d.). *American Heritage Dictionary of the English Language, 4th edition*. Retrieved December 7, 2015, from http://www.yourdictionary.com/muster

[12] A military unit having its own headquarters and consisting of two or more regiments, squadrons, groups, or battalions. brigaded. (n.d.). *Dictionary.com Unabridged*. Retrieved November 02, 2015, from http://dictionary.reference.com/browse/brigaded

48th N.Y. S. Vols. Flank marker
(Courtesy of N.Y. State Military Museum)

Lt. Col. Dudley W. Strickland
(Carte de visite, courtesy of N.Y. State Military Museum)

[*Letter]

Brooklyn   July 28 1861

Dear Friends
     One week has passed since our great defeat & I am glad to say that the frightful report which at first cast our country into @ state of universal anxiety & gloom have proved to be greatly exagerated. In fact I can hardly acknowledge it @ <u>defeat</u> in spite of its disastrous results except in the sense that Sumpter was
     For Our Troops were more than victorious & crowned themselves with undying glory in every instance where they had anything like an equal contest   But Masked Batteries supported by overwhelming odds in numbers aided by deception fraud from which no civilized people have ever been base enough to adopt are obstacles not easily over come
     This whole affair is much to be deplored But still there is @ bright side to every picture although we often fail to see it & <u>this</u> has <u>its</u> lesson to that officious meddling class of people & who not content with leaving their own duty undone are continually prying into other people's

16

business criticising things which they know nothing about & passing judgment upon people whom their narrow minds fail to appreciate I trust in future that military matters will be left to Military men & whether it takes 6 mo^s or 6 years let us abide the result I do not yet learn anything of the future movements of the Mass 5th I see they were in the thick of the Battle & that their Col was wounded & several of the Concord Boys missing It is painfull to be in suspense I suppose the friends are very anxious I see Cyrus Hosmer's name among the missing How do his friends bear it what is the affect upon the pluck of the men as to enlisting   If I could have been certain that Concord would send another company if the other returned   I should rather have waited & gone in that way as @ private than to go from here as I expected to soon as @ non commissioned officer. But in times like these there is @ demand for decision & action & we must not consult too much our own preference or allow our personal desires to stand in the way of our national or public duties. The Continental Guard Col Perry are advertised to go into Camp this week & If nothing happens to prevent I go with them we shall most likely remain in camp about @ month as our recruits are mostly fresh from the country & will need considerable discipline & drilling. I have the promise of 1st Sargeant. It was offered unsought by me by our worthy Capt Strickland who has been Capt of our union Rifles & under whom I have been drilling the last 2 or 3 mo^s My duties I expect will be arduous & I confess as I am comparatively @ novice in the business I shall enter upon them with somemisgivings But with the blessing of Heaven I hope I may soon become with some instruction& study competent to perform whatever may be required of me

If I find I am not equal to the position I presume I shall be permitted to resign & go into the ranks & in the daily routine of @ soldiers life content myself with the idea that I can at least do my Duty. & that all that can be expected of any whether that Duty be to command or to obey. One question of Em's I neglected to answer Sterner Duties have interposed between me & JP Swain & Co & in anticipation of these I have not urged other claims & do not intend to beg for any future favors Ellen Wood has @ daughter doing well The weather here is very warm & sultry. If I go in to Camp as I expect I would be happy to see any of my friends there   I saw Stacy & Geo Hayward here last week on their return from Washington Stacy thinks Prescott will not want to return

Aunt wrote that Ned Barrett had joined the Mass 5th It was @ mistake He was at Washington & went out to witness the Battle But was not @ participant. The effect here is to make the firm firmer & the weak & timid more timid & hopeless still. But our cause is just & As firmly as I believe the "Lord God Omnipotent Ruleth" so firmly do I believe that we shall conquer in the end   I do not think that the people are quite ready yet to look the real issue in the face.   That issue firmly I believe is Slavery or Freedom & The Plagues of Egypt will surely be revisited in some shape upon our people untill they will rise in their might & say "Let my people go" We are daily seeing the fruits of this barbarous system & under the present state of things it surely can not be long before our people will weigh seriously the question whether they will longer permit this deadly

"Upas Tree"[13] to send forth its deadly venom to poison & degrade the hearts of our fellow men. You will see in Henry's tribune @ very good letter from Gerritt Smith to Mr Breckenridge It is well worth reading. There is danger I think in times like these of allowing our sympathies to overpower our Judgment   We must not permit our resentment to settle into revenge & hate   We ought to pity as well as blame the errors of our enemies & endeavour with Christian Zeal to revive their Crucified Consciences. With much
love to all   I remain

Yours very truly
Jas.A.Barrett

If Aunt comes on soon I wish you would send @ small bottle of hot drops[vi] by her & I would like to know what that filter is called that E. Barrett got I don't know whether I can get one here or not But presume I can

> *[Emma Jane's transcription of Emily's journal entry]*
>   Sat. Sept 21, 1861
>   *Brother James has, I suppose gone to Washington. Have not heard from him from there I cannot realize that he has gone to the war but am glad that I cannot as I should feel worse if I did. May a kind Heavenly Father watch over him and bless him.*

[*Letter]
 Capitol Hill, Washington, D.C.
 Camp Sherman, Sept 30 1861

Dear Friends at home
        We are under marching orders. Ere another Sun has risen we may be face to face with the enemy Our Knapsacks are packed & will be left behind. We only take our Blankets Canteens & Haversacks[14]. with 30 rounds Cartridges each. Where we are to march we none of us know But our men are eager to start. We have not turned out so full @ company since we came here as this afternoon after the order came to make ready Those who were on the sick list were by some magic power suddenly restored. I presume that the smell of gunpowder in the Cartridges I dealt

---

[13] A tall tropical Asian tree of the mulberry family with a latex that contains poisonous glycosides used as an arrow poison. Applied to anything baneful or of evil influence. Upas. (n.d.). *Merriam-Webster Online Dictionary*. Retrieved December 7, 2015, from http://www.merriam-webster.com/dictionary/upas

[14] A small canvas bag, about one foot square, used to carry a soldier's food. Typically, these bags were painted with black tar to make them waterproof. Civil War Trust. (2014). Haversack. Glossary of Civil War Terms: Improve Your Civil War Vocabulary. Retrieved November 2, 2015,from http://www.civilwar.org/education/history/glossary/glossary.html

out had @ peculiar charm in it. We are the 1st Company & take the rights of the line. I wish we were better drilled But we must do our best & trust to Providence[15] for the result. I can hardly realize that we are on the eve of battle But if we are called on to go forward I for one do not fear to go. The time was when I shrank from the dangers of the field But I have outgrown that. I feel that my life, my hopes, my duties to my Country my friends & my God as well as my own self respect are now at stake & if any efforts or sacrifice of mine can help to free us from our present troubles I will willingly make them.

I recd today letters from Aunt G Charley & Mrs Bates & heard through them that you were well It is impossible to say where tomorrow night may find us. We may be among the living & we may be reckoned among those who have said their last good night. But whatever the issue We know that He who mindeth the sparrows when they fall ordereth all things well In his hands I am content to stay so long as I feel that I am trying in my feeble way to do my duty faithfully. & I am sure you will feel the same. If I live I shall get an experience that will be worth @ lifetime. If I fall I cannot fall in @ better cause & @ few years of time will count as nothing in the balance

We have prayer meetings nearly every night in camp But I cannot enjoy them much The Methodist element is very strong & they approach @ little too nearly to the Camp Meeting order for my taste I am reminded of the passage in scripture about The Kingdom of Heaven <u>suffering</u> from violence &c We have some exceptions One of the Captains who ranks next to us is @ Methodist Minister & I admire him & our Captain's father who is also our Chaplain is also @ Methodist of the milder stamp

My Health is very good. I passed the medical examination without any trouble 3 of our 100 men were rejected. I am very busy & my time fully occupied I never knew time go so fast as since I came into Camp I sleep on the ground with my rubber under & my blanket over me We draw our Co rations & cook them ourselves which is no small job 123 lbs Beef 8 lbs of coffee 15 lbs of sugar 98 loaves Bread 10 lbs coffee 8 qts Beans 4 lbs. soap 7 candles with vinegar & salt to suit & all to be made fit for use in one day, & last But not least dealt out equally & agreeably to all is no very pleasant task But I try to make the best of it &

if some grumble I put them to carrying water or on guard which generally answers the purpose of stopping their complaints Where is George Please write soon & often don't wait for me give much love to all & breathe occasionally @ kind thought & an earnest prayer for Your Son & brother

　　　Jas. A. Barrett

Direct as before regt NYV Washington DC

[Emma Jane's transcription of Emily's journal entries]

---

[15] God's forseeing protection and care of his creatures. providence. (n.d.). *Dictionary.com Unabridged.* Retrieved November 28, 2015, from http://dictionary.reference.com/browse/providence

Sat. Oct 5, 1861

Letter from James last week telling of his arrival at Washington on the 18th and another, night before last, in forming us that they have orders to march, where they knew not, but he seemed to think they were on the eve of battle, with their knapsacks all packed in readiness to move. He seems to realize that he may have said his last good night but with submission to the will of Heaven. He expresses his willingness to fall a sacrifice, if needful in the cause of his country and his God. Thanks for such a true and noble brother.

James' brother, George Henry Barrett[vii]
(Barrett Collection)

We had a nice long letter from brother George telling of his arrival at Pike's Peak. He was three months on the way. He has not found much gold yet.

Sat. Oct 26, 1861

We had a letter from James last week saying he expected to sail for the south soon, and have since learned that he had gone to Ft. Monroe[16] where he is now, we know not save in the care of a kind Heavenly Father.

---

[16] Fort Monroe is the largest of the Third System fortifications in the United States. Known as the "Gibraltar of the Chesapeake," Fort Monroe was designed to protect the bay's inland waters from attack by sea. A young WestPoint-trained engineer named Robert E. Lee also lived at and played a role in the construction of the fort from 1831 to 1834. U.S. National Park Service. (n.d.). *Stories: Social Injustice in the Landscape*. Retrieved December 14, 2015, from www.nps.gov/cultural_landscapes/stories-Ft.Monroe.html

Chapter 2

Battles of Port Royal and Port Royal Ferry

October 1861-January 10, 1863--Embarks on "Empire City" to Hilton
Head, South Carolina--January 1, 1862, trip to Port Royal Ferry to
destroy rebel batteries--Marches to Seabrook, Hilton Head Island--
Embarks on steamer, "General Scott"--Sails to Daufuski Island--
Builds masked batteries to cut supply lines from Savannah to fort--
April 10, 1862, Captain Gillmore begins bombardment on Fort
Pulaski--Promotion

[Note that all the following transcriptions have been faithfully copied from the original
document, as written by James, except where noted.]

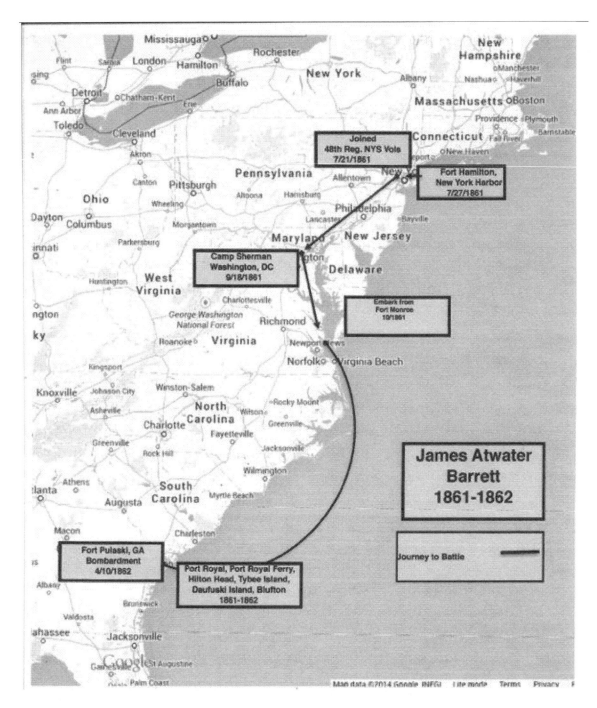

James' travels, 1861-1862
(Courtesy of Google INFGI, 2014)

"Empire City"[17], deck view
(Courtesy of Historylink101.com)

[*Narrative]
& about the last of Oct[r] embarked on a secret expedition 8 companies of our Reg[t] were crowded on the "Empire City"[18] Bunks were built in the hold of the vessel on both sides with a narrow passage between. These were 3 high & each bunk held 3 men I had heard of close packing before but this was my first experience of it   We marched up twice a day past the kitchen to get our cup of coffee pork or beans or rice & hard bread   The facilities for cooking were none of the best & the fare the worse I ever had. Beans & rice were seldom cooked soft   Pork was generally reduced to grease   Crackers[19] often—repulsive But it could not be helped & must be endured   We were 3 weeks on board this vessel & during this time we were exposed to a very severe wind storm & were fearful of being wrecked   Our position if bad before was much worse now   The Steamer was old & leaky many of the men got seasick others were washed out of their berths & their clothing all wet   Our supply of water was scanty & men went about trying to buy from the hands or cooks generally however without success   Our fleet finally gathered again & anchored off Hilton Head S. C.   I never shall forget the sensation I felt when I witnessed the first gun

[17] History Link. (n.d.) *Civil War Ships*: USS Empire City deck view. Retrieved December 17, 2015, from

http://historylink101.com/bw/civil_war_ships/CivilWarEraShipsEF/empi_PICT4396_st3.html
[18] Wooden side-wheeled steamer built in 1850 by William H. Brown. Modeled for speed and very strong, she was said to be the first ocean vessel to have a deck house extending from stem to stern. "March14, 1861. *The New York Herald*: Daily Chronicles of the American Civil War." Web log post. *Chronicles of the American Civil War*. (n.d.) Retrieved November 9, 2015, from www.cw-chronicles.com/blog/
[19] A hard saltless biscuit; a.k.a. Hardtack.

fired from one of our gunboats upon the Rebel works on the 8[20]th of November Then followed the bombardment The scene was terribly grand The gunboats sailed round in a circle delivering their "Broadsides"[21] in rapid succession & sending Death & destruction with them We could plainly see the effect of each shot from either side

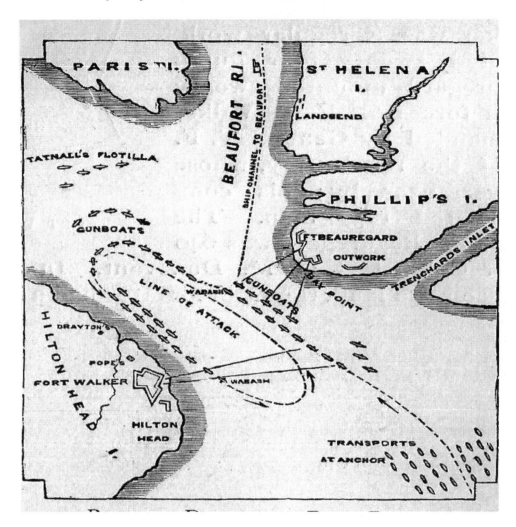

Plan of battle of Port Royal
(*48th Regt. N.Y.S. Vols.*, A.J. Palmer, D.D., 1885)

---

[20] Battle of Port Royal, 1861.
[21] A battery of cannons on one side of a warship that fires simultaneously. broadside. (n.d.) AMERICAN HERITAGE DICTIONARY OF THE ENGLISH LANGUAGE, FIFTH EDITION. (2011). Retrieved November 9, 2015, from http://www.thefreedictionary.com/broadside

Battle of Port Royal (This media is in the public domain in the United States, 2016)

The enemy could not stand it long   Next day the place was ours & on the 10th we landed & took possession   There were no docks there & Landing was performed under difficulties We first embarked in large boats & then waded ashore

All the baggage Equipage & Provisions had to be landed in the same way & carried ashore on the men's backs   This exposure following on our long passage where cleanliness could not be properly attended to soon told on the health of the men & our Sick list averaged about 20% of the command

Large fatigue parties[22] were constantly employed on the fortifications & our drills & parades were closely attended to   Every sunday morning we had regimental or brigade Inspection & drill.

[Emma Jane's transcription of Emily's journal entries]
Fri. Nov 22, 1861

Thanksgiving day was passed with neither of our brothers at home to share its festivities with us—the first time that James was ever absent and we missed his cheerful presence. We had a letter from him at Port Royal where the fleet was in which he had stopped and achieved a great victory in Beaufort, and now I suppose, he is among those who have started another expedition.

[22] Any manual labor or menial duty, other than drill or instruction. fatigue. (n.d.). *Webster's New World College Dictionary*. Retrieved December 14, 2015, from http://www.yourdictionary.com/fatigue

Mon. Dec 16, 1861

Heard from James this week at Hilton Head where he is now located. He has escaped the dangers of the battle field, but stands ready to engage in service whenever called upon. I was busy knitting mittens for the soldiers. George Prescott went from Concord with a company last week on Tuesday.

Sat. Dec 28, 1861

James is still in the enemy's country and we know not whether he is among the living or the dead. Heaven preserve him if it is His will!

[*Narrative]
About Jan 1/62 we made a new years trip to Port Royal ferry to destroy a rebel battery there This was our first experience under fire Our Reg^t was thrown out as skirmishers[23] to feel of the enemy & draw his fire & indicate his position to our Gunboats which finished the work As soon as we were fired upon we laid down flat & thus escaped until our Gunboats could cover our retreat Our part of the work finished we bivouacked[24] for the night without blankets or overcoats (as we had left them on the steamer) or shelter of any Kind & slept as only soldiers can. Next morning we reembarked & returned to camp We did not know exactly what was the object or result of our mission Soldiers never do We generally looked anxiously for the N Y papers to inform us what we were doing I cannot describe in words the eager anxiety which soldiers feel on the arrival of the Mail Those who get letters are very happy Those who do not are worse than miserable.

[Emma Jane's transcription of Emily's journal entry]
Sat. Jan 18, 1862

Another year has fled, filled with sad details of war and bloodshed. Had a letter from James last night telling of his having been in battle with bullets flying all around him, but with no man lost or blood spilt in his company, which seems quite remarkable. Thanks to a kind Heavenly Father for His preservation.

---

[23] Troops, usually of company strength or less, assigned to protect the head and flanks of a main battle formation. Lane, Shannon Hurst *Insiders' Guide to Civil War Sites in the South*, 4th ed. Guilford, CT: Insiders' Guide. (2010). Glossary: Skirmishers Retrieved November 9, 2015, from https://books.google.com/books?id=0762762454

[24] An encampment for the night, usually without the use of shelter (tents or covering). bivouac. (n.d.). *Dictionary.com Unabridged*. Retrieved November 9, 2015, from Dictionary.com website: http://dictionary.reference.com/browse/bivouac

Sat. Jan. 18, 1862

Had letters from the boys. Poor James is suffering from injustice, hardships and vexations[25] from which his true and noble soul revolts.

[*Narrative]

The latter part of Jan'y 1862 We marched to Seabrook, Hilton Head Island & embarked on the Steamer "Gen¹ Scott" & sailed to Daufuski Island Our (right) wing landed in boats & marched all night across the Island   We all supposed there was going to be some fighting. But the battle of Daufuski Island that I have seen spoken of in papers   I think must have been fought without powder   We met no opposition But in the morning found ourselves within sight of Fort Pulaski Ga 4 Companies of the 7th Conn were here

We had orders not to let ourselves be seen from the Fort   Here we went into camp & our comrades joined us in a few days after escaping shipwreck on the "Gen¹ Scott" which stranded & went to pieces on a sand bar near where we landed   We were in this camp nearly 3 months   We sent fatigue parties to Jone's & Bird's Islands on the Savⁿ [Savannah] river to build batteries to cut off supplies from Savannah to the fort. At the same time Gen¹ Gillmore (Capt then) with his Corps of engineers were building masked batteries[26] on Tybee Island[27]

---

[25] The state of being annoyed, frustrated, or worried. Vexation. (n.d.) *American Heritage Dictionary of the English Language, Fifth Edition*. (2011). Retrieved November 9, 2015, from http://www.the freedictionary.com/vexation

[26] A battery artificially concealed until required to open upon the enemy. (Mil.) A battery so placed as not to be seen by an enemy until it opens fire. masked battery. (n.d.) *Webster's Revised Unabridged Dictionary*. (1913) Retrieved November 9, 2015, from http://www.thefreedictionary.com/Masked+battery

[27] By the outbreak of the American Civil War, Tybee would again play an important military role in U.S. history. First Confederates occupied the island. In December, 1861, the Rebel forces would withdraw to Fort Pulaski under orders from Gen. Robert E. Lee to defend Savannah and the Savannah River. Union forces under the command of Quincy Adams Gilmore took control of Tybee and began constructing cannon batteries on the west side of Tybee facing Fort Pulaski about one mile away. U.S. Park Service (2015). *Fort Pulaski: Tybee Island*. Retrieved November 9, 2015, from www.nps.gov/fopu/learn/historyculture/tybee-island.htm

Swamp angel
(This media is in the public domain in the United States, 2016)

Jones & Bird Islands were low & marshy & the high tide covered them   Our men had to work in the mud up to their waist   But in time @ corduroy road[28] was made across, dikes were thrown up & the mud was so soft that it ran back most as fast as thrown up   Slowly we enclosed about an acre

Carte de visite of General Quincy
Adams Gilmore. (Barrett Collection)

---

[28] A log road that is constructed by placing sand-covered logs perpendicular to the direction of the road over a low or swampy area. The result is an improvement over impassable mud or dirt roads. Corduroy road. (2015, November 5). *Wikipedia, The Free Encyclopedia*. Retrieved November 9, 2015,
from https://en.wikipedia.org/w/index.php?title=Corduroy_road&oldid=689258734

Rendering of the corduroy road by A. McCallen (Courtesy of thecivilwarandnorthwestwisconsin.wordpress.com)

The sun baked these banks of mud very hard & the tides were effectually kept out All this had to be done secretly or we might have been shelled out   We worked mostly nights Our men returned to camp daily covered with mud & were relieved by another party Great was the surprise of the rebels when our little batteries one on each side of the river first disputed the passage of the regular supply boat

[Transcription of James' letter from Gerrish Papers Collection]
I enclose @ rough sketch of a gun taken at Braddocks point & now mounted at Jones Island

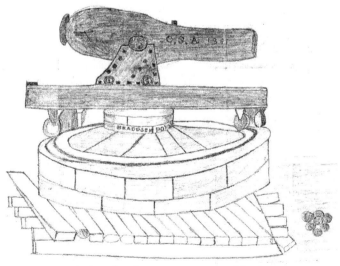

James' sketch of a cannon at Braddock Post
(Gerrish Family Papers Collection)

Dear Charley   Yours of 13th is this day recd I had previously recd those of 6th & 14th & the 11 Boxes all came to hand last sunday   It caused some surprise to hear my name called so often & I believe they concluded that I must be about to open @ store. But I soon disposed of the things & we are to be paid in a few days when I shall be able to send on about 500⁰⁰ to you. I was somewhat annoyed by outsiders coming to buy things   But I politely informed them that they were for Co H   2 boxes of the milk were open & showed the contents & everyone wanted Milk (luckily none was stolen)   But I was @ little too fast for them for I sold out to my tent mate with the privilege of having the refusal of it back again so that I could say it was all sold I sent for it for the Co & I meant the Co to have the benefit of it. about 1 Doz of the linament & 3 bottles of oil & the oysters were broken & the shirts were 6 short   But I shall make enough on the other things to make up the loss & do well besides altho I do not intend to charge very much profit. I get 1²⁵ for the best shirts 1⁰⁰ for the army knives 3⁰⁰ for the dirks 25ᶜ for the gingerine²⁹ etc. I have sold about all now & could sell more if I had the things.   The watches sell readily for 50 perct profit   I am much obliged to you for your trouble & judgement in packing & forwarding these things. When our Co was sent down to *Jones Island (*Mud)   I left that warrant with the postmaster to forward to you as I did not wish to keep it with me & did not know where or when our next move would be. We are still daily expecting an attack to be made upon Pulaskie & then a forward movement upon Savannah & then I think our work is about over & I hope as you say to get marching orders for home soon But "large bodies move slowly" & it may be many mos yet before uncle sam will be through with us   It seems to me that secesh is on is last legs But it dies hard. I think I shall be able to spend 4th July at home. I hope so at any rate I do not enjoy my position here now. Our 2ᵈ was quite modest at first But since he has got his new clothes they (the clothes) go strutting round as if they were entitled to some respect. I have as little to say or do with him as possible & feel disposed to be busy during the hours of Co drill when he goes out to drill the Co. He generally teaches them wrong & always makes @ fool of himself when he attempts to handle a rifle

I think the tailor that gets up @ suit of clothes that cant navigate better than those do had better work for soldiers rather than officers.   The other day at dress parade when he was in command & I acting as Lieut   I quietly & kindly gave several orders & cautions to the men which he omitted or neglected to do thereby saving him from open rebuke & He actualy took offence at it & really got his back up in regular tom cat style   I cared very little about it altho I rather think I did not feel very amiable knowing as I did that I had not exceeded my duty for I always did it with Capt & 1st Licut But I made up my mind to let the Co depend on him exclusively next time & today I had @ chance & took my place at the right instead of the rear & if he didn't get blowed up for blunders I did not hear Straight He didnt know half the time how & when to give the orders & The Adjutant

²⁹ One of the many cures, elixirs, perfumes, and drinks invented by Dr. John Stith Pemberton. Dr. Pemberton's most notable invention was the popular drink, Coca Cola. Pendergrast, M. (2013). *For God, Country, and Coca Cola: the definitive history of the great American soft drink and the Company that makes it.* 3ʳᵈ ed., rev. and expanded. New York: Basic Books. Retrieved November 30, 2015, from https://books.google.com/books?ibsn=0465046991

had to keep helping him. Well when the war is over I am as good as he & I can tell him so too. Perhaps I should be glad to get home again But "I hant afraid to try"

I sympathise deeply with you in your <u>single</u> <u>blessedness</u> I presume Mr F is fully occupied now that he is fairly <u>caged</u> But isn't it rather sudden I thought Mrs H's maternal glances used to indicate @ different state of things

I hope Miss ___ wont go into @ decline & I am afraid J.F. will get lonesome if he dont call round occasionally in his old <u>tracks</u> I think you must have been dissipating somewhat freely the past winter from all accounts. You must not forget Hall's caution about loss of sleep But perhaps the presence of "<u>A very interesting young lady</u>" (& <u>possibly</u> 2 or 3 of them) serves as an <u>antidote</u> for these <u>occasional</u> <u>trespasses</u> upon <u>physical</u> <u>laws</u>.

I think Stratton got decidedly the best of that joke I think James must have felt <u>rather</u> cheap. Served him right. That is the only kind of punishment that <u>tells</u> upon such <u>mean</u> <u>natures</u>. I think you must have your hands full while making so many changes when we come home I would like to recommend some of <u>my</u> <u>boys</u> to you   I have them of various kinds & I think I know who would suit you in any department from Bookkeeper down   I mean to pick one man for father who is @ perfect team to work.

I think what you style "unsalable stuff" on the John Randolph would have sold had it been tried But once when I told him I thought the pickled herrings would sell at a low price inproportion He said he would sell them cheap But did not suppose them salable only took them for ballast etc I never saw any of them offered for sale at all   The weather is getting warm here now & I am glad you did not send more blankets these are about gone & the rest will go   But the demand is mostly over   Many thanks to Mrs Bates for those cakes & also to Ellen for her part she had in them They make one think of old times & are much better than richer cake Of course you know that I appreciate your own share in sending the things without @ formal acknowledgement. Those meats & preserves could not have been selected with better taste. I will not now order further for I think we may not stay down here long enough to make it an object. It would take 6 weeks from now to get anything here & I hope to be home in 2 months. I may conclude to send in @ few days & if I do please to forward promptly for reasons alluded to above. We have just got @ new suit. Sky blue pants & other things same as before I have an entire new suit & am trying to keep it nice to go home in.

I like to have you write about the general feeling north as to the war etc I don't get much time to read & consequently am not well posted They have been preparing @ long time on Tybee for attacking Pulaskie Deserters from Pulaskie report 100 men in irons there for refusing to do duty. All accounts seem to agree in the conclusion that there is @ vast amt of suppressed union feeling among the rebel soldiers which added to the good news which every dispatch brings to us certainly gives us cause to hope that "The night is far spent & that the morning is coming" which will bring with it that sweetest of all sounds o the soldier's ears "Peace"
With much love to all <u>individually</u> & <u>severally</u> I am as ever yours &c

Jas. A. Barrett

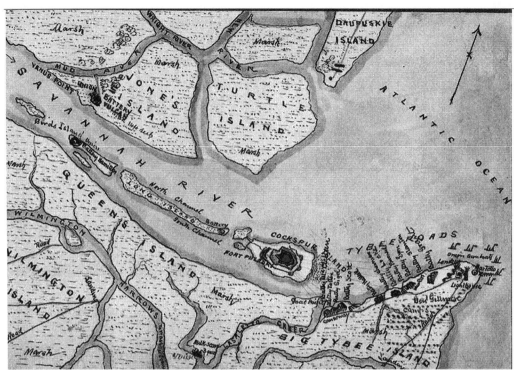
Siege of Fort Pulaski, Savannah River, Georgia, 1862
(Courtesy of Library of Congress)

Mortar Battery Stanton
(Courtesy of civilwardailygazette.com)

[*Narrative]
Soon after this about April 10th Genl Gillmore opened his famous Bombardment & it was one of the grandest sights I ever saw

The firing was made with wonderful precision & attended with a success which surprised every body   Gillmore had been ridiculed by the best engineers in the country for attempting to reduce Fort Pulaski[30] with land batteries

But he did it & on the Apr 11th the Rebel flag no longer floated there The 7th Conn Regt were sent to occupy & in a few days were relieved by ours   We remained here 14 months & had an opportunity to recruit our strength, perfect our drill in Infantry Artillery & bayonet & thoroughly repair the fort   Our Regt came to be considered one of the best in the Dept   While here we made several raids to destroy salt works for plunder &c   On of these we lost our first man

Our Regt also went on the expedition to Pocotaligo[31] & narrowly escaped capture after pouring a deadly fire into a train of rebel soldiers & capturing a flag. I was sick with bilious[32] fever & did not go   I was sick about 6 weeks   This was the only serious sickness I had during my service

Bombardment of Fort Pulaski Currier and Ives rendition of the bombardment
(Courtesy of National Parks Service)

---

[30] The Battle of Fort Pulaski was fought April 10-11, 1862. Union forces on Tybee Island and naval operations conducted a 112-day siege, then captured the Confederate-held Fort Pulaski after a 30-hour bombardment. The battle is important for the innovative use of rifled guns which made existing coastal defenses obsolete. The Union initiated large scale amphibious operations under fire. U.S. National Park Service (2015). *Fort Pulaski* Retrieved November 9, 2015, from www.nps.gov/fopu/learn/historyculture/tybee-island.htm

[31] The expedition's objective was to destroy the railroad and railroad bridges of the Charleston and Savannah Railroad and isolate Charleston, S.C. *Sons of Confederate Veterans*: History. Battle of Pocotaligo 21st, 22nd and 23rd October 1862. Retrieved December 14, 2015, from http://battleofpocotaligo.com/history.html

[32] Affected by or associated with nausea or vomiting/ [colour] lurid or sickly/ [physiology]: relating to bile. bilious. (n.d.). *Oxford Dictionaries*. Retrieved December 11, 2015, from http://oxforddictionaries.com/definition/english/bilious

Breach in Fort Pulaski (Courtesy of U.S. Army Military History) (Courtesy of
http:etc.usf.edu/clipart/galleries/559-miscellaneous-civil-war-illustrations)

[Emma Jane's transcription of Emily's journal entries]
Sat. Apr.12, 1862

We have been busy today working for the soldiers. We had a letter from James this week. He is still on Daufuski Island, but expects to move forward towards Savannah soon.

Sat. Apr. 26, 1862

We had a letter from James last Sunday telling of the surrender of Ft. Pulaski. He seems to flatter himself that he will soon be singing, "Home Again." Would that it might be so!

Sat. June 7, 1862

We have been somewhat relieved this week by hearing from James. He is still at Daufuski Island—is not very well, biliously inclined. We fear he is worse than he tells of us as he is not one who complains much without reason.

Sat. July 26, 1862

Had a letter from James this week saying that he was very well and weighed 160 lbs.—a fact which we were happy to learn. He is stationed at Pulaski still.

Sat. August 16, 1862

Had a letter from James this week through Charles Gerrish saying that he was well which we were happy to learn.

Sat. Sept 6, 1862

Last week on Monday, Becky had just got the clothes put to soak when C. Barrett rode up for her to go down to a soldiers' meeting and stay two days as there was a great call for lint and bandages in consequence of the recent battle near Mannasseh

---

Official Discharge

Form 4

I certify that the within named James A. Barrett, a Sergeant of Captain Dudley W. Strickland's Company (H) of the Forty Eighth Regiment of Infantry. N.Y.S. Vols—Born in Concord in the State of Massachusetts—Aged 30 years—5 feet 8 inches high—Light complexion—blue eyes—auburn hair and by profession a Clerk—was enlisted by Captain Dudley W. Strickland at Brooklyn N.Y. on the 27th day of July—Eighteen hundred and Sixty one, to serve for 3 years or the War and is now entitled to a discharge by reason of Promotion.

The said James A. Barrett was last paid by Paymaster Major Spaulding to include the 31st day of December—Eighteen hundred and Sixty two—and has pay due from that time to the present date.

He is indebted to the United States Eight Dollars and Thirty cents on account of extra clothing, etc.

Given in duplicate at Fort Pulaski, Ga. This 30th day of December, 1862.

Dudley W. Strickland

Commanding Company

Emma Jane's transcription of the original Form 4 (Barrett Collection)

[*Letter to his 13 year old niece, Mary Elizabeth Warren]

Ft. Palaski Ga Jan 10 1863

Dear Lizzie

I rec'd your letter of 21st Dec & Mothers of 16th & was very glad to hear that you are all so well I hope Father is now entirely well I am glad to notice the improvement you have made in writing   When I read your letter I could hardly believe it could be really from Lizzie Warren who could hardly write at all when last I saw her. I am glad to hear of your promotion   Hope you will improve your advantages & learn faster than ever Tell your Mother that she must write @ postscript in all your letters unless she prefers to go it alone & express my thanks to your father[viii] for his <u>kind</u> sympathies for the <u>poor</u> <u>soldiers</u> We have turned away one of the darkies & got 2 more so we have <u>only</u> got <u>3</u> now to attend to our <u>physical</u> <u>wants</u>   But we <u>manage</u> to <u>get</u> <u>along</u>   You know <u>Soldiers</u> must be content to put up with some <u>privations</u>

Who would'not be an orderly Serg^t & fight bleed & ___ for his Country. You can see in the Pictorials[33] of Jan 3^d pictures of our Burlesque parade   we have lately had @ match base ball game between the 47th Reg^t & ours   their 9 & our 9 played here a week ago & ours beat them bad our boys have gone down to the Head today to play the 2^d game & if they get beat they will play the 3^d at Beaufort

We have got @ dramatic association here too & are fitting up @ Stage   we intend to entertain the 48th & their friends 2^{ce} [twice] @ week. Tell your father to serve out another <u>ration</u> of sympathy for us in our trying positions. My health is good & I weigh nearly 170.

I am forcibly reminded every time I get letters from home that you are all doing much more in your Countrie's service than I am even if I do wear soldier clothes. But I cant help it   I can But do my duty where I am & I try to do that We hear of great union Victories   But don't know how much to believe   It don't seem as if this war could last much longer   But I fear we have much more to do than we think

This Slavery question proves to be an ugly customer & dies hard   But it must die even though it have an hundred lives. I often hear from Charles Gerrish   He has been very kind in sending me things from time to time & I shall not soon forget it   I have not rec^d any letter from George yet   Poor fellow   I pity him   I hope he may be successful   I think he has earned success by his untireing perseverance.   It is @ long time since I have seen him & @ longer time still may wear away before we meet again What is the general opinion as to the duration of the war. Tell Ella she must be @ good girl & write again when she has @ chance. I am looking for @ promotion soon   But you need not tell of it at present   give much love to all   write soon & believe me as ever

Your aff Uncle
James A Barrett
Co H 48th Reg^t N Y Vols

I have got @ secesh[34] spoon that I am going to send to you one of these days

---

[33] *Frank Leslie Illustrated Newspaper* was founded in 1852.

[34] Any type of spoon taken by Union soldier found in a Southern home during the Civil War.

Chapter 3

Life at Fort Pulaski and a Romance Begins

January 20, 1863-May 23, 1863—A reminiscence of Thanksgiving Day at Fort Pulaski--Receives commission as 2nd Lieutenant--Given own company--General Hunter in command after death of General Mitchel--Colonel Perry dies--Lieutenant Colonel Barton takes command--Amusements at Fort Pulaski of baseball and theatre--Barton Dramatic Association

[Note that all the following transcriptions have been faithfully copied from the original document, as written by James, except where noted.]

48th N.Y.S. Vols. Regt. on parade at Fort Pulaski, GA
(*48th Regt. N.Y.S. Vols.*, A. J. Palmer, D.D., 1885)

48TH N.Y.S. Vols. Regt. Company E at Fort Pulaski, GA
(*48th Regt. N.Y.S. Vols.*, A. J. Palmer, D.D., 1885)

James A. Barrett

(Please note: The identification of men begins in the back row from left to right)
Fee, Moser, Fox, Taylor, Smith, J.A. Barrett, Lockwood, Nichols, Hilliard, Ingraham, Edwards, Irvine (3D R.I.)

Tantum, Fry (3D R.I.) Ferguson, Paxson, W. Barrett, Eaton, (1st N.Y. Eng.), Humphries, Miller, Swartwout, Robinson, Mulford, Howland, Farrell, Elmendorf, Hale, Green, Barton, Strickland, Gould (3D R.I.), Hurst, Avery, Elfwing, Coan, Lent

THE FIELD STAFF, AND LINE OFFICERS OF THE 48TH REGIMENT N.Y. VOLUNTEERS, FORT PULASKI, GA (*48th N.Y.S. Vols.*, A.J. Palmer, D.D., 1885)

Baseball game is being played in background while photo was being taken
(Barrett Collection)

48th N.Y.S. Vols. Band, Fort Pulaski, GA., 1863 (Courtesy of Library of Congress)
Retrieved April 25, 2016 from
http://lcweb2.loc.gov/service/pnp/habshaer/ga/ga0100/ga0120/photos/377994pv.jpg

James' original first page of letter written to
Jane Farmer (Barrett Collection)

[*Transcription of letter below]

Fort Pulaski GA   Jan 21 1863

Jane Farmer
Concord, Mass

   Dear Friend   I believe you will excuse the liberty I take in thus opening a correspondence unbidden. But shut up as we are here far away from home friends & kindred. You can have no idea how welcome letters are. Our thoughts continually wander to our Northern homes & friends we have left behind us & when a Mail does come & I receive the bundle of letters for our Co it is interesting to witness how eagerly each ear is bent in the fond hope of hearing his name among the lucky few. Or the disappointment that is pictured on the faces of those who are not so fortunate. My correspondents are very few & they are so busy that my letters are few & far between. 18 Months have now elapsed since first I entered the service during that time We have seen something of hardship much of fatigue & a <u>little</u> of Danger When we left our first camp we thought we were going to <u>War</u>. Our reg^t has been under fire twice When it fell to lot our being one of the flank companies to be thrown out as skirmishers to pioneer the way & draw the Enemie's fire The 1st time was @ year ago We then advanced to within about 150 Yds of their battery when they opened upon us & we immediately fell flat on the ground & remained there about ½ hour with the balls whistling all about us when we made @ successful retreat without loss & the Gunboats did the rest We witnessed the capture of Hilton Head But took no part in it The sight was @ grand one & will not soon be forgotten. We claim the most of the credit of taking this Fort inasmuch as we paved the way by planting the batteries on Jones & Bird's Islands which cut off the communication between Savannah & the Fort Our reg^t (or 6 co^s of it) also were engaged in the expedition against the Savannah & Charleston R.R. You may have seen pictures of it in the Pictorials I was sick on my back at the time & was left behind This was in October I will not attempt to give the details of these expeditions, Accounts of which you have undoubtedly read in the papers We also made several excursions to Blufton where we destroyed some Salt works & in one of these we lost one man. @ Corp^l [George Durand][ix] in Co B. This is the only man we have lost from the bullet of the Enemy. Since we came to this Fort last May We have been very comfortably situated We have had @ good deal of work to fix up the place But we have just got it fixed nice.

Thanksgiving day was devoted to Pleasure. Games of various kinds occupied most of the day & prizes were given to the successful competitors   A burlesque Dress parade was the prominent feature of the day   Each Co dressed as comical as possible & the orders that were read were intended to be hits upon the various Officers   All passed off pleasantly. In the evening each Co had @ good Supper in their quarters & the officers had music & dancing nearly all night. Of course there was more or less drunkenness in some of the Co^s & I am sorry to say some of the officers (invited ones) were not <u>entirely</u> <u>sober</u>.

GRAND THANKSGIVING
FETE AND FESTIVAL,

Given by the Officers of the Garrison of

FORT PULASKI, GA., NOVEMBER 27TH, 1862.

PROGRAMME.

DIVINE SERVICE AT 9 O'CLOCK, A. M. THE ENTERTAINMENT TO COMMENCE WITH

TARGET PRACTICE,

Three competitors from each Company. Distance 200 yards. Best string in three shots each. First Prize—Gold Medal, valued at $25. Second Prize—Silver Medal, valued at $15. Third Prize—Bronze Medal, valued at $10. *First Prize taken by Co A*

II. ROWING MATCH.

Distance one mile around a stake boat and return. First Prize—Purse of $10. Second Prize—Purse of $5. Third Prize—Purse of $2 50. *Not decided, Co A thinks taken 2nd prize... When decided*

III. FOOT-RACE.

Three times round Terreplein, and over 12 hurdles, three feet high. First Prize—Purse of $10. Second Prize—Purse of $5. Third Prize—Purse of $2 50. *First Prize taken by Co A*

IV. HURDLE SACK RACE.

100 yards and return; over 3 hurdles 50 yards apart and 18 inches high. First Prize—Purse of $10. Second Prize—Purse $5 00.

V. WHEELBARROW RACE.

Competitors blindfolded, trundling a wheelbarrow once across Terreplein. First Prize—Purse of $10 Second Prize—Purse of $5. *2nd Prize taken by Co A*

VI. MEAL FEAT.

Exclusively for Contrabands; hands tied behind the back, and to seize with the teeth a $5 Gold Piece dropped in a tub of meal. Six competitors, to be allowed 5 minutes each to accomplish the feat. Prize—$5.

VII. GREASED POLE.

Pole to be Fifteen feet high. Prize—$10 00.

VIII. GREASED PIG.

To be seized and held by the tail. Three Competitors from each Company. Prize—Pig.

IX. BURLESQUE DRESS PARADE.

Each Company will be allowed to enter an equal number of Competitors for each prize.

JUDGES AND COMMITTEE ON AMUSEMENTS.

Capt. J. H. Gould.
Lieut. Samuel K. Wallace.

Adjt. A. W. Goodell.
Quartermaster J. M. Avery.

The usual Dress Parade of the Garrison will take place at 4.30, P. M. Ball—8 P. M. Supper—12 P. M. Lunch at all hours.

The 3d Rhode Island Minstrel Band will play at intervals during the evening.

The Band of the 48th N. Y. Regt. will perform at intervals during the day and evening.

☞ A Steamer will leave the wharf at Hilton Head to convey guests to Fort Pulaski at 9 o'clock, Thanksgiving morning.

Program with handwritten notations
(Courtesy of sethkaller.com, 2016)

Greased Pole Competition
(Courtesy of http:etc.usf.edu/clipart/galleries/559-miscellaneous-civil-war-illustrations)

Burlesque Dress Parade
(Courtesy of http://etc.usf.edu/clipart/galleries/559-miscellaneous-civil-war-illustrations)

Thanksgiving Ball
(Courtesy of etc.usf.edu/clipart/11600/11611/thanks-ball_11611.htm, 2016)

Christmas & New Years were also Holidays with us & we endeavored to forget in the pleasure of the hour the troubles which brought us here. Our old Col died soon after we came into the Fort He was @ great favorite in the Reg^t But not with me I never could forget one wrong he did me in promoting @ 3^d Serg^t in another Co over me (when our 2^d Lieut resigned over @ year ago), & that too in direct opposition to the expressed wishes of all my Officers as well as the men of the Co But peace to his ashes He has gone where there is no war to give his final account. Our present Col was very savage at first He had 6 of us Orderlie's under arrest for 10 days for mere nothing once But his wife who is @ very sensible woman came down here & She made him alter his policy. He has got to be quite popular now. He is proud of his Reg^t & well he may be for the 48th are universally admitted to be the best reg^t in this department We are considered as the Bodyguard of the comdg Genl to be called on when wanted. There are several Iron Clads[35] at Hilton Head & we look for something about to be done in this vicinity. Our men are all anxious for action We are perfectly satisfied with this as our Headquarters But are anxious to make some excursions & do something to hasten along the "good time coming"

These are glorious times long to be remembered The year 1863 I think is destined to mark @ golden era in our Nation's history When I first enlisted I little dreamed that we should be here now I thought one year at most would do the work But events have proved that we entirely misapprehended the magnitude & depth of the work before us I believe that the liberty of all nations depends on the issue of this war If Republican Institutions cannot be sustained here Then farewell to the great principle of Man's power to govern himself But we cannot fail. We may

[35] An Ironclad was a steam-propelled warship. It was protected by iron or steel armor plates.

meet mortification & defeat in many battles yet But These will only serve to discipline us & unmask our weakest points & rouse up the dormant energies & patriotism of an indignant people

Emancipation[36] has at last been proclaimed Good for that I now hope to see Fire & the sword do their work of destruction leaving not one stone upon another, nor one rebel to tell the tale of his disgrace & ruin Then we may hope to see thrift & prosperity once more reign over @ happy & united people. Then we may truly enjoy that liberty which we have never yet experienced. Time bids me close If you think this hasty scrawl worthy of an answer, you will confer a favor upon Yours very truly   James A. Barrett
                    Co H. 48th N Y S Vols

                                                                              Fort Pulaski, Ga   Feb 14 1863

Dear Father
                    I have had @ streak of luck & must hasten & tell you about it   My 2nd Lieut Commission came 2 days since having been detained about a week at Braddock's point The Col sent for me & gave it to me himself & several others Mrs Barton among them congratulating me I have bought @ coat & sword & am about ready to appear in Dress Parade I am not assigned to duty yet The Lieut whose place I am to fill has not for some reason or other recd his promotion yet It will most likely come by next mail But I shall soon be in my own Co as Lt Carlton is about to be promoted I have not got used to it yet One thing annoys me I cant move @ peg But everyone must needs be saluting me so that I have to keep my right hand & arm in @ sort of perpetual motion It is all right I suppose But I haven't got used to the "superior officer dodge" yet

                    We were closely inspected by some regular Army officers on Monday The Sergts had to be catechised[37] & Lieutsx drill the Battalion All passed off fine. Our Company got much praised He said he had never seen the manual of arms executed so well except at West Point Since Capt Lockwood came back to us There is not anything here that can touch us in drill Genl Hunter is much pleased with our regt & calls it the best in this department. He says this is his regt & he will take care of them I think we are good for this Fort for @ long time yet or untill Savannah is taken when we are to be placed there to do Provost duty[38]

                    I send you @ paper with local news   But it is getting late & I must close to go to bed with much love to all I remain as ever truly
                                                            Your Son
                                                    Jas. A. Barrett
                                                    Co H. 48th N.Y.S. Vols.

---

[36] The fact or process of being set free from legal, social, or political restrictions; liberation/ the freeing of someone from slavery
emancipation.(n.d.).*OxfordDictionaries*.RetrievedDecember7,2015,from
http://oxforddictionaries.com/definition/english/emancipation
[37] To question or examine closely or methodically. catechised. (n.d.). *American Heritage Dictionary of the English Language, Fifth Edition*. (2011). Retrieved November 29, 2015, from http://www.the freedictionary.com/catechised
[38] Military policing.

Fort Pulaski Ga Mch 1 1863

Dear Mother. I have just written to George & think I will do the same to you. I have now been an Officer nearly 2 weeks & hope I have not disgraced my position   It is not as responsible @ position as the one I left But much pleasanter I fully appreciate the temptations connected with it & have made @ resolution to start with. Not to mingle with or countenance any drunken frolics. For I am sorry to confess that it too often happens that Officers meet together on some extra occasion to celebrate it as they term it with "@ jolly Drunk"   But I have set my face against it from the start. I fully believe now that the influence of whiskey is bad.   & I will have none of it. There were several pros came on yesterday 1st Lt _____ was made Capt & in the evening <u>Wet</u> his <u>Commish</u> The consequence was @ drunken frollick disorderly conduct. One Officer fell off of the Dock into the water   Sentries were bullied & insulted & today bloodshot eyes & several officers under arrest. Good enough for me   If Officers cant behave themselves how can we expect the men to

My Co Officers do drink some as indeed does nearly every one   But do not drink to excess   I believe I have told you that I am now settled in my own Co I am on good terms with the Col.   I told him when he asked me where I wished to be assigned that I preferred @ 2d Lieutenancy in Co H. to @ 1st Lieutenancy in any other Co. & so I would   Co H. is somehow different & more respectable than other Co's & as the Col told me seldom are represented in the guard house. The way things look now My turn will come round before long for another <u>lift</u>   But I shall respectfully decline <u>unless</u> it be in <u>my own Co</u>

You say Officers are singled out as marks in the field. We cant help that   I for one when I enlisted took my life in my hand & run the chances of war. leaving my fate in the hands of He "who doeth all things well" & do not forget even the Sparrow's fall

I think we shall remain here for the present. There was some talk of our going on the Expedition to Charleston which is being fitted out But it is thought that we shall not be called on But if we are I assure you Co H. is on hand & I think will not disgrace themselves.

You speak of knitting   I get no time for such employment   My "leisure moments" can be better employed in studying the Tactics & Regulations than in sewing knitting or washing   I therefore generally engage the services of some color Brother or Tailor in the regt while I am @ Soldier I intend to give My particular attention to my Company & My Military duties. The weather is getting warm here & we are on the look out for the famous Iron Clad ram that we have heard so much about. I moved my Quarters yesterday as Capt. _____ chose them for himself   But I think I will be equally as well pleased with the room I have got   2 other Lts are going to quarter with me & they are both steady & neat   Our Theatre is fairly started we have had 4 performances & expect to have 3 each week changing the Programme every week. We may as well make the best of our fortune & cheer ourselves with some innocent amusements. The acting is good & we have really got @ very pretty little Theatre   The Painting & other work was done by men from the Regt & we can accommodate nearly 200 men in the house. You can tell Cyrus Hosmer that Frank Howland is 2d Lt in this Regt & @ fine fellow he is. I knew him in Brooklyn   Please remember me to all friends write soon & believe me Yours very respectfully

Jas. A. Barrett
Co H. 48th Regt N.Y.S. Vols

Fort Pulaski Ga Mch 8 1863

My Dear Friend

Yours of the 8th ult was recd on the 22d   I meant to have answered it before   I have several times resolved to answer all letters at once as it is much easier to do so   But often turning over @ new leaf I must confess I often find the old story written there   Since I wrote you I have recd @ commission as 2d Lieut & best of all am assigned to duty in my own Co. I had to report to another co for the 1st week until our former 2d (Lieutenant) recd his promotion & during that one week experience I was forcibly reminded that all companies were not alike & was prepared to appreciate the merits of my own old Co "H."   We have 4 good Germans in our co the rest are all Americans & @ fine set of fellows they are too The Col asked me what co I would rather to be attached to. I told him I would rather be 2d Lieut in Co H where I felt that I belonged than 1st in any other Co.

We sent for two presentation Swords some time ago for the Major (our late Capt) & our present Captn they arrived @ few days since & were formally presented. They were very handsome   cost about 230.00 Dollars for the 2   The Sergts have ordered @ splendid one for the Col to cost 25000   This don't look much like war does it? I often think that we get much more credit from friends at home for bravery & self sacrifice than we deserve

I did think when I enlisted that I was going to War. & was in some measure prepared to endure hardships & face dangers   We have seen something of hardship   But very little of danger. Our deaths have been with one exception   the result either of disease or accident

We are called Genl Hunter's "Pet Lambs." We have been in this Fort since last May. & are very comfortably quartered. & live nearly as well as if we were home. Duty is light. only 3 hours drill each day & guard duty. The latteer is new to me as I never was subject to it untill I was promoted   But my time only comes once in 10 days which is nothing to speak of. I think sometimes that if I serve my 3 years out   it will take another 3 years to get domesticated & broken in to industrious habits again   Laziness thrives in camp & Soldiers want excitement to enable to resist its influence   We have our amusements here too   Base ball by day & Theatre in the evening 3 nights @ week   I wish you could see our Theatre   It is pronounced "Perfect." Stage is about 20 feet square   Scenery painted by our own Artists   Orchestra 7 pieces   2 private boxes & seats for nearly 200.   "Richard 3d "Family Jars" "Box & Cox" & "The Idiot Witness" have all been performed to "crowded houses" & each pronounced @ "complete success". "Othelo" is cast for this week   We have @ benefit once @ fortnight[39] to pay expenses   I think it (the Theatre) will be

---

[39] A unit of time equaling to 14 days or two weeks.

illustrated in "Leslie"[40] soon. Col Barton approves of show & has encouraged us all he could in getting this up.[xi]

Second Col William B. Barton
(*48th N.Y.S. Vols.*, A.J. Palmer, D.D., 1885)

You ask "what kind of @ place is Fort Pulaski?" Cockspur Island[41] is 1 mile long & 1/2 mile wide & nearly all @ low marsh   But there is @ Dike constructed round the principle part of it where the Fort is built & there is @ hard road across from the north to the South dock. The Fort itself is built of brick with 5 faces & surrounded by @ moat some 30 feet wide. The men quarter In the casements. The guns that we depend upon mostly are mounted on the Ramparts They consist of 11 to 14 inch Columbiads[42] James Rifle Pieces[43] & Parrott Guns[44] There are nearly 50

---

[40] "Frank Leslie's Illustrated Newspaper", later renamed "Leslie's Weekly", was an American Illustrated literary and news magazine founded in 1852 and published until 1922. It was one of several magazines started by publisher and illustrator Frank Leslie. Frank Leslie's Illustrated Newspaper. (October 16, 2015). *Wikipedia, The Free Encyclopedia*. Retrieved November 29, 2015,
from https://en.wikipedia.org/w/index.php?title=Frank_Leslie%27s_Illustrated_Newspaper&oldid=686086352

[41] The first military use of Cockspur was in 1761 with the construction of an earth and hewn log fort near the confluence of the South Channel and Lazaretto Creek. U.S. National Park Service (2015). *Fort Pulaski: Cockspur Island*. Retrieved November 29, 2015, from https://home.nps.gov/fopu/learn/historyculture/cockspur-island.htm

[42] The Columbiad was a heavy iron artillery piece which could fire shot and shell at a high angle of elevation using a heavy powder charge. Columbiads were usually classified as seacoast defense weapons and were mounted in fortifications along the rivers and other waterways. Melton, Jack W., Jr. and Pawl, Lawrence E., Melton & Pawl's *Guide to Civil War Projectiles* (1996). Basic Facts Concerning Artillery: Civil War Cannon. Retrieved December 14, 2015, from http://www.civilwarartillery.com/BasicFacts.htm

in all besides the casement guns. Each co have its Battery & is responsible for it   Ours is in the Demilune[45] with (3) 20 lb Parrotts & (2) 8 inch Howitzers[46].

Parrott guns
(This media is in the public domain in the United States, 2016)

---

[43] A generic term to describe any artillery gun rifled to the James pattern for use during the American Civil War. Charles T. James developed a rifled projectile and rifling system. James rifle. (December 10, 2013). *Wikipedia, The Free Encyclopedia*. Retrieved November 29, 2015, from https://en.wikipedia.org/w/index.php?title=James_rifle&oldid=585511010
[44] The Parrott rifle was a type of muzzle loading rifled artillery weapon used extensively in the American Civil War. Parrott rifle. (October 21, 2015). *Wikipedia, The Free Encyclopedia*. Retrieved November 29, 2015, from
https://en.wikipedia.org/w/index.php?title=Parrott_rifle&oldid=686880791
[45] Fortifications shaped like a crescent moon constructed as an outwork in front of a fort. demilune. (n.d.) COLLINS ENGLISH DICTIONARY – COMPLETE AND UNABRIDGED. (1991, 1994, 1998, 2000, 2003). Retrieved November 29, 2015, from
http://www.thefreedictionary.com/demilune
[46] A relatively short cannon that delivers shells at a medium muzzle velocity, usually by a high trajectory. howitzer. (n.d.). *American Heritage Dictionary of the English Language, 4th edition*. Retrieved December 11, 2015, from http://www.yourdictionary.com/howitzer

---

Genl Hunter thinks the rebels will improve the opportunity when an attack is made on Charleston to come down with their celebrated Rain & try to drive us out. Our orders are "to hold the Fort to the last at any risk" & "blow up the magazines as a <u>last</u> <u>resort</u>" If necessity should force us to that extremity But we say "Let them come & we will pepper them" We think we can hold this place But time will tell Meantime "Let the world jog on as it will We will be gay & happy still."

We did expect to go on the expedition against Charleston But the Genl thinks we are needed here.

The President Proclamation does not receive that sympathy in this Reg^t that it would in a New England one. The moral tone is not sufficiently advanced Men will be shortsighted None are so blind as those who <u>wont</u> see "Having eyes they see not & having ears they hear not" "the still small voice" which is destined to vibrate through this Land echoing & reechoing its stern & solemn teachings until conviction shall be forced home to every Heart

You allude to an article in the Atlantic There is much truth in the idea that all things have their price But I think there is much error as to the suffering of great men &c

No doubt they do suffer from some <u>petty</u> annoyances or <u>physical</u> discomforts But when actuated with @ great principle & inspired with @ noble purpose they are enabled to look through these little shadows & shades of life & see the triumph that is finally to crown their efforts Does not virtue then bring its own reward? In the highest sense

I think without doubt it does I believe than even from a selfish point of view "Honesty is the best <u>policy</u>" & will finally bring its own reward & the little temporary defeats & discouragements that oppose us can hardly be termed (a <u>price)</u> when we consider the value rec^d I look on this war as a great National blessing It is the natural working out of nature's laws solving the great problem of Justice truth & humanity Anything that stands in the way has got to fall beneath its power. But the Day is dawning & when we behold the "Regenerated glorious life" of tomorrow the little sufferings & sacrifices of today will sink into insignificance

This is a world of progress Wrong & tyranny can not always rule I believe The very men who have been the innocent cause of our troubles are soon destined to be the instruments in God's hands of ending this war hurling retribution upon <u>their</u> oppressors & <u>our</u> enemies

If the principles that Fremont^{xii} advocated nearly 2 years ago (& for which he was so shamefully abused) had been carried out we should not now be entangled in civil brawl The people are now beginning to see that he was right Negroes are made free & formed into Reg^{ts} It will make men of them & at the same time insure to us Peace. They fight well take @ pride in the performance of their duties & it seems to raise them in the scale of being Genl Hunter is forming several reg^{ts} here & as we advance still more will be formed. Once let the slaves fairly understand that their freedom is to be the reward of their efforts & they will flock by thousands to our standard This is the true way to recruit our army. But many of our Gen^{ls} have treated them so roughly & even returned them to their masters that their confidence now is not complete

I am inclined to be hopeful & look on the bright side & altho this war is proving to be a much more lengthy affair than I ever expected still I am reminded that great results are not speedily brought about. "Large bodies move slowly" But it is only a question of time & all we can do is to do our duty & leave the rest to Him who ruleth all things & notes the sparrow's fall What

reg^t & what Brigade is Ned in   I expect he has seen rough times   They all do up there   Please remember me to all inquiring friends   write again as opportunity offers & believe me
Yours very truly

James A. Barrett
Co H. 48th Reg^tN.Y.S Vols

[Emma Jane's transcription of Emily's journal entry]
Sat. May 23, 1863

James is still at Ft. Pulaski with little hope of being released till his three years' term of service has expired. Heaven speed on the day when the ravages of war shall cease, the rod of the oppressors be broken and the happy sign of peace, liberty, truth and righteousness prevail.

Emma Jane pen and ink sketch
(Barrett Collection)

Olympic Theatre handbill
(Barrett Collection)

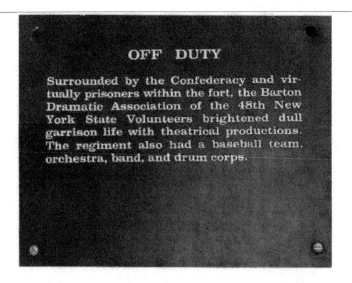

Wall placard[xiii] at Fort Pulaski, GA honoring the 48th N.Y.S. Vols.
(Courtesy of U.S. National Parks Service)

Tour of Fort Pulaski's ramparts with 14 inch columbiads
Left front: Capt. A. Elmendorf; Capt. Elfwing and his dog; Lieut. Smith
Middle front: Col. W.B. Barton and wife; behind: Capt. Lent
Right front: Capt. Hurst; behind: Capt. S.C. Eaton (1st NY Engrs.); Lieut. Nichols
(Courtesy of Library of Congress. Retrieved April 25, 2016 from
http://lcweb2loc.gov/service/pnp/habshaer/ga/ga0100/ga0120/photos/378007pv.jpg)

Chapter 4

Battle of Fort Wagner

June, 1863-September 19, 1863—Sails to St. Helena Island—
Brigaded under General Strong—
Rebels take refuge in Fort Wagner—
General Gillmore builds batteries—
General Seymour's night attack on Fort Wagner fails--Heavy
casualties--Wounded—Returns home for two months

[Note that all the following transcriptions have been faithfully copied from the original document, as written by James, except where noted.]

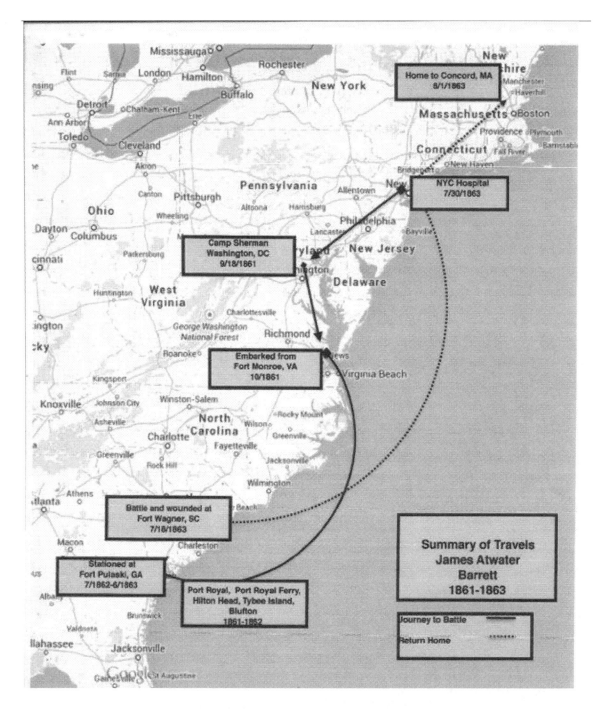

Summary of James' travels, 1861-1863
(Courtesy of Google INFGI, 2014)

Carte de visite of Brigadier General George
Crockett Strong (Barrett Collection)

Emma Jane's rendering of Fort Wagner
(Barrett Collection)

[*Narrative]

In June 1863 we bid farewell to Ft Pulaski leaving 2 companies to man the fort & sailed to St Helena Island[47] where we were brigaded under Genl Strong & drilled   From there we sailed to Folly Island[48] & from there Genl Strong with his Brig except our wing of our Reg^t marched in one direction & crossed Lighthouse Creek to morris Island & charged the rebel works while our wing crossed in another direction & charged a battery   It was rather exciting crossing in boats in constant peril of being upset by the rebel shot. Only one boat was hit & that close to shore   Our party took the battery without the loss of a man. The other wing lost one Capt & several men

---

[47] St. Helena Island is a Sea Island in Beaufort County, South Carolina.

[48] Folly Island is a barrier island in the Atlantic Ocean near Charleston, South Carolina.

Depiction by Emma Jane as inspired by
48th Regt. N.Y.S. Vols., A.J. Palmer, 1885
(Barrett Collection)

<u>What</u> rebels escaped took refuge in Fort Wagner[49] which kept pelting us with shot & shell. The numerous knolls of sand served us many a friendly turn & were our only protection from Wagner's fire   This was July 10th   At daylight next morning an assault was ordered   The 76th Pa[50] led. Our Regt was to support. But by some means the 9th Me was ordered instead.

       The assault failed from the failure of the 9th Me[51] to support it was said   It was a bloody affair & the 76th Pa lost heavily   Genl Gillmore commenced building batteries[52] at

---

[49] Fort Wagner or Battery Wagner was a beachhead fortification on Morris Island, South Carolina, that covered the southern approach to Charleston harbor. It was the site of two American Civil War battles in the campaign known as "Operations Against the Defenses of Charleston" in 1863, and considered one of the toughest beachhead defenses constructed by the Confederate States Army. It was immortalized in the movie, "Glory". Fort Wagner. (2015, November 13). *Wikipedia, The Free Encyclopedia.* Retrieved November 30, 2015 from https://en.wikipedia.org/w/index.php?title=Fort_Wagner&oldid=690393024

[50] During the Civil War the 76th Pennsylvania Infantry Regiment lost a 364 total of troops (9 Officers and 161 Enlisted men killed or mortally wounded and 2 Officers and 192 Enlisted men to disease; which includes 52 in Confederate prisons) out of an enrollment of 1,942. The Civil War in the East: 76th Pennsylvania Infantry Regiment "Keystone Zouaves". (2015). Retrieved December 14, 2015, from http://civilwarintheeast.com/us-regiments-batteries/pennsylvania/76th-pennsylvania-infantry/

[51] Ninth Maine Volunteer Infantry Regiment. The regiment lost a total of 421 men during service; 10 officers and 172 enlisted men killed or mortally wounded, 3 officers and 236 enlisted men died of disease. Retrieved November 29, 2015, from http://civilwarintheeast.com/us-regiments-batteries/maine/9th-maine/

once under cover of our gunboats & several companies of infantry as pickets   The work was mostly done at night   One day when our Reg^t was on picket we had several sharpshooters with telescopic rifles who succeeded in preventing the enemy from working their guns all day by picking off the gunner as fast as he attempted to sight his piece   This seemed to annoy them considerably & they came down that night & attempted to capture us   Our 2 Vidette companies gave them 2 vollies & then retreated on the reg^t at the battery from which we poured forth a galling fire which drove them home.

During this skirmish a portion of the companies had a hand to hand conflict & took several prisoners   Our loss was several captured & I think 2 or 3 wounded   I forgot to mention that while at Ft Pulaski in Jan'y 1863 I rec^d my com^{n}[53] as 2nd Lieut. Col Perry had died of heart disease during the summer before & Lt Col Barton took command. My Capt became Major & I remained in my own company to which I was much attached Col B[54] had a prejudice against promoting Sergeants into their own companies thinking they would be too familiar with their men & often told me that I was too familiar. But I never accepted his version

When I rec^d my first com^n I welcomed it as placing me above the arbitrary will of any officer (Far too many of our officers were arbitrary & selfish especially those who were appointed from civil life & had not served in the ranks[55]) & I pledged myself to temperate habits & to use my position in the interest of the enlisted men I did not think myself too good to go to their quarters & talk with them & never found that I lost either respect or authority by so doing When a reg^t first goes out the men generally prefer their own officers those whom they enlisted under I remember well the first vacancy that occurred in our reg^t Our 2nd Lt resigned when we were only a few months out I as the senior non com^d Officer naturally expected the position Altho my short experience had not made me anxious for promotion

But when an under Serg^t of another Co who had not done half the duty I had & could not drill a company was placed over me & under protest too from my Capt Lt & whole Company I did feel that patriotism had some other trials beside those that should belong

---

[52] The basic unit of soldiers in an artillery regiment; similar to a company in an infantry regiment. Batteries included 6 cannon (with the horses, ammunition, and equipment needed to move and fire them), 155 men, a captain, 30 other officers, 2 buglers, 52 drivers, and 70 cannoneers. As the War dragged on, very few batteries fought at full strength. A battery can also be the position on a battlefield where the cannon are located. Civil War Trust. (2014). battery (n.d.). Glossary of Civil War Terms: Improve Your Civil War Vocabulary. Retrieved November 2, 2015, from http://www.civilwar.org/education/history/glossary/glossary.html

[53] Commission

[54] Colonel Barton

[55] Or commonly known as being "breveted"

to camp life & that sectarianism[56] was not the proper qualification to ensure was not the proper qualification to ensure promotion   My company was enraged & it was with difficulty I restrained them from openly showing it

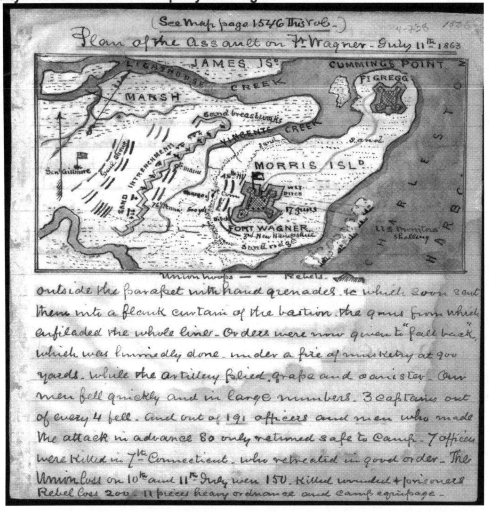

Sneden, R. K. (1863) *Plan of the assault on Ft. Wagner, July 11th 1863* [S.I., to 1865] [Map] (Library of Congress. Retrieved December 4, 2015 from https://www.loc.gov/item/gvhs01.vhs00151)

---

[56] (A person) strongly supporting a particular religious group, especially in such a way as not to be willing to accept other beliefs. sectarian. (n.d.). *Cambridge Advanced Learner's Dictionary*. Retrieved December 14, 2015, from http://dictionary.cambridge.org/dictionary/british/sectarian

But to go back to Morris Island Fort Wagner still remained a stubborn obstacle to our approach to Charleston Our batteries were pushed forward & on the 18th they & the gunboats kept up a terrific fire upon the Fort A night attack was planned We lay on our arms all day & just before sunset (fatal mistake) were formed in column The enemy must have seen us. Just before dark the column advanced under a galling fire up the beach It was an awful hour for young soldiers Our ranks were thinning at every step To our left another column with the 54th Mass (Cold[57]) Col Shaw advanced on the Fort. We waded the moat & scaled the parapet[58] Our loss was terrible sometimes whole companies were mowed down. About half way up the parapet a piece of shell pierced through my right thigh

I knew I was badly hurt but could not stop there & then with victory as I thought so near. I do not think I bled much. I retained the use of my limbs & the excitement kept me up for about an hour We jumped over the parapet into one bastion of the Fort where there were 2 Guns But the firing was too hot to turn them to our use Darkness was upon us & we could see nothing before us Our own men fired upon us. I soon found myself forced to seek a corner & lie down Our little band grew thinner & thinner Our Officers were killed off. A retreat was ordered But somehow it was not altogether understood & quite a number remained doing their best to silence one solitary gun which alone was keeping up its fire I was the only officer left who was able to stand I did not hear when the retreat was made These men called out for an Officer I was weak but could stand & with my sword for support I got up & directed their fire gathering ammunition from the wounded to supply them This soon gave out & only one or two being left I ordered them to cease firing

Then the wounded began to fear their coming fate; resist they could not, neither could they get away I told them to keep quiet & surrender when any one came to surrender to. This corner or bastion was literally filled full of dead & wounded men I crawled over their bodies to the parapet & looked around All was ominously quiet one or two scattering shots whistled past me I determined to make an effort to get to camp With some difficulty- I slipped down & crossed the moat which was nearly full of dead men

A rebel sentry paced the beach I placed my hand to my pistol It was disabled Under cover of the bank I got past him & with my sword for a cane hobbled down the beach 2 or 3 miles to camp My wound dressed & I was helpless as an infant That was a terrible night I little expected to see another Sun rise. Gen¹ Seamore [Seymour] planned the attack & to him belongs the blame

If we had attacked by daylight no doubt we should have captured it. But Gen¹ Gillmore afterwards proved the superiority of his method of taking the fort by gradual approaches & comparatively little loss of men. Our reg went into this charge with 500 men & 16 officers & 300 men & 13 officers were killed & wounded My Company was

---

[57] Abbreviation for colored

[58] A wall, rampart, or elevation of earth or stone to protect soldiers. parapet. *Merriam-Webster*.com. Merriam-Webster (n.d.). April 18, 2016.

reduced from 60 to 22   Poor fellows   I loved them & could not speak of them for weeks without shedding tears

My nerves were unstrung   I rec[d] a furlough & was sent to N.Y. on a hospital Steamer   My comrades who were left in the fort were taken prisoners in about 20 minutes after I left & taken to Charleston   A flag of truce was sent up & those who were able to be moved exchanged & some of them went home on the same vessel with me

Sketch of a flag of truce by Emma Jane
    (Barrett Collection)

[A note from the Cousins: Our Great Grandfather James describes the events of the siege of Fort Wagner with a matter-of-fact account. No melodramatic flourishes, only the facts with some hints of the emotional toll that weighed on him and the 48th. As we researched the events of July, 1863, and found other descriptions that we felt gave a more in-depth account of the assault, we wanted to include them in our book.]

James Moses Nichols enlisted August 26, 1861 as a 2nd Lieutenant in Company G of the 48th New York State Volunteers. He was honorably discharged on September 12, 1864. The New York, Civil War Muster Rolls, 1861-1900 shows that he was discharged with the rank of Captain with Company E of the 48th. In his book that was published in 1886, Nichols includes the following description of the attack on Fort Wagner on July 18, 1863:

> *"The following is the account of the assault, written by J.A. Barrett, who was a second lieutenant of Company H:--*
> *We lay on our arms all day, and just before dark were formed in column by companies, and advanced under a galling fire up the beach. It was a trying hour, our ranks thinning at every step. For*

much of the way the right of our column was obliged to wade in the water. On our left another column composed of the 54th Massachusetts colored regiment, under Colonel Shaw, also advanced on the fort. We waded the moat and scaled the parapet. Our loss was terrible, sometimes whole companies being mowed down at once. We jumped over the parapet into one bastion where there were two guns, but the firing was so hot that we were unable to turn them to any use. Darkness was upon us, and we could see nothing. The supporting columns coming up in our rear, poured in a heavy fire, mistaking us for the rebels. Our killed and wounded kept piling up. A rebel officer for some purpose came among our men, and was seized by a private of the 48th, who called to Colonel Barton that he had a prisoner. To which the colonel replied; 'Take him to the rear.' 'But he won't come,' said the private, who was nicknamed 'Plucky.' 'If he wont yield, then bayonet him,' was the order; when a wounded man dragged himself up, and, with all his remaining strength, plunged his bayonet into the side of the rebel officer, and, falling back, expired. A retreat was ordered, but was not altogether understood, and some fifty of our men remained and continued firing. I was severly wounded in the thigh, but roused myself, and directed the fire of these few men as best I could, collecting ammunition from the dead and wounded. When this gave out, I ordered all who could to go to the rear. This section of the fort was literally full of dead and wounded, piled up even with the parapet. I crossed over their bodies, slid down the slope and crossed the moat, which was filled with our dead. A rebel sentry was pacing up and down the beach, but by keeping near the bank I was able to pass him. My scabbard was shot away, my pistol bent and useless, and, leaning on my sword I hobbled down the beach to camp. The 48th went into this assault with five hundred men and sixteen officers, and three hundred men and fourteen officers were killed, wounded, or prisoners."

Nichols continues, *"While this brief account is valuable, as the brave statement of a cool, self-possessed, and brave officer, who participated in the assault, and was an eye-witness to what he states, no words can adequately describe the horrors of that night…On the night of the assault, July 18, there was no sleep in the 48th. It was past midnight when the last of the men came in from the fort, and the horrible scenes through which they had passed, and the anguish of grief over friends and comrades, maimed and wounded, are lying silent in that pit of darkness and* blood forbade all thought of rest. Colonel Barton was wounded through the thigh, Lieutenant Colonel Green, Captains Farrell and Hurst and Lieutenant Edwards were dead, and Captain Paxson was mortally wounded. Captains Lockwood, Elfwing, and Swartout, and Lieutenants Miller, Barrett, and Acker, were also severly wounded. It was a heart-rending sight when, on the following morning, I visited them on the steamer which was to convey them to Hilton Head. No one could doubt the quality of the 48th now. The heroism of the men was equaled by that of their officers. None could have been braver. All the wounded officers had made their escape with the exception of Lieutenants Taylor and Fox, who were in the hands of the Confederates." Nichols, J.M. *Perry's Saints or the Fighting Parson's Regiment in the War of the Rebellion.* 1886. Boston: D. Lothrop and Co. (169-173)

Abraham J. Palmer included this account on the assault of Fort Wagner: *"It would be unfair to neglect to say that there had doubtless been others who had participated in the defence for some time and who had succeeded in getting to the rear before the surrender; indeed, Lieutenant James A. Barrett, though severly wounded in the thigh, remained within the fort for a long while, encouraging the men to hold the banks, collecting ammunition from the dead and passing it to the living, and his word cannot be disputed that when he determined to go to the rear himself, he ordered all the men within sound of his voice to retire also. Such orders, however, were unheard high up on the bank where the firing was in progress; and if they had been heard it is doubtful if they would have been obeyed. Nothing less than a delirium of patriotism actuated the defiant men, who would not surrender and would not retreat."* Palmer, A.J. (1885). *The History of the Forty-Eighth Regiment New York State Volunteers, In the War for the Union. 1861-1865.* Brooklyn: Veteran Association of the Regiment. (120-121)

Written as a Master's Thesis (2000), Luis M. Evans writes of the assault of Fort Wagner *"After several attempts, the Confederates, utilizing soldiers from the Charleston Battalion, the 51st and 31st North Carolina, and the 32nd Georgia, were now having success in dislodging the pesky Federals. Scores of men in blue began to fall, surrender or attempt to escape. Eventually, only a few Federals were left alive to continue any resistance. Lieutenant Barrett, the last Federal officer still inside the fort, saw the folly of staying to fight and ordered a general retreat. But, the order was not well understood or heard. Some fifty members of the 48ᵗʰ , along with a number of men from the other regiments, remained behind."* Evans, L.M. *So Rudely Sepulchered: The 48ᵗʰ New York volunteer Infantry Regiment During the Campaign for Charleston, July 1863.* 2000. Fort Levenworth, Kansas: U.S. Army Command and General Staff College. (88)

Young Jane "Jennie" Farmer
(Barrett Collection)

[Jane "Jennie" Farmer's First Letter]

Concord, July 21, 1863

Dear James

I have neglected your letter longer than I intended to but we have a numerous household just now and many things to take up our time. We are all at home, every one of the children Judge of our surprise when Ned walked in among us after an absence of nearly five years. We were well nigh astounded, but rejoiced I assure you.

He has a scrofula tumor[59] upon his neck and is home on a furlough, but returns today or tomorrow. Mattie[60] is home, and Lizzy with four of her children.

I see by the papers that the 48th were engaged in the proceedings against Charleston thus far

Edwin "Ned" Farmer in uniform

Martha "Mattie" Farmer Leete

Carte de visites of two of Jennie's siblings (Barrett Collection)

---

[59] Tuberculosis of the lymphatic glands, esp. of the neck, characterized by the enlargement of the glands, suppuration, and scar formation. scrofula. (n.d.). *Webster's New World College Dictionary*. Retrieved December 15, 2015, from http://www.yourdictionary.com/scrofula
[60] Martha and sister, Elizabeth, married two brothers. Martha "Mattie" married Charles Leete and Elizabeth "Lizzy" married George Leete.

Farmer Homestead Concord, MA (Barrett Collection)

I hope earnestly that a kind Providence has preserved you from harm. We shall anxiously look for news from you and till we hear, will try and believe you safe.

We are having cheering news now. It was too bad that Lee's army was not all taken, I hope the War is nearly over, but pray that they may not patch up things with compromises to the slave power. Brother Ned likes in the Army very well, thinks he shall remain now til the war is over. We are so sorry that he should have this scrofula trouble. I presume that army life and habits, diet, etc, brought it on.

Several of the Concord boys were injured in the Gettysburg battles. Prescott's Reg Did bravely. Charles Young Charley Bowers is home quite badly wounded, and amputation of one limb it is thought may be necessary. Frank Buttrick (David's son) has had one limb taken off below the knee. Charles Bowers the father was somewhat injured, also Geo. Prescott, but not seriously I believe, Prescott has not returned I believe.The nine month men under Capt. Barrett are expected home, but how soon I do not know. I suppose you have heard of the soldiers' party on the 4th of July. There was a story that Geo. Prescott has been relieved of his command, but I have not learned the true state of affairs and do not think many have known about it.

Nett Melvin has left us. She was very patient and cheerful to the last. Thomas Tolman is dead. He was suffering from Consumption for some time.

William Brown (James's son) preached last Sunday, very ably, they said, Mr. & Mrs. Reynolds congratulated Mr. and Mrs. Brown.

Was not the N.Y. riot[61] shameful? I think Copperheadism is indeed our worst enemy. I hope we shall hear from you very soon. If you are just a little hurt, you had better come home on a furlough. The folks wish to be remembered. Lizzy sends her love and good wishes. She left Brooklyn last Friday. The riot was mostly quelled then but she felt uneasily about leaving, would not, if Ned had not been there. There is not a bit of the Copper-head[62] about Mr. Leete.

We have seven weeks vacation five after this. I do not think you will find Old Concord or its people very much changed. Drafting has been going on here for the last ten days and yesterday the Actonites? the first drafted here came down to report themselves as their ten days had expired. The 7th district was drafted here comprising some twenty or more towns. Albert Tolman, Edward Damon, John Reynolds Julius Smith, Cyrus Hosmer, Joseph Melvin (John's son) F.R. Gourgas, a youth of twenty. Cyrus Conant of Nine Acre Corner, were among the drafted. Oh George Keyes was another & Cyrus Clark. Most of them will pay or procure substitutes. I presume I am writing you no news and will close now.

Truly your friend

Jenny Farmer

Write soon if you are able.

---

[61] July 13-16, 1863, known at the time as "Draft Week" were violent disturbances in New York City that were the culmination of working-class discontent with new laws passed by Congress that year to draft men to fight in the ongoing American Civil War. The riots remain the largest civil insurrection in American history outside of the Civil War itself. New York City draft riots. (November 15, 2015). *Wikipedia, The Free Encyclopedia*. Retrieved November 30, 2015, from
https://en.wikipedia.org/w/index.php?title=New_York_City_draft_riots&oldid=692362882
[62] The "Copperheads" were a vocal group of Democrats located in the Northern U.S. of the Union who opposed the Civil War, wanting an immediate peace settlement with the Confederates. Republicans started calling antiwar Democrats "Copperheads", likening them to the venomous snake. Copperhead (politics). (November 22, 2015). *Wikipedia, The Free Encyclopedia*. Retrieved November 30, 2015, from
https://en.wikipedia.org/w/index.php?title=Copperhead_(politics)&oldid=691759372

[Emma Jane's transcription of Emily's journal entries]
Sat. Aug 1, 1863

A week has passed, not soon to be forgotten, commenced with anxiety mingled with sorrow and joy. Monday, on looking into the morning journal, I learned that the 48th N.Y. Vols, brother James' regiment had lost five hundred and fifty men with only three officers escaping unharmed so that we immediately concluded that James was very likely among the wounded and possibly among the dead, but fortunately, we were relieved of our suspense as the next day's paper, mentioned his name among the wounded. That afternoon Charles rode over, went down to the post office for me, and brought back a letter in James' hand writing which revealed his intention of coming home directly, so Charles and I rode up home with them. Friday noon, Story ran into the front entry and asked me if I wanted to see James—that he was in the carriage at the door. I rushed out without much ceremony to speak to him. Charles Gerrish came on with him. He was toil worn, and weary and I guess as thankful to get home as we were to see him. I had resolved to go home when he came, but, being house keeper, had to forego my inclination being in the midst of ironing, until night. Here I am, joyous and grateful that my dear brother has been snatched as it were from the jaws of a barbarous and blood thirsty foe.

Joseph Story Gerrish, James' cousin
(Barrett Collection)

Sat. August 15, 1863

James is getting along fine- has been home more than a fortnight, but I have not seen him much as yet—hope to be able to soon as sister Mary is considerably better and talks strongly of going home.

FROM PORT ROYAL—LIST OF THE WOUNDED OF THE 48TH OF BROOKLYN.—The United States transport steamer Cosmopolitan arrived at this port from Port Royal yesterday, after a passage of seventy-two hours. She brought one hundred and eighty-five wounded soldiers from General Gilmore's corps d'armee on Morris Island. Among the number are the wounded of the 48th Brooklyn Regiment, formerly commanded by Col. Perry, but since his death by Col. Barton The list of wounded officers of the 48th on board is as follows:

Col. W. B. Barton, wounded in hip; Capt. N. Elwing, Co. B, leg; Capt. S. M. Swartwout, Co. F, in head; Capt. W. L. Lockwood, Co. H, shoulder; Lieut. Chas. E Fox, Co. A, hip, arm and head (paroled prisoner); Lieut. Joseph Taylor, Co. E (paroled prisoner); Lieut. A. F. Miller, Co. K, leg and thigh; Lieut. J. A. Barrett, Co. B, thigh.

The list of paroled prisoners of the 48th captured by the enemy in the assault upon Fort Wagner is as follows:

Second Lieut. Charles E. Fox, Co. A; 2d Lieut. James Taylor, Co. E; Josiah Sturges, Co. C; John Morton, Co. H; Corporal B. Lenard, Co. K; Wm. Hess, Co. K; C. Roberts, Co. B, Lemuel Roberts, Co. F; Wm. B. Smith, Co. B; James Larkin, Co. A; Charles N. Cole, Co. D; Charles Mills, Co. H; Corporal A. Ellison, Co. K; Sergeant John F. Clayton, Co. H; F. Konklin, Co. K; Corporal James Hyatt, Co. F; James H. Slivers, Co. B; Jas McGurney, Co. H; John Lee, Co. H; John Gluff, Co. C; W. H. Foley, Co. F; C. Smith, Co. E; Corporal W. L. Bredenburg, Co. A; Robert Douglass, Co E; M. B. Conklin, Co. K; W. J. Omers, Co. B; John Burton, Co. E.

The number of wounded still in Charleston, unexchanged, of the 48th is as follows:

Captain Frederick Hurst, Co. K, severe wound in hip; C. Messenger, Co. E; Charles Roberay, Co. B; Cornelius Cadmus, Co. A.

The following have died of wounds:

Amos M. Haven, Co. H; Thomas Kelly, Co. K; Geo. W. Nichols, Co. H; Jas. McPherson, Co. K; C. Ward, (doubtful) Co. K.

All accounts agree that the 48th fought with desperate bravery, and the list of casualties which we previously published and the list now given shows that they were in the thickest of the fight.

The *Brooklyn Daily Eagle*, July 31, 1863

(Retrieved December 4, 2015 from http://www.newspapers.com/image/50412256)

Sat. Sept. 19, 1863

Mary had previously invited the Buttrick girls as the Thompsons went away that day and Aroline and Vina Hunt and Jennie Farmer, at James' instigation, which raised our suspicions a little, as we have joked him considerably about her since he has been home, but cannot get much clue to the real state of the case. He took some pains to carry her home that night and then round to her boarding place to be ready for school in the morning and kept Father and Becky down in town waiting till quite into the evening, wondering why he didn't make his appearance and why caused a little merriment.

Emma Jane's sketch of horse and buggy (Barrett Collection)

Sat. Sept. 19, 1863

A week ago today, James, Becky and myself rode over to Sudbury and spent the afternoon; had a very pleasant afternoon. James went to Boston the Monday before and got his leave of absence. His wound is doing well.

Chapter 5

Return to Duty and a Written Confession

October 2, 1863-October 23, 1863—
Rejoined regiment at Beaufort, South Carolina as a
First Lieutenant—moved to Seabrook on Hilton
Head and assigned to Plantation--Engagement to Jenny

[Note that all the following transcriptions have been faithfully copied from the original document, as written by James, except where noted.]

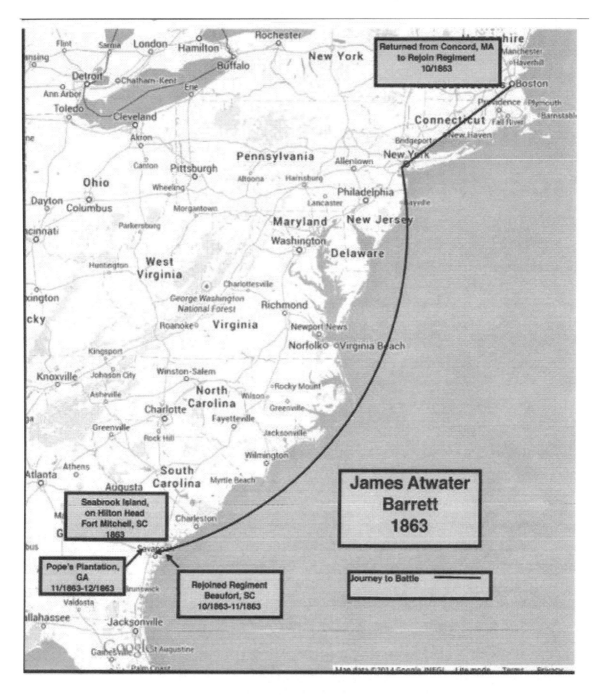

James' travels, 1863
(Courtesy of Google INFGI, 2014)

[*Narrative]

After 2 months at home I returned my reg^t at Beaufort, S. C.[63] having been promoted to 1st Lieut   I was still very lame but able to do Camp duty   I was temporarily assigned to command of Co A. & given charge of an outpost.   We soon after moved to Seabrook on Hilton Head when I was assigned to duty with Co A again, at a post called Popes plantation[64] to do picket duty[65] & had the use of a horse as I could not walk any distance There were about 500 Negroes here & I gained some insight into plantation life & the habits of freedmen.   They were anxious to learn   quiet & peaceful in their habits & perfectly competent to provide for their wants   I see no reason why they cannot make good & useful members of society if they get half a chance

      Everything is against them at the start But if God has no place for the Negro He never would have created him   When Genl Hunter first enlisted black troops there was a great cry against it from our Soldiers   But later when the fighting became the order of the day instead of playing Soldier, they were very willing to let the blacks do their share   But seldom would they render the credit that was due   It will be a long time before the war for equal rights can batter down the fortifications of prejudice & Aristocracy

      But the lesson must be learned & our Country can have no <u>real</u> <u>peace</u> until that time comes

---

[63] The amphibious attack and subsequent occupation of Beaufort made it one of the first communities in the Deep South to be held in Union hands, as early as November, 1861. The Civil War had a dramatic effect on Beaufort, though much of the town was spared from physical destruction, there were many incidents of arson and looting as a result of Union occupation and the early liberation of the substantial slave population. History of Beaufort, South Carolina. (June 19,2015). *Wikipedia, The Free Encyclopedia*. RetrievedDecember1,2015,from https://en.wikipedia.org/w/index.php?title=History_of_Beaufort,_South_Carolina&oldid=667601068

[64] Pope's Plantation was located on Hilton Head, South Carolina.

[65] An advance outpost or guard for a large force was called a picket. Ordered to form a scattered line far in advance of the main army's encampment, but within supporting distance, a picket guard was made up of a lieutenant, 2 sergeants, 4 corporals, and 40 privates from each regiment. Picket duty constituted the most hazardous work of infantrymen in the field. Being the first to feel any major enemy movement, they were also the first liable to be killed, wounded, or captured. And the most likely targets of snipers. Picket duty, by regulation, was rotated regularly in a regiment. Weeks, Richard. *Shotgun's Home of the American Civil War*. Definitions of Civil War Terms. (2012). Retrieved on November 30, 2015, from http://www.civilwarhome.com/terms.html

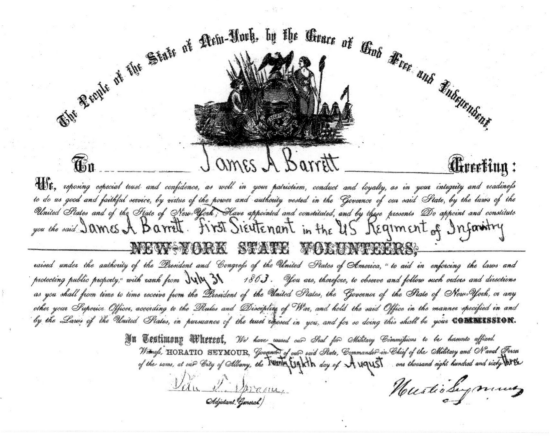

James' 1st Lieutenant certificate
(Barrett Collection)

[This is Emma Jane's transcription of a letter written by James.]

New York   Oct 2 1863

Dear Jennie, I have been very busy since I have been here or I would have written before. I have not found my trunk yet I think I have obtained @ clue to it & the agent for the sick & wounded is doing what he can. I have been very well. I get rather tired, that is all. I have obtained @ pass per Steamer "Arago"[66] which sails tomorrow.

I called at Mrs. Leete's today. She said they had received @ letter from you. She seemed to <u>understand</u> without any explanation from me. Enclosed I send you my photograph in two styles. You can keep the one you like best & do what you like with the other. I also enclose one for Nell. Please give it to her & tell her I would be happy to hear from her whenever she has an hour to spare. I rode out to Cambridge & saw Annie. She was just going to the office with a letter for me addressed to you to forward. She seems to try to forget her troubles in thinking of the welfare of her friends, But it won't last long. I can see how it will end. Outside influence may check for a time but never obliterate. I send you @ ring. I don't know how it will suit your taste. If you prefer a different style, I will get it if you will let me know. Please write very soon, direct to St. Augustine Fla. I will write on board the steamer.

I would have liked more time with you & was sorry afterwards that I had not waited until the noon train & so had you over to the house again. There were many things I wanted to say But I suppose it is all for the best as it is. I remain with much love

Yours very truly

Jas. A. Barrett

P.S. I had almost forgotten to say, But I presume you will be interested to know that I have been appointed 1st Lieut. The Col. informed me of it & that my commission had been sent to the Regiment.

As ever

James.

Photo of steamer "Arago"
(This media is in the public domain in the United States, 2016)

---

[66] USC&GS "Arago" was a survey ship that served in the United States Coast Survey from 1854 to 1878 and in the United States Coast and Geodetic Survey from 1878 to 1881. From October 1861 into 1863 "Arago" was at times attached to the Navy's South Atlantic Blockading Squadron off South Carolina to provide hydrographic support. She was the first ship of the Coast Survey and Geodetic Survey to bear the name. USC&GS Arago (1854). (September 23, 2015). *Wikipedia, The Free Encyclopedia*. Retrieved December 1, 2015, from https://en.wikipedia.org/w/index.php?title=USC%26GSArago(1854)&oldid=682426533

Carte de visites of Jennie's sister, Elizabeth "Lizzy" Farmer Leete
and her husband, George Leete
(Barrett Collection)

[*James' first diary entry]
Sat Oct 3 1863
Sailed about noon. Expect to join the regiment at St. Augustine.

[This is Emma Jane's transcription of a letter written by James.]

AT SEA   Steamer "ARAGO"
12 noon Oct 4 1863

Dear Jennie,

      This is Sunday morning & we have just held religious services on deck But it is very different from the Sabbaths I have passed during the last two months I have enjoyed them, I assure you & expect to be obliged to make them answer for the next year to come. Last Sunday morning I heard Mr. Staples & liked him very much. He has a remarkable conversational style, simple & at the same time, forcible. The little church is just as it used to be except that it is better filled. It has not been altered & enlarged as I suppose, & I think will not be. There was a suggestion of the kind in the Inquirer.

      So long as my nation's burdens remain unlifted, I am content to draw my spiritual & social pleasures from the memories of the past, the prayers of the present & the hopes & promises of the future.

      My time was so taken up in N.Y. that I hardly found time to write & I believe I said that I would enclose a ring (which was to be the certificate of the <u>Prize</u> I <u>drew</u> on Cattle Show day). I afterwards sent it in a separate package   which I trust may reach you safely. I think it will fit, But if it does not, It can easily be made to do so. I presume that our engagement is by this timegenerally known, at least among our friends. I know how such things circulate in a place like Concord. I do not think it will surprise them. Indeed I think some of them have wondered that it has not taken place before. I do not believe in long engagements & I had fully resolved to wait until the war was over before I sought to bind your fate with mine. But every time we met I felt more & more strongly the barrier which separated us, & now that this is removed & we dounderstand each other, I cannot tell you the relief I feel. I only trust & pray that I may be worthy of you.

Now Jennie, I owe you my entire confidence & perhaps I had better commence by explaining something of the past, & the motives which governed me. Fifteen years ago, when we used to go to dances together I loved you & I did then flatter myself that it was in some measure returned. Since then, I confess that I have wavered & diverged at times, But only to return again stronger & more firmly fixed in my loyalty to you. Our relationship did at one time cause me to hesitate, But this has ceased to trouble me, believing as I do, that He who directs our thoughts & affections, knows best what is good for us. I was young then, too young to assume life's responsibilities even if circumstances had allowed. I left home at seventeen & went to Boston only to return again after 9 months experience of city life. I liked the country & always had @ sort of taste for farming. But after living at home several years, I resolved to leave again & seek my fortune elsewhere. Experience & observation both taught me that happiness seldom or never blesses the son who settles at home & I determined that I would not be either the active or passive cause of family discord & I loved you too well to expose you to the fate of most wives who settle with their husband's parents. On leaving home, I was offered @ deed of one half the farm & stock if I would remain. This of course I refused, & many called me foolish. Perhaps I was, But I have never regretted it. Five years in N.Y. taught me something & placed me in @ position where I could reasonable hope at least for independence. Then the War broke out & again circumstances, fate or as I prefer to call it –Providence, changed my course & I hope has watched over it since.

During all this time, I have from time to time sought to intimate to you my intentions towards you, without at any time, seeking to bind or control your action. This I did not feel justified in doing until I could feel confident that I could provide for you @ Home that we might hope to make pleasant & happy. Now Jennie I have tried to be frank. Excuse me if I have been tedious. You were frank & honest toward me. I thank you for it & love you the better. As I said before, at one time I thought you liked me But after that I know how you were joked & teased. Then you very naturally shunned me. I feared you would come to hate me entirely. You said you did at one time like Charley. I did not know it although I am not surprised at it. He is as noble @ man as walks the streets. I think now I can remember the time. But enough of this. I am satisfied with the assurance of the present. I believe I am not of @ jealous nature & if I was, I am sure there is nothing in your character to ever encourage it. A few years past I have felt that you understood me, although perhaps you would not allow yourself to acknowledge it. I knewI had no <u>right</u> to <u>expect</u> anything more than <u>friendship</u> whatever I may have <u>hoped</u> for.

But enough of the past. I am glad you passed that last night at our house. You will feel all the freer to visit there, & feel assured that you will always be welcome at any & all times. You are @ great favorite of all of them. Em began to quiz me the next day & it was only after repeated assurances on my part, that I finally succeeded in making her believe that we were really engaged. How your folks did stare that night! I have thought of it often since. The day I left home, Father again renewed his offer to give up the farm to me if I would come home "when this cruel war is over." I told him I should probably go back to Brooklyn. At Boston, Storey again suggested the idea of my going in with him. I believe I told you that I had talked of it @ few years ago. In N.Y. I also canvassed the chances. Charley and I talked over business matters & alluded to what <u>might</u> be. I also talked with Davis some. Clark (one of our old clerks) has just engaged for 5 years at $2000 a year on the strength of being one of J.P.S. & Co's clerks. But this is neither here or there. I am not at liberty to accept @ chance in business & until I am, it is needless to worry you with these recitals.

We left N.Y. about noon yesterday. We have had fine weather. The boat rolls some & I have felt just @ little inclination to sea sickness—not enough to say that I am sick, But enough to feel @ little uncomfortable. There are some 500 people on board. Among them some 12 to 15 ladies supposed to be teachers of contra bands[67][xiv]. But some of them, no doubt, only use this as @ pretense in order to get @ pass. Indeed, one lady told me so. Her husband is at Beaufort & she is going to pass the winter with him. Damondale is intended to refer to the village, not to @ man named Dale. You remember you asking me to inquire.

Contrabands aboard U.S. Ship Vermont, Port Royal, South Carolina
H.P. Moore, Photographer (Barrett Collection)

---

[67] Contraband was a term commonly used in the United States military during the American Civil War to describe a new status for certain escaped slaves or those affiliated with Union forces. The Army (and the U.S. Congress) determined that the US would not return escaped slaves who went to Union lines and classified them as contraband. Boundless (2015). *Boundless U.S. History.* Retrieved from https://www.boundless.com/u-s-history/textbooks/boundless-u-s-history-textbook/the-civil-war-1861-1865-18/ (See Endnotes)

The boat rolls & my hand is not steady so I really think I may be excused for the shocking appearance of this letter as well as for all mistakes. I believe I told you I received your last letter after I got home, But it was very acceptable nevertheless.

I think I will defer writing of my safe arrival &c until next week or until I hear from you. Hoping this will not be long, I remain with much love to all,

Yours very truly
James A. Barrett
1st Lieut, 48th N.Y. Vols

Oct 7 1863

Arrived safe at Hilton Head. Our Reg't is here on @ steamer going to report to Gen'l Terry at Morris Island.

Direct ---Port Royal or elsewhere. James.

*[*James' diary entries]*
Wed Oct 7 1863
Arrived at Hilton Head 8 A.M. Had @ fine passage. 48th here on
transports bound for Morris Island. Destination changed for Beaufort.
Captain & I join them in the evening. Lt. Smith resigned & gone home.

Thurs Oct 8 1863
Slept very well in Moser's tent. Got mine up to-day. Four companies
gone to Seabrook for @ few days. Board at the restaurant for one week.

Seabrook Plantation, South Carolina.
H.P. Moore, Photographer (Barrett Collection)

[*Letter]

Beaufort, S.C. Oct 9 1863

Dear Friends

I arrived safely at Hilton Head on the morning of the 7th after @ delightful passage. I was just @ little seasick the first day But enjoyed the passage very much after that There were somevery pleasant people on board & among them several ladies. So I managed to drive away the <u>blues</u>

When we arrived at the Head you can judge my astonishment at seeing the 48th N.Y. Regt on board two transports bound for Morris Island. I went out in @ boat to see the boys & was very warmly welcomed by my Co as well as 2 others that were on board with twice 3 Cheers & a <u>tigre</u>[68]**xv** They are very well & in good spirits. But the Lt Col was ashore & there recd orders there to come to Beaufort instead of Morris Island & here we are. Capt & I came up that night & were made welcome in Camp again. Yesterday 4 Cos were sent to Seabrook for @ few days. We don't know how long we shall remain here But expect to be here for some time

All the Officers & men unite in speaking in the highest terms of St Augustine & say it was like leaving @ 2nd home Of course we were disappointed But it is all in the 3 years. The people become very much attached to our Regt and actually shed tears when they came away & also sent petitions for the 48th to come back again Our little theatre was in full blast there & was @ source of much attraction & interest   The whole Regt has got the blues. I think I am jolly compared with them My wound is doing well almost healed. They won't listen to my going on duty at present. I told the Adj that I was ready to go on guard. He said "he did not see it." But I am glad I am here I feel now that I am at my post & I know I can be of <u>some</u> service & that is better than to be <u>idle</u> at home. I met Ellen Barrett & Minnie at Bronxville one night. I supposeCharley has sent @ lot of my Photographs home by this time I left some twenty with him to be sent home

I am appointed 1st Lieut But cant get mustered until the Regt is filled up. I think the Co numbers about 70 who are still upon the rolls We can be mustered with 80 men

I hope we may get that number soon. We have @ very pleasant Camp here I am boarding for @ week at @ restaurant near camp write soon give much love to all & believe me

Yours very truly
Jas. A. Barrett
1st Lt   48th N.Y. Vols.

---

[68] This is a derivative of "Three cheers and a tiger". It was popular to imitate a growl for all festive and joyous occasions. Walsh, William S. (1909). *Handy Book of Literary Curiosities*. Retrieved November 30, 2015, from
https://archive.org/stream/handybooklitera04walsgoog#page/n1056/mode2up (See Endnotes)

[*James' diary entry]
Fri Oct 9 1863

Most too far to walk to meals. Weather warm at noon. Called at Mrs. Judd's in the evening. Reported for duty yesterday, But the Adj. said he could not see it. Wound doing well.

> [Emma Jane's transcription of Emily's journal entry]
> Sat. Oct. 10, 1863
>
> *Had a letter from James saying that he was intending to sail this morning for Hilton Head. May a kind Providence go with him and preserve him from danger. We miss him ever so much. His photographs haven't come but we shall expect them soon.*

[*Letter to his niece, Lizzie Warren]

H.Q. Co H. 48th Regt N.Y.S. Vols
Beaufort S.C. Oct 10 1863

Dear little Lizzie

Now dont be mad cause if you are you will only have to get clever again

I dont know as I have got much to write except to tell you to be @ good girl   mind your mother & be careful how you drive the horses. I sent you @ Photograph through Emma

I shall expect yours soon with that long letter you promised me.

I am doing well   expect to go on duty in @ week. Would do so now   But they wont listen to the idea. I don't know how long we will stay here   It looks now as if we might remain all winter Altho we may go to Morris Island. I think we may be in at the taking of Charleston after all

I have got one very good little Nig   He answers to the name of William Henry with some big name on the end of it   I forget now what it is & Capt has got another. I think mine can lick his though

I tent with 2d Lt Edwards & am boarding for the present in the Village.

We expect to start our theatre here if we stay Tell Ella she must come on as soon as she can get ready. Want it @ pitty she was not ready to come with me? Kiss Georgie for me & tell him I wont sell him

Now Lizzie I want you to play Hail Columbia & @ lot of other patriotic songs for me & learn all your teacher can know before I come home again   You know you are coming to Brooklyn to visit me & I want to be proud of you   you know I should be sorry to be ashamed of you Now don't be mad again because you know

We are getting quite settled in camp   I wish you could take @ peep at me now. We have not commenced to drill yet

The weather is fine   I can imagine you shivering up there while I am enjoying the Sunny South. (All But the enjoy I think I hear you say) never mind   It is all in the 3 years. As I said befor

I have nothing to say. I only wrote to let you know I did not forget you   So with much love to all & hoping to hear from you soon   "Ill dry up" with

> Yours very truly
> Jas.A.Barrett
> 1st Lt. Co H 48th N Y V

[*James' diary entries]

Sat Oct 10 1863
Getting @ little bilious[69]. Mail leaves tonight. Hired @ boy yesterday. He seems to be @ very good one. Called at Mrs. Judd's in the evening.

Sun Oct 11 1863
Went to church in the 56th N.Y. Camp. Dr. Van Wycke preached. Our band played.

Tues Oct 13 1863
Steamer "Carnack" arrived. Burr on board. Mail gone to Augustine. Strickland, Dunbar, Nichols & Ingraham mustered. I shall be.

Wed Oct 14 1863
Regiment paid off to-day. I have to witness Co. A's rolls. 2nd Lieuts. not mustered.

Thurs Oct 15 1863
Joined Moser's mess. Showery to-day. "Fulton" arrived. Another mail gone to Augustine.

Fri Oct 16 1863
They want us to start the Theatre. On board of survey to-day to condemn tents. Dunbar says I am to take command of Co. A. I can't see it. Men drunk—fight in camp. Firing heard to-day.

---

[69] Having or causing a sick feeling (nausea) in the stomach. bilious. (n.d.). *Merriam Webster's On-line Dictionary*. Retrieved November 30, 2015, from http://www.merriam-webster.com/dictionary/bilious

[This is Emma Jane's transcription of a letter written by James.]

Beaufort S.C.   Oct 16 1863

Dear Jennie

The "Fulton"[70] arrived a few days since & sails on Monday. Her mail for the 48th with two before that being directed to St. Augustine went there & we must wait for them to be sent back before we can get our letters.

I am not on duty yet. My wound is gaining very slowly. But I did not come back @ day too soon. Captain & I found the company sadly in need of us to look after them. It is going to get things straight again—about as much as we shall want to do before our wounds heal. We did not get to Morris Island after all. I was in hopes to catch @ sight of the place on our way down but it was evening when we passed Charleston bar & we could see nothing But an occasional flash of @ gun to indicate our approach to the seat of war & the fields where we lost so many of our best men. Our regiment makes @ sorry appearance now on dress parade & roll call is @ sad reminder of the ravages of war, But we are coming out better than I feared & the men are all in good spirits & the kind welcome we received from them on our arrival made us almost forget our temporary disappointment in not going to St. Augustine[71]. They all give the most glowing accounts of the place & only wish to go back. They managed to make themselves very popular there.

It is @ very difficult task to make ourselves contented here. We have @ fine healthy camp & duty is not very hard. Guard duty is the principal thing & that comes pretty often now that four of our companies are away at Seabrook.

Our little Olympic Theatre was in full blast in St. Augustine & we are thinking of starting ithere. The only objection is the uncertainty of our remaining.

What do you hear from Ned? Mrs. Leete said his regiment was ordered to the front. I think Rosecrans is doing splendidly & I believe he will yet turn the tide of fortune in his favor. Spirits like his are not to be discouraged by trifles nor conquered by @ few disasters, But fixed by @ noble zeal, with his past experience to help him & supported & assisted by that brave Gen. Thomas, I believe he will yet obtain @ victory which will be second to none yet gained. We have heard heavy firing all day & think it must be from Gen. Gillmore. His works are said to be nearly completed & when he does open, you may calculate that Charleston is ours.

I made application for some duplicate papers as soon as I landed. I can not get my pay or be mustered as 1st Lt. until I get them, But I apprehend no trouble.

---

[70] The "USS Fulton" (also called the "Dick Fulton") was 123 ton stern-wheel steamer, used as an auxiliary vessel in the U.S. Ram Fleet during the American Civil War. USS Fulton (1862). (April 24, 2015). *Wikipedia, The Free Encyclopedia*. Retrieved December 1, 2015, from https://en.wikipedia.org/w/index.php?title=USS_Fulton(1862)&oldid=659064513

[71] St. Augustine, Florida was under Union control for most of the Civil War. It was only under the brief control of the Confederacy. St. Augustine in the American Civil War. (April 21, 2015). *Wikipedia, The Free Encyclopedia*. Retrieved December 1, 2015, from https://en.wikipedia.org/w/index.php?title=St.AugustineintheAmericanCivilWar&oldid=65 7429745

I had such good times while at home & was humored so much that it is hard to go to work again, But I am getting into it slowly. There has been quite @ talk here of reenlisting for 3 years. But I believe they have nearly all concluded to wait until their present term of service has expired.

I did not write this letter because I had anything to say, But only to let you know that "I still live".

Hoping to hear from you soon, I remain

Yours sincerely

James A. Barrett

[*James' diary entries]

Sat Oct 17 1863

Sutlers[72] arrived. Hard to get their pay. Theatre working at Augustine.
I must write for the things to be sent.

Sun Oct 18 1863

Church in 56th N.Y Camp. Mr. Harris, post chaplain, preached. Very good.
Our band played. "Cosmopolitan"[73] arrived. No mail. No news. Lt. Moser resigned.

Mon Oct 19 1863

Lt. Taylor & Capt. Vidal arrived. No great news yet except the utter defeat of the Copperheads in Ohio & Penn. I am to take command of Co. A for the present.

Tues Oct 20 1863

Assigned to Co. A. R. Order. Called at Mrs. Judd's.

Wed Oct 21 1863

Went on duty to-day—officer of the day. Am most well.

Thurs Oct 22 1863

"Cosmopolitan" came up to-day with sick men from Folly Island. I went down & found my trunk. Will have pictures taken tomorrow. "Arago" due to-day with mail.

---

[72] A person who followed an army or maintained a store on an army post to sell provisions to the soldiers. sutler (n.d.). *Random House Unabridged Dictionary*. Retrieved December 7, 2015, from http://dictionary.infoplease.com/sutler

[73] The "Cosmopolitan" was a troop transport and hospital-steamer. The "Cosmopolitan" was part of South Atlantic Blockading Squadron under the command of Brigadier General H.G. Wright.

Fri Oct 23 1863
Picture taken this A.M. Officer of the day again. Mail in but ours
not received yet. Col. & Capt. Miller arrived. No ___ N.Y.

Carte de visite of two of James' sisters
Rebecca Minott Barrett   Mary Prescott Barrett Warren
(Barrett Collection)

[letter from James' sister, Rebecca Minott Barrett]

Concord, Oct 23rd, 1863

Dear brother James,

We felt very sorry to see that your Reg. was ordered back as we know you are not fit to be there. Hope you will not try to go on duty until your wound is entirely healed and don't walk about a great deal We shall make up your shirts as soon as possible if we can get the flannel am afraid we shall have to get plain blue but will do the best we can Jane Farmer was in and spent the night a week ago last Friday she had rec· your photographs also abby Buttrick has received hers we think them good but the one without the cap very much the best ours have not arrived yet I have written to Charles about them to night I fear they are lost on the way

Rev. (George) Washington Hosmer[74]
(Barrett Collection)

The sabbath school association met here last week   Mr. Washington Hosmer was there, his son James with his new wife a very pleasant person I should think and his daughter Anna and her husband. I believe they had quite an interesting meeting I was not present as I had to be over at the hall preparing for the collation [75]. I carried down half a dozen of my bouquets to ornament the hall and sold them all I could have sold a great many if I had had them done and these am making them now – shall send my first basket full off this week Mrs. Reynolds thinks there is not much likelewards of her getting her photograph with trunk

Doc says he almost hopes you will not find it because you dreamed you had We received the boxes of soap day before yesterday but have not received the bill of them should like to know where you get the balls as Emily thinks we may want more as there are a number want some Sister Mary is rather better but has not much strength yet I do not believe we shall get her away from home at present You did not tell us any thing about your visit at Bronxville   should like to know all about it Anna Story died a little over a week ago So our circle one after another pass away

[74] Rev. (George) Washington Hosmer was one of the most noted preachers in the Unitarian Church of his day. He was President of Antioch College in Ohio (1862-1872). He was Jane Farmer's Uncle and James A. Barrett's second cousin. Hosmer, J. K. *Memorial of Rev. G. W. Hosmer D.D.* Privately printed, 1882.

[75] A gathering, reception or bringing together. Collation. (n.d.). *Merriam Webster's On-line Dictionary*. Retrieved December 1, 2015, from http://www.merriam-webster.com/dictionary/collation

reminding us that we too must soon go may we be as willing and ready to meet our summons as was she

James Wood's youngest child was brought here and buried last week. It was a little over a year old   Father's club meets here tomorrow night   It is getting late and I am run ashore for news so Good night with much love

Take good care of yourself
Yours affectionately
Rebecca

Chapter 6

"Weigh All Things & Hold Fast to that which is good"[76]

October 24, 1863-November 27, 1863--Beaufort, South Carolina--
Mustered in as First Lieutenant--New York and St. Lawrence Riots--
Theatre update--Wound healing--Description of living conditions--
Letters from home--Move to Pope Plantation--Description of
grinding corn--Thanksgiving dinner

[Note that all the following transcriptions have been faithfully copied from the original document, as written by James, except where noted.]

---

[76] Quoting St. Paul from the *Bible*. (1 Thessalonians 5:21). "Prove all things; hold fast that which is good."

[*James' diary entries]
Sat Oct 24 1863
*Mail arrived. Received two letters. New tents arrived & are very good.
Will draw some on Monday.*

Sun Oct 25 1863
*Cold & stormy. Co. A look pretty well on inspection. Col. B. goes around.
Small attendance at church. Went to see 1ˢᵗ S.C on dress parade. They
do well. Lockwood going to Pulaski tomorrow.*

Mon Oct 26 1863
Cold & cloudy. Had to pitch our tents over again.

Tues Oct 27 1863
*Des. list of David White—Ft. Schuyler, N.Y. Clothing a/c Aug. 7/63—Cr.
3.48 Des. list of Erick Leinberg (Errick Limberg) —Annapolis, Md. Clothing
a/c July 18/63—Cr. 14.70 General inspection. Co. A. looks well. Books
behind.*

Wed Oct 28 1863
*Officer of the day. Policing. Negroes rather filthy. Col. is consulting about
who to muster first.*

Thurs Oct 29 1863
Making pay rolls. N.C. under arrest, but work at writing.

Fri Oct 30 1863
*Mustered in as 1ˢᵗ Lieut. Acker also mustered. Edwards & Sweeney are to
be as soon as discharged. New mess tent put up.*

Sat Oct 31 1863
*Mustered for pay. I am on duty with Co. A. but mustered on Co. H roll.
Co. A. looks very well.*

Sun Nov 1 1863
*Inspection of Co. A. Very good. Church in 56ᵗʰ Camp. Preaching by Mr.
Van Wycke. 250 conscripts arrived for several regiments. None for us.
Feel nervous on parade. Legs will shake. Saluted twice this night. Mr.
Harris has @ talk with the Col. about men going to church*

[This is Emma Jane's transcription of a letter written by James.]

November 1 1863

My Dear Jennie

It is Sunday evening—not like Sabbaths at home. We don't have <u>Sabbaths</u> in the army, But Sunday comes once a week with its inspection & <u>sometimes</u> followed by church call & some sort of @ discourse in the vicinity. The Reg^t Chaplain, Mr. Van Wycke, brother to Col. Van Wycke, the senator, preached to day, what I supposed your friend Carrie Hosmer would call @ fine discourse, But it did not inspire me much. I always think it makes one feel better to go to church even if we do not enjoy it altogether. Mr. Hoar used to say he could always gather some wheat even from the driest sermon. I am glad to hear that the bitter Sectarian bigotry[77] in Concord is softening down. I notice what you say about your discussion on the Bible. I like discussions so long as they can be carried on in the right spirit—When friends can agree to disagree & reason with @ candid loving spirit. I know we are very apt to accompany our arguments with @ <u>sting</u> & then we too often allow anger to mount the throne of reason & disarm our better judgments. It is unpleasant, as you say, as @ general thing, to talk upon these subjects with friends with whom one differs widely. As to being settled in one's convictions, I think it is far better to be unsettled with an earnest inquiring mind, than to accept @ passive, lifeless faith on other people's testimony. "Weigh all things & hold fast to that which is good." It used to annoy me to be called heretical[78] or infidel[79], But I got over that long ago.

Captain Lockwood, not <u>conscripts</u>. We want men who come willingly, bringing them whole hearts with them & ready to raise their strong arms to crush this accursed rebellion. I have lately read some detailed accounts of the N.Y. & Lawrence riots. It is enough to make one's blood run cold the many inhuman outrages committed upon unarmed men & helpless women & children. It does seem as if Hell itself was let loose & all the friends & demons of the infernal regions were unchained & granted for @ time full license to their maddened & unbridled passions. I blush for my country when I think she has nurtured such <u>things</u> as these & pray for the speedy downfall of those institutions which so completely ignore our most sacred rights—which take from man his manhood & from woman her more than life. Report says that the siege of Charleston has

---

[77] Sectarianism, according to one definition, is bigotry, discrimination, or hatred arising from attaching importance to perceived differences between subdivisions within a group, such as between different denomination of a religion, class, regional or factions of a political movement. Sectarianism. (October 6, 2015). *Wikipedia, The Free Encyclopedia*. Retrieved December 2, 2015, from https://en.wikipedia.org/w/index.php?title=Sectarianism&oldid=684382516

[78] Characterized by, revealing, or approaching departure from established beliefs or standards. heretical. (n.d.) AMERICAN HERITAGE DICTIONARY OF THE ENGLISH LANGUAGE, FIFTH EDITION. (2011). Retrieved December 1, 2015, from http://www.thefreedictionary.com/heretical

[79] Infidel is a term used in certain religions, especially Christianity and Islam, for one who has no religious beliefs, or who doubts or rejects the central tenets of the particular religion. infidel. (n.d.) AMERICAN HERITAGE DICTIONARY OF THE ENGLISH LANGUAGE, FIFTH EDITION. (2011). Retrieved December 1, 2015, from http://www.thefreedictionary.com/infidel

recommenced. I hardly credit the story But hope that bed of treason & infamy may be laid in ruins. I want to see it reduced to ashes like Sodom & Gomorrah of old (am I right?) Too long it has been the plague spot of our land & breathed its pestilential[80] poison into the very heart of our nation.

I am glad Henry is better. I do not think your mother is very strong.

Carte de visite of Jennie's brother,
Henry Farmer[81] (Barrett Collection)

Do they have Dr. Bartlett? The dear old soul—I love him as @ father. "May he live @ thousand years & his shadow never be less." I wish, we had him down here. It would be easy to get @ position for one like him—always cheerful with @ kind word for all. He is @ regular sunbeam in the sick room.

Dr. Josiah Bartlett
(Carte de visite courtesy of the Concord Free Library, Special Collections)

---

[80] Dangerous or troublesome; harmful or annoying. pestilential. (n.d.). *Dictionary.com Unabridged*. Retrieved December 1, 2015, from http://dictionary.reference.com/browse/pestilential

[81] Henry Farmer joined the 5th Reg. Massachusetts Infantry, Company G. His regiment was engaged in the First Battle of Bull Run. His regiment's term of service was for three months.

You say you dreamed that Charleston was taken & that you gave four cheers by mistake. That was all right. Soldiers always give three cheers & @ tigra which is equal to four & as to the city being taken, you know "Coming events sometimes cast their shadows before."

I had the pleasure last Friday of taking the oath of allegiance for the third time since I entered the service on the occasion of my being mustered as 1st Lieut. I sometimes wonder if the Rebels can feel the enthusiasm that we do. I suppose they must or they could not fight as they do. It is @ pity so much energy should be expended in such a cause.

We are getting good news from the north. Well done Penn., Ohio & Indiana. "The October that has touched our maples with fire has touched our banners with victory," & @ victory that is worth recording too. Let the good work go on until "No pent up Utica confines our powers, But this whole boundless continent is ours."

We have splendid evenings here. How I wish I could convey myself quietly north & take some more rides where the horse would insist on walking. I believe you said you did not sleep well after that ride. If I remember rightly, I was affected in the same way. So that the folks joked me for being dull next day. It was wicked in me to come away the way I did, But I always dread to say good-bye & always feel like @ fool for @ while before. I leave home—I did intend to ride over again, But I didnt & I will submit myself to your mercy when I come home again.

I would ask you to excuse this scrawl, for really I am ashamed of it, But such apologies are worn out & if I should attempt to copy it, I fear I should lose my patience & tear it up, the "Fulton" would sail without my letter.

So Good night, from yours

James A. Barrett
1st Lieut. Co H 48th Regt N.Y. S. Vols.
Port Royal   S.C.

[*James' diary entry]
Mon Nov 2 1863
Dunbar thinks of coming back. I hope he will. Steamer in from
Augustine—four letters about a month old. Sergt. Himrod not come yet.
Theatre likely to be sold. Adj. going down on @ pass. Will try to stop the
sale.

[*Letter]

Head Quarters Co H. 48th Regt N.Y.S. Vols
Beaufort S.C. Nov 2 1863

Dear Mother

Yours of Oct 8th is just recd after traveling on an exploring voyage vainly trying to find @ man about my size down towards the Gulf. That was @ ridiculous fancy of yours to imagine a chap of my humble appearance being assassinated on the wharf for my money   It is as bad as the Old Maid who burst out crying one night while looking into an open fire place. Now dont you worry about me. Under ordinary circumstances I believe I am competent to take good care of myself & under more serious circumstances I am sure Anxiety will only make the matter worse

Evil comes fast enough & it is time enough to dread it when it comes. "Fear not but trust in Providence wherever thou may'st be" Surely the same Providence that has carried me safely through the past can keep me from harm in the future & If it is his will to do otherwise "It is well" & I trust I may be content. It can make But @ few short years of difference any how. I am in for the war & I have not regretted the step. If I live through it I am sure I shall be much more of @ man for the experience I shall have gained. I have weighed the issue & the chances. Without that for which we are contending Life would be But @ burden It would not be life at all "It is not all of life to live Nor all of Death to die". I do not feel that my work is finished & I do long to live to see better days. I feel that there is much to live for. But just so much the more is there much to fight & die for & if the lot should fall on me I hope I may not falter & I know I should have many earnest Prayers

The folks in NY. were all well when I was there Dr Smith did not see my wound. I do not think I am in any way worse for coming as soon as I did & the moral effect is much better than to over stay the time

Geo poor fellow has @ hard row to hoe I think his pecuniary matters are all that kept him out of the Army I do not think it is always the duty of young men to enlist They all know their own business best & must govern themselves accordingly I am glad that Martin is going to stay I feel much easier for father while Martin remains. Father does work too hard I do wish he could sell out & so relieve himself of some of his cares

I often think of Dr Bartlett It always does me good to see his face I often wish we had him here He once asked if I could get him @ place here I think he was joking It would not be @ difficult thing to do

If he should apply at washington with one or two letters He would get @ commission by return mail We are sadly in need of good Surgeons Tell the Dr I should be happy to see him in this department He may always be sure of my welcome wherever I meet him.

I suppose Rebecca is as much devoted to the Soldiers as ever & Em to Charles This is well. Each is doing her work in her own good way

The Harvest will come bye & bye. Tell Father he must learn to hope more He gets too easily discouraged about war matters. We are sailing in the good staunch Ship "Constitution" Liberty propels her wheels & God himself sits at the Helm. We may meet with temporary reverses even as Peter did when he attempted to walk on the water But we will not allow such trifles to shake our faith. Our cause is just. & Justice rules

There is no such thing as fail

I am glad Mary is improving I think if she takes proper care of herself she will be all right.

I get the Independent & Inquirer regular I long for Beecher to return & take hold of the Independent again He gives life to every thing

Direct every thing to Port Royal S.C.   The Fulton leaves tomorrow & I have another letter to write tonight so with much love to all

I remain very truly

Your Son

James A. Barrett

1st Lt Co H. 48th N.Y.Vols

Port Royal S.C.

[This is Emma Jane's transcription of a letter written by James.]

H.Q.CO.H, 48th N.Y.S.VOLS.

BEAUFORT S.C. NOV 2 1863

11 p.m.

My dear Jennie,

I wrote you @ long letter last night, But this eve our mail arrived from Augustine bringing your 2 long looked for letters, one from Mother & one from Lizzie Warren & as I have adopted (strange as it may seem) the rule of answering letters by first steamer, I will just scratch off @ few lines & send by the "Fulton" which leaves in the morning. I am receiving congratulations from all quarters. I really believe I am getting happy in my <u>old age</u> in spite of my <u>gray hairs</u>. I hope you will excuse my not writing you sooner when in N.Y. & also my not writing you first. But I supposed you would hear their letter & I was very busy & not quite ready to write to you. I was going to get @ plain ring & enclose. I was afraid to trust myself to select anything else, But Charley dissuaded me & I finally got Mrs. Bates to go & help me select one. I had full confidence in her taste. The one I sent was <u>her</u> choice & I thought you would like it better than @ plain one... If you do not, just say so & I will get a plain one too.

It seems you do sometimes dream too. If Dr. ever says anything more about my dreaming, tell him I will dream him @ conscript dealing out quinine &c &c I believe I got the best of the whole of them after all their blackguarding me for not giving up my presentiments. You spoke of the coming year being long. I look forward to its termination with very much pleasure, But time seldom drags with me. It is always my good fortune to be kept busy at something & I find days, weeks and months chasing each other away with greatly increasing swiftness, & then I have seen it written somewhere & I like the idea – "Never insult today with @ too anxious longing for tomorrow." "Today is thine & wisely intended to precede tomorrow." But I do not propose to preach in this letter. I did have @ good time in Brooklyn. I did not stay long enough to miss anyone, or I certainly should have missed Beecher[xvi]. Staples satisfied me very well. Mrs. Bates was very kind & made my visit very happy. I called at Lizzie's twice. Martha was not there the last time.

I did think of you very much after I left home & took the first opportunity after embarking when I could be by myself to write to you what I could not tell you at home for lack of time. You and some others give me altogether too much credit. I am not as strong or as stable as you seem to think. I often have reason to regret my own weakness, insignificance & want of decision of character. You do not notice it perhaps. You have no opportunity of doing so, But I cannot let you blindly deceive yourself. On intimate acquaintance, we are often disappointed even in our best friends, & far be it for me to encourage @ false idea of my true character only to have the real truth glare out all the stronger at last.

I cannot help laughing when you speak of sister Emma. She is so confiding, sympathetic & honest & the way she sought my confidence & then would not believe me, I have thought of many times since.

How do you like the new rule I visiting schools? I should think it would cause confusion. So Dr. Barrett is really tied at last! When at home, I heard that he was to be married & I immediately thought of the old adage, "There's many a slip etc" I should think from all accounts that marriage is getting contagious. Capt. Barrett had better fall his men in, <u>Draft</u> a lot of ladies or call for volunteers as leap year is coming and engage @ minister by the month. Only, if he does, I will send <u>you</u> your <u>exemption</u> <u>papers</u> to show that you have got some one totally <u>dependent</u> on you for <u>assistance</u>, <u>encouragement</u> & <u>support</u> &c &c &c   I am glad you have such an accommodating clock. Whether the children were as forgetful, I am doubtful.

I am at @ loss to know what you found to enjoy in that "Nursnack" walk. I am sure I was very poor company that day. I was resolved not to tell you my feelings until after the war &I felt the distance between us & it weighed upon me. You must have noticed. I am sure you did. I could not stand it & afterwards in the 11th hour, took that happy second thought.

I felt provoked when the steamer came from Augustine & did not bring @ Serg^t of the Co I am in command of, who has been left there. The returns & accounts have not been made since June 30 & I can't do anything before he comes & brings the necessary papers. You ask me to define my duties. I rise at sunrise, & attend Roll call, inspect the rations, complete my toilet, attend to the details of the Co. business, sign papers, draw & distribute clothing, go out on inspections & parades & take my turn as officer of the day in camp. In fact, I do most everything except picket duty. I don't like to walk so far. My wound is nearly well now & I shall soon be able to march.

Genl Saxton wants us to start our theatre. It was left at St. Augustine & I think is sold by this time, But we may start again anyhow. There is an old church here that would be a good place.

But here I have nearly filled my 2nd sheet & it is almost one o'clock & I am Officer of the Day in the morning.

Good night; give much love to all inquiring friends, not forgetting yourself & believe me

Yours
James

[*James' diary entries]
Tues Nov 3 1863
Officer of the day to-day. At noon received orders to break camp & proceeded with Co. A to Battery Taylor on the left of entrenchments. Very

pleasant but lonesome. Countersign[82]—"Brandywine". The march stiffened
me some. Lt. Schultz is with me.

Wed Nov 4 1863
Busy cleaning up & getting settled. Must get something to eat. Found @
nigger with @ mule who will go on errands for us & wash & furnish eggs &
potatoes etc. Countersign—"Borodino".

Thurs Nov 5 1863
Visited the other batteries. Col. says Dunbar is relieved. Our battery is the
prettiest. Co. H. is fixing up well. I shall soon go back to H. No
Countersign given. I have relieved the picket at battery Brayton. Fold
Corp. to challenge & get countersign. "Seven Oaks". Hamel here. Smith
did not pay him.

Fri Nov 6 1863
Mail arrived. Medicine sent me! Drill in artillery P.M. Busy writing letters.
Countersign—"Moscow".

[*Letter]

H.Q. Left Detach[mt](Co "A") In the Entrenchments
Battery "Taylor"   Beaufort S.C.   Nov 6 1863

My Dear Jennie   You may think I am putting on "Airs"   Why should[nt] I. I am in command of this Detachment @ Battery of 3 Guns. Big Thing. I really feel quite Independant

Am about 2 miles from the other Co[s] & have a delightful camp   a little lonesome But shall soon get used to it. A Lt. Schultz is with me a very pleasant fellow & we tent together. Altho the Capt[ns] tent is pitched along side & no one to occupy it except our 2 nigs. But it is pleasanter & more social to be together   I furnish a Picket for this & Battery Brayton (2 guns) near by. The Officers of this Co were killed & the 2[d] Lieut who is now assigned here with me is not mustered yet. The new Capt has been away from the Reg[t] on detached service   He is soon expected to return & take command of the Co   There have been no Returns &c made since June 30th & I was put temporarily in command in order to sign for Property & make up the Returns &c but the Co Clerk who has the accounts, was left at Augustine & I can not sign or account for the Property until He returns & now I expect the Capt will be back soon enough to relieve me from the vexation & responsibility   I hope he will   I do not fancy undertaking to straighten out rather perplex affairs. I say nothing of the risk & responsibility. It is bad enough to be Capt in fact. & worse still to be Lieut Com[dg] (acting Capt[n])

---

[82] A secret sign given in response to another sign; password. countersign. (n.d.). *Dictionary.com Unabridged*. Retrieved December 1, 2015, from
http://dictionary.reference.com/browse/countersign

I left our old camp Tuesday & marched out here   My letter of 2^d acknowledged your 2 letters from Augustine. Thank you for them   You see I am answering promptly   I am trying the plan of answering on rec^t of all letters   Can not say how long the fit may last   My wound is almost well. I dont think the Dr has seen it at all. I dress it when I think it necessary & get whatever I want from the Hospital. Have not been sorry that I came when I did you must have had quite a Reunion with all your Buffalo friends   I would like to have seen them   How about those mishaps & adventures   I conclude there was nothing serious as you would have mentioned it

I would like to have heard Dr Huntington   I well remember several of his sermons & lectures   I always liked him However much I may have differed with him of late years.   I am glad your Photographs are on the way. I have been looking for one   I am glad to hear that Ned is doing so well   Please remember me kindly to him & tell him I would be extremely glad to hear from him

I am @ miserable hand to open a correspondence.   But generally try to answer all letters

I am sorry about Rosecrans   Hope soon to hear of his return   He can hardly be spared now   A few more like him & well supported   & the Rebellion must soon be crushed. God grant that it may   But I shall not be discouraged even if Rosecrans Grant & a score or two leave the field   For I am sure that "God will raise up Men to fight our Battles for us"

You say you dread Examinations   I always did.   I well remember what a relief I felt when it was all over But in your case I think your anxiety will all be spent in anticipation.   You say you hope Mr Benjamin will go to the Lyceum[83]   I presume you do not mean (<u>Benjamin Clark</u>)

I believe he <u>used</u> to go and did <u>not like</u> to go <u>alone</u>. I hope Benjamin will go & always have room for <u>one man</u> & I assure you I have <u>no objections</u> whatever to his <u>tucking</u> the <u>Buffalo</u> well <u>around</u> you.   So that you may not take cold

I hope you will just take the <u>fullest liberty</u>. I believe <u>jealousy</u> is not among my <u>vices</u>

If it was it would be just good enough for me to be stirred up a little just to crush that "Green eyed monster"[84] Never fear for my working too hard   There is little danger of it   I am too fond of my ease for that & as for enlisting again I think I will finish my present term of service first & then if the war is not over & I feel that I am needed I hope I may not hesitate to do my duty & my friends must not be the first to throw impediments in my way   I am doing very well on army fare & my quarters are very comfortable My tent is boarded   A cotton sack filled with dry grass with sheets & blankets makes a very comfortable inducement to sleep. 2 rush bottomed chairs a table wash stand & basin & pail for water looking glass & trunk with hooks & a line to hang things on complete the furniture in our Home   Our dishes &c are kept in another tent. If you should peep in upon us at meal time I think you would not fear that we should starve.

---

[83] Organization of Concord, Massachusetts, formed for the purpose of improvement in knowledge, the advancement of Popular Education, and the diffusion of useful information throughout the community. Retrieved December 2, 2015, *Concord Lyceum Records, 1828 - 1928* from http://www.concordlibrary.org/scollect/finaids/concordlyceum.htm

[84] Green-Eyed Monster may refer to jealousy, phrase possibly coined by Shakespeare in "Othello" (Act lll, scene 3, line 169).

Patricia Peterson's illustration depicting James' quarters (Barrett Collection)

My tent is boarded   A cotton sack filled with dry grass with sheets & blankets makes a very comfortable inducement to sleep. 2 rush bottomed chairs a table wash stand & basin & pail for water looking glass & trunk with hooks & a line to hang things on complete the furniture in our Home   Our dishes &c are kept in another tent. If you should peep in upon us at meal time I think you would not fear that we should starve. The 48th have a way of looking out for no 1 & we have a healthy appreciation of what comfort is & intend generally to enjoy it when circumstances will allow.   And so I <u>have</u> found my "<u>Trunk</u>"   This important fact is doubtless made known to you ere this   <u>Dreams</u> do <u>sometimes</u> come to pass

"It will never do to give it up so"   I cannot say how long we shall remain here.   We can not complain of having much to do here   We are to drill twice a day & I think I shall attempt a Dress Parade Sunday night. I can divide the Co up into sections thus making it 4 Cos of it with Sergts for <u>Captains</u>   Myself acting as Col & my Lt as Adjt   I have not fully decided.   The weather here is very mild   We seldom have any frost   Our nights are often chilly & cold   But Days generally mild & pleasant

Our evenings are perfect often almost as light as Day   The "Arago" is expected tomorrow & I shall look for that Photograph

Excuse me I have forgotten again to acknowledge the rect of yours of Oct 27th which is this day recd & now before me   You did not know that I was @ Dr did you? I told the Col yesterday that I wanted some medicine here to use in case of sickness   And today I have recd some Sun mixture quinine & Pills   which I intend to administer as occasion requires   Rather a

limited stock to set up with   isnt it? But perhaps you will say the more limited, the less risk   All right I can Bear it as my shoulders are broad. I recd letters today from Rebecca &
Abbie Buttrick   I laughed well at Abbie's remarks on the Hard tack[85] (issue of 1812) I sent herI will try & answer all today. I also had a letter from one of our discharged men of a year ago who has reenlisted & was wounded at Gettysburg & is now in Hospl in Phila So you see I got enough to do today. With much love, I remain

        Very truly yours   James A. Barrett
                Co H Port Royal S.C.
Yesterday as I was going through @ cotton field   I plucked several blossoms & sent directed to your father   I thought perhaps he might like them
                Yours
                    James A. Barrett
                    1st Lieut & A. Assist Surgeon

48th N.Y. Vols Comdg Detachmt Battery NY.Vols.   Beaufort, S.C.
I believe I have got it nearly all in. You may continue to direct as usual to Co H

James' father, George Minot Barrett
(Barrett Collection)

[Letter from James' Father, George Minot Barrett]

Concord, November 7th, 1863

Dear Son, the rest of the House are so busy for the Soldiers, making wreaths, bokays, &c, that they can not stay to write, so they have urged it upon me, and the difficulty with me is I never have anything to write, we are glad to hear that you are well and have found your trunk, Massachusetts

---

[85] A hard, saltless biscuit, formerly much used aboard ships and for army rations. Also called pilot biscuit, pilot bread, ship biscuit, ship bread. hardtack, (n.d.). *Random House Unabridged Dictionary*. Retrieve December 15, 2015, from http://dictionary.infoplease.com/hardtack

election has come off well 40,000 for the Republicans, we received your Picture with the Cuffe[86] behind safe, the War does not look as well as I could wish, there seems to be a great want of more men, Rosecrans it seams came very near getting his Army cut off from supplys by some mistake of his, but Hooker drove the Rebels from lookout Mountain which saved him, I have got my harvesting done, my Apples geathered and pretty much sold I had about ¼ of a crop, but more net profit than a whole one they have sold at the door for about $250, Henry Farmer has carried them off for me. the President has called for three hundred thousand more men Concord is going to try to raise her quota 19 by paying them $500, before they start it is thought we may raise them, Richard has gorn in with Keyes Assistant Marshal at $1500, a year, Mother and the girls have made you two flannel shirts and sent them to Charles last Monday, Charles sent to them to make them, I showed that Picture with the cuffe behind to Samuel Barrett and he wants to take it and get a photograph taken from it I told him he could take it. Story was up last sunday he says his Mother is getting along very well but he has not seen her yet thinks she will winter there all wish to be remembered to you

     From your Father

     George M Barrett

James with Cuffe
(Barrett Collection)

---

[86] Cuffe/Cuffy/Cuffee was a traditional Creole name, based on African customs, given to a male child born on Friday.

*[*James' diary entries]*

Sat Nov 7 1863

Dunbar rode up. Suggested some improvements. Too much trouble, I think. He won't be here for @ week at least. Himrod back & I must make my returns. I am going to apply for @ horse.

Sun Nov 8 1863

Col. forwarded application for horse. Went to church. Col. talking of reenlisting. Himrod returned last night. I must make returns out right off now. Theatre sold at Augustine $300.00.

Mon Nov 9 1863

Col. called to Hilton Head. In command of H. Hd. Is. 156 conscripts arrived for 48th Co. A. gets 15.

Sat Nov 14 1863

Cleaned camp and Negro quarters. Sensation in Negro camp. Great improvement. Rode in to Seabrook. Duty hard there. One recruit in a bad way. Dr. rather harsh. "Greene".

Sun Nov 15 1863

Inspection. Co. looks well. The boys come up to see me. Capt. Won't be with company for sometime. "Charleston".

Mon Nov 16 1863

Ladies visit plantation. Slow way of grinding corn. One mulatto[87] here, who isquite a lady, will do my washing. I don't think we shall stay here long. Mail not in yet. "Shaw".

Tues Nov 17 1863

Rode down to Seabrook. Serg. Mackellar back from furlough. Voorheef not back. Mail not up yet. Report that five cos. to be mounted. "Vicksburg".

Wed Nov 18 1863

Rode down to Seabrook. Mail in. Received six letters. I make the rounds on plantation tonight. Firing heard to-day towards Pulaski. "Mobile".

---

[87] A term used to refer to a person who is born of one white parent and one black parent, or more broadly, a person of any "mixed" ancestry. mulatto. (n.d.). *Merriam-Webster On-line Dictionary*. Retrieved December 1, 2015, from http://www.merriam-webster.com/dictionary/mulatto

Thurs Nov 19 1863

Weather fine. Shan't ride to-day. Must answer letters. "Pulaski".

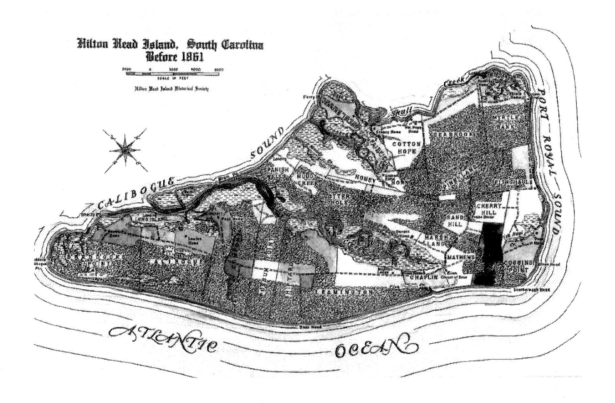

Map of Hilton Head Island Before 1861
(Courtesy of the Heritage Library, History and Ancestry Research Center,
Hilton Head, South Carolina, 2016)

[*Letter]

Head Quarters Co A. 48th Regt N.Y.S. Vols
Pope Plantation   Hilton Head Island Nov 19 1863

My Dear Jennie
        The long looked for Fulton's Mail at last arrived yesterday & I rec'd your two very welcome letters of the 4th & 10th I told Schultz I expected to get at least 6 letters. & I did, 2 from you 1 fr Father 1 from Lt Howland (home sick), 1 fr Srg't Sparks (home wounded) & one from the wife of one of my wounded men asking after him. I was rather disappointed in not getting that picture But it will all be right by the Arago. Steamers leave N.Y. regularly one day later each week The Fulton left the 13th   The Arago will probably leave the 21st & so on once in 8 days. I like it here

exceedingly The men are getting the chills considerable But I am taking all the precautions I can to guard against it. Lt Schultz is a very pleasant fellow & we get along nicely together. He is dreading the Capt^ns return. As he thinks they wont hitch so well together as we do. I have become quite used to this co & flatter myself that I have their good will. I certainly have if I can believe what they say. But you know There is always "Policy in war". We were short for rations the other day & I had occasion to reprimand one man for some remark which I fancied reflected on me. He said they had better get an Officer who would look out for their rations

But he apologized & assured me that it was the Orderly he meant & afterwards came back again to reassure me of his & his comrades good will respect &c &c I told him I could not allow him to speak disrespectfully of the Serg^t & there the matter ended. Schultz is engaged to an Augustine lady. As I am writing He wishes to be remembered & promises at some future time to pay us a visit with his tropical plant which he proposes to transplant to northern soil. I suppose your School is now about finished. You will enjoy the change & I presume I am beginning to think of Thanksgiving one week from today This letter will just about reach you bythen. You may if you please reserve room for me in your circle that evening I will be with you in Spirit. I wish I could be there in person. Our Indian Summer lasts all winter I expect it will be hard to acclimate myself to Northern winters. Not having seen any for 3 years But I am very willing to try. I don't think I shall enlist again until my time is up. I hope there will then be no further need of it. It does seem as if the large bounties offered ought to furnish men sufficient to crush the rebellion in the next 9 months. Col B is very anxious to reenlist his Regt. There is some chance of his getting to be Brigadier

If so my old Capt will be Col. & probably my present Capt may be Maj. It would depend on circumstances whether your humble Servant would in that event try for another bar But this is all premature. I certainly am not anxious I presume I am as independent in my present position as I can ever be in the Army I had some visitors the other day Two ladies rode up here & asked to be shown around the place. Of course I did what I could to make the visit pleasant Our clusters of Orange trees are very pretty with once in a while a Fig tree. The Orange trees grow something like Your Cherry trees The Fig trees something like your Quince only if possible more scrawling. The Negroes here are nearly all field hands & do not seem to understand house keeping very well. They however look about as well as certain classes in the North. They need some watching & care to make them keep clean & &c You can very readily distinguish those who have been House Servants There are a few families here. They are neat & clean & keep their floors scrubbed. & their children neatly dressed.

There is one Mulatto who has a husband in the 3d S.C. Reg^t who is quite a lady. We went in talked with her some time. She does my washing & If I stay here I am thinking of taking my meals there as she is a very good Cook She seems to be doubtful whether she is really free

They all seem to live in today & take little thought fur tomorrow. In one corner of their rooms you will generally see a bin of corn & they have Sweet Potatoes & in heaps covered with earth in their yard Their pigs are almost as numerous as their children and generally after the harvest run about loose. They catch some fish But live mostly on sweet potatoes and Corn cakes. They have an exceedingly primitive way of grinding their corn. Two miniature millstones about 2 feet in diameter do the work. One end of a stick is passed through a hole above & the other end placed in a socket on the edge of the upper stone. With this they turn the stone putting the corn in the centre. They grind a half peck in about an hour. You say Henry Wheeler has sent for Books He can do much good if he works right. The negro is pretty tractable easily influenced & many of them learn easily. I have often been surprised to see how well they apply themselves. When they become soldiers they seem to have an Inspiration breathed into them

Slaves of Rebel Gen. T.F. Drayton, Hilton Head, South Carolina
H.P. Moore, photographer (Barrett Collection)

If I was going to stay here long I think I would get a lot of cheap jewelry to award to the best & those who kept themselves the neatest.

We lived rather poor at Battery Taylor We had a man detailed to cook for us   But between him & our niggers we could have nothing decent   We could hardly tell which was the most slovenly[88]. The Co Cook now caters for us & we go out & take our meals under a little shed. We have Bread & butter cheese Sweet potatoes Onions & Pork or Bacon & we have either coffee or Tea 3 times a day with milk in it. We intend if we stay to get something better. Altho we do not complain of our present fare. That quotation from Whittier is certainly Soul Inspiring. I do not often read Poetry But there are a few writers who have a peculiar fascination. I hardly know who they are   I seldom have noticed Authors. In fact I never read much.   I suppose Lizzy Cheney has been married ere this An unhappy match I fear   I think she sold her happiness years ago & discovered her mistake when too late

---

[88] Untidy, as in dress or appearance. /Marked by negligence; slipshod. slovenly. (n.d.). *American Heritage Dictionary of the English Language, 4th edition*. Retrieved December 15, 2015, from http://www.yourdictionary.com/slovenly

I never could understand Mrs Cheney's motives in that affair. It seems to have been a blessing to Charley & a curse to Lizzie. I think she loves Charley best today. I predict for her an unhappy & aimless future   I think that life has lost for her its charms   It is sad to think so But I think it is true

I am afraid Stonewalls flank movements will not avail him in the other world. But it is hardly a subject for punning   But we can hardly expect any good thing out of Secesh[89]

I don't see where that "silly" comes in I presume you left it out. I am glad you like the ring I always feel almost afraid to select anything of that kind. You ask "when did I change my mind." I hardly know.   But I know "I could not touch you with a ten foot pole" & of course could not enjoy myself in your society all on account as I felt of that <u>unspoken</u> <u>word</u>. I remember how the Girls laughed one day when we passed the afternoon at your house & you gave up your seat & was obliged to cross over & sit near me You was as shy as a Mountain Deer, I thought I knew the cause   You would not commit yourself until I spoke the word The rest you know. I am not sure but Anne was partly responsible   You are perhaps aware that we <u>talked</u> some that week She stayed at our house & some of our conversation was about <u>you</u> & I was very frank in expressing my opinions   All very well perhaps But under the circumstances hardly warrantable & if repeated you might have thought we took too great liberties with your name. I did it at the time all in fun But "there is many a truth spoken in jest" & beside Although Anne & I understood each other (for I believe I learned her secrets although I did not tell her mine) I found <u>some</u> were inclined to misconstrue our confidence. I therefore decided to be <u>selfish</u> <u>once</u> more & try & have an understanding. & not let <u>others</u> be <u>deceived</u>.

My former conscientious scruples are all over come now & if I come home a <u>cripple</u> I believe you assumed that <u>War</u> <u>risk</u> in my 3 years <u>policy</u>.   So Em wanted to see the whole letter. Well I guess there was not much to hide She is somewhat curious I did enjoy getting her on a string. I told her the truth & She would not believe it, & when she did She wanted to know the How When & Where Circumstances Details &c &c

Of <u>course</u> I <u>told</u> her – <u>over</u> the left   She is so frank   I like to plague her that is try to. For she is so honest & matter of fact that you cant plague her. As to the Draft I would not even for selfish motives, have you consigned to this miserable climate

I can in some measure account for the bilious dispositions of S.C. Public Men. Pity the State cant be sunk.   I was however inclined to purchase some of these lands which wereadvertised for sale But the sale has been stopped not to live on. I would not be hired to live here after the war is over. When I was home I had no good chance to get any little trifles in shape of a present & besides I don't know what to get I enclose $20[00] of the filthy leucre. [90]   Which

---

[89] Derogatory term for Confederates and Southerners. secessionists. (n.d.). Atwater, G.M. (2005). *Civil War Era Slang and Terms. A Writer's Guide for the American Civil War*. Retrieved December 23, 2015, from
http://freepages.genealogy.rootsweb.ancestory.co/~poindexterfamily/CivilWar.html
[90] Money, especially, gained in a dishonest or dishonorable way. lucre. (n.d.). *Oxford Dictionaries*. Retrieved December 1, 2015, from
http://www.oxforddictionaries.com/us/definition/american_english/lucre

please do me the favor to accept & use for what you may like best I much rather you would select as I do not know What you would like   When I come again I will try to & get you something. Hoping to hear again soon, I remain with much love

Yours very truly

James A. Barrett

1st Lieut Co.H 48th Regt, N.Y.S. Vols

You can read such portions of this as you may see fit to my folks   I have written to Father But I do hate to write the same things twice.

[*James' diary entries]
Tues Nov 10 1863
Regiment soon going to H. Hd. Conscripts[91] assigned to companies. Mail in from "Arago". No letters for me. Summoned on court martial. Charges against Poulson withdrawn. They would hang him. Returns finished Inventory

Muster-In Roll
(Barrett Collection)

Wed Nov 11 1863
Ordered to Seabrook. Extensive luggage. Pitched our tents.

---

[91] To enlist someone compulsorily, typically into the armed services. conscript. (n.d.). *Dictionary.com Unabridged*. Retrieved December 1, 2015, from http://dictionary.referenxe.com/browse/conscript

Thurs Nov 12 1863

Ordered to Pope's Plantation[92]. Like it much. Independent. Horse. Fish. Niggers many & not clean. Pitch our tents. Make the rounds. Mess with Co. Doing well. Very pleasant place. "Burnside".

One of Pope's Homes on Hilton Head Island
48th Regt. N.Y.S. Vols., A.J. Palmer, 1885
(Barrett Collection)

Fri Nov 13 1863

Rode to Seabrook. Good horse. Rations scarce. We expect to move again soon. Co. H. at Fort Mitchell. Very pleasant. Want me back. Packing dead men's things. Inventory, etc. Tent boarded. "Scott".

Confederate ten cents note from No. Carolina
(Barrett Collection)

*[*James' diary entry]*
Fri Nov 20 1863
"Tybee".

---

[92] The Popes were a prominent family. They had three homes located in various locations on Hilton Head Island.

Sat. Nov. 21, 1863

Have letters quite often from James, don't know but he thinks he must write to us as often as he does to Jennie but I think we should not be jealous if he favored her a little. I suppose it is natural.

[*James' diary entries]

Sat Nov 21 1863

Fee assigned to A. Edwards to C. I. to remain until Dunbar returns. Fee not coming. Vidal assigned here. Marriage here this evening. I am asked to perform the ceremony. Elfwing did it. Great dancing. "Corinth".

Sun Nov 22 1863

Negroes continue to shout. Fee temporarily assigned to Co. H. Lippincott to be 2ᵈ Lt. Co. H. I think I will like him. Col. B. trying to reenlist the regiment. Co. A. can give some. Co. H. none. "Beaufort".

Mon Nov 23 1863

Rode to the Head to get certificate of leave of absence. Must go next week again, near getting wet. "Arago" due tomorrow. Company fixing up for Thanksgiving. "Newbern".

Wed Nov 25 1863

Capt. D. lays out his plans on the plantation. Expects to return soon. Inspection. Property condemned. Baking pies and crullers[93] &c for Thanksgiving.

Thurs Nov 26 1863

Thanksgiving day. Very pleasant. Roasting our pig. Getting up games. Good dinner & supper & very good time generally.

---

[93]A rich, light cake cut from a rolled dough and deep-fried, usually having a twisted oblong shape and sometimes topped with sugar or icing. cruller. (n.d.). *Dictionary.com Unabridged.*
Retrieved December 1, 2015, from http://dictionary.reference.com/browse/cruller

Emma Jane's embellishment
used to decorate one of her
transcriptions (Barrett Collection)

[*Narrative]
While at Popes we had one good Thanksgiving dinner which if not quite as elegant as we
used to enjoy at home certainly relished as well.

[*Letter]

Head Quarters Co A. 48th N.S.Y. Vols
Pope Plantation Hilton Head Is SC
Nov 26th 1863

My Dear Jennie   Your doubly welcome letter freighted with two of your Photographs came to
hand Yesterday I like them much I can not say which is best. Each one is perfect. The Vinette is
listening & the other just going to speak. When You arrived & asked me to call round I was sorry
to be obliged to say that Military duty would oblige me to defer it untill after Thanksgiving. I can get
up quite a little party now But what is very uncommon where there are so many ladies Present I
have to do most of the talking. Please send me a copy of that Poetry or that Essay that Your Face
tells me you have been writing for some Periodical You may wonder howl discovered it. You dont
know how good I am at reading thoughts. We have a beautiful day for Thanksgiving I was afraid
it might rain as it has been threatening for some time. I was nearly wet through last Monday riding
home from the Head. I have got to go down again next Monday to have my leave of Absence
examined & get a certifficate that is all right. I have been trying for it ever since I returned & can
not get my ten months pay without it.

Evening I was interrupted by the call to dinner Our table was laid under the arbor we had built in
the Orange Grove We had Roast Pork 2 kinds of potatoes boiled Onions Pies & Rice Pudding.
Over the table hung the State Flag with the inscription "New York expects every man to do his
duty." At the entrance there were Stacks of Muskets with Wreathes containing the Co pictures.
Boards were arranged for seats & the Men's dishes scoured & placed on the table

 All eat with a relish & then of course we had to say something in response to some Cheers they
gave us. Lieut Schultz & I get on finely together He dreads the Captains return. After dinnerI
offered several prizes for shooting running &c which took up most of the afternoon At supper we

had Pies & Cakes and Coffee & then 2 fiddles & some dancing & <u>Negro Shouts</u>[94]. Several Officers came up this evening & had to give in that Co A beat them all. I meant to do it. The men are disposed to give me the credit for it They say they have had the best time they ever had. But my 1st Serg[t] deserves the most praise. I simply encouraged & helped <u>him</u>. I have just dispersed them all to their tents & all is quiet again & another Thanksgiving is over. I have often wondered where my next one will be passed. But I would not look behind the veil of what <u>is</u> <u>to</u> <u>be</u>.

"Oh the blindness to the future kindly given &c." Oh I must tell you what Schultz said when he saw your picture. He said you would outlive me.   As you had a Widow's lock as he called it on your forehead I hope you wont allow this to trouble you I would not have said if I had thought you superstitious

I hope Lizzie Cheney may be happy But I fear. I don't know whether I should enjoy such a large wedding I suppose I should leave it to my friends. Charley will probably call upon them But I do not think he will often do so.

I accept your <u>apology</u> for <u>writing</u> Just make another excuse will you I don't know why you should say the picture looks better than you. They say the Camera wont lie. I think it looks exactly like you. I wish I could hear some of those lectures It would be a treat I understand now what you meant when you spoke of Beecher's work abroad I have been reading his speeches They are capital. It does seem as if he was inspired. I have thought so before. I do not believe that Inspiration was confined to old times I believe we all have our moments of Inspiration. Rec[d] a long letter from Anne with @ Vinette[95].

> With much love, believe me
>
> Yours
>
> James A. Barrett

P.S.   Joy will be mixed with sadness. I have rec[d] notice of the death of one of our men who was in Hospital at Beauford   Sick with Chronic Diarrhea. I will not tell the men until tomorrow. Let the dance go on. I like to see them enjoy themselves when they can.

---

[94] A frenzied "shout" apparently bursting forth at the climax of a rousing sermon in a primitive church. It was also a rhythmic testimony that must continue in fever heat until the final note. *The Negro Spiritual Inc.: The Shout*. (2015). Retrieved December 1, 2015, from http://www.thenegrospiritualinc.com/article_the_shout.htm

[95] A small illustration or portrait photograph which fades into its background without a definite border. vignette. (n.d.). *Oxford Dictionaries*. Retrieved December 15, 2015, from http://oxforddictionaries.com/definition/english/vignette

James' mother, Elizabeth Prescott
(Barrett Collection)

[letter from James' Mother, Elizabeth Prescott Barrett]

Concord Nov 27th 1863

My Dear Son,

you will perceive by Date that yesterday was Thanksgiving Story came up and Marys family. Deacon Warren & Wife went to Boston so you see our number was quite small   your Father was quite anxious to have us invite Jane to come and spend a number of days but we thought that she would feel that she must come, and that it would be too bad to leave Ellen at home and as you were not here there would be no attraction. Your photograph arrived day before yesterday and those pictures from Concord N.H. last week. Emily sent by Charles to Boston to get an album to present to Rebecca. Jane happened in a little after and she thought it as very handsome. She left her picture for us which was put beside yours in the album. When she was gorn I said I was going to write to you Friday and I should tell you that you must get one and present to Jane, and we would get Mr. T to get one like R and we could give it to her your Father said he did not know but he should give her one he was affraid she would get one before we could get one and he wanted R to let him have hers and so he wrote her a note and sent it to her she appeared very much pleased Emily gave it to her night before last.   Lizzie was up here making baskets but she persuaded herself that she had an errand. I suppose the secret was she wanted to see how it would be received how did you spend Thanksgiving.   we missed you but hope the War will be over so that your place will not be vacant again. We had a letter this week from GH dated Nov. 10. he has not worked on his Lode for 2 months His Neighbour has sold out and the Company were expecting to put up an engine this fall but he thinks its so late that they wont before Spring. so he don't want to take all the water and so he took a shaft to sink and had to work very hard at twenty dollars a foot one foot a day but he expected it would be harder so that he should not be able to do more than half a foot in one day. in his last letter he says in the last 20 days he has made clear of expense one hundred and 82 dollars but he finds he has worked too hard and has quit it and is expecting to commence working by the day (instead of the job) for three. fifty. his board one dollar a day He sent a draft for one hundred to your Father saying he felt bad that he had not been able to send it before and could not spare the other hundred at present unless your Father needed it as he wanted to get some clothes and poor child he must feel dreadfully to be in debt and have to work so hard all the time. I wonder if Dakin feels troubled any thinking of his debts. I don't see how George can help feeling that he has been to blame and I should think unless he has secured himself that he must have a hard time to get along with his large family. I cannot help feeling that he has done wrong in some way and poorly has to suffer by it.

Doc Bartlett came to us on Sunday and wanted to know when we were going to write he wanted you to go to Hospital No 3 and enquire after Alonzo Munroe who he thought died the Tenth of this Month what was the matter with him if he suffered much and if it could be ascertained where his Body lays, that he could be removed if they wish to send for it. please write in the first letter even if it is to Jane. George says he was taken by surprise at your engagement though he had always suspected it might be some time   He said he was very sorry to have you go back to your company before you got well. We are having fine weather now your Father has all his Cattle home and through harvesting and making cider   has hired both Philip & Tommy I was very much afraid he would not hire Philip he asked so much but he concluded I suppose that a bird in the hand was worth two in the bush wages are high and scarce I think it is better to give more and keep good help than to give less and get those who will stop work the moment the boss is away I think the latter much the more expensive. your Father sold a Rooster for eight dollars he was so importuned [96] that he finally set his price, So high notwithstanding he thought he would not sell it at any price. Story went to see his Mother last Wednesday morn staid with her

---

[96] To ask someone pressingly and persistently for or to do something. importune. (n.d.).
Retrieved December 1, 2015, from
http://www.oxforddictionaries.com/us/definition/learner/importune

two hours she appeared nicely and felt rather disappointed in not comeing up to Thanksgiving. I wonder she did as she had not
even seen Story before so I think she may be up before Spring. We have not given your trunk picture to Jane yet but have told her we meant to keep it a while of course she would not object. Emily has not distribute your photographs yet. I think your Father did not mention that James Brown Brother William was ordained at Sherbern I think not quite so far off as Boston. Deac Warren and Mr James Brown were sent Delegates. Doc Bartlett wished me to remember him to you said you was a fine fellow. You said you wanted your shirts fix up some. You were too late they had been sent a number of days and were made entirely plain and we forgot to mark them perhaps its well as you may not heed them as you found a supply in your trunk so you can sell them. there was seven yds eighty cents a yard. I mention this that you might know what to ask for them.

From Mother

p.s. I forgot to say that Charles came over last night and staid until this afternoon. Mary is getting better.

Chapter 7

Taking Command

November 28, 1863-December 31, 1863--Pope's Plantation--Update on Grant victories and Bragg's retreat--Description of leaving Pope's Plantation with a Shout--Christmas Day celebrations, 1863-- President Lincoln's Proclamation applauded— Mustered by Major Coan

[Note that all the following transcriptions have been faithfully copied from the original document, as written by James, except where noted.]

Fri Nov 27 1863

Picket at Spanish Wells fired us from Chimney Point. Must be vigilant. "Taylor."

Sat Nov 28 1863

Gunboats gone up to shell Chimney Point. Two companies went along to recounoitre[97]. Lockwood going to buy some pine lands. Pickets frightened. Dark night. "York."

Sun Nov 29 1863

Rainy. Returns finished. Found a stove—will have it fixed tomorrow. "Chester."

Mon Nov 30 1863

Rode to Hilton Head & had my leave of absence examined. All right. Will get my pay next pay day for one year. Very cold day & windy. Conscript missing—Colonel's Orderly. "Derby."

Tues Dec 1 1863

Cold night. Lockwood gone to sale of lands. May purchase for me. Good news from Tennessee. Bragg whipped. Capt. Ferguson resigned. Lt. Fee signed for property. Capt. Lockwood alone now. Wants me back. "Ohio".

> *[Emma Jane's transcription of Emily's journal entry]*
> Tues. Dec. 1, 1863
>
> *Jennie called this morning and read some letters received from James. I begged the loan of one which was quite interesting to read to Charles (Charles Thompson). She hesitated a little at first but finally consented. He made her a present of a photograph album. We hardly knew how to account for it in him as he seldom makes presents.*

*[*James' diary entry]*
Wed Dec 2 1863

Lots of rockets seen & guns heard last night. Some boats seen near Pinckney Is. They seem to quarrel. Some excitement. I have ordered the pigs shut up. "Alma."

---

[97] A French term, meaning "to explore."

[*Letter]

Head Quarters Co A. 48th NYSV
Pope Plantation Hilton Hd Is   SC
Dec 3^d 1863

Dear Jennie

  You see I am still here I have been expecting to go back to my Co in a <u>few</u> <u>days</u> for so long I am getting tired of repeating it. In fact this Co are beginning to talk about <u>swapping</u> off their <u>Capt</u> <u>to be</u> for the <u>1st Lt that is</u>

  Between them & my own Co I believe they are likely to spoil me. Each <u>pretends</u> to want to keep me Of course I "shall not go back on my own Co" I intend to stick to <u>them</u>   Yours of 22^d "together with one from <u>another</u> <u>correspondent</u>" came to hand today Just to test your capacity for Jealousy I will enclose it. The Style is evidently original. Spelling & all & not to be criticized by the common standards.

  I would advise your Father to invest his <u>Cotton</u> <u>fund</u> in <u>English</u> <u>Stocks</u> unless Beecher succeeds in raising the premium an Greenbacks[98].

  My Battery was not near enough to "War" to be <u>very</u> dangerous. There are about 3000 troops at Beaufort

  Dont be too much attracted by my "Titles" They don't amount to much

  Battery Taylor was one of the Outposts at Beaufort. My Dress Parade ended as it begun in <u>talk</u>. I concluded that it <u>would</u>^{nt} pay. I care not how my letters are directed so that I get them Once in a while I get one directed 1st Serg^t & I believe I am more proud of that title than any. For It was the Index of 18 months of rich Experience, which now that it is past. I often think of with pleasure notwithstanding its hardships cares & vexations. Dont be too confident about the <u>Capt</u>. There are 6 1st Lieuts Senior to me & only 2 vacancies of Capt yet. I shall not strive for further promotions unless it be in Co H. If Col B is promoted I suppose Capt L will be In that case I <u>might</u> be tempted to play my <u>Trumps</u> & try to <u>jump</u> my <u>Seniors</u>. It would only be paying off an <u>old score</u> which I have not <u>forgotten</u> yet. But to speak the honest truth & throwing competition one side I think <u>one</u> <u>bar</u> <u>becomes</u> me better than <u>two</u> woulds

  I do not think you need fear any trouble with your large bags. I believe you are pretty cool & you must know something of human nature by this time

  My experience has taught me that I could govern others easily just about in proportion as I succeeded in governing Myself.

  We have had quite a cold snap lately   I have found an old Stove here   But it smokes so badly that it is little Comfort   I think our evenings here are splendid

  We have the "same moon"   But it is more brilliant So Abby is going to teach again. I hope my <u>6 mos</u> wont become <u>12</u>   Lest "Hope deferred make the heart sick" Poor Girl She

---

[98] The term greenback refers to paper currency (printed in green on one side) issued by the United States during the American Civil War. Greenback (1860s money). (October 20, 2015). *Wikipedia, The Free Encyclopedia*. Retrieved December 2, 2015, from https://en.wikipedia.org/w/index.php?title=Greenback(1860smoney)&oldid=686693288

depended too much upon Ned's coming this year. She does not seem to realize the <u>uncertainties</u> of <u>War</u>

I had a long letter from Annie which I answered last mail   I need not tell you   <u>You</u> <u>can</u> <u>see</u> <u>that</u> for I believe you <u>waived</u> <u>Jealousy</u> in this case. It seems <u>Ned B</u> is home   I expect to hear <u>more</u> notwithstanding Annie's <u>resolutions</u>   I think I can see how it will <u>end</u>   Romances generally turn <u>out</u> about the <u>same</u> <u>at</u> last. Annie is a good Girl   But is so very sensitive & sympathetic that she allows trifles to trouble her   She needs to cultivate her <u>will</u> & act more upon her own responsibility independent of what others may say or think

Rumor says we are going in to the Head in a day or two   I hope not   I have got used to this sort of independent life & do not care to go back with the reg^t again. It would seem like coming down several pegs   Besides I had just made arrangements to have good living here. But it is all in the 3 years, We have had some excitement out here lately. The Rebs over the way made quite a display of fireworks in the shape of Rockets &c a few nights since & their boats were seen quite near our Pickets 2 miles below here. They seemed to quarrel among themselves by all accounts

We were on the sharp lookout for them   But they did not come within the range of our Rifles   We heard of Grants recent Victories from Rebel sources & the Fulton confirmed the account

Today the National Salute of 34 Guns has been fired from all our Batterie's about here   Of course we are all happy. Braggs[99] much dreaded Army seems to be almost entirely routed & Lee also in retreat

It seems almost too good to be true   We have been at war so long   It seems hard to realize signs of approaching Peace   But It does seem as if Day was at last dawning. The recent Elections. Beechers work abroad & now the Rout of Braggs boasted Army is surely enough to kindle hope even in the most desponding breast

I have been busy all day in getting off Final Statements of deceased Soldiers & I feel very stupid tonight & besides my stove smokes so badly that it almost blinds me. So I must bid you good night for this time   I will try to be more endurable in my next. With much love I remain

Yours
James A. Barrett

*[*James' diary entries]*
Fri Dec 4 1863
Commenced to board with "Alice". Hot biscuit, sweet potatoes, chicken, venison, apple pie, S.P. pie &c &c &c. Good living

---

[99] Throughout these campaigns, Bragg fought almost as bitterly against some of his uncooperative subordinates as he did against the enemy, and they made multiple attempts to have him replaced as army commander. *The Civil War Trust: "General Braxton Bragg"*. Retrieved December 2, 2015, from http://www.civilwar.org/education/history/biographies/braxton-bragg.html?referrer=https://www.google.com/

Sat Dec 5 1863

Capt. Findley 76 Penn. Vols Comes up this evening to relieve us as we start for Seabrook at five in the morning—thence to Hilton Head. I will ride in. Negroes shout for us. Sorry to have us leave.

Sun Dec 6 1863

Negroes come out with eatables &c for the men. March at five, arrived H. H'd entrenchments about ten. 47th N.Y.V furnish coffee. I rode in, sent Wm back with horse. Pitch our tents & mess with Westerodt—(Ingraham, Moser, Acker, Edwards, Schultz, Wyckoff and I) West & Rily cook. Five drills this week.

Mon Dec 7 1863

Cold. Have to move our tents again to make the streets wider. Making frames to set the tents upon. Lockwood going to remain at Ft. Mitchell (Fort Mitchel)[100]. My wound breaking out again.

Tues Dec 8 1863

Repitched our camp. Looks well. My leg very sore. Still quite cold.

Wed Dec 9 1863

Quite lame. Weather milder. Detailed for guard tomorrow but sha'n't go on. Capt. Dunbar back. I will get back to Co. H. this week. Little George[101] very sick brought to hospital from Mitchell [Mitche].

Hospital at Hilton Head, South Carolina
H.P. Moore, photographer (Barrett Collection)

---

[100] Fort Sherman and Fort Mitchel were two additional forts built in 1862 by the Union Army to continue the defense of the Union blockade and to prevent Confederate assaults.
[101] George E. Jones "Little George", a musician, died from Congestive Chills and was buried at Hilton Head. This is noted under the Register of Deaths in the Company "H" 48th New York State Vols. Account Book. (Barrett Collection)

Thurs Dec 10 1863
Little George died at 3 A.M. Taking a/c of property etc. Men from Pulaski
all returned to regiment. Lt. Robinson[102] tried to-day. I think he will get
clear. "Arago" in with mail

[*Letter]

Headquarters Co "A" 48th Regt N.Y.S. Vols
Hilton Head S.C. December 11, 1863

Dear Mother

Yours of 27th is recd I should have been very happy to have got that Album But it seems Father got ahead of me. Never mind   I wont be <u>jealous</u>. I am very glad you all seem so well pleased with my <u>choice</u>. I did not ask your consent That is not my way altho I believe I knew pretty well what your minds were. That did not influence me however.   I am glad to hear that George is well hope he will not work himself too hard   I have not had a letter from him But I suppose he is too busy to write. I do hope he will strike a <u>rich</u> vein soon   I think his perseverance deserves success.

As I am not at Beaufort & it is difficult getting a pass I have written to the Surgeon in charge & will send you his answer. I think you will get along well this winter with your present help. I am glad you have secured the same men They seemed to be very good & willing & they know what is to be done better than strangers. I think it is cheaper to pay good wages than to take up common help. What kind of Rooster was that that Father sold for Eight Dollars. I should call that a big price.   It would pay to raise chickens at that price. I am glad to hear that Aunt Gerrish is getting better I think it would be a good place at Mrs Stowell's for her to board if she would take her. I hope she will soon be well enough to return home again altho I guess she is as well off at Summerville as anywhere for this winter. Please remember me to her when you see her.

The Shirts have arrived & I like them very much. I enclose $15.00. Please pay the bill for the Shirts out of it & give the rest to the children I was short when I left home & did not give them anything as I Intended I am very much obliged to whoever made them & shall be happy to do as much in return when opportunity offers I shall <u>not</u> <u>sell</u> <u>them</u>. I can make them useful when those I have now are shrunk too small to use myself. I can always find room to pack my things in the Co Box if my trunk is full

What did Mrs. Reynolds say to my Trunk & darkey

I am still with Co A But the Capt has retnd He is sick in Hospital here now I have made out all my Receipts & Invoices ready to turn over the property & Co to him It rained today or I should have done it today. I expect to do so tomorrow & return to my own Co who are stationed at Fort Mitchel near Pope's 9 Cos of us are here now & have just got nicely settled in camp It is a long time since we have been together. Col Barton wants to start a Theatre again I dont know but he will But I can't do anything

---

[102] Lt. Henry W. Robinson was accused of exhibiting cowardice during the Battle of Fort Wagner.

about it as I shall be with Co H. 7 miles off. You see I am to be independent again after all. I have felt quite humble since I have been here after being My own <u>Boss</u> so long. I rec^d orders last Saturday at Pope's to march in & join the Reg^t at daylight & from there we came in here about 7 miles I <u>rode</u> in on my horse before I turned him   over to my Successor & sent him back with my darkey.   I was sorry to leave Popes.   We had got nicely settled & everything went on smoothly. The darkies asked permission to have a good <u>Shout</u> the night before we left. They were all sorry to have the <u>Cap</u>ⁿ & <u>his</u> <u>boys</u> go away. They said that our Co treated them better & behaved better than any other Co had done. They did not steal anything.   I let them dance & sing for 2 hours & then sent them all home. Early in the morning we got some coffee & started singing John Brown's body &c   A lot of the darkeys came out with cooked sweet Potatoes Peanuts &c to give to the men as they left & to bid us good bye

        I hope the Co that relieved us will treat them kindly Poor creatures they need good treatment & encouragement to make anything of them they are not so big fools as many think. They show many signs of ingenuity & skill & I believe with proper treatment they might become good members of Society

        But I can see in them all a Shiftless careless & loose sort of habit which is only the legitimate fruits of the accursed Institutions in which they were born & bred. I am not surprised at it I only wonder they are not worse. I used to try to make them appreciate that they were not longer Slaves & subject to a Masters will But free men & women & I told them that they must learn to act & do as free people should. Truly the ways of Providence are often mysterious I often wonder what the future may develop in this people. They surely have never had half a chance But they seem to have good sense & good hearts. They are respectful and obedient. I know they are lazy But so are white folks in this climate

Please remember me to all inquiring friends & believe me

                    Yours very truly
                    James A. Barrett
                1st Lieut 48th Reg^t N.Y.S. Vols.

[*James' diary entries]
Fri Dec 11 1863
Rainy. Making up invoices & receipts &c. Big boil on my wound broke last night and I am better to-day.

Sat Dec 12 1863
Bid Co. A good-bye this morning. Got three cheers etc. Expect to leave to-day.

[*Narrative]
I was soon relieved from Co A. & returned to my own Co H. The Capt was on detached duty & I had com^d of a small fort (Mitchel) with 4 Guns & a magazine with necessary ammunition This was built to prevent the Enemy running out through Calabague Sound   In Decr 1863

we commenced reenlisting our men as Veterans My company reenlisted almost to a man 46 came forward & renewed their Oath. This entitled them to 30 days furlough & I was appointed one of the officers to go north with them & help get them their bounties

*[*James' diary entries]*
Sun Dec 13 1863
Joined my company. Rode by Pope's. Niggers quite happy. Sent for again about the theatre. Rode back & stopped with Dr. Mulford. Came back next morning.

Mon Dec 14 1863
Rode from H. H'd. to Ft. Mitchell before breakfast. Good exercise. Capt. Gone to the Head to-day.

Tues Dec 15 1863
Inspection to-day—Maj. Metcalf. Pieces look well.

Wed Dec 16 1863
Rainy.

Thurs Dec 17 1863
Co. drill to-day. Recruits march well. Will soon work in with the Company. Lt. R. being tried.—Will probably go home.

Fri Dec 18 1863
Rode to Pope's to buy hogs. The niggers don't seem to care to sell. Old Bob will find some. Men arrested at Pope's/ Released again.

Fri Dec 25 1863
Christmas pleasant but @ little chilly. Co. H. 47th N.Y. V & Lt. --- came out to dinner. Clean sweep! Rather dull day. Two men missing. Patrolled around Pope's. Found some loafers at Alice's & heard of some at Rachel's. Lts. Avery & Hale called to see us. Some men drunk. Small mail received.

Head Quarters Co. H 48th Regt N.Y. Vols.
Fort Mitchell Hilton Head S.C. Dec 25 1863

My Dear Jennie

Yours of 12th inst. Came to hand this day & it was all the more welcome because unexpected. It came on @ transient boat. The regular steamer is expected tomorrow. Another Christmas day is over. I am glad of it. I hope it is the last one I shall spend in this climate. We had Co. H. of the 47th here to-day to dinner. We had roast beef, roast pork (fresh), two kinds of potatoes, boiled onions, apple sauce, apple dumplings & doughnuts & cheese with ½ bbl. of ale to wash it down. We officers had roast chicken &c I did not expect to enjoy the day. I never do when there are so many to look after—130 or 140 men. There are always some who are piggish & some will get liquor & get drunk. But it is over now & considering the number here & things went off very well. We are going to give our company @ big oyster stew tomorrow to finish up with. The 47th have invited our reg. down there New Years.

I don't find it so very agreeable "out of the reign of King Frost" as you imagine. We find the weather about as hard to bear here as at home. The days are mild but the nights very cold & chilly. Water often freezes over in our tents. I am writing now with my overcoat on. Your weather is more uniform & one gets used to it.

Reenlistments are going on quite lively in our regiment. None of our company have enlisted yet. I think it very doubtful if the 48th go home in @ body at all next fall. I think the regiment will go right along & officers enough be retained to officer the men. You know every time we are promoted, we are mustered for three years.

There is a wonderful power in that "keeping cool policy" you refer to in Gen. Butler. I have often felt it even in my experience. The man who keeps the coolest, wins the day in everything. We used to have lessons in tactics, But it was soon given up. We have @ school for our non-commissioned officers twice @ week when we have two or three pages recited. It is @ good thing in the company But I abominate it in the regiment. Officers are supposed to learn their duties without these school boy recitations!

I am curious to see how the President's Proclamation will be received in the rebel states. I do think that President Lincoln is proving himself the <u>right</u> <u>man</u> in the <u>right</u> <u>place</u>. He has carried @ <u>burden</u> the last three years such as <u>no man</u> in this world has ever done before & how <u>nobly</u> he <u>stands</u> <u>to-day</u>! He is <u>emphatically</u> the "<u>Moses</u>" of our day leading this American people out of @ worse than "Egyptian bondage" into the bright "Canaan" of Liberty, Prosperity, & Peace. The hallowed name of Washington which we have always been taught to look upon as the embodiment of all that is good & noble, will here after be only too proud to be associated with the honored name of Lincoln & we shall find deeply engraved on the hearts of all Americans "Washington & Lincoln—the father & preserver of our country." Others, many others there are whose names will justly shine on History's pages, But the names of these two will be imperishable as Time itself.

With much love, I remain as ever Yours very truly
James A. Barrett

Sat Dec 26 1863

Quiet day—@ little cloudy. Wrote @ letter. In evening @ steamer passed without giving signal. I rode to Seabrook on new horse about it. We came near giving @ shot. It proved the "Croton" & all is quiet.

Sun Dec 27 1863

Company inspection. Mail received—three letters. Christmas box coming. 76th Pa officers called.   Reenlisting going on brisk. Expect Maj Coan up here tomorrow

Major William B. Coan
(*48th Regt. N.Y.S. Vols.*, A.J. Palmer, D.D., 1885)

[Emma Jane's transcription of letter fragment to unknown recipient from James]

"I am surprised that Mr. Emerson should say anything derogatory to England. He has always been very English. America surely ought to be great. We have all the elements of greatness among us & if we do not make ourselves universally respected, it is because we fail to "make use of those means which the God of nature has placed in our power." We, as @ nation, have been fearfully remiss in our duty & now are reaping the fruits of our sins in @ harvest of blood. We have sinned with our eyes open, suffering ourselves to be bound by @ fancied obligation to the support & protection of an institution which both reason & conscience condemned as infamous, forgetting, or at least ignoring the fact that there is no bond strong enough to justify us in wrong doing. I think the

President's message[103][xvii] is capital. Short & to the point. Very encouraging!   Jeff seems to indulge in fault finding. I think he is finding that "the way of the transgressor is hard." Still I cannot help But admire his pluck. I am only sorry it is not put to @ better use.

Carte de visite of Jennie's neighbor,
Ralph Waldo Emerson
(Barrett Collection)

[*James' diary entries]
Mon Dec 28 1863
Captain gone to the Head. Stormy—partially cleared in P.M. Co.drill. Two 76th officers called. Some excitement about the reenlistment. Want to hear about bounty. Made @ little desk to-day.

Tues Dec 29 1863
Pleasant. One man has four hours knapsack[104] for going off without pass & two men to clean bayonets for absence from drill. Col. Hall and three ladies & gentleman call at the fort. On council of administration this P.M. to order sale of deceased men's clothing.

Wed Dec 30 1863 *Rode to the Head. Stopped for meeting of B.D.A.[105] [Barton Dramatic Association] Returned by 9 ½ P.M. Dark night but good horse. Rained soon after I got back.*

---

[103] President Lincoln in his annual message to Congress in December, 1863, outlined a model for reinstatement of Southern states called the ten percent Reconstruction plan. Ten percent plan. (November 27, 2015). *Wikipedia, The Free Encyclopedia.* Retrieved December 3, 2015, from https://en.wikipedia.org/w/index.php?title=Tenpercentplan&oldid=692695884
[104] A punishment meted out by superior officer. In this case, a soldier marches for four hours with a knapsack loaded with stones. *American Civil War Life: Union Infantryman – Life In Camp X* Retrieved December 2, 2015 from http://hubpages.com/education/American-Civil-War-Life-Union-Infantryman-Life-In-Camp-Hygiene-Sanitation-and-Illness-and-Crime-and-Punishment

Thurs Dec 31 1863 *Mustered by Maj. Coan. He gives the Company a very good name. Steamer "Alice Price"*[106] *comes down from Pulaski without the signal. We bring her to by loading one of the Parrotts. She gives the countersign & goes on.*

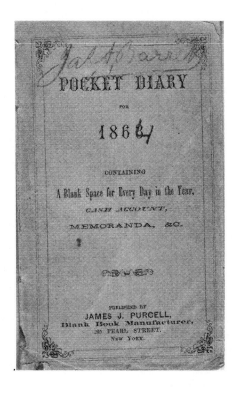

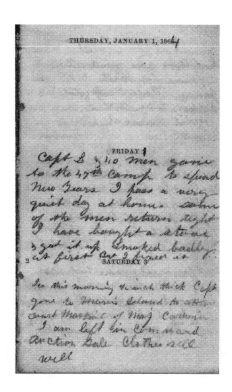

Front cover and first diary entry of
January 1, 1864 (Barrett Collection)

---

[105] March 1864, enlisted men of the 48th New York Regiment (part of the Second Brigade, as was the Third New Hampshire) formed the Barton Dramatic Association and opened the "Union Theatre" at Hilton Head.

[106] The "Alice C. Price" was a side-wheel steamer with a very shallow draft. She was an ideal vessel for carrying troops and supplies on the St. Johns River. On July 19, 1864, she was struck by a torpedo and quickly sank. Martin, Richard A. (1993). *The Great River War on the St. Johns.* Retrieved December 15, 2015,from
http://mapleleafshipwreck.com/Book/Chapter2/chapter2.htm

Fri Jan 1 1864
Capt. L. & 40 men gone to the 47th Camp to spend New Years. I pass @ very quiet day at home. Some of the men return tight. I have bought @ stove & got it up. Smoked badly at first, but I fixed it.

Sutler's Row at Hilton Head Island
H.P. Moore, Photographer (Barrett Collection)

Chapter 8

A Letter from James

January 1, 1864—Fort Mitchell, Hilton Head Island, South Carolina—
Letter to Sunday School children at the Second Unitarian Church,
Brooklyn, New York—Recounts his experiences during his time from
enlistment in 1861 through 1863 in the 48th Regiment of the New
York State Volunteers

[Note that all the following transcriptions have been faithfully copied from the original
document, as written by James, except where noted.]

[*Letter]

Head Quarters Co. H. 48th Regt N.Y. S. Vols.
Fort Mitchell   Hilton Head Island S.C.
New Years Day 1864

My Dear Young Friends of the 2nd Unitarian Sunday School Brooklyn

As your Supt has asked me to write you a few lines. I will spend a portion of this pleasant New Year's day in wishing you all a Happy New Year & telling you something of Soldier's life I suppose you have enjoyed your Holy days very much as you always do. I often think of you & the pleasant hours I used to spend in your little Sunday School room. 3 years have nearly passed since then & they have been long years. It seems as if we had lived a lifetime in these few months. God grant that another New Year may find our troubles ended & we be permitted to once more enjoy our Holy days in the midst of our friends at home. Home that is a blessed word. None know better than the Soldier how truly to value it   Each successive mail is looked forward to with eager expectation.   Every one hoping to receive some tidings from home or some cheering news fur the cause we hold so dear. You who have always lived at home can hardly appreciate how you would miss it when you are removed fur away from the scenes & the friends you love so well. I presume you are enjoying your cold weather I read accasionally about your skating grounds & how you improve them We seldom see ice here Once in a while the water will just freeze over lightly But our nights are quite chilly nevertheless I sometimes think we feel the cold as much here as any where I expect you all feel an interest in the Soldiers. As this is a Brooklyn regt perhaps some of you have friends in it & would like to hear something about it No doubt you think it hard to live in Camp, But you would be surprised to go through our regt & see how Comfortable the men make themselves. Where there are 5 or 6 in one tent they have to make the most of their room. The new Recruits find it difficult at first   But they soon get used to it.

The old Soldiers are not many hours in Camp before they fix up some rude bunks to sleep in. A table, Shelf, stools & sometimes even a fireplace. Our food, though not very palatable at first we soon learn to eat with quite a relish.   & Many a man who has been accustomed to cast dainty glances at his well filled board at home will now make a hearty meal off of his 3 hard crackers a piece of pork and cup of coffee. Our 1st Christmas, (in 1861) was spent at work on the entrenchments on this Island   The capture of which nearly two months before (or rather the bombardment attending the capture) was one of the grandest sights I ever witnessed. The following New Years we were exposed to the enemie's fire at Port Royal Ferry. Here we witnessed another Bombardment It was something long to be remembered. The bursting shells & burning houses dispelled the surrounding darkness & lighted up the whole heavens about us. It was a sight which can not be described. It must be seen to be appreciated.Then came the labor of erecting the Mud Batteries on the Savh River. Most of which was done by our Regt.

Then Pulaski was taken & our Regt occupied repaired & fortified that   Here we remained 14 Months & from here we went on several expeditions to destroy Saltworks, Bridges & Railroads to Blufton Pocataligo &c in several of which we had a skirmish with the enemy. Here the 4th of July Thanksgiving & Christmas of 1862 & New Years of 1863 were duly remembered & very appropriately celebrated We had our amusements too. When off drill our Parade ground was used for playing ball & other sports. We also fitted up a place for a Theatre outside of the Fort where we spent many pleasant evenings. We believe it is well for Soldiers to make themselves as cheerful & happy as circumstances will allow them to do consistently with their military duties

View of Fort Pulaski, Georgia
H.P. Moore, photographer (Barrett collection)

Last June we took the field again & were engaged in the capture of Morris Island & also in the bloody night Assault upon Ft. Wagner where we lost many of our men. This last was much the most terrible scene we have ever been engaged in. It is horrible beyond description to see your Comrades falling all around you to hear the groans of the wounded & dying & to witness the many scenes of cruelty & suffering which meet our gaze on every side without the power to assist or relieve them

For it is the Soldier's duty to press on & strive to accomplish the task before him regardless of the havoc & destruction that may be going on about him. It is enough to make the strongest man weep to think of it when the excitement of the battle is over.

We are now very comfortably situated in Camp Our Co (H.) is occupying this Fort. The other 9 Companies are at Hilton Head 5 or 6 miles from here. How long we are to remain here or where our next field of labor will be no one can tell Soldiers learn to make themselves at home in any place they may be sent to & are always ready to "take up their beds & walk" at a moment's notice. I must tell you how I have spent the Holy days. Thanksgiving day I was stationed at Pope's plantation about a mile from here with one Co. We gathered a lot of greens & made a bower under a beautiful Orange Grove where we spread our table We found brick enough to build an Oven in which we cooked a large quantity of Beef Pork Pies &c & really had a very sumptuous feast. In the afternoon we had various games & in the evening we collected the Negroes together for what they call a shout. It consists in singing & dancing & is very amusing to those who never saw anything of the kind These Negroes (There are about 4 or 5 hundred on the plantation) are not as helpless as you may suppose. They need teaching But they are amply able to take care of themselves They build their own houses out of timber & slabs which they themselves cut & split in the woods Their Chimneys are a sort of wicker work Covered over with Mortar made from burnt oyster shells They live mostly on Corn, Sweet potatoes, Rice & Pork. Some of the Negroes can read pretty well.

I sometimes used to see little children teaching quite a class of children their letters. It is something new for them to be free & permitted to study.   & they seem anxious to learn & when they get a book they study it faithfully I have often been surprised to see how well they apply themselves.   When they become soldiers, they seem to have an inspiration breathed into them.Christmas day the 48th entertained the 47th N.Y Reg[t]   Each Co. inviting its own corresponding letter. Co H came out here & they enjoyed the day very much. Today our regt are invited to the 47th camp to make a New Year's Call partake of the good things provided for them & enjoying the day in a social manner. A portion of our Co have gone We could not all leave I am spending the day very quietly at the Fort.   I suppose you are all much interested in our late Victories Perhaps some of you may often have wished you were large enough to shoulder your Musket & help to "show how fields are won"

I well remember when I was a little boy how much I enjoyed listening to my grandfather [107] as he told us about the Revolution It seemed to me a sacred privilege to have been permitted to live in those Glorious days. Little did I then think that we were so near to the brink of another Revolution which is destined to surpass in Magnitude & importance anything the World has yet seen. Truly these are Glorious times Let us thank God for them & that it becomes our blessed privilege to live & participate in the events that are now transpiring.

Our part may seem to us insignificant & unimportant But Every Man, Woman & Child has certain duties to perform.   & so long as they do those duties well there is no part that is unimportant The smallest of you can do something if it is only to speak a kind word or to cultivate a cheerful disposition You know the old adage "Greater is he who ruleth his temper than he who taketh a City". There is much truth in that. There is many a man high in station who loses much of his power by not controlling his passions. It has been said to be "a Glorious thing to die for one's country." But it is equally glorious to live for it if that life is made radiant with good deeds I know there are many things in times like these to make us sad Very few there are who will not be called to mourn the loss of friends But count them not last. Their memory is doubly sacred now.   For

---

[107] James is referring to his Grandfather, Major James Barrett III (1761-1850) telling him about the actions of his Great Great Grandfather, Col. James Barrett (1710 – 1779) and his Great Grandfather, James Barrett Jr. (1732-1799) of Concord, Massachusetts during the Revolutionary War. Col. James Barrett was elected by his fellow citizens and bestowed the rank of colonel to the command of a Middlesex, MA Militia Regiment. On April 19, 1775 he ordered the Militia to march to the North Bridge. It was an instrumental act that was to begin the American Revolutionary War. For further reading: Rasmussen, A. W. (2015). *Colonel James Barrett: Consummate Patriarch of Revolutionary Concord.*

they have gone to join the noble army of Martyrs in a better land It is hard I know to think that the faces of those we have been accustomed to meet we shall see no more. But when we think of the noble cause for which we are contending Our Flag dishonored our commerce disturbed—& the

very life of our Nation threatened   There is no sacrifice so great no hardships so severe & no danger so terrible   But we should cheerfully meet them all in defense of Liberty & Justice & call it gain. No one would welcome peace more heartily than Soldiers would

         We long & pray for it But we would rather die & leave our bones to bleach on southern soil than to accept an ignoble Peace subjected to oppression & tyranny Our fathers staked their lives in defense of their liberties & their homes. Let us their descendants keep the holy fire of Patriotism still burning in our breasts & transmit to future generations a spotless inheritance. Thank God our prospects are brightening & Victory seems to be perching upon our banners The good old Stars & Stripes which we have always been taught to look upon with reverence now waves in every state. Let us hope the time is not far distant when we may again beat our swords into plough shares & our spears into pruning hooks & the proudest words we can speak will be "I am an American Citizen" Once more wishing you a Happy New Year, I remain Very truly your friend

James A. Barrett

Photo of the Unitarian Church in Brooklyn
(Barrett Collection)

Chapter 9

The Demon of Intemperance

> January 2, 1864-January 30, 1864--Fort Mitchell--Construction of
> new theatre going well--Barton Dramatic Association--Drunkenness
> of enlisted and officers recounted--Letter from cousin Charles P.
> Gerrish recounts sermons of a "Mr. Longfellow"

[Note that all the following transcriptions have been faithfully copied from the original document, as written by James, except where noted.]

Sat Jan 2 1864

Ice this morning ½ in. thick. Captain gone to Morris Island to attend a court martial of Maj. Corwin. I am left in command. Auction sale. Clothes sell well.

Sun Jan 3 1864

Inspection goes off well. Forage for horses received for January. "Fulton" expected. Coppied letter to S.S. (Sunday School) Mail arrived. "Berlin."

Mon Jan 4 1864

Rainy day. Sent for the mail. Can't get it till tomorrow. Changed cooks. Getting up reports of deceased men's effects sold at auction Gerrish is engaged. "Dresden."

Countersign "Dresden"
(Barrett Collection)

Tues Jan 5 1864

Sent for mail again. Had to lecture M. this morning for lying. I must change my mode of living. Think I will have Parker cook for us after this week. Mail rec^d "Vienna."

Wed Jan 6 1864

Sent to turn in my condemned property. Rainy day. Capt. at the Head.
Theatre progressing. Borrowed $60.00 from Barney to get costumes. We
are to be relieved soon. "Munich."

Thurs Jan 7 1864

Rainy day. Writing letters. "Paris."

[Emma Jane's transcription of letter fragment to unknown recipient from James]

"Our Port Royal Theatre is progressing rapidly & the Barton Dramatic Association expects to reopen in their elegant new building with new scenery, new attractions & new acquisitions to their former unequaled stock company with the popular pleas of ------ on Feb. 1/64. The B.D.A would respectfully inform their friends & the public that they intend to sustain the high reputation heretofore enjoyed & would solicit their continued patronage. You will hear from this theatre from other sources yet. It is bound to be one of the institutions here. Our worthy doctor is President & your humble servant is Vice President & Treasurer. I will send you from time to time copies of the "New South"[108] which may contain notices of it. Our new building will hold 500 & we are promised that Gen. Gillmore will honor us with his presence the opening night.

I see that Lord Lyons predicts the end of the war in three months. My faith is not equal to that But I do believe the most of our fighting will be done within the next six months. The Herald is pushing forward Grant's claims for the next Presidency. I think Uncle Abe will have a vote or two in the matter."

*[*James' diary entries]*
Fri Jan 8 1864

Cloudy—Maj. Coan & Dr. M. came up to swear in some men. Co. H. has
10 Reenlisted.

Sat Jan 9 1864

Reenlistments going on. Rode into the Head. Called on Miss Wakeman,
Mrs. Barton, & Avery. Saw brigade drill. 34 veterans reenlisted in Co. H.
Think the company will go north soon. Mail arrived.

---

[108] Union postmaster Joseph H. Sears published the "New South" newspaper out of the post office building on Union Square in Port Royal, S.C., on a weekly basis beginning in March 1862. The paper was moved to the town of Beaufort sometime in 1865 and remained there until it ceased in 1867. *The New South Newspaper, 1862-1866*, Retrieved December 2, 2015, from http://library.sc.edu/digital/collections/newsouthabout.html

Sun Jan 10 1864
Pleasant day. Captain gone to the Head. He is to be Brigade Inspector.
"London."

[*Narrative]
  A soldier is proverbially free with his money. The Veterans were paid about $500 Dollars each & I suppose ¾ of them spent every dollar during their furlough & many of them in the grossest dissipation. Once released from restraint they would commence by getting drunk & finish no one knew how This Demon of Intemperance was the Rebel's strongest ally It was the prime cause of half of our defeats It ruined many of our Officers & demoralized our men.

  It is a shameful fact that many of our officers led a life of debauchery & I have known men to offer $20.⁰⁰ for a bottle of whiskey. It is a true saying that "when whiskey goes in sense goes out" & I think it as true that a drunken man is literally & "truly possessed of a devil"

[This is Emma Jane's transcription of a letter written by James.]
Head Quarters Co.H. 48th Regt. Veterans N.Y.S.V.
Fort Mitchell Hilton Head Island S.C. Jan 11 1864

My Dear Jennie
  I am happy to inform you that I expect to be home next month. Enough of our company have reenlisted to take us north to recruit & see our friends. I have decided to stick with <u>my boys</u>. I have been battling with selfishness about staying But feel easier now the thing is settled. I hope the war will soon be over & not make it necessary for us to remain three years more. But however that may be, I know it is <u>my duty</u> to remain & I am sure you will not object. If our country is worth anything, it is worth fighting for & the man who is not willing to sacrifice something for the general good, plainly shows that he does not value & appreciate republican institutions. Our country can now easily be made the Eden of the world. The eyes of all nations are turned upon us! Shall we at this hour allow the fire of Patriotism to wane or grow dim? No! a thousand times No! The very shades of our ancestors would rise up to confront, rebuke & drive us to our duty. The monumental piles of Concord, Lexington & Bunker Hill are still eloquent with their historic teachings to every true American heart & certainly should inspire us to defend & protect with our last breath & sinew & transmit unsullied to future generations, that blood bought inheritance we received from our fathers.
  I see the time is about to be extended to the 1st of March for veteran volunteers. The soldiers in the field are coming up with remarkable unanimity[109]. Whole brigades are reenlisting. The old members of our company who are competent to reenlist, have all but three, put down their names for three years more. The old company tie is very strong and Co. H. is bound to stick together or sink in the struggle. After a few had taken the lead, they concluded that

---

[109] Agreement by all people involved; consensus.

their officers must go north with them and to this end they worked until the "leaven had leavened the whole loaf." One other company has the required number & only 70 more are needed to take the regiment home. Whether we shall wait for the regiment or not I do not know. We have made our application to be ordered north & expect to go about the 1st of Feb. I do not know if I can come east at first. If not perhaps I will send for you to try to make a visit in New York & I would return with you. You see my "Bone" theory is working. I told Mrs. Bates I could not get my teeth fixed for want of time then, But that I had a sort of presentiment[110] that I should be in N.Y. again before long!

I suppose I shall soon have to sign myself Lieut. Com dg (Commanding) Co. H. Fate seems to say "Barrett you must do it." Capt. Is to be Assistant Inspector & Instructor for the division—a proud position. Do you remember how you read his character? I have got to sign for the company property etc. I do not particularly fancy the honor of being Lieut. Com dg. I try to get the appointment in "H" nevertheless, if Captain L. gets to be Major.

I do not have much chance to be of service to the contrabands. My duties will not allow of it. An officer must be very careful what he does and says & how he conducts himself. It is best for many reasons not to have too much to do with the contrabands, except of course, as opportunity may allow. One's motives are often misconstrued & I think it sometimes best to put a check upon the good you might do, rather than give a handle for the tongue of scandal to work upon. I sometimes think I am too cautious, But better this than rashness.

I think I understand what you mean when you say "there is something sad in the flight of time." I have felt it too But I am like this man in the wilderness—each stop brings me so much nearer to the light & although I must not shirk from to-day. I will confess that I often find myself anxiously reaching forward for tomorrow. Not that my time hangs heavily. I never knew it to fly faster, But soldiering does not fit me & I am getting grey in the service. I do not care for this either, I like grey hairs but I do so long for civil life when we can once more throw aside the arbitrary rules of military law & man meet man as Christians and brothers should. There are often little events to discourage & disgust one in the army. You have all kinds of men to deal with. Last night several of the men got real crazy drunk. Luckily I was not far off or there would have been a regular knock down. As it was, I was obliged to have one man tied until he got over his raving. Some men will get drunk every chance they get & many officers set them the example. I wish every officer who so far forgets his manhood as to barter it away in this manner could be cashiered & dishonorably discharged. I have no pity or sympathy for them & I am sure they are unworthy of trust or honor.

With much love, I remain as ever

Yours

James A. Barrett

---

[110] Intuitive feeling about the future, especially one of foreboding. presentiment. (n.d.) RANDOM HOUSE KERNERMAN WEBSTER'S COLLEGE DICTIONARY. (2010). Retrieved December 2, 2015, from http://www.thefreedictionary.com/presentiment

Mon Jan 11 1864

Captain gone to Head. 42 veterans enlisted. Mail expected.—Mail arrived.
Captain going to be detailed as Inspector. I am to take possession of the
company property. Several men intoxicated.

[A letter from James' cousin, Charles P. Gerrish]

New York   Jany 412 1864

Dr¹¹¹ James

Yours of 3rd inst is at hand with and enclosed letter for the Sunday School. and first let me say that I have read your letter to the children, and am delighted with it. it is good enough to be published in the Inquirer, and if you will give permission I will have it inserted in a portion of it if I can It is simply, and very interestingly written, and contains sentiments that do you great credit. It makes me feel how much your experience has enriched your nature -- how much you have grown during these last three years, and it makes me feel how little I have accomplished, and gives me fresh resolution and fresh courage for the future, so you see you have done me good see, if the seed sown will only ripen to the harvest. it will I know be interesting to the children, and will exert some good influence which you nor I may never perhaps see some influence incorporated in to

some youthful soul which shall purge the branch, that it may bring forth more fruit, I thank you heartily for the promptness and the completeness with--which you have answered my suggestion. It will supply some of my shortcomings to my school. You know if one cannot of ones self do something, the next best thing is to find someone who can do it, And I have often thought as I possess so little faculty to talk to the

---

¹¹¹ Dear

Sunday School· that I could in a measure atone by finding some one who could talk or write to them· I often think, were I away somewhere, amid scenes of interest I could write them a letter that would interest them I wish I could find some one who would take my place as superintendent, and I would then take a class· I feel better fitted for such a position, I taught a class last Sunday morning, and although my preparation was in a great measure impromptue I nevertheless enjoyed it very much, and the youthful questions and answers, seemed to thoroughly arouse me·

Mr· Staples is I fear hopelessly ill· he seems to have lost the use of his voice, and his nervous system seems unstrung and seems to be wearing physical frame, He is going to Fayal, and I hope he may recover·Mr· Longfellow [112] has preached for us the last two Sundays & very acceptably, Mr· Collyer preaches for us four Sundays very soon· When I heard Mr L and saw him in the same place as formerly, I could not but wish he might return, and be our pastor again

He preaches great and solemn truths and he seems in spirit to be in close communion with the spirits of those who listen· He has had such deep religious experiences that he is eminently fitted to teach, instruct and console others· Everything connected with the war looks prosperous· I now anticipate a speedy termination of it, the most encouraging feature is the reenlistment of veteran regiments It shows a lofty patriotism, and a determined spirit of which we may be justly proud, and which may cause those to tremble, who have anticipated
and hoped for the downfall of our Republic· It is a severe
blow to Copperheads· [The rest of the letter is missing]·

---

[112] Mr. Samuel Longfellow (1819-1892) was the younger brother of Henry Longfellow.

Beginning of Charles Gerrish's letter and signature.
(Barrett Collection)

[*James' diary entries]
Tues Jan 12 1864
Stormy day. Issuing clothing. The reg^t. only lack 70 men to reenlist to send them home.

Wed Jan 13 1864
Rainy

Thurs Jan 14 1864
Pleasant. Capt. Lockwood appointed A.A. Insp. Gen. I sign for company property dated 15th. "Geneva"

Fri Jan 15 1864
Captain L. left the company—going to live at the Head. Christmas box arrived—2 albums, cake, pie &c Very nice.

Sat Jan 16 1864
Rode in to the Head. Col. Anxious to get more veteran recruits. Officers can't go with companies. Men allowed 35 days home. Lot of papers to make out. "Mary Benton"[113] stopped—two shots fired.

Sun Jan 17 1864
Pleasant. Making out furloughs & discharges, &c Stoney reenlisted. Edwards wants to & Pedro too if they hear from home. 45 veterans now. Arrested two boys in a boat & sent them to Seabrook. Kept the boat.

Mon Jan 18 1864
Rainy. Can't ride in today. Mail expected tomorrow.

Tues Jan 19 1864
Rode into the Head. Can't go home. More papers to make out. "Fulton" in Brigade drills. 48th inspected today.

Wed Jan 20 1864
Sent for mail. Rec^d it. Must ride in with my papers. Edwards wants to enlist. Gave the oath to Pedro. Murdick has enlisted.

[This is Emma Jane's transcription of a letter written by James.]

My Dear Jennie

The Captain has left me & I have moved into his tent. I have a good stove & am fixed very comfortably. I was really surprised the other day to find that I weigh 180 lbs. My cough does not trouble me. Sometimes the sentry in front of my tent says he hears me cough some But it is not much. I am rather lonesome as I am the only officer here But am too busy to mind it much. I use my horse pretty often now. I ride into the Head several times a week, besides riding about when I like. Am getting quite fond of riding.

We have 45 veterans in our company. I wrote you that I was coming north. It was a false alarm. I owe you an apology. Captain & I are entitled to go having reenlisted over ¾ of our company, but I believe we are to be disappointed as we have been home so recently. I presume it is "all for the best." I am the only officer with the company now & those who are left will need some one to look out for them.

---

[113] A vessel used as a transport during the Civil War.

My Christmas box came all safe. I have two albums, I devote one to my military friends & the other to my underline home friends. They are very convenient. There were apples, pears, cake & two splendid mince pies—one from Aunt Ann in a large pudding dish about two or three inches thick. It was a little nicer than anything I have tasted in this department.

Who is that man who has named his child Jeff Davis? I think the child will kick some at the baptism, if indeed the parent dares to blaspheme Heaven by presenting him at the altar with such a name. I pity the little innocent. No doubt he will take an early opportunity to have his name changed & put his profane father to the blush. I think it is a right which should be granted him even while he is a minor.

I like that quotation at the close of your letter very much. Who wrote it? It is certainly soul inspiring. In the hour of danger when one feels naturally inclined to shrink from the task before him a few such thoughts as these serve to drive fear from his heart & give strength to his harm.

> "Lord we have wandered forth in doubt & sorrow
> & Thou has made each step an onward one;
> & we will ever trust each unknown morrow,
> Thou wilt sustain us, till its work is done."

I am sorry now that I wrote that I was going north, But it seems that we can't be spared. Very consoling thought. One likes to know that his services are indispensable, But nevertheless, I will confess that I did feel disappointed, But as I said before "it may be all for the best." No doubt it is. I don't know as I ought to complain. There are some who have not been home at all & perhaps we who have, ought to give way to them.

I think our coldest weather is nearly over. Our days are as mild now as ours in April or May.

With much love, I remain   Yours

James A Barrett
1st Lieut C. H. 48th Regt N.Y.S. Vols.

*[*James' diary entries]*

Thurs Jan 21 1864
Edwards has taken the oath as private. Colonel told him last night he would have him detailed as a teamster. Rode to Seabrook to see about clothing. Took tea with Capt. Richmond.

Fri Jan 22 1864
Capt. L. inspected the company today. Said it looked better than any he had seen yet. He left his horse & took mine. I am going in tomorrow to get another.

Sat Jan 23 1864
Rode into the Head. Worked my passage on white horse. Rode my own back again. The Capt. will draw one. Ordered to take the Veterans in to be mustered[114] in the morning.
Issuing clothing.

Sun Jan 24 1864
Hailed the "Mayflower" & went to the Head to have the company mustered. The company make a good appearance. Rode out on horseback with more papers to make up. I think I will go home with the company.

Mon Jan 25 1864
Rode in & turned in condemned property. Capt. has drawn a horse. I ride him out to break for him. Young, skittish & lively. Edwards hold of him. Will be paid soon.

Tues Jan 26 1864
Very pleasant. Made up my monthly returns &c Rode to Seabrook. Fired on the "H.A. Weed"[115] & brought her to. She gave the signal. 76th scouting on Pinckny. I am getting ready to go home.

Wed Jan 27 1864
Mrs. Barton & another lady & a Lieut. rode up to the fort. Sent Edwards to the Head. Mail not arrived. Capt. called out here. I am going home sure. He may. Boats very polite now. Paymaster expected tomorrow. Lost children[116] expected soon.

Thurs Jan 28 1864
Rode into the Head. "Atlantic" in. Mail not sorted yet. To be paid tomorrow. Going home on "Atlantic."

---

[114] The term muster designates the process or event of accounting for members in a military unit. This practice of inspections led to the coining of the English idiom pass muster, meaning being sufficient. When a unit is created, it is "mustered in," and when it is disbanded, it is "mustered out." It also included the change of military rank. Muster (military). (2016, June 9). In *Wikipedia, The Free Encyclopedia*. Retrieved 18:39, September 29, 2016, from https://en.wikipedia.org/w/index.php?title=Muster_(military)&oldid=724522358

[115] "H.A. Weed" was a transport ship that was destroyed in May and June of 1864 by submarines in the St. John's River.

[116] Referring to Enfants Perdus, a French term, meaning lost children or soldiers in dangerous post.

Fri Jan 29 1864

Rode into the Head & brought out the pay rolls & mail. Left Capt.'s horse & took mine. Signed for the horses & trappings.

Sat Jan 30 1864

Took the "H.A. Weed" & went to Hilton Head with the veterans to be paid. Arms &c Nine of the lost children going to our company. Lt. Wyckoff gone to Ft. Mitchell. We sail tomorrow. The men provided for in camp.

Emma Jane's depiction of soldiers at ease

(Barrett Collection)

Chapter 10

A Visit Home

> January 31, 1864-March 4, 1864--Traveled home via steamer
> "Atlantic"--Arrived February 3rd in N.Y.--Stopped at Brooklyn then
> on to Concord, Massachusetts--Surprises all--Attended military ball--
> Diary entries while at Concord--March 5th, Regiment reassembles at
> Montague Hall, Brooklyn

[Note that all the following transcriptions have been faithfully copied from the original document, as written by James, except where noted.]

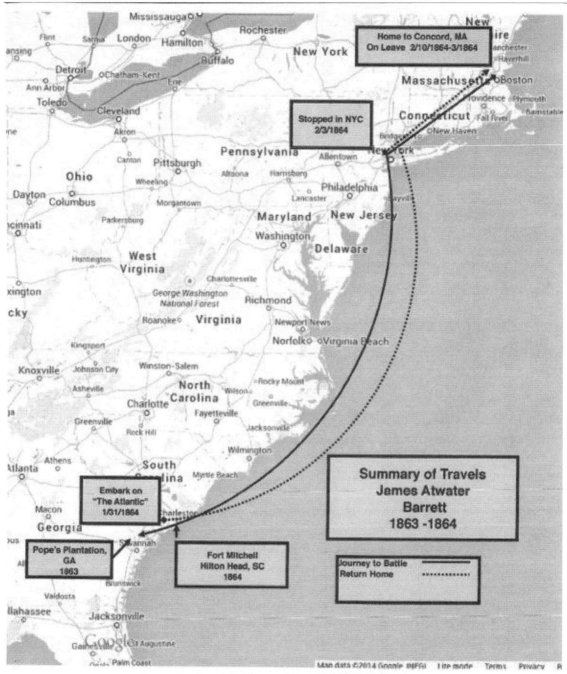

Summary of James' travels, 1863-1864
(Courtesy of Google INFGI, 2014)

*[*James' diary entries]*

Sun Jan 31 1864

Formed & marched to the dock. Brigade escorted us down. Embarked on "Atlantic". Very much crowded. I have a room with Hilliard. Sailed about 3 PM

Mon Feb 1 1864

A little sick. Not much appetite Table not well attended Making good time

Tues Feb 2 1864

On duty this A.M. Feel very well. Getting colder Some gambling on board. Men do not like to be molested

Wed Feb 3 1864

Arrived in NY at daylight. Went ashore & got breakfast. Took a good while. Marched to Brooklyn in companies. Left the knapsacks in Montague Hall. Filled up the furloughs & obtained the bounty for the men promptly. Some drunkenness. Dismissed to meet March 5th

Thurs Feb 4 1864

Took the people by surprise. Henry Warren going south. Sat for photos. Made calls.

Fri Feb 5 1864

Went to Bronxville. Mr. Swain hurt.

Sat Feb 6 1864

Returned from Bronxville & spent the night with Wm Wood. Henry with me. Very pleasant visit.

Sun Feb 7 1864

Attended church at the little chappel. Mr. Staples' funeral in the afternoon. Very solemn & affecting. Took tea at Mr. Leete's. Spent the night at Mr. Bates.

Mon Feb 8 1864

Went to dentist. Henry left for Hilton Head. Went for my pictures. Very good. Called on Charley's lady—like her very much. Went with Mrs. Bates to hear Miss Dickenson[117] lecture.

Tues Feb 9 1864

Took steamer for Fall River.

Wed Feb 10 1864

Arrived in Boston. Met Story & went to see Howland. Took the noon train for Concord. Took them all by surprise. Went after Jennie. She will stay at our house while I am home

Thurs Feb 11 1864

Received invitation to a military ball.

Fri Feb 12 1864

Went to Ball—first rate time. Went home at 5 A.M. Carried Jennie & Nell.

Sat Feb 13 1864

Rather stupid today. Spend afternoon & evening at Mr. Farmer's. Nell at home.

[Emma Jane's transcription of Emily's journal entry]
Sat. Feb. 13, 1864

> *Last Wednesday had the pleasure of welcoming brother James unexpectedly as we had given up seeing him. We saw a carriage turn up to the door and recognized Mary and Georgy but wondered who her escort could be. Were up in Father's room and started to go down to the door when we discovered the soldier through the window, Mother's eyes stuck out pretty well when he entered the room. We soon dispatched him for Jennie, and intend making her our guest while he stays.*

---

[117] Miss Anna Elizabeth Dickinson (1842 – 1932) was a well-known American orator, lecture and gifted teacher. She was an advocate for the abolition of slavery and woman's suffrage. Miss Dickinson was the first woman to speak before the United States Congress. Anna Elizabeth Dickinson. (November 8, 2015). *Wikipedia, The Free Encyclopedia*. Retrieved December 4, 2015, from https://en.wikipedia.org/w/index.php?title=AnnaElizabethDickinson&oldid=689684946

[*James' diary entries]

Sun Feb 14 1864
Attended church. Mr. Reynolds preached. Very few there in the afternoon.

Mon Feb 15 1864
Attended Miss Martha Monroe's funeral. Very solemn. Aunt Gerrish came home this noon. Boards at Mary's.

Tues Feb 16 1864
Getting cold. Snowing.

Wed Feb 17 1864
Coldest day this winter. Takes hold some. Aunt Gerrish & Mary spend the day at our house.

Thurs Feb 18 1864
Very cold but the wind has gone down. After leaving Jennie at school. Carried Mrs. Reynolds to ride. She is getting better.

Fri Feb 19 1864
Cousin party at Mrs. Hosmer's. Annie Buttrick came up—seems very happy. Jennie goes home tonight on account of company.

Sat Feb 20 1864
Dined at Mrs. Farmer's. Jennie & I called up & took tea at Mr. Wood's. Met several others. Found Mr. Thompson at home. Em happy, of course.

An Emma Jane embellishment
(Barrett Collection)

[*Narrative]
During our absence Our reg^t what there was left of them about 300 men (We had been recruited up) were sent to Florida & fought at the battle of Olustee[118]   This counted one more slaughter for Genl Seamore & he was relieved & sent to another Dep^t much to the liking of the Troops of our Corps who had no confidence in a Genl who called them "nothing but <u>Damned Volunteers</u>".

But we all loved Genl Gillmore & I do not think his services have ever been half appreciated.

*[*James' diary entries]*
Sun Feb 21 1864
Attended church. Minister from Stowe. Sermon rather agitating. I like
them. Some discussion in evening at home. Jennie is fully as radical as I.
Story in town till Tuesday.

Mon Feb 22 1864
Attended Mary Wood's examination with Jennie & Nell. Very good! Dined
at Mr. Farmer's. Went home to tea & attended a fair in the evening.
Danced a little. Did not stay late as Jennie did not dance.

Miliscent Hosmer Farmer   Jacob Brown Farmer
Jane Farmer's Parents
(Barrett Collection)

---

[118] The Battle of Olustee or Battle of Ocean Pond was fought in Baker County, Florida on February 20, 1864. It was the largest battle fought in Florida during the American Civil War. Battle of Olustee. (October 1, 2015). In *Wikipedia, The Free Encyclopedia*. Retrieved December 4, 2015, from https://en.wikipedia.org/w/index.php?title=BattleofOlustee&oldid=683592913

Tues Feb 23 1864

Sherman Barrett died this morning. Took noon train for Waltham. Stopped at Mr. Bacon's. Found them all out. Was delayed & missed the return train. Went to a fair with Mrs. Bacon & spent the night at their house. He is to send me some watches. Ancient wedding.

Wed Feb 24 1864

Returned to Concord on early train. Found the folks anxious. Jennie thought I was left. We all went to Mr. Farmer's to tea & spend the evening & meet the cousins. Living rather fast these days. Missed the Lyceum this evening.

Thurs Feb 25 1864

Left Jennie at school. Examination today. Carried Rebecca & Mrs. Hosmer to the S.A. society & took Annie B. to ride. Had a good time returned. Made several calls—took tea at Mr. Darby's. Examinations passed off well. Sherman Barrett buried today. I went to the funeral. Left the girls home.

Fri Feb 26 1864

Took Jennie down to Emma Moore's examination. First rate. Dined at Mr. Farmer's. Called at Jos. Clark's & at Mr. Brown's. Went to an exhibition in the evening.

Sat Feb 27 1864

Rebecca helping Jennie today on her dress. She is to spend Sunday at our house.

Sun Feb 28 1864

Mr. Reynolds preached today two capital sermons. Found Mr. Bacon at Mary's with my watches—very pretty. Gave Jennie hers—she likes it very much. Our regiment have been in a fight in Florida—suffered a good deal. My company not much.

Mon Feb 29 1864

Carried Jennie home to get ready to go to New York with me tomorrow. Mary comes up to spend the P.M. Lizzie busy getting up theatricals. Father & Mother getting smart.

Tues Mar 1 1864

After saying good-bye to all, Father carried Jennie & me to the morning train for Boston. Made several calls & took the 4 P.M. train for Fall River & N. Y. Very pleasant journey, altho it snowed hard.

Wed Mar 2 1864

Arrived in N.Y. 8 A.M. also took a carriage for Mrs. Leete's. Most all got the mumps. Did some business. Charley called in the evening & I went home with him & spent the night. Mr. Bates suffering from rheumatism.

Thurs Mar 3 1864

We went to the Sanitary Fair this A.M. met Charley [Gerrish] & Fanny & dined together at the New England Kitchen. Decidely ancient. Jennie & I then went over & took the cars for Bronxville. Found the people all assembled at Uncle's. Very polite. Jennie got along finely. Aunt Ann & Nell Prescott very attentive.

Fri Mar 4 1864

Invited over to Kate's [Mrs. Swain] where we dined & then took the noon train for N. Y. Stopped at Central Park & rode around for an hour & visited Trinity Church & took a peep from the steeple. Returned to Mr. Leete. Rec^d a call from Charley & Fanny in the evening. I borrowed his key & went to Mr. Bate's to spend the night.

Sat Mar 5 1864

Bid a hasty good-bye & reported at 10 A.M. at Montague Hall where our regiment were to assemble. Dismissed untill 8 A.M. tomorrow. Made arrangements about the baggage etc. & passed the night at Mr. Leete

Chapter 11

Heading to Hilton Head Aboard "Arago"

March 5, 1864-March 15, 1864--Emily's journal entry--Spends few
days at Fort Schuyler, New York City--Soldiers allowed to vote

[Note that all the following transcriptions have been faithfully copied from the original
document, as written by James, except where noted.]

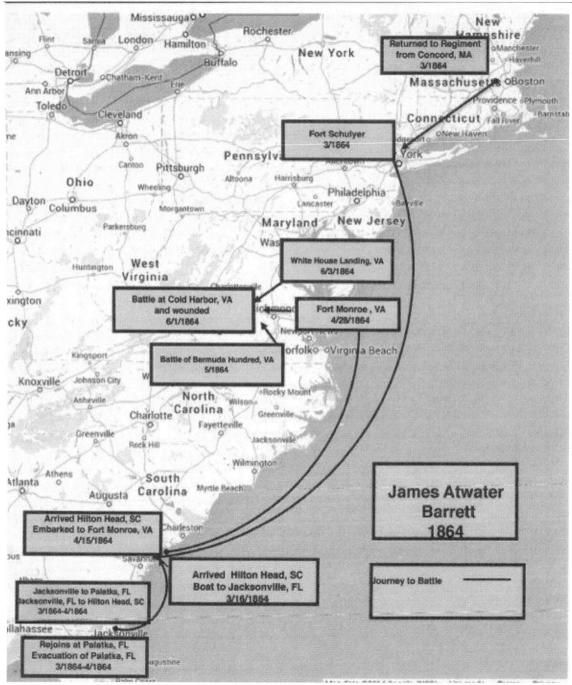

James' travels, 1864
(Courtesy of Google INFGI, 2014)

Photo of steamer "Arago"
(This media is in the public domain in the United States, 2016)

[Emma Jane's transcription of Emily's journal entry]
Sat. Mar. 5, 1864

Stern winter has passed and spring ever welcome, has stepped in this time unheeded for sad thoughts were brooding and tears flowed freely as we spoke that bitter word "good bye" and saw our dear brother again leave us for scenes of blood and carnage, for his regiment has been engaged lately in an unsuccessful conflict in Florida so that we can hardly realize the danger into which he may be going. Charles came that day and though usually all sadness takes flight at his presence, I could not quite obliterate those last few words so earnestly spoken as poor James took me one side in the back room just as I was drying up my tears that I might not make him sad and requested that if he should get chopped off down there, he wanted we should remember Jennie. Heaven forbid that his life should be sacrificed. Jennie accompanied him to N.Y. where she intends passing her vacation. James was home about three weeks, but we seemed to see him very little as he was going for and with Jennie night and morning and usually did not always appear till with her again, but poor child. I resolved that I would do all in my power to help then to enjoy each other for it is a sad engagement at the best, made so from the uncertainty of their ever meeting again.

[*Narrative]

Our furlough over, we gathered our men with some trouble altho quite a number failed to appear & the word "Deserter" stands recorded against their names.

[*James' diary entries]

Sun Mar 6 1864

The 13th Reg. escort us over to the battery this morning. Only about 100 men reported. We go to Fort Schuyler[119] for a few days. The men have good accommodations. Officers not extra. I feel rather dull & blue— nothing strange. Found a mess finally & borrowed some blankets.

Mon Mar 7 1864

Nothing to do. Decidely dull. I expect to get a pass to go up to the city tomorrow if we remain here. Nothing about sailing yet.

Tues Mar 8 1864

Can't go today. No more officers back yet. Awful dull here—nothing to do. Took a look round the island & all over the fort. Strong place. Lt. Hutchinson back in the evening. I will try to get to N.Y. tomorrow.

Wed Mar 9 1864

General won't give me a pass this morning. Lt. Hilliard comes down at noon. The Colonel says I can go up. I take the noon boat. Find the folks all pretty well. Pass the night at Mr. Leete's. Gerrish comes over to tea. Mr. Leete is going west. I pass a very pleasant evening. Jennie is well as usual. Mattie curious & quite domestic.

[This is Emma Jane's transcription of a letter written by James.]

Fort Schuyler
Mch 9 1864

Dearest Jennie,

I have not yet been able to get off from here. I applied to Gen[l] Brown this morning for a pass & he refused me. I shall make a desperate effort today, But if I do not see you again, it will not be my fault. But I think I shall. I am still depending on my luck. We have about ½ of our men here. Our accommodations are poor. I sleep on the floor. You may imagine that I dream some. Perhaps you may guess who about. It makes a fellow feel rather blue to be kept here just in sight of friends without being able to see them. But I suppose it is all right. It won't last always. The war will be over one of these days & then—"Richard is himself again." Until then, I will try at

---

[119] Fort Schuyler is most well-known for its use during the Civil War as a hospital and prison, and as a training ground for soldiers bound for fields of war. Fort Schuyler is located on Throgg's Neck, the southeastern tip of the Bronx. It guards the eastern entrance to New York Harbor.

least to be resigned to whatever Providence may order. Charge it all to the "General Good" & take my pay in the satisfaction of having <u>tried</u> to do my duty. I cannot tell you how anxious we all are now to get off. Once started, soldiers like to reach their destination & fret at anything like delay.

I wrote to sister Mary that I should sail this week. I wish you would write to some one after you find that I have gone, & I shall depend on getting a good long letter from you on my arrival. You don't know how refreshing your letters are to me, & they will be doubly so in the future. I feel that I never half knew you before.

Good news this morning. Soldiers are to be allowed to vote! Thank God for that! Lincoln will be our next President & then let all rebels and Copperheads bid a long farewell to their long cherished hopes that the North will fail to give their unconditional support to the cause of Liberty & Humanity. Excuse me Jennie, if I have written in a gloomy mood, But it is very natural to feel dull after having such a good time as I have had & then being shut up in such a lonesome place as this. But I shall soon get over it. It is not my way to indulge in gloomy thoughts. I am going now to try to get up to the city for the last time. If I succeed, all right. If not—let this be my good bye until better days, & with much love, believe me as ever

Yours

James A. Barrett

1st Lieut, 48th Reg^t N.Y.S. Vols.

Please write me a line by the "Arago". She sails Friday I think. We expect to go on her.

[*James' diary entry]

Thurs Mar 10 1864

I have taken cold. No appetite. Not very well this morning. Jennie & I go out for a walk. Met Col. S. and Capt. L. "Arago" sails tomorrow. Called in Took a picture of Jennie in military. Met Dr. Guy in Lizzie's sitting room. Left at 2 P.M. to go to the boat for Ft. Schuyler. Can't go today so returned. Start in morning.

Photo of Jennie taken in military uniform
(Barrett Collection)

Fri Mar 11 1864

Feel better this morning. Take an early start. Must take a boat at 8 A.M. Jennie walks to the ferry with me. Good-bye to all. Arrived at fort by 10 A.M. Left about noon for the "Arago." Went on board 2 P.M. Officer of guard. Relieved at 6. Lucky! Most all our men here. Crowded! Good state room 16 with Hilliard. Wrote a line to send up by tug. Foggy.

[*Letter]

At Sea Steamer "Arago" Mch 11 1864

My Dear Jennie.

I am just off duty. I was detailed Officer of the Guard upon coming on board (about 2 P.M.) & was relieved at 6. (<u>Luck</u>) My successor takes 12 hours duty. Upon reaching the battery this morning, I was told that the steamer was not going to Fort Schuyler but to Rikers Island[120], But the Captain finally kindly offered to see that we were sent there. So after reaching Rikers Island He hailed a tug & (10 men and 3 officers of us) proceeded to join our Reg^t. I did not see Genl Brown—thought I would not report to him. All hands were glad to get out from under his rule. I was not the only one who had reason to dislike him. We took a steamer about 12 M. (miles) & proceeded to the "Arago." We find it rather crowded I have a first rate state room. The same room that I went on in last fall was given me But I exchanged it so as to be with one of our Lieuts. There are a number of officers on board whom I know.

Only 2 <u>ladies</u> have been seen I do <u>not</u> know them <u>Dont</u> <u>expect</u> <u>to</u> So you wont be jealous. Will you? Our men are nearly all here—about 20 absent. The Lord help them. They will get fits when they are caught.

My appetite has returned (I think I fed on <u>something</u> <u>else</u> <u>when</u> <u>at</u> <u>your</u> <u>house</u>) My spirits are good. Perhaps it may be partially owing to my laughing two women (wives of Soldiers) into good humor on board the boat that brought us here. They were dreadful low spirited at the prospects of their husbands going off again. But I fairly got them to laughing.

<u>Alas</u> I believe they relapsed again afterwards. But I am faced <u>South</u> now & I feel as if I am really a Soldier again I don't want to come north again until I come to <u>stay</u>. Did'nt I feel blue last Sunday though. After leaving Brooklyn. Well I never felt quite so worthless before I could not think of anything except the <u>past</u> & that was only an aggravation then as I was leaving it with the prospect of being kept at Fort Schuyler for a week & no certainty of getting a <u>pass</u>

But that is all over now I did get a <u>pass</u>. & now I feel better & am ready to go back & finish my work in the army

I am reminded that the lights must soon be put out. & I must close I just thought I would write a line & send to you by the tug in the morning We are now lying off in the Harbor. Shall sail

---

[120] Rikers Island is located in Queens, New York. The island was used as a military training ground during the Civil War.

during the night. I am so glad I got that picture. It is a real prize   2 or 3 who have seen it admire my taste

No more at present Good night—

Yours
James A. Barrett
1st Let 48th NYSV

[*James' diary entries]
Sat Mar 12 1864
Sailed about 6 A.M. Very pleasant. Took a good bath this morning &c &
feel tip top. We have a schooner in tow & are making very poor time. A
little inclination to sea sickness but I take my regular meals. Slept several
hours today & retired early.

Sun Mar 13 1864
Slept well last night. Feel first rate this A.M. Weather very pleasant.
Sermon by Dr. Parker of Boston in the cabin 11 A.M. On deck at 4 P.M.
by another young minister & a Catholic priest.

[This is Emma Jane's transcription of a letter written by James.]

At Sea   Steamer "Arago"
Mch 13 1864

My Dear Jennie,

I wrote you a hasty note Friday night in hopes that it might be sent by some tug before we sailed. But I understand that no letters were sent.   So I suppose that it will go in the same mail with this. We are having delightful weather, But having a schoo'r in tow, are making slow time. We shall not reach the Head before Wednesday at our present rate. We sailed Saturday morning 6 A.M. I got a room at first with Lieut Hilliard away aft. After looking at it, we were troubled with visions of sea sickness so I asked the Purser if he could not give us a room in the middle of the boat where there would not be as much motion. He gave us parts of 15 & 16 & then we exchanged & got together in one of the best rooms on the ship.   I thought I was going to be sick yesterday But I got bravely over it. I slept soundly until late this morning. Strange what makes me sleep so. It must be owing to those restless nights at Fort Schuyler.

Today is Sunday & the sun is shining warm & pleasant. We are soon to have services in the cabin. This afternoon there will be services on deck. How I would like to accompany you to hear our old friend Mr. Longfellow preach. I suppose you are just about starting now. But all in good time. I am impatient to get back to my post again, where my time will be occupied & I shall not find it dragging heavily. It is a blessed thing to have something to do. I miss the daily papers. I want to hear something about the army movements. I expect great things from Genl Grant. I think he is in his right place now.

It is church time & I must stop for the present. Perhaps I may get inspiration from the sermon to give me a few ideas.....I wonder if he is any relation to Theodore. He says not. The

165

text was, "Seek ye first the kingdom of God", &c He drew a very good parallel in the shape of loyalty, & disloyalty or Rebellion. He spoke of the inspiration we felt in the consciousness of being in the right. It is an interesting & earnest sermon. I wish I could listen to one as good every Sunday, But when I can't, I must do the next best thing.

By the way, I must praise you a bit for your pluck. It did me good to see you when we parted. I do dislike <u>scenes</u>. It was really distressing to witness some at the boat. But I always expect to see you strong. Few have disciplined themselves as well as you have. I sometimes think I have wasted my life when I see how much others accomplish. But I won't weary you with my shortcomings. I believe you don't listen to them very well.

Write often & believe me most affectionately
Your most obedient
Jas. A. Barrett

[*James' diary entry]
Mon Mar 14 1864
Passed Hatteras early. Rough this forenoon. Smooth towards night.
Wrote some & played a few hands at Euchre[121] & Whist[122].

[This is Emma Jane's transcription of a letter written by James.]

Mch 14th 1864

My Dear Jennie

We passed Hatteras during the night & it is a little rough today. I feel inclined to keep rather quiet. But have taken my regular meals so far. There is something sublimely[123] grand about the ocean   I like to look upon it Especially such a day as this   The weather is delightful with a fresh invigorating wind from the N.W. & The deep blue of the water dotted here & there, as far as the eye can reach, with white foamy caps makes a picture which I cannot but admire. The poet tells us "Man's control stops with the shore", but when I see our noble Ship plowing its way so bravely & riding so gallantly & securely over these angry waves,
while I am forced to acknowledge man[s] weakness & littleness still I am also reminded how man's energy has done. For if he cannot "Control", he surely has succeeded in bridling the waves & in

---

[121] A card game in which each player is dealt five cards and the player making trump must take three tricks to win a hand. euchre. (n.d.) *Merriam-Webster Online* Dictionary. Retrieved December 15, 2015, from http://www.merriam-webster.co/dictionary/euchre This is the game responsible for introducing the joker into modern packs.

[122] A card game for four in which the two sides try to win the balance of the 13 tricks: forerunner of bridge. whist. (n.d.). *Collins English Dictionary*. Retrieved December 15, 2015, from http://www.collinsdictionary.com/dictionary/english/whist

[123] Of high spiritual, moral, or intellectual worth. sublimely. (n.d.) AMERICAN HERITAGE DICTIONARY OF THE ENGLISH LANGUAGE, FIFTH EDITION. (2011). Retrieved December 3, 2015, from http://www.thefreedictionary.com/sublimely

making them serve his purpose. So it is in life   We are continually meeting with difficulties opposition trials.

But these are all portions of life's lesson & according as we learn it well shall we prove ourselves worthy of our trust.

The more difficult our task the greater will be the satisfaction of having accomplished it & rather than yield to discouragement or to hesitate in our course. Let us buckle our armour tighter about us & thank God that He has thought us worthy of our mission. Never doubting "That as our day is, so will our strength be". But I am getting prosy[124]. I hope you will be able to read this scribbling I know I am making awful work of it   But I cant help it.

Surely the world is moving   Yesterday afternoon we had services on deck & I saw five ministers, all of different denominations, & one a Catholic too. Apparently in perfect harmony & fellowship. It does me good to witness these evidences of progress. I like to see these different Theologians shake up their views together. It gives them a healthy airing.

Last night I got hold of a book by "Timothy Titcomb"[125] It was a real treat. I looked for it today in vain. Have you ever seen his letters?   I suppose we shall get off Charleston bar tonight or tomorrow morning. I hope it will be daytime so that I can see the sights there. I was quite amused the other day at the patriotism of one old man in Co. G. He was a little tight, But sober enough to know what he was about. We were just about to start & I spoke to him as I was passing. "Ain't I proud," said he in speaking of going back. It really did me good   I think we can often learn valuable lessons from even the most ignorant of men I certainly often think when I see what the poor privates endure & suffer how little I have gone through in comparison

I notice it on Shipboard more than anywhere else for well do I remember my own first experience in the fall of 1861   But hard as it was I would not sell the memory of it for any price

The law of compensation is always working after all. & Each one is pretty sure to get his reward I suppose our lots are not so different as they sometimes appear

I think I like your picture better & better the more I look at it. It almost seems to speak to me. I intend to give it a prominent place in my writing desk when I get into camp   I have a fancy picture I will send to you   I will try & write more when I get to the Head. Please excuse this scribble & believe me as ever   Yours
                                James A. Barrett

[*James' diary entry]
Tues Mar 15 1864

---

[124] Showing no imagination; commonplace or dull. Prosy. (n.d.). *Oxford Dictionaries*. Retrieved December 16, 2015, from http://www.oxforddictionaries.com/us/definition/english/prosy
[125] Josiah Gilbert Holland (July 24, 1819-October 12, 1881) was an American novelist and poet who also wrote under the pseudonym Timothy Titcomb. Josiah Gilbert Holland. (October 12, 2015). *Wikipedia, The Free Encyclopedia*. Retrieved December 4, 2015,
from https://en.wikipedia.org/w/index.php?title=JosiahGilbertHolland&oldid=685455809

*Pleasant this A.M.   Wind with us. Schooner has her sails up & we are
making better time. Passed Charleston bar about 6 P.M. Could see the
sunken "Housatonic"*[126]*xviii. Also Sumter & see firing from Wagner.*

[*Letter]

Wednesday morning arrived all right   Start for Jacksonville today

At Sea   Steamer "Arago"
Tuesday evening   Mch 15 1864

My Dear Jennie

We passed Charleston bar a little before dark & I assure you I used my eyes dilligently. The besieged city was plainly seen in the distance   While the guns from the long to be remembered Wagner could be easily heard at short intervals sending their compliments & reminding them that the "mudsills"[127] from the north now commanded their respect. Sumpter still stands & continues to insult humanity with its rebel flag.

How much I would enjoy a visit to Wagner   The four short hours I passed there served to give it a place in my memory never to be erased. But how different it must appear at the present time   Our noble Flag now waves where then then the dispised rag of treason floated. & the very guns that dealt out death so cruelly to so many of my poor comrades now daily take the oath of allegiance to our common country & hurl back defiance & scorn as a just judgment from Heaven upon those who have so foully rebelled against the best government that the world ever knew. The Fleet that fills the Harbor reminds me that none but a disordered brain would ever dominate a "paper blockade". Tomorrow morning I expect we will arrive at the Head. We have had a splendid passage Altho an unusually long one   I will write again as soon as I get settled at camp But not in season for this mail.

You were saying the other day that you dreaded going back east. If you go alone You can stop in your Stateroom at Fall River until morning if you like & then proceed to Boston in a Morning train   Many do so rather than to be broken of their sleep

I merely mention it as I happened to think of it.

I picked up the December Atlantic today & was very much interested in one article—"The Man without a Country". I dont know who wrote it. But it is a good a tribute to Patriotism as I have seen for a long time. I presume you have read it. I was talking to a Capt today who was well acquainted with Uncle Barretts family in Rutland

---

[126] The Sinking of "USS Housatonic" on 17 February 1864 during the American Civil War was an important turning point in naval warfare. Sinking of USS Housatonic. (January 26, 2015). *Wikipedia, The Free Encyclopedia*. Retrieved December 4, 2015, from https://en.wikipedia.org/w/index.php?title=Sinking_of_USS_Housatonic&oldid=644207806

[127] A Southern derogatory term for a Northerner meaning to be at the lowest level of social position. Mudsill. (n.d.). *Merriam-Webster Online* Dictionary. Retrieved December 3, 2015, from http://www.merriam-webster.com/dictionary/mudsill

It is pleasant to meet with people in this way   I often do & always enjoy talking over familiar things. I dreamed last night of being home in Pear time. Do you think that means next fall?

Somehow I have not my usual faith in my dreams now

I have enjoyed so much the last few weeks that it is very natural that this should affect my dreams

I take lots of comfort now in thinking over about those times. But they will come again. A few short months & we shall be no more needed here. Until then I crave your Prayers. I know I shall have them & feel sure that He who has promised to hear & answer Prayer, will watch over me in the future as the past.

& Now Jennie accept my good night Kiss & may God bless & protect you is the sincere wish ofYours Very Truly

James A Barrett
1st Lt 48th N.Y.V.Vols
Hilton Head S.C.

Chapter 12

Palatka

March 16, 1864-March 31, 1864--arrives at Hilton Head aboard
steamer "Dictator"--Rejoins regiment after Battle of Olustee--
General Seymour relieved of duty--General Gillmore takes reins of
leadership--Receives orders to march north to camp on St. James
River--Life at Camp Palatka--Skirmish with two companies of
Dickson's Cavalry--Letter from Jennie

[Note that all the following transcriptions have been faithfully copied from the original document, as written by James, except where noted.]

[*James' diary entries]
Wed Mar 16 1864

Arived at Hilton Head. Reg^t landed until 4 P.M. Took a steamer "Dictator"[128] for Jacksonville. Saw the new theatre. Met Henry. He looks well. Theatre just started. Much liked.

Thurs Mar 17 1864
Started during the night. I was lucky & got a state room & slept well. Arrived in Jacksonville (Florida) in afternoon, stopping at [Fort] Fernandina on the way. Passed "Maple Leaf"[129] which sailed six hours before us. Got our equipments & proceeded on the "Maple Leaf" to Palatka, Fla. Where we arived early next morning

Fri Mar 18 1864
Arived at Palatka early & joined our reg. Very pleasant camp. My tent is up. The men's tents not here yet. Lt. Wyckoff gone home. Many things lost. I miss lots of my little things. Two stoves gone.

[*Narrative]

We rejoined our Reg^t at Pilatka Florida soon after the battle of Olustee but were soon ordered north after several slight skirmishes with rebel cavalry to join Butler in Virginia stopping at Hilton Head to be paid off We went to Gloucester point on James river where we went into camp & prepared for field service, turned in our camp equipage & extra baggage, obtained shelter tents & fully equipped ourselves & sailed for Bermuda hundred where we took up our march carrying all our baggage on our backs except one small Valise to each officer which the Quarter Master carried.

The road on the line of march soon became literally covered with blankets, tents & clothing of all kinds. 50^{lbs} on one's back gets very heavy to carry after the 1st 5 miles & every time we halted for rest, say once an hour, the men would examine their Knapsacks & throw away the things they could spare best, & it followed that the well filled Knapsack of the morning was often nearly empty by night.

---

[128] "USS Dictator" was a single-turreted ironclad monitor. USS Dictator (1863). (October 12, 2015). *Wikipedia, The Free Encyclopedia*. Retrieved December 4, 2015, from https://en.wikipedia.org/w/index.php?title=USSDictator(1863)&oldid=685374283
[129] The "Maple Leaf" was a wooden side-wheel steamer built to carry passengers, freight and mail. Maple Leaf (shipwreck). (August 25, 2015). *Wikipedia, The Free Encyclopedia*. Retrieved December 4, 2015, from https://en.wikipedia.org/w/index.php?title=MapleLeaf(shipwreck)&oldid=677852596

Emma Jane's sketch of regiment marching
(Barrett Collection)

[*Letter]

Head Quarters Co. H. 48th Regt N.Y.S. Vols.
Palatka Fla Mch 18 1864

Dearest Jennie

I arrived at this place early this morning   We are in Camp on the St. John River about 100 miles from its mouth. I have been busy today trying to straighten out things

Lt Wyckoff whom I left with the Co has resigned & gone home   So I find things in a rather unsatisfactory condition   But I shall soon fix it up   We have a beautiful place to camp   But no tents for the men except such as they can fix up from what they find. My tent is here & up   Our Regt has suffered much more than the papers stated

Barton's Brigade had the most of the work to do & did it well. I recd your 2 letters of Feb 1st & 8th & also yours of 9th inst when I arrived at Hilton Head

I went into our Theatre at Hilton Head It was a splendid affair It opened last Monday or Tuesday Tremendous crowd only a few of our association are there & they had to get some men from elsewhere to take parts   So it was not as good as of old. But the performance was well liked after all. They did not play the Wednesday night I was there as they could not have the band. I met Henry at Hilton Head   Just as I was going in to the Hotel to write to him   He was looking tip top

He has taken his plantation back again & is going to work it as much as he can this year. It seems quite natural to get back in camp again. I expect to be very busy for two weeks to-come. I felt myself "very near to you" while at Fort Schuyler   I did last night also. You know I believe somewhat in these spiritual manifestations. I do not often speak all I think. But I believe you are aware of what my ideas are.   I am perfectly willing that you should visit Mr. Lewis or any other Mr you may wish. & You need not fear my being "jealous" I have the fullest confidence in your discretion as well as your constancy   I have often thought that you might have found someone more deserving your love than my humble self

But still now that you have committed yourself I feel secure. & If you are the loser   I am just selfish enough to cage the profits.

Mrs. Barton is living here with her Husband & seems to enjoy it much. It is very interesting to hear the men talk about the Battle. Our Pickets occasionally see a few Rebels   But there are not many about here   Our Reg^t went out a few days since & destroyed a Rebel Camp

They talk of going out after some Horses before long about 50 of our Reg^t have been mounted for outpost duty

The duty here I expect is going to be pretty hard   I find many things missing   I guess I have lost nearly $50.00 worth of private property & lots of Company stuff. The latter I can get out of. The former I shall have to stand myself.   I have got in to my old mess & live better than I have since I left New York   We have to put up with hard tack except when we bake biscuit   I don't patronise the Hard tack much   Crinoline on the brain[130] still rages   There seem to be quite a number of patients. It is not <u>dangerous</u>. But some cases are attended with a frequent waste of <u>sighs</u> & an occasional droping of a <u>tear</u>. Your humble servant does not <u>often</u> indulge in the latter. It would be useless <u>denying</u> the <u>former</u>.   Mr. Hutchinson of whom I spoke to you as suffering from this disease does not seem to improve much   His case is a very obstinate one & baffles the best of treatment

He just stepped in & wished me to send his love. I have heard from my black boy   But have not seen him yet. I dread to see my sick list of tomorrow. Many of our men have dissipated so hard during their furlough that exhausted & abused nature demands relief.

It is strange that men will make brutes of themselves as so many do. But if they will do so they must suffer the consequences. The great law of compensation is always working   I notice it more & more every day I live.

I am going to enclose a card of Mr. Dickson   Our base Drummer. He is our old Stage manager in the Theatre. He played Iago in the Play of Othello

You need not feel obliged to put all these pictures in your Album that I send home I send them more because I cant very well keep so many with me that anything else. I intend to send the most of all our Reg^t Officers if it would not be too much <u>trouble</u> for you to take care of them for me. You see I prefer to fill my Album up with <u>Ladies</u> mostly & my <u>particular</u> <u>personal</u> <u>friends</u>

But Tattoo is beating which reminds me I must begin to think about "<u>Atlantic SV</u>"[131]. So with much love to all & an <u>extra</u> <u>share</u> for yourself I will bid you Good night. & believe me Yours very affectionately

<u>Direct to Hilton Head or elsewhere</u>   James A. Barrett

---

[130] Men during the war were unable to perform tasks as they were thinking about women. Probably the most distinctive signature of this time period is the hoop skirt, named for the structural support of wire hoops or whalebones called "crinolines," worn under the skirt to hold its shape.

[131] The "Atlantic" was used by the Union as a transport ship during the American Civil War.

*[*James' diary entry]*
Sat Mar 19 1864

The men have rigged up some rude huts & have an appearance of comfort.
Duty is going to be hard. Can't stay in my old mess—too many. Getting
along the best I can untill Hilliard starts his mess.

[Emma Jane's transcription of Emily's journal entry]
Sat. Mar 19, 1864

 Had a letter also from Jennie this week saying that James
probably sailed last Saturday so that the painful separation is
over and they must feel it deeply after enjoying each other so
much.

*[*James' diary entry]*
Sat Mar 20 1864

Turned out at 4 A.M. & skirmished two miles& back in search of spies.
Found nothing. Returned about 7. Took a good wash. Inspection at 10.
Rather tired.

[*Letter]

Hd Qtrs Co H. 48th Regt N.Y.S.Vols
Palatka Fla Mch 20 1864

Dear Jennie

 I like this place very well   It is a beautiful place. I was ordered out this morning at 4 A.M. (Co E. G. & H.) turned out to search for some rebel Spies   2 men were seen to go through our lines. We Skirmished about 2 miles & returned tired & wet with tramping through the bushes & swamps   We discovered nothing

 I am out of my old mess as it was full & am now living from hand to mouth   the best I can I have made arrangements to join another as soon as the things arrive. Hard tack goes rather against my inclination I have not fasted myself into condition to relish it very well yet   I expect to be called up nights pretty often while here

 Rumor says there is a church & preaching here   But I am too tired today to feel like looking it up. Our nights are quite chilly   But the days are warm   I went in bathing in the river after coming in this morning & found the water very agreeable

 The Orange Trees are in blossom & some have fruit upon them. The blossoms are very fragrant   I will enclose some   But I fear they will lose all shape, smell & beauty before reaching you

 The whole atmosphere is filled with the perfume from them   I keep a sprig in my tent all the while. If you see Charley ask him if he sent that album to Lieut Schultz of our Regt   I gave it to him to send when I first went home. Lt S. was just in my tent & I showed him my pictures   He thinks your military one is a much better picture than the cards. We have good chances to get Sweet potatoes, eggs, fresh Pork etc from natives who live across the river. They came over & trade considerable   I enjoy going round among my men & hearing them tell about the Battle

They (My Co) did nobly   Not one flinched in Co H.   There was some sculking in the Reg^t of course   One Serg^t of Co G. was reduced for cowardice. The Maj had to drive him up several times. He did get wounded at last   But that did not affect the charge of cowardice

It is not positive evidence that a man is brave that he is wounded

I heard the Maj speak of quite a number whom he had to drive to their post   But I have not heard a word against any of H. Co   I must say I am proud of them

One Irishman of H had his Blanket slung across his shoulder & I counted 23 bullet holes in it   He was only slightly wounded after all of & is on duty again ready for another brush, I hear good accounts generally of our Officers

I tell you Jennie when I see these numerous manifestations of Bravery & Patriotism and often among the ignorant & lower classes too   It makes me think meanly of myself

For I know I am not brave   It always requires a struggle for me to nerve myself up to wrestle with danger & these people many of them seem to think no more of it than any ordinary duty   Many of them too have families at home dependant upon them. Truly sacrifices such as these have made ought surely to entitle them to wear the crown of Patriotism

I really feel ashamed of myself for ever having entertained the idea even for a short time of quitting the service before my country's wrongs shall have been avenged

I feel Jennie that I owe a prior duty to the country that had given me my nativity--& I thank God that I have no ties so strong as to induce me to withhold what little strength & talent Heaven has blessed me with in this hour of my country's need. I am constantly reminded that the utmost extent that I can do will be But a mere mite in the balance compared with what others have done are doing & are willing still to do for our common cause. My earnest Prayer is that Providence may give us all the required strength & courage to do our whole duty faithfully & will to the end & in doing this I believe we are serving our own personal interests far more than if we were contented to remain at home in these "hours that try men's souls" Now Jennie you need not feel jealous of me. I am thankful that we are not married   For I have not sufficient confidence in my Patriotism to feel that I should be satisfied to remain in the Army leaving a wife at home. But think not that I do not appreciate your Love

I feast upon it   I dream about it   It makes me better stronger happier.
Your letters are company for me & the thought of you inspires me to renewed effort. But Our time is not yet & until then   "It is all for the best" as we are. I thank God for the glimpses of sunshine He has given me. & will try to be content to leave the future in the hands of Him who has so kindly protected & blessed me in the past

I am unable to tell anything about the Steamer sails while I am here But I shall try to write often enough to be sure & catch them all. You must excuse my scrawls   I know I make lots of mistakes   But it is such a bore to copy anything. I cant do it.

It is so long since I have written any letters It is awful hard work

Ideas wont come. But enough of this. Please write often   I want to hear about Mr. Lewis I am afraid Mattie works to hard. Stopping after school every night. I hope she will not break down. But I guess she will stand it. I must close now with much love   I remain

Yours as ever

Jas. A. Barrett

*[*James' diary entries]*
Sun Mar 21 1864
On fatigue today with Lt. Hutchinson & 150 men. Rained in afternoon. Attacked in the front by Dickson's Cavalry. Sharp skirmishing. No one hurt. Rained hard all night. Very tired. Hope we shall not have to turn out tonight.

Wed Mar 23 1864
Finished returns for Feb. Must make up forms for ration money. Ordered co. cook stove etc. Price $55.00 Paid Paddock the amt

[This is Emma Jane's transcription of a letter written by James.]

Hd Qtrs Co H 48th NYS Vols
Palatka Fla   Mch 23 1864

Dearest Jennie

I did my 1st day's duty Monday, at work on the fortifications. They ran about 1 mile with a Battery planted at short intervals. It rained in the afternoon quite hard But we kept at work until sundown.

During the afternoon our Pickets were attacked by a Co of Dickson's (Dickison) Cavalry[132] & driven in a little ways until covered by our guns. We then took our arms & the 47th & part of the 48th went out to the front A good deal of ammunition was expended But not much harm was done Our Regt burnt several houses. We lost no men I returned with my party to my work after the 1st alarm. It rained very hard all night. But we did not have another alarm. I was thankful for that I assure you. For I was tired & mad & wanted rest. Yesterday it cleared off pleasant again. Our camp is in a beautiful grove of fine oaks They look very handsome with large quantities of long, heavy moss hanging from the branches. The foliage is very green & the gray moss looks fine in contrast. This moss is used for hair in stuffing chairs &c It is cured by burying it for a season when the outside comes off & it then looks very much like horse hair. We have a Volunteer Chaplain,
Mr. Taylor, temporarily attached to our Regt. I believe he is Presbyterian. I went to hear him Sunday night. I like him very much. He is a young man & not afraid to go into the field with the Regt. I hope we shall keep him. There are several churches here. There must have been quite a place in its day Yesterday I found quite a number of my things which I had given up as lost. Some of the books were soaked with kerosine but I guess that will dry after a while. I found out my sheets & Blankets so I slept comfortably between two sheets last night. It really seemed like

---

[132] John Jackson Dickison (Dickson) (March 28, 1816-August 20, 1902) was an officer in the Confederate States Army during the American Civil War. He was better known as the "Swamp Fox." Dickison is mostly remembered as being the person who led the attack which resulted in the capture of the Union warship USS Columbine in the "Battle of Horse Landing". John Jackson Dickison. (October 14, 2015). *Wikipedia, The Free Encyclopedia*. Retrieved December 4, 2015, from https://en.wikipedia.org/w/index.php?title=JohnJacksonDickison&oldid=685653493

living. How much we depend for happiness upon little things. You don't know how badly I felt when I thought all my little trifles were gone & how glad I was to find them. It is the little things after that go toward making up the sum of human happiness in this world. I have often been reminded of it. I just stopped a few minutes to put up my stove. My Co. clerk came in & said he thought a fire would be very comfortable. I find it so. It is very chilly after a rain. I expect to get my new mess started today. I have got so that I can eat Hardtack or anything that comes along. Pork with liver on it is thought nothing of & as to sand, that is thrown in.

One of our gunboats returned Sunday from an expedition up the river with 150 bales of cotton & a lot of sugar etc. She has been gone a week. I am going to appoint Corp¹ Pearsall, (the one you said Serg^{t)} in a few days as soon as I can get the proper data. I have not written except to you & one letter home since I came here. I am very busy getting my accounts settled up. I find a great many mistakes have been made. I shall try & write often to you at any rate & some of them will be sure to catch the steamer

I am going to have a lot of small copies of Pulaski views   I shall send them to you when I get them. Is your Album getting full.   "My gentleman from Africa" has not arrived yet. I miss him much But I managed to get another Lieut's boy to do my work or part of it

When I get my work done up   I shall try & catch up my correspondence. I have been thinking I am sorry I did not have all my letters at home. I may do them up & send them home yet

Would it be any trouble to you to keep them for me   The most of them are yours   But perhaps you would like to read some of the others. I have got a large piture of my co at home. You can take it if you want it   I shall look for letter in a day or two. Please write often & give much love to all   Take good care of yourself & believe me   Yours faithfully

James A. Barrett

Direct to Hilton Head as usual

[*James' diary entries]
Thurs Mar 24 1864
Finished my commutation of rations & papers issuing clothing. On board of survey to put prices on blankets issued as rubber. Decided that they are painted. Price $1.27

Fri Mar 25 1864
Rained hard during night & this morning. Cleared off pleasant. Work is still pressing. Horse race. One man fell off & broke his leg.

Sat Mar 26 1864   *On fatigue today with Lt. Acker &100 men. Good deal of work done in P.M. Check each load. Building Abertee[133] [Abatis] Mackey (Pvt. Frederick) died at 71/2 P.M. in hospital.*

---

[133] A defensive obstacle formed by felled trees with sharpened branches facing the enemy. abatis (n.d.). *Merriam-Webster Dictionary*. Retrieved April 10, 2016, from http://www.merriam-webster.com/dictionary/abatis

Sun Mar 27 1864

Took a good bath in the morning. Made arrangements for funeral in afternoon. Mr. Taylor conducts the services. Very touching. Church in the evening.

Mon Mar 28 1864

Mail in. I hear from 3rd quarter of '63 Ordinance. Made up final statement of Mackey & wrote to his friends. Pickets fired on. No one hurt.

[This is Emma Jane's transcription of a letter fragment written from James.]

Palatka, Fl
March 28, 1864

Dear Jenny

I had the pleasure of a letter from the Ord^{ce} Dep^t saying that my returns for the 3rd Quar. Of 1863 were correct.--- One of my veterans died suddenly on Saturday of Typhoid fever[134]. Yesterday we laid his remains in their final resting place. It seemed very sad to lose him so soon, after his return. I have just finished his final statement & written to his friends. His mother is a widow & my heart fairly ached for her as I wrote to her the sad tidings of his death. I tried to soften the blow a little But it is sacred ground to tread upon.

We sent out an expedition for a scout across the river the other day & brought in 10 prisoners. Did not learn much. I never lie down at night feeling sure of a good night's rest, But alarms are not as frequent now as they were before we came back. The Officers did not undress at night then. I have my bed on one end of the tent, a large box with two sides partially knocked off, with legs nailed on for a table where I have my Co writing desk. Beside it, I have another table for my Co clerk. A cracker box makes a very nice seat & my trunk another. On the other side is a long gun box which makes a good sofa & I have my little stove put up behind me. Overhead a pole is suspended where I hang my coats, towels, &c. My album is constant company for me & Your commission lies in a little drawer in my desk. Do your ears burn? I keep you pretty constantly on <u>duty</u>. If I see you putting on airs, I shall reduce you to the ranks. I was so glad that You enjoyed coming to Brooklyn. I don't know what I should have done without you. Besides we got better <u>acquainted</u>. I did think I knew you pretty well before I went home, But I find that I never half appreciated you.

---

[134] An acute infectious disease characterized by high fever, rose-coloured spots on the chest or abdomen, abdominal pain, and occasionally intestinal bleeding. It is caused by bacillus salmonella typhosa ingested with food or water. typhoid fever (n.d.). *Collins English Dictionary*. Retrieved December 15, 2015, from
http://www.collinsdictionary.com/dictionary/english/typhoid fever

I have not been on guard yet But I go on Wednesday. I have been on fatigue twice. I was lucky. I am going to start a bakery here & have soft bread. I broke one tooth the other day eating a hard cracker.

I will send you a copy of the Palmetto Herald.. Guess "I have written as much as will pay for you to read" so with lots of love to <u>everybody</u> <u>using</u> <u>discretion</u> of course. May God bless and prosper you---&c---

[*James' diary entries]
Tues Mar 29 1864
Finished monthly & quarterly returns. Coming out nicely. We are going to start a bakery here & have soft bread. I like that   I broke a tooth out the other day eating a hard cracker.

Wed Mar 30 1864
*Made quarterly returns of deceased soldiers & men joined. Went out & lay in ambush in
afternoon. Returned at dark. Saw no one. Missed picket today. Gave Mr. Taylor a call for Chaplain.*

Thurs Mar 31 1864
Sent off my returns. Went out to the front—lay in ambush a while. Attacked on right by cavalry. Advanced & joined them. Had a pretty lively skirmish. I threw my company out to the left. Some whistling. No one hurt.

[A letter from Jennie Farmer. This is a transcription by Emma Jane that she included in the family collection.]
        Brooklyn, 31st March 1864

Jimmy Dear,
        Your three blessed letters are just rec'd. I have enjoyed them very much. I hardly dared expect them today. They were dated the 18th, 20th, 23d. I wrote you last Thursday and I directed to Jacksonville. I hope you will get it all right. Miss Norton came in for a few minutes just now. She has given me her picture and will send one through Charley, she said. It seems to me that you have a great deal to say about <u>trouble</u> in your letters, about it's being a <u>trouble</u> for me to receive <u>pictures</u> etc. Do pray, dear Jimmy, give me every chance I can to do anything for you, will you not? Is there not something I can send you? You spoke of Timothy Titcomb's letters, wouldn't you like them?
        I like so much your patriotic spirit. I feel indeed ashamed that I have done so little. I almost wish myself a man. May an Infin—Love protect you, and lead you through all the way of duty by His unfailing strength. I think it well that we are not married James

dearest, but I know you would be faithful to duty even then; at least I think so. I hope the crinoline disease will not prove fatal in any case. I think it would be a doubtful compliment to any lady; yet I am sure we are thankful to be thought of and we will try to be worthy of an occasional sigh (we will never speak of tears) but we know that God loveth a cheerful giver, and for every sacrifice of present blessings, or what may seem to be such, He will repay a hundred fold.

Mattie caught a bad cold staying after school at night. Mr. Lewis was slightly indisposed or so much so that he did not attend school and found it necessary to send Miss Farmer a note as to her duties, etc. (that is the way I conclude your letters when I entertain the folks with parts of them. They are rather saucy about my skipping, but they behave pretty well.) Lizzy is nicely, the baby not very well. Georgy calls himself Mr. Leete and puts on airs. He had a letter from his
father today. He was at Fort Kearney, Nebraska. He had four days more of stage journey before reaching Denver. He thought they were having a tough time in the stage for it was crowded and he had had no sleep for three days & nights. Georgy and Will have just gone to bed. Georgy sends his love...G. has been superintending this last page. I lay one blot to his account. Don't say a word about your writing, or I shall have to use a half a page in each letter with apologies. You did not
tell me if you were well. How large a force is there at Palatkin? I found a place that is spelled Palatka[135] on the map. Is it the same? My kind regards to Lieut Hutchinson, if you please.

Last Friday night Mattie and I went to Williamsburgh. We were thinking of spending Sat. afternoon with Mrs. Bates but the rain prevented. Mattie came home Sat night. I remained until Monday morn. I had a very pleasant visit. I should have said we. I do not wonder at your admiration for your cousin Nell Wood. What a wonderfully sweet temper she has. I told William that you thought his wife as near perfection as they made them. He said he thought so too and he is not given to flattery. How well he keeps posted on the War! I think they live very happily. I should not like to attend the church they do or be connected with the Sunday School that they are. We met Miss Mattie Lyman there. As I was returning Monday, I called at Mrs. Bates. She was out but Mattie and I called Tuesday afternoon and were persuaded to stay to tea and had a nice time. Mrs. Bates was very social and entertained us with a story of the "Present for Ellen" in a way that made us laugh. Charley was home that night. Miss Norton returns next week Tuesday. I may go with her. I told Charles if he were going, I should be afraid of being a third party, but he says in that case (which is doubtful as he may not go) there will be a third one beside me, a Miss Richardson. I think I shall accompany them. Miss

---

[135] Palatka (pronounced puh-lat-kuh) is a city in Putnam County, Florida.

Norton sent love or remembrances to you. I cannot be <u>bothered</u> with so <u>many messages</u> of <u>this kind</u> from <u>ladies</u>!

I had a letter from Nell Farmer yesterday. She says that you need not be troubled any more about <u>her health</u>. She is not going back to Bedford. I think <u>she</u> sends her love to you. She says R.W. Emerson, Wm. Brown and J.B. Farmer are chosen members of the School Com., that they are to have a meeting next week deciding when schools will commence, that Miss Davis, Moore and Taylor have resigned, that the Report speaks <u>very well</u> (that is the way she wrote it) of me. I thought <u>you</u> would like to know. Nell does not say it, but I think she would like a school in Concord. I should not wonder if she got one. Nell writes that Rebecca has been sick, but was out to church. She says James Wood's wife and Ellen Skinner are expected. She had a grand time in Boston, commissions me to buy her a dress, with the advice and consent of the sisters, thinking it will require our united talent to do it. I wore my new black dress out to Williamsburgh. Lizzy sends love.

Good night, <u>dear boy</u>, pleasant dreams and a glad realization of them one of these days, is the prayer of your own

Jennie for you.

I shall look Anxiously for news of you. Thanks for the orange blossoms. They are as fragrant as possible.

Carte de visite of Jennie's sister, Nell Farmer
(Barrett Collection)

*[*James' diary entry]*
Fri Apr 1 1864
Ration returns altered to 22 cents per day.

Chapter 13

It Would Be a Sin

April 1, 1864-April 15, 1864--After two-hour skirmish, all six
companies safe--"Maple Leaf" blown up by torpedo--April 13th,
receives orders to move to Jacksonville--Discovers old gallows--
Theatre closes--Jeff Davis is hung in effigy--Steamer "General
Hunter" blown up by torpedo

[Note that all the following transcriptions have been faithfully copied from the original
document, as written by James, except where noted.]

[*Letter]

Palatka Fla Apr 1 1864

My Dearest Jennie

I have not rec^d your last letter yet am expecting it tomorrow. I must write now & tell you about our skirmish yesterday. There are quite a number of Rebel Cavalry about here & they are in the habit of making a dash & trying to capture our Pickets. On the 30th ult ^{136}about 200 of our regiment went out to the front under our Maj. Coan   to lay in ambush for them   But returned at night without seeing them. Yesterday after dinner we went out again—6 Co^s—4 to the left & 2 Co^s to the right. Our plan was to let the advance mounted Pickets draw them in & then we close in their rear & cut them off   But there were two or three premature shots fired by some of the 115th N.Y The Rebs drove in our Pickets on the right—a few shots were fired as I said before. This disclosed our presence   We then advanced—4 Co^s of us deployed as Skirmishers (I was on the left).   We had quite an excited time of it—a pretty sharp skirmish for some two hours. There were 2 Co^s of them—their shot fell all about us but hit no one. We had about 200 men. the others were on duty. These were divided into 6 Co^s. I had the misfortune of having some green men of Co. B. in my Co & they did not understand Skirmishing But on the whole they all behaved well. I only noticed one who seemed to falter & he said he was "sick." I presume he was. He was not of Co. H. Well we all returned about dark Safe—thank God for that.   & if we were not tired & hungry I would not say it. I only wonder how we escaped being hit. We could not see the enemy very plain on account of the woods. I really could not swear that I saw them at all Altho I saw their shot strike But they attacked the right of the line worse—they saw them plainly, so you see I have not killed my man yet. I had a six shooter all ready, But I don't fire without taking aim at a Mark. I presume there will be plenty of chances yet. We have some Cavalry here now & I guess we will bag some of them in a few days.

Emma Jane's drawing depicting picket duty
(Barrett Collection)

Report says that we killed the famous Capt. Dickson [Dickison] on a former raid. We came up to one house with a big woman in it. She said she wished we would find some other place to do our

---

^{136} A date from the previous month

shooting except round her house. She told us that there was a heap of them there. I have been sorry ever since that we did not burn her house & let her come inside the town to live. I believe our tents are to be sent for so we may be here quite a time. Our position is strong. It makes us feel kind of soldierly to smell gunpowder. I think one feels himself more of a man afterwards. Of course it is only natural to dread & shrink from it at first.

I think we are getting pretty good schooling. We may need it one of these days. It is interesting to see how the men will spring in at the word just as if it were only Partridges they were after. They will dodge their heads occasionally when a ball strikes pretty near & then go right on the same as before.

I have sent all my old letters & papers to Charley   I thought if anything should happen to me it would be better so. I wrote something about sending them to you   But I concluded that it might give food for scandal. They will be safe with him.   You may have them if you want to keep & examine too if you would like. I have got all my returns off now & am feeling easier   I am coming out splendidly. Am over in almost everything

I intend to carry a gun home with me to pay for my Stewardship.

That Lt Hutchinson who has the "brain" trouble had several Photographs of his lady. I met her once at Ft. Schuyler & know her father very well in the Reg^t   So I appropriated one for my album. He was asking me the other day if I would not get him one of yours   I told him I did not think you would send one where you were not acquainted

He seemed to think I might get one. I expect to get Staleys Picture this mail   My Orderly Lacappidan is to be 2nd Lt in my Company soon   I have been all alone   I need someone. I found my Books & Rolls made up with a good many mistakes. I met our Brigade Ordnance Officer last night   He is 2nd Lt. in the 55 Mass Reg^t (Lt. Bradish)   He was in the 44th Reg. at Newbern. He knows the Bartletts very well.

I will write again when I get my mail untill then I must bid you an affectionate adieu

from yours

James A. Barrett
1st Lieut 48th Reg^t N.Y.S. V.
Com^dy Company H.

[*James' diary entries]
Sat Apr 2 1864
10 men &14 horses of Reb Cav captured last night by Co. H. 115th N.Y up the River. We are going out again this P.M. 240 men went to the front. I did not go. My Co. was not taken. Nothing seen. Mass. Cav lost 4 of their men last night.

Sun Apr 3 1864
"Maple Leaf" blown up by torpedo near Jacksonville early Thurs. morning. Five lives lost. Mail saved. On picket today. Nice day.

Mon Apr 4 1864
Relieved. Took a wash etc. & feel fresher.

[*Letter]

No 1.

Palatka Fla   Apr 4 1864

Dear Jennie

I am just in from Picket   have taken a wash & will write you a line. This is my first full tour of guard since last July   I had a fine night & saw no Rebels. Friday The Provost went up the river on a Gunboat & Captured 10 men & 13 horses & equipment—But as an offset

The Rebs gobbled up one of our outer Cavalry Picket post here   1 Srg^t–& 3 men with horses &c of the Mass Cavalry & Thursday morning one of our Steamers from here to Jacksonville "Maple Leaf" was blown up by a torpedo about 15 miles this side of Jacksonville   I think the Rebs are pretty smart. I have not been out on another skirmish since the one I wrote you about on Thursday. I expect some of my letters may get lost between here & Hilton Head. I am going to begin & number them. I am daily expecting letters But the "Arago's" Mail is not here yet. Genl Gillmore has gone north   I believe to be attached to Genl Grants staff <u>Chief</u> <u>Engineer</u>   Genl Vogdes is now in Command I believe. I hear reports that our Reg^t is going to the Potomac before long to be attached to Genl Seymour's Brigade. I hope not   But it is all the same 100 years hence. Anything to end the war   Send us to the Potomac Texas N.C. anywhere   Only let this little business be finished up. One of our wounded men returned to Co the other day. That hard case I told you about (a Substitute)   He is a regular Billy Wilson[137] Chap   But there are always two sides to every picture. He was very brave at Olustee & was 1st to catch up the good old flag when its bearer was shot down. I must tell you something about the ideas of these outside barbarians down here (Natives)   A short time since we sent a scouting party across the river. They took several prisoners & They inquired with a good deal of surprise if our men were real <u>Yankees</u>   They did not expect to see Yankees looking so much like human beings. I am even told that some of the Natives here think the Yankees have horns & tails like beasts. This does not seem possible   But I am assured it is true. I have found a boy at last & am going to put him on his good behavior for a week & see if I like him.

It seems real hard to wait so long for news. Our latest news from N.Y. are to the 19th & no knowing when we shall hear again. If the rebs are going to sink torpedoes much   They will cut off our communication & we shall be forced to evacuate & cut our way through somewhere

I think we can do it. We can cross the river & march to Augustine if necessary

But I am not going to borrow trouble   We don't travel nights any more   So we can look out for breakers ahead   I am going to enclose a Photograph of Lt Edwards formerly 2nd Srg^t in Co H. He is soon to be 1st Lt

---

[137] This is in reference to Edgar Allan Poe's main character in his short story published in 1839 entitled "William Wilson".

Are these pictures getting to be a bore to you? If so say so

I expect you have commenced your school by this time   write me all about all these little every day things. On Picket last night I found myself getting very sleepy   "Atlantic St" seemed very near   It was pretty hard work to keep awake.

With much love I remain yours sincerely

James A. Barrett

[*James diary entry]

Tues Apr 5 1864

Mail arrived. Torpedoes & prisoners captured near Jacksonville. We expect to go north soon. Commence to drill. N.C.O. school.

[*Letter]

Palatka Fla Apr 5 1864

Dearest Jennie

The mail has at last arrived & your welcome letter of the 24th ult was read with a good deal of interest. You seem to enjoy every thing you see & then you remember so much so as to be able to tell about it afterwards. I think it is an excellent way to fix a thing in the mind to talk about it. I have often noticed in your letters how much you seemed to enjoy what you saw & heard. This War is truly developing many valuable scenes & lessons for Historie's page

But as you say. There are many unwritten pages recorded only in the hearts of the Actors & with the All seeing one. But even these are not lost. They are silently But surely weaving their silken threads into the very texture of Society—

The Economy of Nature will not permit to be lost a single Heartthrob Noble impulse or Heroic deed. Every tear that is dropped   Every drop of blood spilled   Every Sacrifice that is or has been made in this great struggle is so much incense offered to Heaven from the Altar of our Country.   & The seed thus sown in sorrow will ere long be reaped in Peace & the Souls of those who have fallen will join with us in one great Chorus of joy & thanksgiving

I was struck with one little circumstance this morning. A large Crane sat on a log in the river opposite our Camp for a long time with its wings partly spread towards the camp. As if invoking the blessing of Heaven upon us   It reminded me at once of a Minister asking a blessing for his people. But a number of sticks were thrown at the bird which drove her off   She soon settled again on another log however in the same attitude. Here again she was pelted   I could not help saying to a Lieut who wanted to shoot her. "It would be a sin"   But so it is
We are continually resisting a driving off circumstances & opportunities which come to us laden with choicest of Gifts

We refuse to "entertain Angels unawares"   I would not have you think me superstitious.

I am merely pinning the train of thought suggested by this little circumstance   Did you read Mr. Collyer's sermon after the death of Mr. Staples   I have & it is very beautiful.   Is it uncommon then for Charley to have 2 nights rest. I must look after him. But I am afraid my courage would fail me in any attempt at interference. I can face a battery But not a woman's wrath. A pair of black eyes would be too formidable to fight against.   Well I guess I had better not have said that. But it is out now & I don't retract   I am glad to hear that you are all so well at Brooklyn. I think Mr Leete will be glad to get home again. I am very sorry to hear that Mattie & Miss H. are resolved to have a duel. You ask me what weapons. Well I would recommend that they both be put on bread & water diet & the one who stood it the longest win the game.

Don't speak of this for the world for I should be called an accomplice & dueling is positively forbidden in the Regulations. & I know you would not wish to have me dismissed. We had an Officer's Call the other day to see if any of us had given duplicate discharges to soldiers. None had. If we had   Our names were to be sent in for dismissal

We have been somewhat anxious of late about our communications since the Maple Leaf was blown up. We heard today that 10 torpedoes & 50 rebs had been captured near the place   I am afraid this is exaggerated   But cannot say at present. The impression is getting strong here that our Reg^t is going to Washington soon. So you may be prepared to hear of my "change of base" Well there would be some advantages. I think I <u>dread</u> the <u>disadvantages</u> <u>more</u>. Visions of marches   fatigue   Hunger &c &c &c   rise before me. But it is all in our 3 years. I guess we can go through with it. I don't know whether we shall go to N.Y. or not   If we do I don't suppose we should stop anytime. We have made great changes here during the short time we have been here. Whole forests have burned to the stern decree of "Military Necessity" & No longer stand to obstruct our view & give protection & shelter to our Enemies. Last Sunday I was on Picket. My first was close by some graves near which a rude Gallows was lately constructed to hang some Negroes & I think several whites   It is all cut down now   There are 2 graves   I don't know how many are in them   You will see it alluded to in the paper I send you. But I must close. With much love believe me as ever yours
James A. Barrett

[*James' diary entries]
Thurs Apr 7 1864
*Reg^t inspection by Col. Barton. Battalion drill in afternoon. Capts. Nichols
& Ferguson & Moser, Lts. Tantum, Acker & Barrett called on to drill the
Reg^t. Firing bad. Dress parade down town. J. Hoxie made a speech.
B.D.A. returned to the Reg^t. We had officers call the other day to see if any
of us had given duplicate discharges to soldiers. None had. If we had, our
names were to be sent in for dismissal.*

Fri Apr 8 1864
*Col. Barton talks of sending me to the Head about our theatre. He wants
us to start something here. We talk of doing so. Moving our struts &
pitching our tents. Property being condemned.*

Sat Apr 9 1864
Fixing tents today. Boards & nails scarce.

Sun Apr 10 1864

Company inspection. Look well. Fine day. Col. dont want me to go to the Head tomorrow. Sent in the names of Pearsall & Freeman for promotion. Last Thursday we had a regiment inspection by Col. Barton. I was very much pleased afterwards to hear that Co. H. was put down _best_ .

[*Letter]

Head Quarters Co H. 48th NYSV

Palatka Fla   April 10 1864

My Dear Jennie

The boat goes down at daylight & I will just drop a line   I have not rec^d the "Fulton's" mail yet. I heard that the mail that was on the "Maple Leaf" when she sunk was saved   I was very glad to hear it   All my returns were in that mail   Last Thursday we had a Reg^t Inspection by Col Barton. It went off very well. I was very much pleased afterwards to hear that Co H. was put down <u>Best</u>. (It is a fact I am not bragging.) Well why shouldn't we   We always have been a No 1. In the afternoon we were taken out to drill & Your Humble servant was one of the victims who were called out to drill the Battallion.

I got through with it the best I could   I had to bite my lips once or twice to think of the proper orders   But managed to <u>escape permanent disgrace</u>. Our Theatre is closed. All the Actors were ordered to join their Reg^t. We still owe $2000.00. The building is worth $5000.00 if it don't burn down. It was very popular at the Head

I was going down tomorrow to arrange some security—But cannot spare the time

Col B wants to send me   But I could not get back in less than 10 days or 2 weeks & I do not like to leave my Co alone so long. Col B wants us to start some amusements here

Perhaps we may. We have selected a very suitable place if we remain here. I think it is very doubtful about our going to the Potomac

This is a beautiful place to live The Climate is perfectly delightful   Geraniums live here all winter out in the gardens. We are getting to live better now   The sutler has got his goods up

I have just purchased an Army range for my Co to cook with. It makes the other Co^s look upon H Co as <u>favored</u> above them   Our tents are here at last   The men are pitching them as frames raised on posts 2 feet from the ground. We are really fixed up quite nice. It is always a sign when we begin to fix up nice I believe I shall not fix my tent much   Serg^t Stayley is going to have some cards & I will send you one by next mail

I have just appointed that Corp^l you saw Serg^t. Tomorrow we have another Inspection Next week still another   I hope we will have enough of it bye & bye. But let them come on <u>Co H. is ready</u>, any day. There is to be a sham fight tomorrow between Capt James's light battery & Maj Stevens 1st Mass Cavalry. It will be inspection with us so I cant see it. The worst of it will be. Some one is bound to be hurt.

Our Chaplain has gone north   I did not go to ~~home~~ church today. But I read a splendid sermon in the Independent (Beechers) of Mch 17th

I don't hear much about the Rebel Cav^{ly} lately. We are going out one of these days to stir them up a little   But the Postmaster is waiting for this & I must close this very uninteresting letter   Please do excuse it   I should not write now only to tell you I am well. So good night with lots of love

From Jas A Barrett

[*James' diary entry]
Mon Apr 11 1864
*Inspection of arms by Maj. Eddy. Moved my tent. Capt. Ferguson is out of
the service. This will put me on the left flank 115th N.Y One piece of
artillery & a company of the provost went out to the front. Nothing new.
Arrival of 3rd N.H mounted.*

Tues Apr 12 1864
*Mail arrived with papers to Apr. 4th. Florida beef very poor. Commencing
to evacuate Palatka. On fatigue. Loading "Dictator" with QM stores.*

[*Letter]
Head Quarters Co H. 48th NYVols
Palatka Fla   Apr 12 1864
Dearest Jennie

Your welcome letter of 31st ult is just rec^d (11 ½ PM) & I will just answer it before I retire & then if I am ordered to the front I wont leave debts unpaid behind. I rec^d the letter directed Jacksonville last week. We are really getting settled here now   Our tents are all pitched on platforms 2 feet from the ground. Some Officer has to come round every day & give orders about fixing up   I get disgusted sometimes   I came out to do a Soldier's duty. Not to spend my time in seeing if every tent was just on a level. I asked the Q.M. today if he could fill a requisition for a Square. Spirit level. & a lot of <u>Red tape</u>   I am down on <u>Humbugging</u>. I am glad I am to receive Fannie's picture I had almost given it up   I notice what you say about "trouble"   Well I am just going to <u>bother</u> <u>you</u> all <u>I can</u> <u>after</u> <u>this</u>

But just now my wants are very few Unless I presume to <u>bother</u> <u>you</u> <u>with</u> <u>messages</u> from <u>my</u> <u>lady</u> <u>friends</u>   But on the whole I think you may tell them to <u>do</u> <u>their</u> <u>own</u> <u>writing</u>. It would save so much "<u>bother</u>"   So you sometimes wish yourself a man. I <u>don't think I do</u>. Altho there is a vacancy in my Co now & some of the men seem <u>proud</u> of their <u>new</u> Lieut. Do you intend to come down & claim your Muster. The Crinoline disease is in no way dangerous   Altho I am constantly finding new developments   A Mr. Sears in our Mess who has been thought <u>proof</u> has lately expressed the desire to get <u>just one letter</u>. "<u>Just one</u>." That is what thousands have said. But they could not stop there

I hope for Mattie's sake that Mr Lewis is better   It must of course make her <u>duties</u> <u>so</u> <u>much</u> <u>harder</u> & then I presume she has to trot round then semioccasionally   But she is of age. So I wont borrow trouble about her   I think you will have to snub "Mr Leete"   You ask "How large a force is there here"? We have 2 Brigades. It just occurs to me however that this is a forbidden subject. The following information is positively forbidden to be written from this Dep^t

Names of Div Brig or Post Commanders. Strength of the same except after a fight. Number position of Reg^{ts} Brig Div^{ns} Batteries etc   Kind & quantity of Arms Cannon & Ammunition. Number of transports & kind of supplies   Description of any movement or any suggestions of an expected movement or attack except after it has taken place   Scouts or Reconnoiasances Position of Camps Batteries Pickets Roads Outposts Publication of Official Reports etc

Violation of the above will be met with the severest punishment known to Military law in the field

Now if you expect to get much information from me   You must expect that I am <u>rebellious</u> But I have yet to see the one who complies with it strictly. This place is spelled Palatka here. I know it is Pilatka on the map. We all spell it with an A.

Lt H desires to be remembered   I thought you would like cousin Nell. I don't see how any one can help it. She has been brought up in the old school But is growing into larger views. I am glad you are likely to have company home. It is so lonesome to travel alone. I am very glad to hear of that good "<u>report</u> <u>of</u> <u>you</u>" I expected nothing <u>less</u> I do "like to know" Please wave any feeling of reserve in writing about <u>yourself</u> even if it is complimentary

You know I will take it in the spirit it is written   I have not been out to the front since that little fight we had on the 31st. Our Theatre was closed last week & the men sent back   we are going to start one here. I am going down to the Head tomorrow to secure our building & make some arrangements   I don't fancy leaving my post with my Co. But Col B. want me to go. I may see Henry there.

After every mail arrives A man from one of the camps comes round with Herald Times Tribune & several other papers. It really seems quite natural. I wrote my last 2 letters to Concord. I did not know exactly   But I guess I was not much out of the way

I don't remember what I said about Schultz in connection with Lucy B. I think you are thinking of Serg^t Stayley.

You may show it to Lucy & tell her that he will be commissioned in a few months   He is just as fond of her picture as ever. My Album will open right at <u>that place</u>.   I rec^d a very <u>loving letter</u> for Mackey that died from a lady in Conn. (A Teacher) enclosing a Photograph. I think I shall return it. Of course I shall have to send a <u>letter</u> of <u>transmittal</u>. You wont care will you

I want to hear all about your visit & your safe return &c &c If you have any more pictures taken you must send me one. My health is first rate   This is a beautiful Climate. No one has a right to get sick here. We have a good many men on our sick list   But their sickness is mostly the result of carelessness & imprudence & dissipation[xix] while at home. "The law of Compensation" It is universal. "What we sow that shall we reap"

I have not read the papers yet   But I am very hopeful for the spring campaign. I hear nothing more about our leaving. I guess we will stay here a while yet. Please remember me kindly to all inquiring friends & with much love I remain

Yours as ever

James A. Barrett

13th I am not going to the Head today   Our Reg[t] is going to move somewhere   Orders are here   I believe   I don't know where we are going   I hope we will be successful this time   I will write again before long   James

[*James' diary entries]

Wed Apr 13 1864

Order to move. Packed up our things & sent them on the "Delaware"[138].
My tent is struck. The men's tents still standing. I sleep out doors tonight.

Thurs Apr 14 1864

All hands hungry. Fatigue. Men jubilant. Jeff Davis hung in effigy.
Embarked on the "Delaware" for Jacksonville. Evacuation of Palatka.
Pickets all called in. Natives taken off. Horsemen seen by the gunboat.
Not molested[139].

Fri Apr 15 1864

Arrived in Jacksonville. Landed. Drew ten days rations. Cooked four.
Embarked on board the "Ben Deford" for Fortress Monroe. Very much
crowded. I have good quarters. Good living.

Sat Apr 16 1864

Pleasant day. News of the loss of steamer "Gen[l] Hunter" by rebel torpedo.
She left Jacksonville last night. Blown up early this A.M. She came down
with us loaded with troops from Palatka Lucky for us that we escaped.
Col. B. sends for the B.D.A. (Barton's Dramatic Association) to come on to
the Head. Our steamer must wait at the bar until tomorrow for high water.

Emma Jane's illustration of the "Ben Deford"
(Barrett Collection)

---

[138] "USS Delaware" (1861) was a steamer acquired by the Union Navy for use during the American Civil War. USS Delaware (1861). (October 30, 2015). *Wikipedia, The Free Encyclopedia*. Retrieved December 4, 2015, from https://en.wikipedia.org/w/index.php?title=USS_Delaware(1861)&oldid=688253291

[139] Not harassed or pestered

Chapter 14

Starting for the Potomac

April 16, 1864-April 22, 1864--Living and travel conditions of poor
privates--Disgusted with General Seymour and Florida expedition--
Massacre at Fort Pillow--Theatre sold

[Note that all the following transcriptions have been faithfully copied from the original
document, as written by James, except where noted.]

[This is Emma Jane's transcription of a letter written by James.]

Direct
48th NYV 10th Army Corps
Washington DC

Steamer "Ben Deford"
Mouth St John River   Apr 16 1864

My Dear Jennie

I have really started for The Potomac   We evacuated Palatka on the 14th   Arrived at Jacksonville yesterday morn

Embarked on this Steamer last night & here we are waiting for high water to cross the bar. We just escaped being blown up   The Steamer "Genl Hunter" came down from Palatka with us loaded with troops   She left Jacksonville last night for Picalatta & was blown up early this A.M. The Torpedo was undoubtedly placed there for us to run on to after they heard that we were evacuating. It was really Providential that we escaped. I can hardly realize now that we are really going to the Potomac. We may stop at the Head even now. & go into Camp there. But I think the B.D.A. will give @ farewell entertainment at our Union Theatre. Monday night. I expect to get @ mail at the Head. This is @ fine Steamer   The men are pretty well crowded   But the Officers have pretty good quarters & tip top living

It is hard that the poor privates have to put up with such usings. I well remember my own first trip & what I suffered & I know how to pity them   But it cannot well be helped   Truly when I see the rank & file of our noble army endure & suffer so much & all for $13.00 @ month & such living & useage as they generally get   It makes me think that there is some patriotism left & Our country will be safe as long as men will sacrifice so much in her defence

Our Officers are generally too selfish   Many of them never experienced these privations themselves & therefore do not know how to appreciate them or allow for & guard against them

My men are packed so thick that their legs have to lap together. It is hard   But I cannot help it. The Col was going to put even more down there   But I protested   If we could have bunks built it would be better. Our Regt are in good spirits. They are generally disgusted with the Florida expedition. It is another of Genl Seymour's smart exploits (Mutiny) (Don't tell of me) Deliver me from fighting under him. His Ambition seems to be to lose large numbers of men. I am willing to fight

But when I run big risks I want to see some possible chance of some possible good to come from it   If we are really going to the Potomac I think we shall for once get on to the winning side

I have the fullest confidence in Genl Grant & Gillmore & think I can foresee the speedy capture of Richmond. "Onward to Richmond" has @ more than historic interest to me now I did expect to have @ hand in taking of Charleston   But that city seems to be destined to be put on probation for @ while longer   Perhaps I intended to represent Finnegan the famous Rebel leader in Fla. I must close now as it is time to put out the lights   I will write more before I mail this & tell you where to direct So good night with much love I remain

Yours ever   James A. Barrett

Sunday Afternoon Apr 17 1864

We are still detained here. Expect to get off tomorrow   We are having beautiful weather But it is dull to be waiting. Now that we are started I want to see my journey's end. Col Strickland brought out three promotions this morning

He rec^d them at Palatka   But forgot to publish it (just like him) Lt Edwards to be 1st Lt. My Orderly of Co A & Co H to be 2nd Lt. My Orderly will soon receive his appointment & then I shall have a Lieut with me. One of our Senior Captains has resigned   This will put me on the left flank I have been with Color Co ever since we went to Morris Island. I don't like the left flank much   But think I shall not be there long.

When we get north I expect to leave my trunk behind & take only @ Valisse

My Negro can carry this   I expect to live with my Co on junk & Hard tack

I have got @ very good boy   He can wash all my clothes & does them real nice   I never trusted my boy to wash before. I told you in @ previous letter that I had sent all my letters home But they have not gone yet   The man who was going to take the package has not gone   I find the same boy on this steamer who waited on me going home on the "Cosmopolitan" last summer when I was wounded

He knew me & is just as handy as ever. This has been @ very dull quiet Sunday   I have read one of Beechers Sermons that helped to pass away time   How I long to again enjoy my Sabbaths as I used to at home   I suppose you have been to church today & heard something to think about. Probably you are now dreading the coming week's work. I merely judge you by myself   I know I used to look forward to Sunday with @ good deal of pleasure & fairly mourn its approaching end & the coming Monday with its cares & toils

I know it is not the true way of viewing things   But it was the way I indulged in. How do you get along with your school   I suppose you have some new faces

How I would like to walk in upon you this evening   But it is useless to speak of impossibilities

I did receive@ letter from Charlie with his & Fannie's Photos by last mail after all. I think them very good. Charlie is curious to know how you all like Fannie

I told him that you liked her very much from what little you had seen of her. Did I say right? Lt. Roberson of our Reg^t (The one who showed the white feather[140] at Wagner) is still under arrest. His case has gone to Washington for decision

He is with us But does not have much to say to any one   Of course he does no duty   I do think he is to be pitied

I always speak to him   But I cant respect him   He don't expect that his case will be settled for several months. & does not seem to care. Now Jennie you may imagine me with you every Sunday evening. For I am in spirit at least

Different Officers passing send their respects according to usage. Your Picture in uniform is very much liked.

With much love Adieu

James

---

[140] Exhibiting cowardice

*[*James' diary entry]*
Sun Apr 17 1864
Col. B. sends for B.D.A. But as our boat expects to go, we do not send them. Can not get off. I go on guard tonight.

[Letter from Jennie]
Concord, April 17, 1864
Dearest James

I rec'd yours of the 1st yesterday. What an age it takes for a letter to come from Florida but I suppose communication is not always regular from Palatka to Hilton Head.

I should think you had a post of much danger. I hope the Reb's will keep out of your way, and yet I suppose you want to do all you can to annoy them. Nell rec'd a letter from you this week. She laughed at me because I did not have one that mail too. I thought that hers must have come by an extra steamer as it was dated only a day later than my last but one.

Our snow has nearly disappeared. I hope we shall soon have pleasant weather. Nell and I ran in to see Mary yesterday. She was busy ironing and was wondering why she did not get a letter from George. He is still sanguine[141] of success, thinks he may come home next winter. Mary has written him, posting him up on Emmy's affairs. Mary says Mrs. Gerrish is delighted with Fanny and so is Story. He never expected to get any one so nice. I am sure it is pleasant all round. I did not see Mrs Gerrish as she had a caller in her room. Lizzy Warren has commenced the study of Botany, which she likes very much. She has Eliza Hosmer for a teacher. Lizzy Skinner undertook the Primary School near her, but gave it up after one day's experience and Nelly Brown has taken it. Nelly boards at home and rides back and forth with her father.

Monday morn.
I am waiting to go to school. It is a splendid morning. The folks are going to do house cleaning. I went to church yesterday afternoon and heard Mr. Salloway of Billerica at whose ordination I was present. He is not very talented but he is real good. We began to be pretty good friends in Billerica. I had a grand experience in school life there, but I would not care to go back again. I rode from church with your folks last night and lent them your last letter but Jimmy, I shall not always do it.

---

[141] Optimistic or positive, especially in an apparently bad or difficult situation. sanguine (n.d.). *Dictionary.com Unabridged*. Retrieved December 3, 2015 from http://dictionary.reference.com/browse/sanguine

Is not the capture of Fort Pillow[142] sad? and the massacre of all those negroes. Methinks they will reap the whirlwind yet, the desperate, maddened South seems rushing to their own destruction, for I am sure these things must make the North more decided in their course. How shameful that we should have representatives in congress like Long and Harvis? I suppose you have read their traitorous language. It makes me mad that they bear with it as they do. I received the Palmetto. Thanks for that. I see there is quite a puff in it for Col. Barton.   (*The rest of the letter is missing)

[*James' diary entries]
Mon Apr 18 1864
Relieved this A.M. Crossed the bar at 5 A.M. Arrived at H. Head about 7 P.M. Our mail gone to Jacksonville.

Tues Apr 19 1864
Sent the B.D.A. ashore & started for Beaufort SC coal. Paymaster arrived at noon & paid us off. Called at Mrs. Judd's. Pleasant call. Bivouacked for the night with my men.

Wed Apr 20 1864
Reembarked on "Ben Deford" & started for H. Head about 11 A.M. I went ashore to get Dfts etc. Theatre sold. I am secure. $50.00 notes. Good joke on me. Detailed men called in. Started at about 5 P.M.

Thurs Apr 21 1864
Received our mail. Capt. Elmendorf is discharged. This gives Co. H. the right flank. I don't like the left flank. I have been the color company ever since we went to Morris Island. All our officers are mustered at last. Fixing up papers.

Fri Apr 22 1864
Made out one copy of my Apr. return   Wrote several letters. Made up rolls for veterans to get state bounty.

---

[142] The Battle of Fort Pillow, also known as the Fort Pillow Massacre, was fought on April 12, 1864, on the Mississippi River in Henning, Tennessee. The battle ended with a massace of Federal black troops, some while attempting to surrender, by soldiers under the command of Confederate Major General Nathan Bedford Forrest. Military historian David J. Eicher concluded, "Fort Pillow marked one of the bleakest, saddest events of American military history." Battle of Fort Pillow. (December 1, 2015). *Wikipedia, The Free Encyclopedia*. Retrieved December 4, 2015, from
https://en.wikipedia.org/w/index.php?title=BattleofFortPillow&oldid=693324496

[*Letter]

At Sea Str "Ben De ford
Apr 22 1864

Dear Jennie   Yours of 7th & 13th were recd at Hilton Head on the 20th   I was very glad to hear of your safe arrival home & of your pleasant journey   Altho I regret the cruel necessity that obliged you to tare yourself away from such pleasant associations

I think Aunt Gerrish must have nearly devoured Fannie with her maternal affection

I have duly appropriated & assimilated all the love you sent from the various sources   I shall have to be careful if my influence is to be so important I hope there is no harm done I presume not if they all keep good time   I am sorry that Annie's eyes are no better. I like to get @ return letter occasionally. I presume Abbie will not teach this year   Who has her school

I agree fully with you as to teachers wages. When @ woman does the same duty as @ man She should get the same pay. I like to hear of the improved state of public sentiment as indicated in the tendency to fellowship together by our Concord Churches

How different from @ few years ago. I have answered that letter of Nells. I presume she has recd it ere this. I am very glad that Mrs. Derby is going to board you again   I think it would be difficult to get another place so pleasant & convenient. I accept your apology about your letters But I have not the slightest fault to find. I read your letter over 3 times before I could find the "repetition". All right I guess there is no harm done

I have been puzzling over that "something to turn up" What kind of @ Trump is Nell going to play now   Can it be that she has been throwing herself away & without consulting me too   I decidedly object But I am so far away I suppose my protest will not avail much

Your father must be pretty busy with all his various duties. But I think likely that he will prefer it to working all the time on the farm   How does Henry prosper at Lowel   Does he visit the vicinity of Acton any now   I have concluded to change the Programme & not stop round at the School house nights any more   It interferes too much with the discipline of the School so you need not expect me until into the evening after Tea. I hope your friends will continue to be your neighbors During the summer you have so much more time that it must be pleasant to have some one to associate with

My health has been first rate since my return. I shall endeavor to be prudent & not needlessly expose myself. Our Col Barton was in command at Palatka (2 Brigades) & I believe he is still going to command @ Brigade in Va. Your humble Servt is still in Comd of H Co. & the prospect is that I shall remain so for the present at least. Mr Leete will be glad to get back again   I am curious to hear how he succeeds & what he thinks of the country

I did not think Father would get well so quick. I never really thought there was anything serious between Mattie & Mr Lewis   You are not the only one who has been glad you came to Brooklyn I have dwelt in memory often & long upon those pleasant days   I can sympathize fully with you in what you say about being welcome   It is the most natural thing in the world Popularity is sometimes dangerous   But like wealth is always sought for. How different are the means taken to obtain it. I like the taste you exhibit in your selections

I have been busy getting my Co matters into shape   I believe I am about ready for whatever may turn up now

I cannot say where our destination is to be   But think we are to have @ hand in taking Richmond   We sold out our Theatre at Hilton Head & I am again square with the Dramatic world. We are going to play in @ very different Drama now. Our two senior Captains have succeeded in getting their discharge & are now going home

This makes Lockwood Senior & puts Co H. on the right flank. Our old position. I like this It is the best place in the Reg^t. Some of these women at home play the mischief with their fellows in the field. Several of our Lieuts have girls at home who are continually urging them to resign & come home. I don't think that shows @ very patriotic spirit. Do you? If they can do nothing else for the war they can at least (like Artemus Ward[143]) "Consent to give all their relations"

I believe my friends have <u>none</u> of them attempted as yet to persuade me to turn from the beaten path of duty

I honor them all the better for it & love them far better than if they yielded to @ Selfish weakness

I will write again as soon as I can we shall arrive at Fortress Monroe during the night. Direct to 48th Reg^t NYSVols 10th Army Corps Washington DC   Good night with much love from yours

James A. Barrett

---

[143] Artemus Ward was the nom de plume of Charles Farrar Browne (April 23, 1834-March 8, 1867), an American humorous writer. Artemus Ward. (2015). ENCYCLOPÆDIA BRITANNICA. Retrieved December 1, 2015 from http://www.britannica.com/biography/Artemus-Ward

Chapter 15

The Bermuda Hundred and the Cast Iron Brigade

April 23, 1864-May 31, 1864--Arrives at Fort Monroe--Six men
transfer to Navy--Battle of Chester Hill--Heavy skirmish with rebels
at Drury's Bluff forces abandonment of Richmond--Lee driven to
Richmond by Grant--Heavy hand to hand combat--James writes
letters to Jennie recounting details of battle--Proceeds up York River
to White House Landing, VA

[Note that all the following transcriptions have been faithfully copied from the original
document, as written by James, except where noted.]

Sat Apr 23 1864

Arrived at Fort Monroe. Sent our letters ashore. Steamed up to
Gloucester Point opposite Yorktown. Landed & bivouacked for the night.
One wagon to @ Reg^t. Must send trunks &c home.

Sun Apr 24 1864

Took our position on the right of brigade. Co. H. right of Reg^t. Pitched our
tents. Lt. Sears assigned to Co. H.

Mon Apr 25 1864

Making up payrolls. We are to have shelter tents. On fatigue to go with
wagons after wood. Wm Rogers & @ man of Co. E. deserted. Supposed
to have gone to N.Y.

Tues Apr 26 1864

Inspection by Capt. Lockwood. The men do not look as well as usual.
Shelter tents issued. Old ones packed to be stored at Norfolk. Our trunks
sent off

[*Letter]

Head Qt^{rs} Co H. 48th NYSVols
Gloucester Point Va   Apr 26 1864
Dear Jennie.   I can hardly realize that I am in Va. But the air is much more bracing here. I have sent my trunk to N.Y. We have drawn shelter tents & I intend to employ 2 <u>Colored</u> <u>Gents</u> to <u>assist</u> me in carrying my things on the coming campaign. I am feeling very humble now. I had begun to feel like bragging a little now that Co H. is back again on the right flank. They really do march proudly in their old position. But I am subdued   One of my men has <u>deserted</u>   I really feel much mortified about it

He is the one that I told you about as being a bad man & one whose influence was so injurious to the Co

But he was not all bad   He caught the Flag up once when the bearer was shot

One man was taken who tried to get off with him & we found out something of him. I think he has not gone to the Enemy   But made for N.Y. He was a Substitute

Today I lost 6 more men to be transferred to the Navy. If they take many more away they may perhaps muster me out. I guess I should have to enlist then for @ few months as Private & finish up the muss   I see that the states are volunteering their militia for 3 mo^s This looks like business. We are very active here making preparations to move   My bones tell me to hope on & trust for better times soon. My Presentiments are of @ much more cheerful nature here than they were in Florida   It did really seem to me while there that I was to be the victim of some misshap or other   But we are on @ different road now & expect soon to sing "Onward to Richmond"

I suppose there is @ letter from you at H Head for me now   But I guess I shall get it as soon as if I was at Palatka. I have 2nd Lieut assigned to my Co now (Lieut Henry H. Sears) @ very clever fellow. He is the author of the <u>name</u> "Crinoline on the brain"

My health is first rate. It always is when I rough it. I do not feel quite so much out of the world here. I am very busy getting my Co into shape to march with the smallest possible amt of baggage   We are to have one wagon to @ Reg^t. Of course we must all carry our own things   I must even leave my Co Desk & papers behind except the last Pay Roll & one copy of last return.

We get New York papers the next day here. Quite @ comfort   I am disgusted with the N.Y. Fair for its giving that sword to McClellan[144]

The Rebs are about 6 or 8 miles to the front & we are some 60 miles from Richmond

I think I wrote that our 2 senior Capt^{ns} had resigned. They came up here with us But went back as far as Fortress Monroe & from there to N.Y. I do not envy them their peace of mind. I should feel real mean to leave in a time like this. These are the 2 Capt^{ns} who were left at Palaski when we went to Morris Island & One of them has never been advanced from his original grade & never been in @ battle or skirmish & now to leave just on the eve of battle. I should feel ashamed of myself   Would not you of me?

I am getting up my Pay Rolls now (@ Big Job.) Am in hopes to finish before we move

You must not worry if you do not hear from me at all until after the campaign   Our letters may be detained. But you can write all the same whether I do or not

Hoping to hear from you soon   I will bid you @ hasty but hearty good night & God bless you   from your sincerely

James A Barrett

[*James' diary entries]
Wed Apr 27 1864
6 men gone to be transferred to the navy.

Thurs Apr 28 1864
On guard today. Not much to do. Discharges to be made over with dates left out.

Fri Apr 29 1864

---

[144] James was to learn later that the sword was actually awarded to Ulysses S. Grant. This was a fundraiser for the U.S. Sanitary Commission. The U.S. Sanitary Commission was a private relief organization that supported army hospitals and sick and wounded soldiers during the Civil War. It was held in New York, New York on April 23, 1864. The "voting" at the Metropolitan Fair became a real contest between Grant and George B. McClellan who was politically connected and very popular in New York. "Votes" cost a dollar a piece; encouraging individuals to cast multiple votes for their candidate. The contest was followed closely through detailed coverage by newspapers.

Finishing up pay rolls. Drawing and issuing clothing.

Sat Apr 30 1864
Muster   finished up my rolls—recapitulation & all.

Mon May 2 1864
Finished up my returns.

Tues May 3 1864
On guard in place of Lt. Edwards. About noon received orders to pack up to march out on picket. Started at 3 P.M. Marched seven miles. I am posted on the right on the Severn River.

Wed May 4 1864
Pleasant country—people polite. Oysters eggs milk & butter. Packed up again about 3 P.M. & marched in. Drew & issued clothing & embarked on the "Delaware" bound for _____ Started about 2 or 3 in the morning. Englehart, Hanselman & Maier missing.

Thurs May 5 1864
Pleasant morning. Slept well last night—shoulders very lame. Steaming up the James River. Wrote several letters & landed about 2 in the morning.. Some foraging—the chickens & pigs suffer.

Fri May 6 1864
Commenced our march about 10 A.M. Marched slowly making on 6 miles & bivouacked. Rations getting out. Grant been fighting for two days. Lots of clothes thrown away. Wagons make slow progress.

Sat May 7 1864
Aroused at 3 ½ fell in about 5 & took up our march. Commenced skirmishing at 1 P.M. & went into @ fight at 2. Charged across R.R. & fought 2 hrs. Drove the enemy back But was too much exhausted to go further. Returned to camp 9 P.M. tired and hungry. Drew 3 days rations. I am about played out. (Battle of Chester Hill[145])

Sun May 8 1864
Slept well. Drank @ cup of coffee & feel better. Took @ good bath. Pitched our tent. Moved our camp 100 yds. Pitched tents again. Resting

---

[145] The Battle of Chester Station was fought on May 10, 1864.

today. Lost 1 killed & 3 wounded yesterday—Nodal, Freeman, Carman &
F. Miller. Making out lists of deserters.

[This is Emma Jane's transcription of a letter written by James.]

James River, Steamer Delaware
May 5, 1864

Dearest Jennie,

I am sure there are several letters for me somewhere but I have not received any since I left Hilton Head. I guess you had better direct to Fortress Monroe, Va. In future.

When our marching orders came, I was out on outpost picket some 7 miles in a very pleasant place. I had just made the acquaintance of a family who cordially invited me to board with them while my company remained there. The ladies played on the piano and seemed very friendly.

I once in a while, see green fields now. It is refreshing, I assure you. We had in our charge one rebel formerly a Lieut in the Rebel army. I had a long talk with him and his sentiments were southern, but he was very gentlemanly to me. He seemed to think that Slavery was an institution ordained by Heaven and quoted from the scriptures to defend it. Oh, how easy it is to borrow the livery of Heaven to worship the Devil in. Self interest often so completely weaves itself into our moral natures as to completely blind us to the calls of duty & justice & often masks the grossest evils behind some Scripture phrase cruelly tortured to meet the "Southern views."

Shame on Nehemiah Adams[146]! A man with his intelligence and opportunities who can distinguish himself in no better way than to defame the "Word" he has sworn to preach, had better always remain "Unknown", "Unhonored." He surely will be!

My health is very good. I am feeling rather stupid today marching 7 miles with my pack on my back 2 days in succession & having lost considerable sleep for 2 or 3 nights back, I was glad to sleep all this afternoon. I shall very soon get used to it but my pack makes my shoulder rather lame in the beginning. I do not know where we are going to land. I presume the papers will give you all these facts. I think it very doubtful if I am able to write very often so you must calculate accordingly and not feel anxious on my account even if you do not hear for a month. I shall try to write often, but our communications must necessarily be limited, and there is no knowing how often I shall see my valise. I hope to hear from you. YOU can write anyhow and I shall get them sometime. I do hope this campaign will prove successful. I often get disgusted with the way things are done. Little fools with uniforms on, like to put on airs and give commands. I have made up my mind to stand on my <u>dig</u>[147]. I won't be spit upon and then have it rubbed in. <u>So be prepared</u>. I <u>may</u> get <u>dishonorably</u> <u>dismissed</u> some of these days. I can be led anywhere, but when one attempts to drive

---

[146] Nehemiah Adams wrote *A Southside View of Slavery* (1854). In his book he touted that slavery was beneficial to the Negroes' character. In retort to his many critics; he wrote a second book entitled *The Sable Cloud, a Southern tale with Northern Comments* (1861).

[147] Dignity

and domineer over me I am rather rebellious. I came into the army to fight & not to be humbugged[148]. But one of these days, we will all be even again. I don't want you to think that I am about to be rash or anything but I do have to bite my lips sometimes.

I suppose you are getting along finely with your school. I want you to write me all about it. I like to hear about little daily occurrences. I believe you do not like to speak of things that trouble you. I don't know why. Perhaps I might be of some service. If so, I should be very happy to give it.

My presentiments are all very favorable for the approaching campaign. I did have some dark forebodings while in Florida, but it seems I escaped any threatened dangers. I expect to spend the 4th of July in Richmond. If so, we will have a grand Union jollification & make the very stones echo the song of our thanksgiving. We are expecting a Chaplain to join us soon. There was a Mr. Taylor from Staten Island with us awhile but his leave of absence expired & he has gone home to try & get relieved so as to join us as our Chaplain. He is a fine fellow and I hope he will return to us.

Now Jennie I must close. Give lots of love to all friends & do not forget to reserve the lion's share for yourself, & believe me as ever

Yours faithfully
James A. Barrett

Hatches Plantation Va   May 8 1864
Dear Jennie

Here we are about 6 miles from Fort Darling[149]. I expect we are destined to lay siege to that place. We landed in the evening of the 5th about 2 miles above City Point on the James River. Yesterday was my birthday & I was in considerable of @ fight. There is @ Battery on the R.R. about 5 miles from here. One Brigade attacked it on the 6th & were repulsed. Our Brigade & part of another advanced & felt of them yesterday. 4 Cos of our Regt (H included) skirmished up nearly to the R.R. & then assembled on the Battallion at 2 P.M. & the Brigade charged across a meadow & up @ steep hill, tore up the R.R. track & the telegraph lines & had @ hot fight for 2 hours. It was very warm & some of our men were sunstruck & all of them very much exhausted. Our rations gave out in the morning & many of the men had hardly tasted food that day. We were faint & weak & could advance no further. We drove them before us like sheep But did not take the Battery.

When we arrived back to our Co around about 9 P.M. we found rations waiting for us. I spread my blanket & throwing myself down, was soon asleep. My Sergt woke me to drink @ cup of coffee & then I slept till morning. I took @ bath this morning & feel very well again. With @ little more rest we will be ready to try it again. There was @ good deal of confusion on account of the different Regts getting mixed up in the charge & some men in the rear would fire ceaselessly & shoot our own men in spite of our caution. My Co lost one killed & 3 wounded. I myself was about

---

[148] Fooled
[149] The same location which went by various names: Fort Darling, Drewry's Fort or Drewry's Bluff. It was a Confederate military installation.

played out but I believe I managed to keep at my post until the ordeal was over. My men expressed their fear that I would break down knowing that I was not feeling very strong But I am all right now.

I have plenty of coffee, the soldiers support & the next time we go into @ fight I think we will do better. The heat is excessive but cannot continue so. I did not get @ scratch. Our Major was just grazed on one ear. We have work before us But with God's help we will take Richmond before July 4th. I changed my clothes before I left the boat & don't know when I can get another change as my valise is left behind. We carry everything on our backs. I carry my overcoat & blankets & let my boy carry the tent. We also have to carry 3 days rations But I have got used to this. This life is new to us But I guess we can stand it.

It would make you stare to see the water we drink. On @ march on a warm day, we are glad to dip our cups into any puddle we come to. I would never have believed that muddy water could taste so well. I am anxiously waiting for letters from home. It seems an age since I heard from you But of course I don't complain. I know that they are on the way somewhere. I am anxious to hear of Grant's movements. Genl Gillmore is here with us. I think we have at least one month's work ahead of us But we have some good troops & they feel the importance of success now. Our Cavalry captured 2 picket posts—about 7 or 8 men. They seemed happy & contented as prisoners. They are generally very young. The whole South is drained of their young men. I don't see how they can hold out much longer. Richmond taken & the Rebellion is broken. I saw many very large fields planted here which shows the enemy did not expect to be molested on this side of the river. But this is Gillmores tactics. Now Jennie, do not worry. Trust that the same kind Providence that has hitherto cared for me will one day return me to you safe & well. If it shall be otherwise, I trust you will say, "Thy will be done."
With much Love, I remain truly Yours as ever
Jas A Barrett

[Note from the Cousins: We felt this fragment of a letter would be an appropriate addition at this point.]

[No date]
This is a copy of a letter to me from my sister [Clara, Mrs. Frederick W. Peterson] telling of a conversation an elderly Civil War Veteran had with Dr. Peterson. He said he came late into Father's Regiment, the 48th N.Y. Vols., and was under his command toward the end of the war.

-Emma Barrett Lothrop

This old soldier said that Father was a very fine man, but being way above him in rank, he did not know him intimately, and could not talk to him as to one in his own rank. Once he was able to assist him after a long, forced march; and that Father, though on horseback, seemed even more tired that his men who had to march so fast.

He almost fell off his horse in a corn field at the end of the march from weakness and weariness, and this soldier helped him and tried to make him comfortable with his own knapsack as a pillow. The horse was all in also, and of course he, himself was tired too.

The soldier was quite old, spoke slowly, and said his memory was poor. He told Fred to tell his wife that he had remembered her Father as a man to be proud of calling one's father. I was sorry that I did not see him, but he left the next morning and I was busy with the children.

Fred did not get to the G.A.R. Convention as he wished, so he did not see the soldier again. The soldier knew Father as Captain and Major though he said he got his last commission toward the end of the war.

Another soldier, not in the 48th, said he remembered the 48th as a well drilled Regiment. At Fort Wagner, his own regiment came up at an angle, and could look across at the 48th and could see what a fine looking regiment it was.

The address of the soldier who helped Father was C.W. DRISCOLL from Hartford, Connecticut.

-Clara Hosmer Barrett Peterson

[*James' diary entries]

Mon May 9 1864

On fatigue on the entrenchments. Several men sunstruck. Retuned to camp, ate our supper, packed up & moved up the entrenchments. Lay by our arms. Col. Howell driven in a little way. R.R. occupied by our troops. I am called up to patrol & watch for spies.

Emma Jane's pen and ink sketch of artillery fire (Barrett Collection)

Tues May 10 1864

At work on battery. Called to the front, lay there till night & returned. Fire in the woods. Our artillery did great execution at the front this A.M. Rebels ask for time to carry off wounded. Gen. Foster meets the truce. Shocking sight! Lee driven to Richmond by Grant. Grant following up closely. Heat very oppressive. Gen. Gillmore very active at the front.

Wed May 11 1864

Slept well. Refilled haversacks. Moved back to old camp on cornfield. Very dusty. Rained in afternoon. 3500 cavalry arrived. Mail arrived. I am making up final statements of Clark (Private David) & Pearce (Corporal Benjamin B.)[150]. Richmond papers say their loss was heavy on the Potomac.

Thurs May 12 1864

Ordered out at 4 A.M. –two days rations. Light marching orders. Gen. Butler rode to the front & captured @ courier with dispatches. Skirmishing at the front. Very wet day. We are reserves. Saw Fort Darling. Our troops advancing. Artillery not at work much yet. Activity at the front. Retired a short distance to bivouack. Picket firing. Lawson of Co. A. wounded.

Fri May 13 1864

Ordered to the front. Bivouacked in the woods. Several lines of battle. Skirmishers feeling the enemy. Good news. One Div. and 40 pieces captured by Meade. Chaplain Taylor returned to us warmly welcomed. Sent for rain blankets. Raining still.

Sat May 14 1864

Advanced across the first row of rifle pits & lay there in reserve all the day. 115th N.Y & 76 Pa. skirmishing at the front. Pretty sharp firing all day. Lee's forces abandoned his works in front of Grant. Grant advancing. Roads heavy. Sharpshooters at work. Two fired at me within 15 min. One gun firing uncomfortably near
to where we are lying. One rebel line come over 90 men. Another line of rifle pits nearly taken. Our Regt relieves the 76th at the front. Raining at intervals during the day.

Sun May 15 1864

Skirmishers firing pretty sharp. Our first party relieved. 2nd relief are getting wounded in the arms & hands. Two of my company—Owen & Liming—At night all quiet. We do not send out any men. Artillery moved.

[*Narrative]

We soon found the need of fortifying our position & encased ourselves safely behind a strong line of works which formed the "bottle"xx spoken by Genl Grant in his

---

[150] Private David Clark died at Richmond, VA on March 18, 1864. Corporal Benjamin B. Pearce [Pierce] died at Richmond, VA on January 9, 1864.

report concerning Genl Butler   From here we sallied forth from time to time feeling of the enemy until about May 15th   we advanced on the works at Drury's Bluff.   took two lines of works when Genl Gillmore wanted to play his trump & fortify   But Genl Butler was in command & objected   Next morning May 16 was very foggy & the enemy took advantage of this & made a furious attack in force on our left then our right & centre & finally forced us to retire & abandon the capture of Richmond for the present

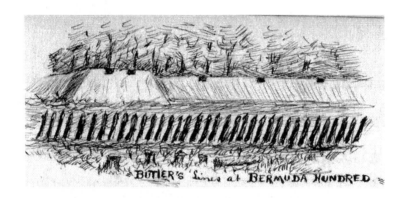

Depiction by Emma Jane of Butler's lines at Bermuda Hundred
(Barrett Collection)

*[*James' diary entries]*
Mon May 16 1864
Firing commenced early. Rebs assault our right. Loud shouts. Drive them back. Left repulsed them three times & then they turn that. The center on my right is exposed. They dash down. The Reg^t on my right run & I get @ hot flank fire. Four Cos of us forced back. Rally & go up again. Retreat by order & advance again but are forced to make good our retreat. Arrive in camp about 9 P.M. Took @ good wash, change my clothes & slept well. Lim fought well. 6 men wounded.

Tues May 17 1864
I was reported wounded. Capt. Moser killed. Lts. Hilliard & Edwards wounded. Resting today. Men cleaning & washing up. O'Brien & Himrod received commissions. D'Arcy—1st Lieut. The Rebs very strong yesterday at Darling & Chester Hill. They gave whiskey to their men & read them flattering news. Cavalry gone out to destroy supply trains. Driven back. Sharp firing heard during night. Two days' rations given for that last Reg^t.

[This is Emma Jane's transcription of a letter written by James.]

Old Point Comfort Va   May 17 1864
Dear Jennie

      I came back to camp last night after being at the front since the 13th. We got along first rate until yesterday when we had @ very severe fight & were driven back. Thursday morning we were ordered to march at 5 A.M. with 2 days' rations & in light marching order. We did not even take our blankets. It rained very hard a good portion of the day. Our Regt was the reserve & did not go under fire But could plainly see the fighting. The enemy was driven back & some prisoners taken. We bivouacked that night & made ourselves comfortable by sitting around small fires. & changing sides occasionally for we were soaked. Friday about noon, we were ordered to march & our Brigade was to be in the advance. After several miles we took position in some woods. We had @ vast body of troops arranged in successive lines of battle. Some shells came over us But as our position was not well known, we did not suffer.

      Next morning—Saturday—2 Regts of our Brigade—115th N.Y & 76th Pa took the first line of rifle pits & passed to attack the 2nd. We followed within supporting distance. The skirmishers suffered considerably that day. We lay all day in @ hollow, narrowly escaped several shots But not hurt

      At night, our Regt & the 47th went to the front & relieved the others. It was pretty quiet that night & the Sunday following. The Rebs had sharp shooters in trees who picked off all they could. Our boys hunted them like squirrels & brought several down. 2 of my Co were wounded that day—one in the foot & the other in the hand. Others were wounded also. The skirmishers had to cover behind logs & stumps. & when they are loading, are often hit. I did not go out on this duty & Lieut & 60 men were detailed at @ time & it did not come my turn. Rather more like hunting than fighting to distribute men along behind logs &c & let them watch for @ man to show himself. Our artillery did good service But they were removed Sunday night to the rear because of information recd which convinced the Genl that he would have to withdraw or be gobbled as the Rebs were being strongly reinforced & we were not strong enough to hold our own. Monday morning early we were ordered to arms. The enemy rushed with mad shouts upon our right. We finally drove them back & I think they must have suffered very heavily. We were about in the center & I could only hear the screams & hard firing. The Rebs were mad with whiskey & encouraged with accounts of @ great victory over Grant. These Graybacks have @ sort of fiendish shout or yell— very different from our Union cheer. Our left was then attacked But Genl Perry drove them back 3 times with great slaughter.

      Our Brigade then recd notice that our skirmishers were driven in. We were protected behind some logs we had piled up. Our Regt was on the right of the Brigade & my Co on the right of the Regt. An open gap of some 200 yds had been somehow left at my right. This was partially filled by the skirmishers. I gave my men the necessary cautions & awaited the issue. We did not wait long. They rushed down just where this gap was. The troops broke & ran. This gave them

@ chance to get an enfilading[151] fire upon us. The distance could not have been over 50 yds. My men stood their ground well as did the whole Reg^t but the way we were placed & the way the enemy was firing was a little too much for human endurance & I ordered my men to fall back for a better position. I tell you the balls flew about there kinder careless. 4 Co's were forced back but we soon rallied & took our positions again. Another Reg^t was thrown in to protect our right & we awaited their 2nd coming. Next time they attacked on the left & drove back the 47th. We fell back with them by order @ short distance & they rallied again & charged back. By this time it became evident that we must retire or be captured. There was no Artillery to support us. We retreated in good order But it was slow work. The roads were muddy & our wagon trains had to be protected. Our Artillery in the rear was soon in protecting range. We are now within our entrenchments & we think secure. I don't know what has happened But this is just what we have been afraid of. Beauregard has received about 15 or more reinforcements from Lee.

A good many Rebs came in across our line after the first charge. I don't know how many prisoners we have But fear we have lost more than we have taken. We lost 6 pieces of Artillery. The Rebel loss in killed & wounded must have been enormous. We fairly mowed them down. They were full of whiskey & dead to fear. They rushed on with reckless speed regardless of our tremendous fire. I tremble for the wounded who were left behind. My Co was very small. I had about 30 men. None were killed. 6 were wounded besides 2 the day before. I do not acknowledge that we were whipped. I think we have punished them the worst But the star of the 48th does not seem to bring us much good luck yet. We seem always to be repulsed. We hoped that Butler held the key to Richmond But our hopes are now somewhat chilled. I guess Grant will be there first, But Richmond is bound to be taken. It is only @ question of time.

Our roads are awful with mud about @ foot deep & when it is not muddy, it is dusty. I escaped this time again without @ scratch. I don't know how. One time I was behind a stump & I fired my pistol several times. The stump was chipped pretty well But I was unharmed. I expect to get into another brush soon & am getting quite used to it.

I got one letter yesterday from Charley. That is the only one since I left the Head Apr 24/64. We get N.Y. papers in 2 days. Mail comes every day. Please direct 48th Reg^t, 10th Army Corps, Fortress Monroe, Va. Please let this answer for @ letter home & save my writing another. I spend as much time as possible in getting rest. Our Reg^t lost one Capt killed, 2 Lieuts wounded, 8 men killed & 62 wounded.

Now Jennie, good bye. Do not feel anxious for me. Write often & believe me with much love

Yours faithfully
James A. Barrett

---

[151] Gunfire directed along the length of a target. enfilade. (n.d.). *Webster's Revised Unabridged College* Dictionary. Retrieved December 3, 2015, from http://www.yourdictionary.com/enfilade

Wed May 18 1864

Inspection by Maj. Eddy. Ordered to the front. Hard shower. Only 21 men in Co. to go. Halted & got coffee & then took the advance line of skirmishers. My Co. are in @ belt of woods & cover behind trees & in pits dug for the purpose. We met @ hot shower of bullets & shell in advancing. The Rebs within rifle range. Pretty quiet during night. Good moon. I can hardly keep my eyes open.

Thurs May 19 1864

Firing commenced early. Bullets pretty thick. A battery opened on us. Fearful shelling. We hold our ground. Our left attacked by @ body of the enemy. Sharp fight. Enemy driven back. More shells. Corp. Laxey joins Co. Relieved in the evening & retire to camp. Some fault found with the Reg^t for not coming in together. Got some coffee & retired to sleep 10 P.M. Turned out at 12. Soon dismissed. Men exhausted.

Emma Jane's portrayal of a sharpshooter
(Barrett Collection)

Fri May 20 1864

Made requisition for clothing. Drew my papers. Ordered to the front. Men very much played out. I feel poorly but must go with the company. Formed column in rear of entrenchments. Short for officers. Port Royal mail received. Rebs attack us. We repulsed them with great loss. Gen. Walker wounded on our hands. Our loss considerable. Bivouacked for the night. Fatigue parties at work.

Sat May 21 1864

Pleasant day. Our artillery opened. 48th on fatigue. Returned to camp at night. 97th Pa & 13th Ind Regts badly cut up. Lacoppidan's commission rec. Called out at 11 P.M. by heavy firing. Soon returned.

Sun May 22 1864

Called out at 3 ½ A.M. Went to the front at 5. All very tired. I am detailed for fatigue to work on the road towards the landing. I am getting some rest. Heavy roads mean something. Returned to camp. Called out at 3 A.M.

Mon May 23 1864

Had one night's rest. Joined the Regt at the front in the morning. Nearly all on fatigue. Sharpshooters at work. Lying off in the field. Returned to camp. Retired late & ordered to turn out at 3 A.M. to move camp. Dikeman missing since yesterday morning.

Tues May 24 1864

Turned out at 3 A.M. Packed up & moved camp about one mile to the front. Pitched tents at double column. Crowded. Arranged to mess with Lippincott. Regt sent out on picket at 4 P.M. Rebs very near. Stormy first of the night.

Wed May 25 1864

Very quiet night. No firing. Rebs in plain sight but they don't fire. Papers exchanged. Cheering heard in camp. Grant still victorious. Relieved by 7th Conn. Flag of truce. Curiosity. Returned to camp. Capt. Lockwood resigned. Clothing to issue.

Thurs May 26 1864

Raining, straightening up our camp, writing letters. Signs of moving, orders to be ready. Mail to be received, cooking rations. Good news from Grant.

[*Letter]
Camp of 48th Regt N.Y.S. Vols
In the field   May 26th 1864
Dear Jennie   This is the 1st chance I have had to write since my last & now I may not be able to write But @ few lines. The papers say that Butler is safe in his entrenchments <u>resting</u> his men. This is the first intimation I have had that we were <u>resting</u>. I wont say how much I have gained by the information. I have been on @ continual go & had to get my Co Clerk to write twice for me   I recd your 2 letters directed to Port Royal & one from Washington & 1 from Fortress Monroe @ few days since   We get our mails pretty regular I wrote you last after my return to camp from before

Fort Darling the 17th   We were in camp that day   The 18th we were inspected & ordered to the front & our regt sent out to take charge of the advance line of Rifle pits[152]

We relieved another regt just at dusk encountering @ heavy fire of ball & shell in our advance   But as we were deployed as skirmishers we escaped harm. I was stationed in the edge of @ belt of woods. during the night some of the men threw up little heaps of dirt to protect them & others arranged themselves behind trees   I had @ big tree in the rear of the Co where I could watch opperations. We were pretty quiet during the night   But at daylight the pickets began firing at each other   The 2 lines were from 1 to 300 yds apart. & an almost continual firing was kept up all day along the lines. & at times it was very brisk   Some of my men fired 100 rounds. once during the morning a Battery of about 8 guns about 100 yds off opened on us & the way they poured Shells grape & canister &c into those woods for about an hour was @ caution to all Cowards & non combattants I assure you. Fortunately most of their firing was high   We were none of us hurt. They sent us a few more in the P.M.   My men were eager to fire But I had to check them a good deal & caution them against firing at too long range I tell you I was glad to get relieved on the evening of the 19th   Those who relieved us were driven back that night & we have not wholly recovered the line yet. I did not get to bed until 10 P.M. at 12 we had an alarm & were ordered to the front. We were not needed & turned back to camp rested until 3 ½ & formed line again & marched to the entrenchment & lay as @ reserve in an open field   That night & next day we sent out fatigue parties to strengthen our works. It was the 20th that The Rebs attempted to advance on our works   They met a warm reception from our Infantry & Artillery & were repulsed with very heavy loss   Genl Walker[153] was wounded & fell into our hands   Our regt was in the reserve & not in the fight. 21st we were on fatigue and returned to camp that night after being away 2 days & hoped to get a night's rest   But firing at the front called us out at 11 P.M. Nothing serious & we were dismissed   22nd At 3 ½ ordered into line & at 5 went to the front   I was sent on fatigue with 75 men mending roads. I rested some that day while my details were at work. & returned to camp at night with my detail   The regt did not come in. 23d turned out at 3 A.M. & joined the regt at the front. (Our camp was nearly 2 miles from the entrenchments) where we remained that day   Our men all on fatigue on our batteries. The enemies sharp shooters occasionally picking off @ man. returned to camp in the evening drew rations & prepared to move camp at 3 next morning one mile nearer to the front. That afternoon 24th our Regt were ordered out to our advance line on Picket

---

[152] A pit or short trench sheltering sharpshooters. Rifle pit. (n.d.) WEBSTER'S REVISED UNABRIDGED DICTIONARY. (1913). Retrieved December 4, 2015, from http://www.thefreedictionary.com/Rifle+pit
[153] General William Stephen Walker was wounded on May 20, 1864.

Illustration, artist unknown
(This media is in the public domain in the United States, 2016)

We found ourselves in rather close proximity about 200 yds to Mr reb But there was an understanding that we would not fire upon each other unless attacked or advanced upon. So we passed our time away very quietly   The Rebs came out in plain sight talked to each other &c one man met them & exchanged papers.   This was against orders   he was sent in to headquarters paper & all   It was @ Petersburg paper of 24th

We returned last night & have been in camp <u>resting</u> today.   When we go to the front we take Haversack Canteen & Rubber blanket & really make ourselves <u>independant</u> as you please

This way of roughing it takes hold of @ fellow at first & makes the men growl some. We have quite @ good many on the sick list   I have felt pretty well played out at times   But my health is tip top. I fancy that my clothes & belt are getting a little loose   But I have got @ pretty good stock on hand & can afford to loose @ little flesh. Capt Lockwood resigned yesterday & has gone home. Of course I expect to get another bar soon unless I get dismissed   Butler is pretty rough on Officers & dismisses them for slight offences. Now I am contrary as @ mule & may say or do something that may not suit some of these days One Lt was reduced to the ranks the other day for falling back from those rifle pits the night after we were relieved

I am beginning to learn something about soldiering   Our Brigade get it pretty rough   We are called "Cast Iron Brigade" "Bartons Flying Brigade" or "Barton's foot Cavalry"   One thing is certain   We have been on the move pretty constantly since we came here. I recd Nell's letter & will try & answer before long   But my time is limited & I <u>must</u> sleep some

She need not wait for me to write   I like to get letters even if I have to <u>owe</u> for them   I also recd one letter from Annie I think I shall have to cut all my correspondents until after this campaign is over. I hope they will write all the same. We are getting good news from Grant. You get as good accounts & better in your papers of our movements than I can give. I will try & keep you posted as to my welfare even if I have to get my Co Clerk to do it fur me

I was very glad to get my back letters I assure I like to have you write me little details   I enjoy reading them   It gives me some idea of what you are doing. I sometimes relent in my resolutions to remain until the end of the war anyhow. If this Campaign succeeds as well as we hope & the war should tarry along with not much to do I might convince myself that I was not needed. & I sometimes get disgusted too   just as sure as we are one day in camp   Col B has to be round & criticise something or somebody   Tents have to be moved or something done of no earthly use except to keep the men to work when they need rest. I dont believe in fancy work in the field   But it is all in our 3 years. I enclose @ piece of Telegraph wire on the turnpike that we cut down. I don't value such things   But some do If you do can keep them. or throw them away. But I must close My tent has got to be moved just so many feet & on the line

      Please give much love to all friends & believe me as ever

      Yours most sincerely   James A. Barrett

[*Continuation of letter dated May 26th]

Dearest Jennie

      It has commenced to rain & I cant move my tent so I will write @ word more

      I notice you say you think I took a certain Poem   I shall plead "Not guilty" & apply for @ full acquittal   We have just rec^d orders to cook 2 days rations   I guess we are going to Petersburg. I notice what you say about nothing happening to us except by God's permission There is much comfort in this thought   He knows what is best for us   We are safe in His hands Let us have faith & say Thy will be done. If I get wounded I am not far from home & if necessary my friends could meet me

      Lieut Ingraham came out Corp^l in Co G was promoted to Q.M. Serg^t & then 2^d & 1st Lt. A very clever fellow   He was acting QM for our reg^t some time & is now in command of Co C as the Capt was killed before Ft Darling

      Father seems to be having @ hard time of it. I do wish this war would end & then I could get him settled somewhere where he would not have so much to do   He has too much care for one of his age & He will not give up.

      I should think you would often find it convenient to have a supernumerary school marm as you say

      Perhaps Nell wont think so Tell Nell I will give her credit for decision now. I am glad you have found some Cottages. No knowing how soon We may want one if Grant & Sherman follow up their successes   Poor we seem to have the luck against us   We draw the enemies fire & hold them here while the others reap all the victory. But we must be content to obey orders. do our best & leave the rest to Him who doeth all things well

      I may meet Ned yet in my travels   Who is he with now   I want to know & then if our Corps meet I can look him up   Or he can seek me if opportunity offers   My orderly has his commission & I have appointed Stayley 1st Serg^t He has not been well lately   campaigning tells upon him. Please write often & don't think strange I do not reply often   I will write as often as I can & if I cant write my Co Clerk will write to father. Again assuring you of my undying fidelity—I remain

                Yours

                   James

[*James' diary entries]
Fri May 27 1864

Turned out under arms 3 A.M. stood until daylight. Reg^t inspection 3 P.M. Left camp with everything packed about 5 P.M. Bivouacked near Bermuda Hundred. Slept well. Secrecy seems to veil our movements No one knows where we are going.

Sat May 28 1864

Preparing for a move somewhere. Expect to join Grant. Mail received. Started at 6 P.M. Marched slowly for Point of Rocks. Roads very bad. Progress slow & tiresome. Crossed the Appomattox about 12 P.M. on pontoon bridge. Some men fell out exhausted.

> *[Emma Jane's transcription of Emily's journal entry]*
> Sat. May 28, 1864
>
> Should like to hear whether James is alive and safe. Jennie had a letter from him last Saturday written after a hot engagement with the enemy the Monday before at Bermuda Hundred, telling that he was safe and yesterday we had a letter from his company clerk saying that he was well but suddenly called to guard the entrenchments that morning so that we feel quite anxious.

[*Narrative]

Genl Butler then retired to his "Bottle" & not needing all his troops lent out our Division which was the fighting division (2nd Div 10th Corps) to Genl Baldy Smith of the 18th Corps & we marched across & embarked for White House[154] where we landed & drew 3 days rations But were ordered to march before we could issue them all & we were obliged to abandon most of the meat We took good care to secure our coffee & sugar which is the soldier's "staff of life" I never knew how to value coffee until I went into the army. When a Soldier is all tired out from a long march it is wonderful what an effect a good cup of coffee has. It must be experienced to be appreciated

*[*James' diary entries]*
Sun May 29 1864

Arrived near City Point at 3 A.M. & bivouacked. Arose at 5 & marched to near the dock. Embarked on steamer "Claymont" about noon. Started down the river about 2 P.M. We now belong to the 18th Corps.

---

[154] White House Landing.   It is located on the Pamunkey River in New Kent Co., Virginia.

Mon May 30 1864

Pleasant. Passed Ft. Monroe at 10 A.M. Proceeded up York River to White House [Landing]. Pleasant country.

Tues May 31 1864

Arrived at White House at 10 A.M. Landed. Drew three days' rations & marched heavy marching orders at 4 P.M. Hot & dusty. Very tiresome march nearly all night.

Chapter 16

Wounded at Cold Harbor

June 1, 1864- September 05, 1864--Receives slight wound in right shoulder--Captures one rebel female artillery captain and finds other women dead--Receives hip and back wound--Waits two days to be ambulanced to White House Landing--8,000 wounded waiting for transport--Takes steamer "Wenonah" to Washington--Enters Hospital--Family Notified—Returns and recuperates at home in Concord, Massachusetts

[Note that all the following transcriptions have been faithfully copied from the original document, as written by James, except where noted.]

Illustration depicting the Battle of Cold Harbor
(This media is in the public domain in the United States, 2016)

[*Narrative]
We marched all night & next forenoon arrived at Cold Harbor about 2 P.M. & being <u>so called fresh</u> troops were immediately ordered to charge the works without even leaving Knapsacks behind   Our Brigade charged gallantly   captured one line of works & 500 prisioners We charged through a piece of woods & many of the men would stop behind trees & commence firing to the great peril of those of our side who were in advance   While rallying these stragglers I rec^d a sleight wound in the right shoulder but not sufficient to disable me   Among our prisoners one Capt of Artillery was a woman & I believe our burial party found several women among the rebel dead[155]. It was about 10 PM. before we were relieved & allowed a little rest

---

[155] There were just shy of 400 documented cases of women who served as soldiers during the Civil War, according to the records of the Sanitary Commission. Women from both sides chopped off their hair, traded in their dresses for guns and fought for the side they believed in. Their contemporaries often looked upon them as outcasts in a society where men and women had completely different roles. People were quick to say that the only women who would have enlisted were mentally unbalanced or prostitutes. In 1865 *The United States Service Magazine* stated that "those who generalize on the impropriety and unladylikeness of such conduct, are unquestionably in the right, according to the practical parlor standard of life."Brown, Olivia. (2012). *Women Soldiers of the Civil War*. Retrieved April 8, 2015, from www.historynet.com/women-in-the-civil-war#soldiers

Wed June 1 1864
Battle of Cold Harbor. Marched all the forenoon. Came up to the 6th Corps about 2 P.M. Men very tired. Advanced on enemy's works about 4 P.M. Made 3 charges. Lots of prisoners taken. Hot work. I got slightly scratched in shoulder.

Early next morning June 2nd our Regt advanced to the front to thicken the lines under a hot fire   I had but just got into my position when a ball from a sharp shooter struck me just behind the right hip & went clear through coming out at the left hip a distance of 11 inches & shattering the lower part of the backbone in its passage, after piercing through about 20 thicknesses of my rubber blanket which hung in my belt at my side. Two of my men helped me to the rear where there were about 8000 wounded men waiting for transportation to White House

Pen and ink illustration by Emma Jane of soldiers at the Battle of Cold Harbor
(Barrett Collection)

[The Cousins asked Dr. William Dietrick for his professional opinion regarding James' description of the injury he sustained at the Battle of Cold Harbor and why it was not a mortal wound.]

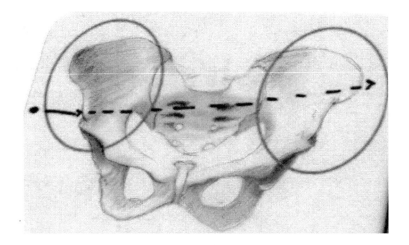

The ball entered above the right hip along the lower ilium and traveled across the sacrum and out the left side. The ball was a low velocity bullet which scooted along a trajectory that paralleled the sacrum rather than penetrate the bone. It missed the arteries, the sciatic nerve and its branches, along with colon and the bladder. The ball took pieces of the rubber mat and cloth from Lieut. James Barrett's uniform and fragments of the bone (exfoliation) with it which resulted in chronic infection in the wound site.

William Dietrick, MD
October, 2016

[*Letter]

Hosp^l in Field near Richmond
June 2 1864

Dear Mother
    I was wounded this morning (not serious) in the Hip. Am doing well. Expect to be sent home soon.I have to ride 25 miles to White House in Ambulance. We have had rough times. Thank God it is no worse.
                Yours JasABarrett

[*James' diary entry]
Thurs June 2 1864
Reserve during the night. I go into hospital till morn. Went to the front early & joined Reg^t. We rally our men & go to the front. I soon get @ shot

in the back & hip—bad flesh wound. My men help me off & Newhart
dresses my wound. Taylor wounded in arm. Lippincott fixes up a tent for
us all. Raining.

[*Letter]

In Hospital in the field
Grants Army 6 Miles from Richm^d
June 2^d 1864

Dear Jennie

      We arrived at this place yesterday afternoon after marching all night & went almost at once into a Charge upon the Enemie's works

      We made our Brigade 3 different charges took 520 prisoners & were partially repulsed at last about dark   I was hit slightly in right arm. Not hurt. After it was over, I went to the rear & remained untill early this AM when I rejoined my Co & after collecting & forming our Reg^t about 100 men went to the front. It was not long before a ball run against me near back bone & came out at the hip. <u>Flesh wound</u>   My men helped me off & I am doing well. Shall go to White House & Fortress Monroe very soon & then probably get @ leave to go home. I am rather sore & stiff & can't help myself much   I think I might with crutches. I walked nearly all the way off the field by leaning on 2 men But my left leg is <u>Game</u> for the present.

      I think I can get home as I did before by getting Charley to attend me from N.Y. rec^d @ letter from you a few minutes since   Dont worry for me   my wound is not dangerous   Hoping to see you soon

          believe me   Yours

James A. Barrett
1st Lt 48th N.Y.S. V.

[*James' diary entry]
Fri June 3 1864
Men exposed. Prospect poor for getting off. Ambulances all busy at the
front. Those who are able, must walk down to White House [Landing]..
Taylor & Lippincott have started. It rained all night. Men poorly cared for.
No covering. Rebs make @ desperate charge in the afternoon, another in
the evening. 6th Corps engaged. Rebs repulsed with heavy loss. Artillery
engaged.

[*Narrative]
After lying on the ground 2 days, I was taken in an ambulance to White House & in several days more on a Steamer to Washington & sent to a Hospital

      Where I just missed my family physician, Dr. Bartlett of Concord Mass, whom my father had sent to hunt me up, but who had returned thinking that I had gone in another direction   He passed across the very boat I was on.

White House Landing, VA
(This media is in the public domain in the United States, 2016)

*[*James' diary entries]*
Sat June 4 1864
Started in ambulance 2 P.M. Left my pistol with Maj. Coan & belt with Dr. Liets. Officers send expressions of good will & confidence. Chaplain Taylor very kind. Corp Turnbull & @ Capt. of 188th Pa. Vol in our ambulance. Corp. lost @ leg. Journey very tiresome. Arrive at White about midnight. Sleep in ambulance all night. Sanitary Commission very attentive.

Sun June 5 1864
Removed to hospital tent. Straw beds on the ground. Pretty comfortable. Hard fare & not much prospect of being sent away. Pretty noisy crowd. Lt. Hubbard of 4th Regt battery makes much fun. My appetite not very good. Can't relish the food, But we must get along. There are @ good many here.

Mon June 6 1864 *Christian Commission & Sanitary Commission[156] agents come round. Issue what clothing is needed. Most of their efforts are made for those just arrived.*

---

[156] The Christian Commission (USCC) was an organization that furnished supplies, medical services, and religious literature to Union soldiers. The United States Sanitary Commission (USSC) was a private relief agency created by federal legislation on June 18, 1861, to support sick and wounded soldiers of the U.S. Army. United States Christian Commission. (November 16, 2015). *Wikipedia, The Free Encyclopedia*. Retrieved December 4, 2015,from

Tues June 7 1864

Dr. Fowler promises to get us off first opportunity. All anxious to go.
Nearly flooded out last night. Beds wet. Mine not so bad as some, as my
rubber was under bed.

Wed June 8 1864

Steamer "Wenonah" loading with slightly wounded cases. Dr. says six of
us can have beds & as many more may go as will take their chances. We
all go. Nearly all fix beds outside. I slept in cabin. No bad cases allowed
in cabin. I guess I should have done as well outside. Dr. Pretty mad to see
severe cases come down. Dr. Fowler makes it all right.

Thurs June 9 1864

Getting along very well. Rather tiresome. The cabin girl looks out for my
meals. I get all the lemonade I want.

Fri June 10 1864

Arrived at Washington about 1 P.M. Sent to Douglas Hospital. Pleasant
place & well arranged. Stopped the ambulance at Mr. Clark's store. Saw
Ben's brother. Irene gone north. Ryan of Co. C. recognized me.
Appeared glad to see me. He is in invalid corps. My wound probed by
doctor in charge. No bones hurt.

[*Letters]

Douglass GenHosp¹
Washington D.C.
June 10 1864

Dear Friends

  I have just arrived here by Steamer "Wenonah" direct from White House [Landing]. I tell
you it seems good to get into @ comfortable bed

  I am doing very well. I have to depend on others for help. I think I might go home if I had
some one to take care of me I have to lie down all the time. I am told that I can get @ Leave of
Absence to go home in 3 days any time. The ball went in on the right side of the back bone &

https://en.wikipedia.org/w/index.php?title=UnitedStatesChristianCommission&oldid=6909255
33 United States Sanitary Commission. (October 6, 2015). *Wikipedia, The Free Encyclopedia*.
Retrieved December 4, 2015,
from https://en.wikipedia.org/w/index.php?title=UnitedStatesSanitaryCommission&oldid=6844
03188

came out at the left hip. There are no bones broke. & I do not suffer much. Let Jennie see this I cant write very well

Yours

JasA.Barrett

I think I shall get on to crutches in a day or 2. If I happen to meet some one here that I know who is going east I may go with him But I cant think of anyone I am going to write Gerrish Perhaps he can come on after me.

James

[Emma Jane's transcription of Emily's journal entry]

Sat. June 11, 1864

This week has brought the sad intelligence that brother James is again wounded though not serious we trust. Father brought home a letter from Mr. Swain Wednesday night with an account of the battle near Richmond in which it stated that James was severely wounded in the spine which made us feel exceedingly sad and anxious, thinking that he would be a sufferer probably for life. The next morning Father went to town and started the doctor right on for him, and to our great relief and joy, found in the morning's mail a few lines from the dear boy himself saying that he was wounded in the hip, not seriously which gave us great cause for thankfulness. The Doctor [Dr. Bartlett] has returned tonight with out him concluding he was on the way home from all he could learn but unable to find him so that we shall hope to see him soon, Providence permitting.

*[*James' diary entries]*

Sat June 11 1864

Well cared for. Mr. Bates called—says Dr. Bartlett & Gerrish went home last night. I get to telegraph to N.Y. Dr. thinks I can go home. J.B. Brown called—is going to get me cherries & ice cream. I drink considerable milk.

Sun June 12 1864

Very pleasant. Good many visitors. The Clarks called to see me. Mr. C. brought some cherries. Mr. Bates' friend called.

Mon June 13 1864

Pleasant day. Rested well. Ryan of Co. C. now of invalid corps called to see me. Brown called in evening.

Tues June 14 1864

Slept poorly—took morphine & drowsed all forenoon. Headache & feverish—can't eat anything today—drink lemonade freely. E. Wheeler,

Blaisdell, N.H. & A. Barrett called. Blaisdell brought some cherries. Charley arrived & called with Bates. My leave signed here. Bates will put it through in morning.

Wed June 15 1864

Feel better this morning. Get my leave all right for 30 days. Expect to start tonight.

Special Orders #147
(Barrett Collection)

I telegraphed a friend in N Y. who came on & took me home   He had hard work to get a sleeping car for me as they did not allow wounded men in their beds. But I told him I would go if I had to ride on the Cowcatcher

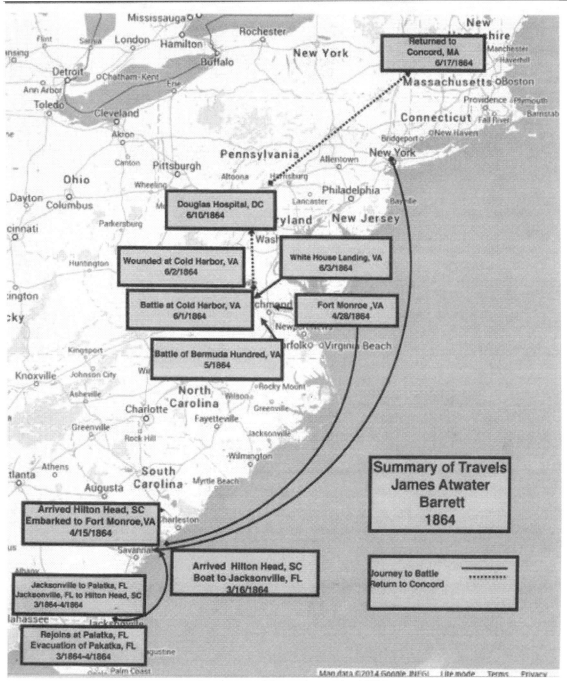

Summary of James' travels, 1864
(Courtesy of Google INFGI, 2014)

Fri June 17 1864
 Arrived home pretty weak.

Certification of promotion of rank of Captain
(Barrett Collection)

[*Narrative]

  This time I remained home 3 months where I had the best of nursing which enabled me to return in Sept & get mustered as Captn   But I was on light duty 5 months more before I was able to take the field again.

[Letter from Charles P. Gerrish]

New York July 8th 1864

Dear James

  I received your letter of the 5th inst yesterday, I must, to be perfectly sincere and frank, accuse both your family and my own, of great remissness in not writing me one word about your health since my return, Not a line from your folks not one word from Mother or Story about you since my return from Concord, I began to fancy I had been in a profound dream for thirty-one years, and that I had been dreaming, that I was born in Salem, and at the early age of 5 months went to Concord to live, that I had a mother & brother, uncles & aunts, cousins, relatives & friends, that one cousin had joined the army, had been wounded &c &c. I queried whether my own existence was a myth or not, what it was that was doing the thinking that I imagined myself to be doing, in short I found myself in a very skeptical mood when your letter arrived, dispelled these illusions, and made me realize, that you were yourself again. I did not expect _you_ to write, and I presume there were good reasons, why I should be neglected, I have not written the above in any spirit of Anger, but felt it my duty to administer a mild reproof to my relatives generally, I am glad your trunk arrived safely, it must have gone to Concord N·H· first, or you would have received it sooner, I hope the charges were less than by express, they ought to have been,- Allow me to congratulate you in your promotion, it will serve as an excellent medicine, to you· I should advise you to take it three times a day in a little brandy & water· I speak reverently, for my 4ᵗʰ of July experience teaches me that stimulants should be avoided by those who are healthy and strong, and should be indulged in cautiously and moderately by sick & feeble, but it does seem to me that a glass of pure country milk, a fresh egg, and a little port wine, or brandy, or Jamaica[157], is just what you need to keep up your strength, I am aware that this advice if especially, if followed, will occasion one of the severest hurricanes, the old homestead under the stately elms, ever experienced, but you know the law distinctly says we must do our duty, though the heavens fall- You

---

[157] Rum

took an opiate- in Washington to make you sleep, you did not desist because Dr. Stone of that city- is drunk all the time from the effects of opium,

Convivial drinking, such as we see in bar rooms, I abhor. I spent 4th of July at Patchojue and sailed from there to Fire Island, and was disgusted. with the scenes of drinking that I saw there, I am equally disgusted with gluttony, which probably kills more people, than anything else, by cutting short their lives, when they should be in their prime, and in the midst of their usefulness, Excesses of all kinds should be faithfully guarded against, and when the tendency is the greater, the caution should be the greater I believe the best drink for man in a healthy condition, is water, pure water, in spite- of a worthy gentleman's remark that he used it only for washing, an artificial life, which enfeebles, and debilitates the human frame, creates the necessity for tea & Coffee, and other stimulants, hence, follows a craving for them

I send you today the "Times" of yesterday which contains some casualties in the 18th Corps. Also the Times of to-day, which contains some severe strictures in Col. Barton's management in a recent action, The Times of yesterday also contains a note from Frank Barlow, which may interest you I will hereafter send you the papers from time to time, Boston papers never seemed to me to contain much news, Mrs. Bates & Martha desire to be remembered to you, Geo. H. is still in Washington, but is expected home this week, Have you ever received the shoulder straps I sent you from Washington? I have not yet had time to make up your Acct with the firm will do so soon, Hadn't you better invest some more money in the Concord Bank for savings for savings, you have about $1000 in Governments and if the country does go to pieces, which I do not for a moment believe, and the debt should be repudiated massachusetts in such an event, would probably pay her debts, and be solvent, I do not think well of having your eggs all in one basket, unless you want to set a hen, and have not more than a dozen eggs.

Yours aff.

Chas P. Gerrish

P.S. My kind regards to all

Have you had a letter from Lieut Edwards? He called down to enquire about you, and took your address. I am sorry to hear that the bone was touched, but from the fact that it does not pain you, and you can use your limbs I look for the most favorable results

Application for leave of absence
(Barrett Collection)

Lieut James A. Barrett   Co. *H* of the *48th*
Regiment, *N.Y Volunteers* having applied for a certificate on which to ground an
Application for leave of absence, I do hereby certify that I have carefully
examined this officer and find that

a ball passed across the sacrum entering on the right side and coming out on the
left side near the end of the ilium, traversing a course of ten inches. Exfoliation
of the bone and profuse discharge through the whole track of the wound now exist
He was wounded June 2, 1864 at Cold Harbor

And that in consequence thereof, he is, in my opinion, unfit for duty. I further
declare my belief that he will not be able to resume his duties in a less period
than+ *some months* ~~days~~ and is unable to travel without incurring the risk of
permanent disability.

Dated at *Concord*, this *eighth* day of *July, 1864*
Sworn to before me,   *Josiah Bartlett M.D.*
July 8, 1864   *Joseph Reynolds, Justice of the Peace*

*Here the nature of the disease, wound or disability, is to be fully stated, and the
period during which the officer
has suffered under its effects.
+Here state, candidly and explicitly, the opinion as to the period which will probably
elapse before the officer
will be able to resume his duties. When there is no reason to expect a recovery,
or when the prospect of a recovery is distant and uncertain, it must be so stated.

[This certificate to be made out in triplicate.]

[Emma Jane's transcription of Emily's journal entry]
Sat. July 9, 1864
Three weeks yesterday since James came home and happy we
were to see him after expecting him all the week. Jennie is off and
on, is quite devoted to her unfortunate lover who is obliged to
keep his bed, but is as comfortable as could be expected with a
wound ten inches long mostly out of sight.

*Carte de visite of
Colonel George Lincoln
Prescott
(Barrett Collection)*

> *Another of our brave soldiers has fallen. Col. Prescott
> was buried last week on Wednesday under military honors.*

[*James' diary entries]

Thurs Sept 1 1864

*Rode round the square carrying Jennie to school. Took the girls to the
Soldiers' aid, went after them at night, stopped at Mr. Farmer's to tea. I
have @ colic pain, put on @ mustard plaster all night*

Fri Sept 2 1864

*Better this morning am going home to dress. I have got to pack my
valise. I take the noon train for Boston. The Leete children go to Mrs. F.
with me. Jennie going as far as Boston. Called at Hovey's. Story gone
home not very well. Called at Mrs. Hosmer & Mrs. Wood took N.Y. train
home at 5 ½ P.M. Great crowd no state rooms But good supper & no
colic.*

Sat Sept 3 1864

*Arrived at N.Y. Folks all well. Met Maj. Elfwing—did some business &
went back to Mrs. Wood Pleasant call passed the night with Gerrish. All
well.*

> *[Emma Jane's transcription of Emily's journal entry]*
> Sat. Sept. 3, 1864
>
> *Another sad time we have experienced in parting from
> dear brother James who left us yesterday noon to return to his
> regiment but not at all fitted to endure its hardships as his wound
> is not healed yet and he has a weakness in his hips and back
> which I fear will trouble him for some time if not always, so that
> the parting from him was somewhat alleviated by the feeling that
> he was not going to be exposed to real danger. I miss him ever so*

much as I have seen and enjoyed him so much the last two months and a half that he has been with us—the last time perhaps that I shall ever see and enjoy him so long in my home again. So it is in life! We must exchange and not multiply our joys!

[*James' diary entries]

Sun Sept 4 1864

No church on Sunday . Went to Mrs. Leetes in the afternoon. Returned in the evening to Gerrishes. Charles quite confidential. Had @ long talk with him. It rained all day. I think it is the equinoctial[158].

Mon Sept 5 1864

Rainy. Took the 10 AM train to Bronxville. Charley met me at the depot. Nell did not come. Found Uncle's folks all well. Also Mattie Lyman is going East Keep ---- with ---- ---- in Bronxville. Swain family away.

---

[158] Happening at or near the time of an equinox. equinoctial. (n.d.). *Dictionary.com Unabridged*. Retrieved December 4, 2015, from http://dictionary.reference.com/browse/equinoctial

Chapter 17

Crinoline on the Brain

September 6, 1864- September 27, 1864--Being detained in New York--News of fall of Atlanta and rebel army demoralized--Reports of rebel John Morgan killed--Barbarity of slavery--Sets sail on steamer "G.C. Collins"--Letter from Jennie which speaks of Sanitary Commission--Wound continues to give problems--Mrs. Major Pauline Cushman--Back in a field hospital

[Note that all the following transcriptions have been faithfully copied from the original document, as written by James, except where noted.]

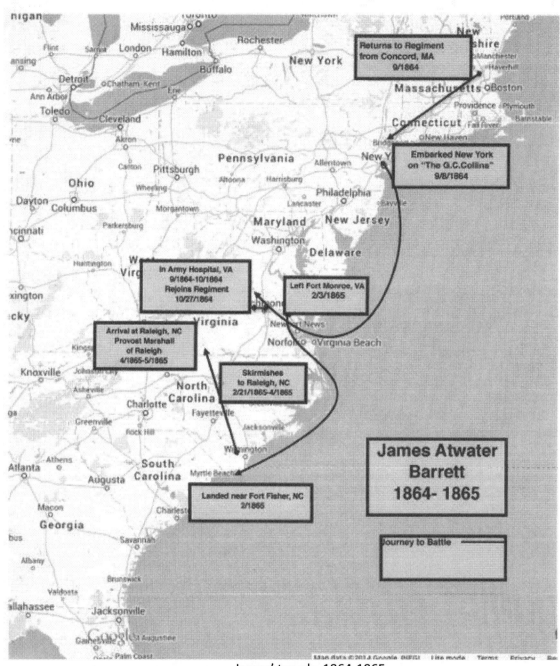

James' travels, 1864-1865
(Courtesy of Google INFGI, 2014)

[*James' diary entry]
Tues Sept 6 1864
Still rainy. Returned to N.Y. on noon train. Applied for transportation. Said
our boat had just gone, But we could have passage on another next day.

[This is Emma Jane's transcription of a letter written by James.]

New York   Sept 6 1864
My Dear Jennie   I presume you may have looked for @ letter before this   But I have really been very busy. We had @ very pleasant passage on   We all had to sit on separate seats I was so crowded & on the boat Staterooms were out of the question   I think the girls had to lie on the floor

I finally crept into @ berth & slept very well   I could not help thinking of the time I came on last   But we cant <u>always</u> have things to <u>our</u> <u>minds</u>   I hope you got home safely

I have been about considerable & met quite @ number of people in my travels   Our Major who resigned has been reappointed & is going back   I shall not go with him   He is going by rail to Balt^{re}   I expect to get passage by Steamer tomorrow

I came near going today   But could not well get on board

Mattie is home & very well   Lizzie has quite @ large family now   Mary is home & has improved very much. She is quite @ young woman

I have had several inquiries after you   You made quite a <u>favorable</u> <u>impression</u>   Uncle cant quite forget the <u>cousin</u>

He asks if you are not a cousin   Altho he knows perfectly well, I went to Bronx yesterday & returned today   I was real glad you went to Boston   I did not give you that ticket home after all. I will make it square sometime   I believe I owe you $50.⁰⁰ on a bet   Do you remember it. I do   But time enough yet, I did really enjoy our walk about Boston   I was only sorry it was not longer   I thank you ever so much for your candor   I feel that I know you better now & I can understand & appreciate your feelings   Do not think I am surprised or disappointed or that I shall love you less for it   It is perfectly natural. You have done me much good during the past year & I would not give up my experience with you for any price   I hope you will continue & be frank with me & whatever your feelings may be Or however they may change   The truth can never <u>harm</u> <u>us</u>

Altho perhaps it may <u>sometimes</u> <u>appear</u> <u>bitter</u> for the time   The fall of Atlanta is hailed with joy by all except Copperheads   The latter stock is dull just now   Rumor says McClellan will not accept the nomination

I am waiting anxiously to hear where Hood's army has gone. Rebel Pickets say Hood has lost 40000 men   The paper says the Rebel Army is demoralized

Times will tell   Grant is tightening his grasp & will be heard from soon   But I must stop as Gerrish is waiting

I met an old member of our Reg^t the other day & he almost eat me up   He was dreadful sorry I would not drink with him

Now Jennie don't worry about me   keep up a brave heart & drive dull care & gloomy thoughts away   Mrs Bates says she will <u>board</u> <u>us</u> <u>One</u> <u>Year</u>   I did not <u>engage</u>   But good bye   I must go   write often & believe me as ever

Yours

Jas A Barrett

[*James' diary entry]
Wed Sept 7 1864
The rebel, John Morgan[159] is killed & his staff taken prisoners at Anderson (Andersonville)—their sufferings are said to be intense. One of the worse things about this war is the rebel's treatment of our prisoners, But I suppose it is a natural result of their institutions. The <u>barbarity</u> of <u>slavery</u> has never yet been half exposed. What causes physical suffering in the slave, works out & develops moral degradation in the master. I hear that the Rebs are jubilant over the nomination of McClellan & that just in proportion as they show it, our own soldiers are set against him. Late news has made a great change in public feeling here. I see that Lincoln has requested prayers of thanksgiving to be offered in all our churches. I like this. It seems to show that he recognizes a higher power. "Man's necessity is God's opportunity." I have long felt a strong stimulant to my faith in the feeling that God is at the helm & that He will give us peace in his own good time.

[This is Emma Jane's transcription of a letter written by James.]

James River Va   Steamer "G. C. Collins"
Sept 11ᵗʰ 1864

My Dear Jennie

I am at last nearing my destination. We left N.Y. at 4 P.M. on Thursday & have had a very slow passage. A hole was found in our boiler soon after leaving & we had to anchor off Sandy Hook nearly 24 hours. This is a miserable old tub anyhow She has rocked so much that I have been seasick nearly all the way and have not been able to take my rations   I recovered however & ate a hearty supper last night and since then, have been able to punish my share   My wound discharges almost none at all   There is a Capt & Lieut of colored troops on board—very clever fellows. The Capt was in Maryland last year & knew Miss Ball & Brigham

---

[159] John Hunt Morgan (June 1, 1825-September 4, 1864) was a Confederate general and cavalry officer. Morgan is best known for Morgan's Raid when, in 1863, he and his men rode over 1,000 miles covering a region from Tennessee, up through Kentucky, into Indiana and on to southern Ohio. This would be the farthest north any uniformed Confederate troops penetrated during the war. Civil War Trust. (2014). John Hunt Morgan (n.d.). Retrieved December 4, 2015, from http://www.civilwar.org/education/history/biographies/john-hunt-morgan-1.html?referrer=https://www.google.com/

There is also a Serg^t who is returning to his regiment   We four are all the passengers on boardRather lonesome you may think But I have been busy reading "What will he do with it" by

Bulwer[160] I have read three vols Like it very much. The idea is that it does not depend so much what our chances are in life as <u>what we do</u> with the opportunities we have. How true this is I was thinking it over a long time as I stood on deck last evening—a splendid place for thought by the way. The arched Hearons overhead, the broad ocean on every side,--there is something soul inspiring in it. There is no place I know of, except perhaps it be a terrific thunder storm, where a man is brought so intimately in communion with his maker   as when alone on the broad bosom of the ocean I can sit for hours & the scene does not lose its charm.

Have you taken any rides around the back square lately   I am sorry we did not take that ride to the Cliffs, But never mind it will be pleasant to have some new places to go to <u>some other</u> time.

I sometimes think I am too lukewarm & allow myself to be too easily led away. I have been sorely tempted to leave the service   I am afraid I am not giving to my country one half the real true manly zeal that I get the credit for   You are not the only one Jennie, who at times think they hate themselves I have often despised myself So don't worry yourself with thinking you are different from others. Nothing perhaps is more natural that we should often feel dissatisfied with our best efforts. But enough of this.

I am now getting anxious to get to my journey's end & see my boys. If I am able, I intend to stay with them & I know God will watch over and keep me. I shall consult our surgeons and if they advise it, I may resign and be with you in time for Em's wedding

But I must close this and write a short note to Charlie. Poor fellow! Few know how much he has suffered But he mourns more for the pain he may have been instrumental in causing another, than for the part he has borne himself. He is a noble fellow. Gladly would he bear a double cross, if only the burden could be lifted from her. He is above anything mean or dishonorable and while some may blame, I can only pity him.

[This is Emma Jane's transcription of a letter written to James from Jennie.]
Concord   Sept 13 1864
My dear Jimmy,

We are having some more snow and it is very welcome. I presume we shall have a long time of it. They say that droughts are usually followed by cold winters

---

[160] Edward George Earle Lytton Bulwer-Lytton, 1st Baron Lytton (May 25, 1803-January 18, 1873), was an English novelist, poet, playwright, and politician. He was immensely popular with the reading public and wrote a stream of bestselling novels which earned him a considerable fortune. He coined the phrases "the great unwashed", "pursuit of the almighty dollar", "the pen is mightier than the sword," as well as the infamous opening line "It was a dark and stormy night." Edward Bulwer-Lytton. (November 6, 2015). *Wikipedia, The Free Encyclopedia*. Retrieved December 4, 2015, from https://en.wikipedia.org/w/index.php?title=Edward_Bulwer-Lytton&oldid=689319055

so we must prepare for one this year. I am longing to hear from you. Becca told me they had had a letter from Charley Gerrish telling of your sailing on Thursday.

I must tell you of Mr. Reynold's discourse last Sunday. It was very good. He said he went out feeling that his visit would be a sad one but he was surprised at the spirit of cheerfulness that pervaded scenes of suffering and death. Another thing that struck him was the self sacrifice of the soldiers—leaving of home and home ties. He said he heard a black preacher speaking to his colored brethren of their homes and the comforts they had left behind them and he thought if this were true of the poor black, how much more was it true of our N.E. men. He felt that we did not realize the sacrifices. Some gentleman who has been at the head of the Sanitary Commission for a long time, in speaking of bounties, said if a man came out and did his duty as a man and Christian should, we could not do too much for him. Another thing on which he dwelt at length was the manliness of the soldiers and the fortitude in sickness and pain. He saw from 11 to 15000 sick and wounded soldiers and did not hear the first groan. It was wonderful. He told of a little boy of thirteen who was sent on a message to General Sheridan and rode three miles after being shot in the leg, delivered his message and was then sent to the hospital. He saw him and he was as bright as a cricket—perhaps a trifle proud but that was excusable.

The profanity of soldiers is talked of a great deal but he has been 24 hours at City Point before he heard or noticed an oath from a soldier. There was ten times as much to be heard by the Captains, mates and sailors who were bringing stores to the place.

Then the black race had some words of interest. Although he had always been anti slavery in principle, he thought he had had something of a prejudice against the race, but when he saw them in the hospital, so patient, so grateful, he felt drawn toward them. It was the best place for overcoming such a feeling. He spoke of the great work of the Sanitary Commission. How great and yet how quiet was its work. He felt that he must try to do more for it than he had ever done before. Of the prospect of the close of the war, he said little but he spoke hopefully and as though he believed that it would soon close.

I do not think of much that is new. Mr. Howard was here Sunday and inquired for you. Abby is to board at Mr. Pierce's. It is a long way for her. I suppose she will not always go home for dinner. Mary Wood has about twenty scholars this term greatly to her delight. My school is very pleasant now although small. I do not know whether I shall be able to attend the tin wedding[161]. I would like to.

Good bye dear with <u>much love</u>

Jenny

---

[161] Tenth wedding anniversary celebration. Tin symbolizing flexibility. The give and take that makes a relationship strong. Tin also symbolizes preservation and longevity.

Carrie Hosmer expressed great admiration for a gentleman of my acquaintance. Don't reciprocate enough to make me <u>jealous</u>. I am going to cure myself of too much jealousy if possible.

[Fragment of letter written to Jennie from James on the 13th of Sept 1864. This is a transcription by Emma Jane that she included in the family collection.]

Your very welcome letter of 4th was here awaiting me when I arrived yesterday. The cars run from City Point nearly up here & then I rode in an ambulance. In the afternoon I was mustered as I am now a full blown Captain. I was very kindly received and welcomed back I found the reg^t much more comfortable here than I expected. Petersburg is in plain sight about a mile away. The front line is about ½ mile away. Yesterday there was a pretty hard artillery fire kept upon our left. I shall have to wait for the N.Y. papers to learn what it was all for & what army of the Potomac are doing. Our old men whose time is out and
who did not reenlist are daily expecting to be mustered out. They are very impatient & it makes me very homesick. We have only eight officers fit for duty & several of them are trying to push their resignation.

Capt Nichols is out of the service and has started home today in fine spirits. There is only one captain besides me here & he is not able for duty. If Col Coan goes home on leave, the command of the reg. would fall on one of us if we were on duty. I found my little nigger here with Lt Lacoppidan. He seemed very glad to see me back again. I found Pearsall in the ranks. He was reduced for being absent without leave. He went over to another Corps to witness an execution. There are doubtless <u>other</u> <u>reasons</u>. He has got the name of being a coward & everyone seems to think he deserves his sentence.

There is a lady in the 2nd Corps who sometimes takes command & gives orders to the reg. I have not seen her But some of the boys have. I think it is Mrs. Maj Pauline Cushman who used to speak last summer in Boston.

Our reg. has to work pretty hard now. They go out to the front 48 hrs. and then have to furnish fatigue parties after that. When the Jonnies attack us, they will find that they have stirred up a hornet's nest. One of our new officers walked right into the rebel's line a short time since while visiting his vidette[162]. It was the first time he went on duty. The Rebs sing out once in a while, "Send us over another officer." "If Capt Nichols will come over we will give him his haversack" &c.

Please give much love to all & accept an extra share for yourself

Yours

Jimmie

---

[162] A mounted sentry positioned beyond an army's outposts to observe the movements of the enemy. vedette. (n.d.). *Oxford Dictionaries*. Retrieved December 4, 2015, from http://oxforddictionaries.com/definition/american english/vedette

[*James' 'diary entries]
Wed Sept 14 1864

*Heavy firing this forenoon in our front. Heavy on our left in the afternoon.
Sent off 2ⁿᵈ Qr. Ordnance. Capt. Nichols' resignation accepted.*

Fri Sept 16 1864

*Rather stiff today. Wound broke out afresh. Discharges @ good deal. Lt.
McKellar's resignation returned disapproved. He is trying another tack.*

Sat Sept 17 1864

*Old men gone home today. Col. Coan with them. Capt. Hilliard in
command. Dr. Leete says I must not stay here. I have finished my last
return*

Tues Sept 20 1864

*Getting papers straightened. Regᵗ come in tonight. More of the W.R.R.[163]
taken. I am going to hospital soon. Can't stand it here.*

[*Letter]

> Hd Qtrs Co H. 48ᵗʰ Regᵗ N Y S V
> Near Petersburg   Sept 20 1864
> Yours of 17ᵗʰ is recᵈ

Dear Jennie

I have read it several times   I admire some of your sentiments   I can sympathize with you in the beauty of that Trusting Faith, which enables us to bear trials patiently & even happily

I feel that I have gathered strength & courage from it in the darkest hours

You need not think you owe me any thing perhaps the balance would be the other way Mattie Lyman does continue her school

Were those peaches good   I believe I <u>dreamed</u> they were <u>not</u> <u>very</u> <u>nice</u>.

I should think Lizzie would have a pretty large family   Altho I remember she said that when there were so many one more did not make much difference

I don't think I did think of <u>the</u> <u>circumstances</u> on the 16ᵗʰ   I was rather miserable that day My wound broke out at both ends & has been discharging profusely since   I have fixed up my accounts (all But the <u>Pay</u> <u>master</u> I have not seen him yet) & am going to Hospital tomorrow   I don't know where   perhaps Fortress Monroe   perhaps Annapolis   <u>perhaps</u> <u>somewhere</u> <u>else</u>   I will write & keep you posted   My letters will follow me

They do not want me to resign. My boys beg me to remain & come back to them if I am able. They offer to nurse & wait upon me &c   I am not suffering   My wound is rather uncomfortable as it discharges so much & I cant attend to it here as I could at home   Some joke me & say I have "<u>Crinoline</u> <u>On</u> <u>The</u> <u>Brain</u>"

---

[163] Weldon Railroad

You must not expect me home I may get there But I doubt if they will let me I hear they send all Convalescent Officers to Annapolis & put all who are able on duty of some kind   I am perfectly willing to do anything I am able to if I can feel that I am giving an equivalent for my pay, There has been a good deal of cheering at the front about the news from Sheridan   Isn't it good? He is really stirring them up finely

Pretty good <u>Peace</u> <u>documents</u> <u>those</u>   Deserters frequently come in   They all say they have had enough of charging our works   They say they are not going to lay in those trenches this winter

I have not heard from home yet   Are they all well   tell them I am still connected with the army of the Potomac   Do they hear from George (Barrett) or Henry Warren   Did Annie get a letter from Phil^a   I <u>dreamed</u> she did   But I believe in the dream she was not in any Hosp^l yet, I get my pictures out once in a while everyone likes that cos (costume) one of you the best   How does Nell get along at Bedford   Hartwell show what am I writing   Miller beside of me sends his <u>respects</u>   I think it is <u>respects</u>

Do you like a word of <u>fewer</u> letters better   If you have any occasion to teach Natural History you must study the habits & dispositions of <u>Bears</u> & how to manage them. It might save you from "<u>trembling</u>" sometimes   There is so much to attend to before leaving that I must close now   with much love

Good Night from Yours

Jas. A. Barrett

[*James' diary entries]
Wed Sept 21 1864
Hard to leave the boys. My wound does not discharge so much today.

Thurs Sept 22 1864
Went down to base hospital. Very comfortable here.

Fri Sept 23 1864
Rained last night. Found Barnes, Eckel, Erfurth & Dickson here. Sammy has gone to Fortress Monroe. Dykeman going into the navy.

Sat Sept 24 1864
Stormy still. Very heavy cannonading heard at the front this morning. My wound is getting very comfortable again. Read a letter from Stayley.

[This is Emma Jane's transcription of a letter written by James.]

10th Army Corps Hospl near Petersburg Va
Sept 24 1864

My Dear Jennie

I left or tore myself away from the reg· day before yesterday   I am now near Point of Rocks. I am afraid I shall miss my <u>regular</u> letters until I find where I am to stop. My men were very sorry to have me come away. It was really hard. Such devotion is not to be trifled with,   I almost felt as if I could lead them yet—cripple though I am. They would not listen to my resigning. They want me to come back & stay about even if I can not take the field.   I am not yet decided   I may be detailed at Fortress Monroe on court martial duty or something of that kind. If I can do any duty I feel I ought to be willing to do it. I should so like to see the end of this struggle. I do not think it is far off and I would like to go home with my co at last   But time will tell. I have about made up my mind that my fighting days are over   I doubt if my wound will allow me to march for a long time. But still I think that God has some purpose in sparing my life.

One of our Lieuts received a letter of dismissal last week from his lady. He showed it to me & told me all about it. He felt pretty bad & could not sleep. I comforted him all I could. One of my men came to me one day & gave me a long account of his family troubles. His wife had proved false to him. Poor fellow! He had suffered everything. He is leader of our band But had taken a musket & engaged in several severe fights just from desperation. He asked me if I could not get him a furlough to go to look after his children, But I could not do that. I told him to cheer up and hope for the best. The war cloud could not last much longer. Thus it is! As we travel over life's path, we little dream of the feelings which agitate the minds of those with whom we daily meet. If we did, should we not be more charitable? How often should we withhold our censure & give pity or praise instead!

Burr is nearly well again of his wound & is back with the co.   I found poor Sammy Hallsted—you may have heard me speak of simple Sammy—hardly able to crawl & still he was on duty & went to the front. I had him sent to hospital and I think he will be discharged or sent to the invalid corps. Sergt Garaghan will soon get his commission & will remain in my co.   I gave him several lessons & charged him above all, to look out for <u>my men</u>. He promised   He is a good fellow—a little childish perhaps But <u>brave</u> as the <u>bravest</u>. I expect to turn over my property to him when he is mustered, <u>unless</u> I am able to go back <u>myself</u> & take charge of the co.   There was a prospect that all co. clerks would have to go into the ranks so I got Miller detailed as brigade postmaster. He will be my clerk too.   Lt Lacoppidan is soon to be Capt. He used to be my Orderly Sergt. He wants to come back to Co H and now he thinks I may go out of the service. He offered to take my property off my hands, But I did not see it. My boys do not want him for Capt. I intend to see who my successor is to be before I give up my office, if I give it up at all.

Jennie I have thought several times of what you said to me one night about joining the church.   I do not think I expressed myself then as fully as I ought. I always feel a delicacy in advising in such matters, But still there are times when we all feel that we need an encouraging word from some dear friend to whom we can open our hearts. I have often thought of how you spoke to me & it has troubled me to think that I did not meet your question with the candor it surely deserved. I would by all means recommend you to the join the church if you feel a desire to do so. I know you are in every way fitted for it and the church would gain a valuable member and I think you would feel happier & more settled & anchored in your belief. I do not consider that you would be any better for doing this But you would in this manner take your stand, show your colors, & "let your light more clearly shine." Excuse me for speaking so tardily but better late than never. Please write often. Give much love to all friends & with a hearty God bless you I remain

Yours very affectionately
JamesA.Barrett

*[*James' diary entries]*

Mon Sept 26 1864

Adj. Maylow discharged. I rode up to the Reg^t. They are in camp in the rear under orders. Expect to be paid soon. Lt. Williams is discharged. Dickson deserted from North Line   Lacoppidan wants my co. I can't see it. The men say I must stay. A boat load of sick sent off. Roads are poor. Our corps some expect to go to N.C. Cheering heard at the front.

Tues Sept 27 1864   *One Capt. of 24th Mass. mustered out Another gone to try it. Returned @ citizen. More arrivals of sick etc. Flying hosp^l ^{164}moved down here.*

[*Letter]

10th Army Corps Hosp^l
Near Petersburg Va Sept 27 1864

Dear Mother

Your nice long letter of 20th inst reached me yesterday & right glad I was to get something to relieve the dullness of life here   Nothing to do is an intolerable bore I have been here nearly a week. I live well & am very comfortable   Yesterday I rode over in an ambulance to where the Reg is in camp. Our Corps has moved to the rear & are under marching orders. No one knows where they are going

Some say North Carolina   Some say south   Some again declare that they are going to Washington. I want to stay about here until the Reg^t gets paid off so as to help the boys send their

---

[164] By June of 1864, Clara Barton was appointed by the Army of the James Commander Major General Benjamin F. Butler to be in charge of diet and nursing at the X Corps hospital, dubbed a "flying hospital" because of its frequent moves to be close enough to the battle to help the wounded but not so close as to be overrun. Historynet. (n.d.). Clara Barton. Retrieved December 4, 2015, from http://www.historynet.com/clara-barton

money home. I also want to see the Col when he returns from the north. I shall then make some move for myself either to <u>do</u> <u>some</u> service or <u>leave</u> it My men declare they will desert if I leave them They say they want me to remain their Capt even if I cant do duty Only come & see them occasionally & keep a sort of fatherly care over them They say perhaps they may get into camp somewhere soon where I can be made comfortable &c &c Now don't repeat this nonsense I ought not to write such trash My wound is very comfortable now & discharges very little I only keep a patch of sticking plaster over it to prevent chafing I have some returns to make on the 30th I am getting restless with this idle life If I find any position I can fill I may get detailed I cant quite feel satisfied to leave the service now when Victory seems so near Almost every day brings some good news & if my feeble efforts can in any way aid our cause I surely can not withhold them I should think the McClellan party was pretty small if they are ashamed to come out like men & own up to their colors I think some <u>accident</u> might happen to the <u>flag</u> just to see who would care for it, I am glad to hear that the Indian troubles are quelled   What do you hear from George   Is he coming home

   Lizzie must have been pretty busy Did she get any premium? If not She must change her occupation & take to writing   I will vote her a premium She knows my address

   Pity that Mary cant get over that <u>chronic</u> <u>difficulty</u> of hers   I was in hopes she would get quite <u>smart</u> I have known a good flogging to drive away laziness before now   I am no Doctor   I dont presume to prescribe   I only <u>suggest</u> I have considered Em's case & <u>knowing</u> <u>something</u> as I <u>do</u> of her <u>forlorn</u> & <u>destitute</u> condition (Visions of days away)   I feel inclined to be magnanimous I therefore excuse her for all seeming neglect <u>in</u> not writing to me under existing circumstances & will endeavor to take the "will for the deed" so long the present claims upon her time continue

   I want to hear all about Cattle Show   I believe I was home last year on that occasion What did you all do for a Rendesvous   I presume Mary did not open her house

   I thought father was not going to attend this year

   Could not stay away   I see   Well I dont think I could myself   One of my men (a Frenchman) deserted to the Rebs the other night while on Vidette duty Another man saw him go But was so frightened that he did not think to shoot him I guess he will find that he has taken "a hard road to travel"   There is a very strong feeling among Army officers who have served 3 years against being kept in the service from their last muster   Many officers are determined to get out & they work all sorts of ways to do so   2 in this Hosp^l have been mustered out since I have been here & others are anxiously waiting Every effort is being made to return to duty every man who is able to bear arms

   It seems to be the general opinion that Grant is about to make some decisive move He has got John'y by the throat & is going to hold him

   When he contracts his hold   look out for that "last ditch" This Rebellion is fated <u>to</u> <u>die</u> <u>on</u> <u>this</u> <u>line</u>

   We wont have to wait long   The death blow has already been measured out   Only the "Crathure dont saim to be altogether sinsibil of it".

   We heard considerable cheering last night & there was a report that Petersburg was evacuated But I guess it was @ false report as I have heard nothing of it today What is the name of the Hosp^l where Sallie Barnes is I may visit Baltimore some time & I would like to call on her

There was a boat load sent from here yesterday   I think I could have gone if I had tried   But I am not ready yet

You need not feel at all uneasy about me   I am very well off here My wound is not so near well as I supposed when I left home & I rather suspect that my fighting days are over   But I have Youth Health Strength & a good constitution still & I am not yet convinced that these are entirely unserviceable in the Army even if I can not take the field I have rec^d Jennie's letter of the 20th   will answer soon It is now near supper time & the cook likes us to be punctual   I like to keep on the right side of the cook   So please give lots of love to all & believe me as ever

Yours very truly

James A Barrett

Direct as before

Chapter 18

Evacuation and Recuperation

September 28, 1864-October 23, 1864--Embarks on Monitor--Lands
in Bermuda Hundred, Virginia--Life in field hospital--Clara Barton
busy as usual--Descriptions of the wounded--Approaching
Richmond--Riot in Richmond--Cousin Ned Farmer is prisoner--
Deserters surrender and tell of conditions of rebel army--Description
of gallant colored troops--Upcoming Presidential election--
Sheridan's victories

[Note that all the following transcriptions have been faithfully copied from the original
document, as written by James, except where noted.]

*[*James' diary entries]*
Wed Sept 28 1864
Packing up to move. 10th Corps start at 3 A.M. The sickest sent north. Balance of us embarked on the Monitor165 & spent the night. Short for food. Managed to get some supper.

Thurs Sept 29 1864
Started early. Capt. can't give us breakfast Got some coffee at last from the steward below. Landed @ little above Bermuda166 About noon. Hospl established about a mile from landing. Gale is one hand with something to eat. News from front Boats sent for to get wounded men. Two lines of works taken, three forts, sixteen guns—10th & 18th Corps still advancing The troops first in Richmond to get 6 mos. extra pay Some wounded brought in here Spirits good. Report says that our troops are close to Richmond. Beds fixed up for us—very comfortable About 1000 convalescents here. Dr. Porter very active. Miss Barton 167 busy as usual. Several doctors sent to the front.

[James writes a letter to unknown recipient. This is a transcription by Emma Jane that she included in the family collection.]

Sept 30 1864

"Spring Hill"   "New Market Heights"   "Fort Gilmer"

We are now on an elevated position about a mile from Jones' landing & about four miles from Bermuda. The 10th & 18th Corps are "Onward to Richmond."   Three lines of works were taken yesterday. On the second line there were three strong forts mounting 16 guns. These were

---

165 "A monitor was the class of relatively small warship that was sometimes used as a generic term for any turreted ship that was neither fast or strongly armored. This type of warship was used from 1860 to 1870. Monitor (warship). (2016, December 27). In *Wikipedia, The Free Encyclopedia*. Retrieved December 27, 2016, from
https://en.wikipedia.org/w/index.php?title=Monitor_(warship)&oldid=756904802
166 A settlement founded by Sir Thomas Dale in 1613 and became the first incorporated town in the English colony of Virginia.
167 Referring to Clara Barton (December 25, 1821-April 12, 1912), U.S. philanthropist and pioneer nurse who founded and organized the American Red Cross in 1881. She was born Clarissa "Clara" Harlowe Barton. In addition to being a nurse, she worked as a teacher and patent clerk. During the end of the Civil War Clara worked at a hospital she built helping the people at the Andersonville prison camp where at least 13,000 people died. Clara Barton. (December 3, 2015). *Wikipedia, The Free Encyclopedia*. Retrieved December 4, 2015, from https://en.wikipedia.org/w/index.php?title=ClaraBarton&oldid=693588646

taken with small loss to our side—the enemy being completely surprised. Our loss later in the day, before the third line was considerable. I cannot give details yet. I am waiting anxiously to hear from <u>my</u> <u>orphaned</u> <u>boys</u>. I might have gone north with the other officers, But I want to linger near to my reg, until they are paid & I can put things into shape to suit me & benefit my men. Poor fellows! I fear they are having pretty rough times. There have been several of the wounded brought here. They speak very hopefully. Our troops are supposed to be within four miles of Richmond.

We are hardly settled here yet. It is a great job to move a hospital like this, with its tents, bedding & stores. It is quite a problem to feed them all. There are about 1000 men here in the convalescent camp, besides all the sicker ones in the several wards and sections. My section has 14 officers in it. We occupy one half the room or section which is four large tents joined together. Three of these sections make a ward and we have six or eight wards besides the surgeons', cooks' and ladies' tents. There are three ladies who follow the hospital and they have one large tent. I don't know what they do. I have seen one of them—a Miss Barton—going about among the men considerably & making herself useful. I do not think it a very good place for ladies.

[*James' diary entries]
Fri Sept 30 1864
Slept pretty well. Good breakfast   Gale gave us ham   potatoes   bread tomato   mince pie & coffee. Square meal   We pronounce Gale a trump Rather cloudy. Nurses very busy leveling off the tents before it may rain. Rained hard in afternoon   Our brigade in action at the front.

Sat Oct 1 1864
Stormy still. Our troops advancing towards Richmond.

Sun Oct 2 1864
Walked down to wagon train   Saw Paddock & Hutchinson. Corp. Walling captured. Lt. McKellar discharged. Lt. Himrod dismissed for being in the rear. Several officers of other Reg^{t}s fare the same. Butler rules. Capt. Finley 76th Pa was dismissed & he had surgeon's excuse.

An Emma Jane's pen and ink embellishment
(Barrett Collection)

Mon Oct 3 1864
Paymaster to pay the men tomorrow   Stoney has brought me my letters.
Stormy day.

Tues Oct 4 1864
Nothing from Reg^t today. Finished reading the "Cavalier." Wrote @ letter
in afternoon. Q.M. moved over the river. Has got to come back.

Wed Oct 5 1864
Weather clear & warm. All quiet.

Fri Oct 7 1864
Heavy firing heard on the right   Wounded cavalry come in   11th Pa. cav
badly cut up. Our infantry check & repulse the enemy with great loss to
them. 400 deserters come in. Some very bad wounds.

Sat Oct 8 1864
Dr. Mulford assigned to duty here. Lt. Edwards joined Reg^t yesterday not
knowing he was discharged.

> *[Emma Jane's transcription of Emily's journal entry]*
> *Oct. 8, 1864*
> *Had a letter from James this week saying that he was in
> the hospital. His wound was discharging more than when he left
> home and he thought his fighting days were over, but he might be
> able to do some detail service.*

*[*James' diary entries]*
Sun Oct 9 1864
Wrote some letters for wounded men. Very cold weather. Several
commissions   received for regiment also 30 recruits arrived   I have
some pleurisy[168] today

---

[168]Pleurisy is an inflammation of the membrane that surrounds and protects the lungs (the pleura). Inflammation occurs when an infection or damaging agent irrates the pleural surface. As a consequence, sharp chest pains are the primary symptom of pleurisy. pleurisy. (n.d.) *FARLEX PARTNER MEDICAL DICTIONARY*. (2012). Retrieved September 29 2016 from http://medical-dictionary.thefreedictionary.com/pleurisy

Mon Oct 10 1864
*Heavy firing heard near Petersburg   Riot in Richmond   49th Corps
expected at Bermuda   Lt. Edwards left for home. Dr. Mulford assigned to
our ward   One division of cav from Sheridan came in this morning.
Weather cold.*

Tues Oct 11 1864
Weather milder.

Wed Oct 12 1864
*Several left today   Rainy in afternoon   Col. Coan back with Capt.
Ferguson   Recruits expected   My wound discharging some*

Thurs Oct 13 1864
*Wound comfortable   Col. Coan talks of going home   Lt. Seward returned
to duty   Capt. Ferguson returned to Reg^t Can't muster yet. Rumor says
that many deserters are coming in   Several Lts. left hospital for their
regiments   Our right advancing   Fighting all day.*

Fri Oct 14 1864
*Our loss heavy yesterday 1st & 3rd Division engaged   About 1000 killed &
wounded. One fort taken on right. Deserters come in fast. Had @ talk
with the surgeon in charge. He thinks I can find something to do soon.*

[Letter from Charles P. Gerrish]

New York October 15 1864

Dear Jim

I have received your letters of the 24 ultimo[169] and 3^d inst, and should have written you before, but I have been very busy indeed, and have found it difficult to keep up my correspondence· You ask me to advise you what to do· Now if you are unfit for active duty, and your wound would do better at home, than where you are, I think your duty is plain to return, but in the other hand if you can be of service where you are, without endangering your health, and without neglecting the means to restore your health, you would consult the good of your

---

[169] Of the previous month.

country by remaining, and perhaps would gain nothing by coming home·
It is hard for me to advise you, as I have done so little for my country·
it might not seem very consistent in me to advise you to remain·   Did
any opportunity for business open you might feel differently, because as
you are no longer a fighting man, the success of the Campaign does not
depend upon you as it otherwise would, I will endeavor to enroll your
name next week, and then send you the necessary blanks, I see that
soldiers in Hospitals are furloughed home to vote·   Had you not better
come home, vote, and advise with your friends what to do·   One thing
seems imperative, that you should take the best care of your health·
Just at present, business is very quiet, and will be probably until after
the election,   we are going to elect Lincoln and Johnson by an
overwhelming vote· and the rebellion must soon cave in,   have you seen
Jeffs speech delivered at Macon Ga· that tells the Story· Mrs· Bates is
at Plymouth making a visit, Martha is housekeeper, Bates is deep in the
Petroleum business, expect now to make a fortune,   Rockwood has been
here for the last few days,   Flora meets my highest expectations except
in her hind legs, she interferes badly & I have had to boot her   They tell
me colts are apt to until they get their gait,   Is this true?

Yours truly

C·P· Gerrish

[*Narrative]
During all this time My reg^t was constantly active & fought at Strawberry plains, Petersburg, Chapin's farm &c   I spent my time in camp or in field Hosp^l when the reg^t was on the march as I could not march

[*James' diary entries]
Sat Oct 15 1864
Sent home to Gerrish $500.00 in 73/10 treasury notes viz:--
Aug. 15, 1864 no. 69310—3 yrs.--$50.00
Aug. 15, 1864 no. 69313—3 yrs.--$50.00
Aug. 15, 1864 no. 69316—3 yrs.--$50.00

Aug. 15, 1864 no. 69319—3 yrs.--$50.00
Aug. 15, 1864 no. 69334—3 yrs.--$50.00
Aug. 15, 1864 no. 69337—3 yrs.--$50.00
Aug. 15, 1864 no. 92653—3 yrs.--$100.00
Aug. 15, 1864 no. 92656—3 yrs.--$100.00
These all made to my order—interest payable every 6 mos.

Sun Oct 16 1864
Pleasant quiet day. Firing heard during the night. Discussion on the merits of Christian & Sanitary Commissions. No lives lost!

Mon Oct 17 1864 *Weather cool but pleasant Occasional firing heard*

Tues Oct 18 1864 *Made up returns of ordnance for 3rd Quarter & C.C. & G.E. for Sept Drew stationery for October*

Wed Oct 19 1864 *Drew up application for furlough for @ man in hospital. Rode up to the front in ambulance Stopped with Regt two hours Our works very strong Graves very thick along the way. The works that our troops carried were protected by two lines of abertee I can't see how we took them.*

Thurs Oct 20 1864 *Heavy firing heard towards night in our front. It is said to be in honor of Sheridan's later victories*

[This is Emma Jane's transcription of a letter written by James.]

10th Army Corps Base Hospl Oct 21 1864

My Dear Jennie

Yours of the 15th is today received. I am very sorry to hear that Ned is captured. His lot must be a hard one It is useless to disguise it A prisoner among barbarians can not hope for much comfort But I think he is better off there than if he were farther north, especially as cold weather is coming on. I am very hopeful that Sherman will soon be able to release our poor fellows who are famishing in those Southern prisons I see he has Hood on the jump again. Hood thought he could out General Sherman and cut off his supplies, but he did not sufficiently weigh the ability of his adversary. He hoped to crush Sherman and came very near being himself crushed instead.

Last night the heavy roar of cannon announced another grand victory for Sheridan—our brave hero of the valley. Deserters continue to come in freely. They all tell the same story—short rations and insufficient clothing for the coming cold weather. We have again lost our corps commander—Gen. Birney died at Philadelphia of a malignant fever a few days since. I wish we could get our old and tried Gen. Gillmore back again, but I suppose there is little hope of that so long as we remain in Butlers command.

I rode up to the front the other day and saw where so many of our gallant colored soldiers fell while storming the enemy's works on the 29th ult It was an awfully hard line to take—a double line of abertee. Fallen trees & thick underbrush obstructed their progress;   but they pressed on resolutely and finally drove the panic stricken hordes of F.F.V. (First Families Virginians) before them.   Little mounds of fresh earth thickly dot the place.   These are soldiers' graves.   No monument marks the spot—not even a head board to record the names and deeds of those who slumber there. But the recording angel is ever at work and every word & deed receives at that upper court its proper name and value, and Nature will plant her choicest flowers to bloom over those nameless graves.

I found my company pretty comfortable in camp just in the rear of our breastworks. They have improved their time in making their position impregnable.   They seem healthy & tough.   I am intending to go up to spend a few days next week with them and help make out the payroll. We are expecting 300 recruits in a few days. So you see I am likely to have some work to do and whether I remain or not, I should hardly be able to be present at Em's wedding.   I would be very glad to be there but in these times, we must ignore personal desires & devote our talents (even though it be But one) and energies to the public good

I admire your enthusiasm in the coming Presidential contest.   What a pity you could not "just wear the breeches" for a little while,   but I rather think it is better as it is after all. Look out that Benjy votes "all right" and "let your light shine etc, etc." I wrote today for some ballots to enable me to vote   I don't intend to lose my vote. Agents are busy in the army collecting the soldiers' votes, but I have not been able to get any local tickets and I intend to go the whole ticket. I am afraid we have a few unsound cousins. Can't you discipline them? No harm in trying.

We get considerable reading, such as it is.   We manage to make our time pass pretty rapidly.   Your quotation is an eloquent eulogy, or rather description of a well spent life. There are very few such positive characters to be found.   We find too many of actual negative characters instead.   We are too apt to allow some few sprigs of wheat we feel conscious of to blind our eyes to the multitude of thistles that are also scattered through the field.

You may expect great things during the next month.   The election of "Old Abe" will give fresh vigor to our troops and at the same time carry terror to the hearts of our enemies.   I shall not be satisfied with simply victory.   I hope to hear of overwhelming majorities so that there shall be no room for a rebel to base @ hope upon. Look out for Benjy and the cousins and satisfy yourself that you have voted. Now Jennie good bye with lots of love from

Yours affectionately
James A.Barrett

[*James' diary entries]
Fri Oct 21 1864
Writing all day   Received four letters   Chaplain Taylor returned Took tea with us

Sun Oct 23 1864
Cool & pleasant   Chaplain Taylor is to have quarters here

                                                                    Mon Oct 24 1864
[James writes a letter to unknown recipient (possibly Jennie). This was transcribed by Emma Jane and included it in the family collection.]

I sent up word this A.M. to have a place fixed for me. My reg· are now in charge of a fort recently built on our line of works and have no picket duty to do. I am going to see how I stand it. The boys think they can make me comfortable and I am tired of lying off. You may depend that "all is for the best.".... I am glad to hear that Dr. Bartlett thinks it worth his while to keep up his interest in me. I value his friendship very highly.   Sheridan's victories rush upon us thick and fast   He is indeed a hero.   He fairly snatched victory out of the very jaws of defeat.   Sheridan absent –his army was forced back in riot and confusion.   Sheridan present-order at once took the place of chaos and his war worn veterans, inspired by the presence of their chief, returned to the contest and hurled back with interest upon the surprised and astonished foe,   the panic and confusion which so lately infected <u>them</u>. Well may the country be loud in the praise of Gen. Sheridan. Grant says, "He is one of our ablest generals" and nobly has he won the title. I am getting jealous of Sheridan, Sherman and Farragut. But be not impatient. Our Gen- is not to be outdone. He is <u>the great</u> planet yet and surveys from his orbit all his minor luminaries! His plan comprehends the whole! Richmond is tottering before his iron will and Rebellion itself is destined soon to humble itself and acknowledge in him its master.

It is getting pretty well along towards election   I am very much afraid the 48<u>th</u> are under bad influence and we'll pull a great many votes for McClellan. I am anxious to get up and try to turn the tide a little. A little thing will sometimes turn the current of public opinion   No harm in trying anyhow.....

I have subscribed to Fowler & Wells[170] monthly. I think I will send them to you after I have read them if you would like them.

A Christian Commission man has just brought in some grapes   They were very good. Somehow my thoughts seemed to wander to Annursnack's <u>quiet</u> <u>shade</u> where they used to hang so <u>plentifully</u>. <u>Strange</u>, wasn't it?

So Annie did tell you all about the "little minister." She told me as a profound secret and charged me not to speak of it even to you. I laughed and told her she could not keep it from you, but she declared she could. Time has told the story and I see I was right for once.

---

[170] Fowler and Wells published *Herald of Health*, a monthly magazine.

Chapter 19

I Have No Taste for Army Life

October 26, 1864-November 23, 1864--Returns to regiment--
Executes vote--Witness of hatred of abused Negroes--Grant's push
into Richmond--Lincoln reelected--Sister Emily's wedding--
Description of living quarters

[Note that all the following transcriptions have been faithfully copied from the original document, as written by James, except where noted.]

Wed Oct 26 1864
Returned to regiment.

Thurs Oct 27 1864
General movement of our troops   Our regiment left in charge of fort.
Fighting in our front   Wounded men come in

Fri Oct 28 1864
Commenced pay rolls   Our Corp. returned   We have lost several hundred
Rumor of victory on left

Sat Oct 29 1864
Officer of the day   At work on pay rolls   Two rolls done   our right drove in.
Line reestablished.

[*Letter]
Hd Qtrs   Co H 48th Regt N.Y.S.Vol.
New Richmond Va   Oct 30 1864
My Dear Jennie

Yours of 23d recd yesterday you rather mistake my ambition I stand no chance I could not be mustered without a Surgeon's Certificate. There is a late order forbidding it. I have just executed my Vote. I consider it a Religious act. I never considered my vote so important as now. I need not tell you how I voted. I look forward to the Election as The Harbinger of Good or Evil to this Nation. The great battle field of this Campaign is now stretched out before our people like a huge Panerama. Oh that every man who has @ vote to cast could see the conflicting views in the background   One or the other of which is to be stamped upon this canvas of our national life by that simple (But oh! how powerful) act. The Ballot. I do feel anxious for the result. The issue of @ Battle before Richmond is as nothing compared to it. Did you go to Sudbury? If so I hope you appreciated your responsibility There is nothing like having a right start you know

I am happy to hear about Ned I only wish it was to learn of his escape   You must feel anxious about him altho it is a relief to know that he is well

You say you "found a note from your Mother" Where is she? So you have got into new business (Refooting Stockings) I object! Please record it. I think you have enough to do to "Teach the young i- - - - " Dressmaking corresponding (for yourself & others) &c &c &c &c. Besides of course Benjy requires some attention. I see you must be busy. I see I will have to get a furlough. But this cant be done. Never mind I guess I can risk things a while longer.

I have just done an unpleasant duty. I have given the Oath of election to a man who voted for McClellan   But fair play is a jewel & I cant refuse a vote But I have cancelled it by another for Lincoln. You must discourage the notion Annie has that she cant succeed with Sarah

She must learn to be Self reliant to assert her own individuality & earn her title to it The greater the difficulty the greater the satisfaction in overcoming it. If you look on your map on the North of the James River you can locate me about 5 or 6 miles from Richmond & south of it

I was on camp duty as Officer of the Day yesterday There was not much to do   I was some tired at night I do not undertake anything I cant do. Our Corps returned yesterday. Did not accomplish much this way But lost 3 or 400 men   I believe they had better success on the left I presume that was where Grant intended to win & meant this for a diversion or feint[171]

I hear that he took the South side road & several thousand prisoners.   But as to these details as usual we must wait for the N.Y. papers to tell us what we have suffered & what we have gained. The army does make a sort of machine of men We execute orders without even knowing their object. & then have to wait for the papers to tell us whether or not we have executed them or not Since I left the Hospl an order has been recd there to allow patients a leave of 15 days to go home & vote

But I have just fairly got broke in Nov& I don't know as I care to go home for so short a time It would only make me homesick for another month We were all turned out yesterday afternoon to man our works   Our pickets were driven in on the right But our line was reestablished

Our works are very strong here We can hold our position until the Rebs are grey. I must close now & work on the muster Rolls I will answer Nell's letter soon also Becky's I inspected my Co this morning   They are pretty well off I would like to go to church with you this P.M. But live in hope. Good bye for this time with much love from yours affecly

Jimmy

[*James' diary entries]
Mon Oct 31 1864
Mustered by Col. Moore 203rd Pa   Finished my rolls all myself

Tues Nov 1 1864
Made up returns for C.C. & G.E. for October   Executing votes

Thurs Nov 3 1864
1st Div. left yesterday   It is said that an attack was made on our works at Bermuda three times yesterday & repulsed

Fri Nov 4 1864   *Sent the companies out for logs to build quarters. Storm has cleared away & the sun is out again.*

Sat Nov 5 1864   *Gen. Butler & several regiments gone to N.Y. We can hear the Rebs cheering in our front about something*

---

[171] A misleading action or appearance. feint. (n.d.). *Collins English Dictionary*. Retrieved December 16, 2015, from http://www.collinsdictionary.com/dictionary/english/feint

Hd Qtrs Co H. 48th Regt Infy N.Y. S. Vols
In the Field Near Richmond Va Nov 5 1864

My Dear Jennie

Your very welcome interesting letter of 1st inst arrived this morning It rather took me by surprise as it came one day quicker than usual. Our mails are very regular now. It seems to me that it takes a long time for my letters to reach you. I think you are getting quite <u>domestic</u>. Have you a <u>taste</u> for it? Or are you only <u>breaking in</u> view of "<u>Coming</u> events &c &c." I think you must have had considerable fun over at Sudbury. I laughed over your account of Dinner. I dont see but Em has got a pretty good "start" "What will she do with it" remains to be seen I hope she may be happy I think she will. But perhaps she anticipates <u>too</u> much I hope <u>you</u> wont think <u>me</u> quite such a lump of <u>perfection</u> as <u>She</u> does <u>Him</u>. I should dread the process of <u>Disenchantment</u>. Don't you fear for my army attachments.

When the <u>time</u> <u>comes</u> the links will be broken like threads of Glass. I am no military genius. I have no <u>taste</u> for Army life. But I have a work to do here & I shall thank God when that is finished. Whatever success I have been blessed with I owe to a fair knowledge of human nature an easy temper & the Blessing of God.   The condemnation which Mr. Reynolds applies to a Party is applicable I think to many more than that party embraces   It is almost discouraging sometimes to witness how universal the hatred to the abused negro is.   Few very few have manhood enough to openly acknowledge him as One of God's children & entitled thereby to all the rights which belong to <u>American</u> <u>Citizens</u>. I should think these people thought that God made a serious mistake in creating the black man. This war <u>is</u> for the black man.   just as truly as the ancient <u>war</u> against Pharioh was for the Israelites But it is not yet judicious to declare it in that light. Christ did not declare the whole truth The people were not ripe enough for it. "The (whole) Truth is not to be spoken at all times"

Our struggle has commenced I trust the 1st lesson is well nigh learned & that our great national wound is <u>cauterized</u> almost enough   But the great questions of Citizenship Suffrage Social position &c &c are yet to be met.

Do you think you would enjoy a school in Bedford as well as your own. Changes are generally <u>experiments</u>

Poor Charlie Bowers I pity him Is he out of the service? I understand that Genl Butler & Staff & several of our Veteran Regts have gone to N.Y.   It is supposed to quell <u>riots</u>   How shameful it is that such @ caution should be necessary in this our <u>boasted Free</u> & <u>Republican America</u> I do wish that <u>suffrage</u> was limited (at least) to such as can read & write   Our foreign element help us some in fighting our Battles   But they are an element of weakness in our Government. None can deny that

They are the stock from which Riots are born. We are under marching orders Last night we had orders to cook 3 days rations & pack our baggage ready to march at @ moments notice We were up late expecting to leave for some part unknown (There is a good deal contained in that word) But I guess we shall remains here after all I understand that an attack was anticipated & that our caution was for the Defensive

We think Lee is anxious to gain some success soon to influence Election   We are proceeding with our work on Winter quarters.   A few days more & the result of the Election will be known to us   God grant that it may be such as to cheer our hearts.   Can it be that we have drank the bitter cup of experience for the past 3 years in Vain? Heaven forbid   But if it should be so

There is a just God in Heaven still. & He will not suffer a Sparrow to fall without his notice   That we may always be submissive to His will is the earnest Prayer of

Yours sincerely
James A. Barrett

[*James' diary entries]
Sun Nov 6 1864
Heard two sermons—one by Mr. Taylor & one in 203rd Pa

Mon Nov 7 1864
Rainy. Splendid bow   On the alert for an attack.

Emma Jane's embellishment for November
depicting the election campaign for President and Vice President
(Barrett Collection)

[This is Emma Jane's transcription of a letter written by James.]

Army of the James in the Fields
Hd Qtrs Co H. 48th Regt N.Y.S.Vols
Near Richmond Va November 9 1864
Dear Cousin Story

Yours of 4th inst is recd I should have gone to your rooms when in B if I had had more time But I could only have called anyhow. I suppose you are happily over Election   I say happily   For I do not consider the result as doubtful. I feel certain that Lincoln will be reelected by a tremendous majority. I should much deplore any other termination to this exciting Campaign   Our Brigade gave Old Abe 24% majority-. Truly the right of suffrage is a Sacred right this fall. I was glad that my Vote counted in N.Y. I think it is not needed in Massachusetts I am glad to hear that you are up to the times & doing what you can for the good cause. People are too selfish We have too little real genuine Public spirit among us.

Prejudice is deeply rooted in our natures & very readily joins its influence to that of Selfishness Together they make their rounds & Many (otherwise) noble natures have been blighted by their withering touch We are too often influenced by policy or some other unworthy motive & almost if not entirely lose sight of the Eternal principles of Truth justice & Humanity. One would think that after the scourgings we have had We should cease to "Harden our hearts" & listen to the "Lessons of the hour" Surely it seems to me they are written as plainly as were "The Commandments of old on the tablets of Stone" on every passing event & Yet Alas for the blindness or stubbornness of our people We allow these priceless tablets to be dashed down & broken before the Altar of @ popular prejudice gainst a poor despised & downtrodden Race

God grant that the Election of yesterday may prove that there are yet enough "Righteous men" to save our Country from the utter Ruin & Moral Degradation that has so long threatened to destroy us. The approaching National Thanksgiving will be a fitting tribute to this joyful news which I feel confident will so soon greet my anxious ears

Well would I like to be with you on that happy anniversary as also the equally happy event of coming week which is to join two loving hearts in one sole bond of Union. But I bow submissive to the stern decree which bids me deny myself his pleasure & walk yet a little longer in the less attractive path which which Duty & Providence have marked out for me. But though absent in person I shall be there in spirit join my humble Prayer with yours & others that the Blessing of Heaven may rest on those assembled there.

My health continues good my wound has healed But I dare not yet attempt full duty

My back bone still seems weak & I dare not yet attempt to ride Horseback. Captains on full duty have to serve as Brig Officers of the Day & this obliges them to ride considerable But we are stationed now in charge of a Fort here & I find a good deal that I can do. We are very short of Officers now especially those who have had experience. We have been having considerable stormy weather of late But it is fine now We are building winter quarters They will be very comfortable. Our Post is impregnable. With much love I remain Truly yours

James A Barrett

[*James' diary entry]
Sat Nov 12 1864
Received letter from P.M. S.N.Y. Maj. C.W. Gulick N.Y.S. P.M. is in the field paying bounties Signed for the property of Co. A

[*Letter]

Hd Qrts Co H. 48th N.Y.S.Vols
Novr 12 1864

My Dear Jennie

Yours of 5th & 8th both arrived this morning   I suppose Election has interfered with the mails   But I will not complain considering the result   Isnt it splendid. Now we will soon see this thing ended & Our Country "Born again" into a higher nobler life than we have ever yet dreamed of. I think we ought to establish a mission to Colonize all the Crestfallen Copperheads in some out of the way place with a view of civilizing & Christianizing them. I am glad you appreciate Stayley's letter   Perhaps he could be induced to stop chewing (My Sergt & (Lt Now) Garaghan has) by a little gentle influence. I have Em's card   I think it is very plain & neat But too large. I shall not be there except in spirit   But I shall not forget the night nor to breath an earnest God bless them in their new relations. I sign for the property of Co "A" again today. They profess to be pleased that I am to assume the charge of them once more   I am pretty smart   I do everything here except Brigade Officer of the Day. That is too much for me at present   Our winter quarters are nearly completed   The men have very comfortable little houses   But I doubt if we enjoy them long There is a strong prospect that our Corps will go to South Carolina. I presume to take Savannah & open communication with Sherman. It may be nothing But rumor But things look that way now. Our Chaplain was telling the other day about a wounded Rebel in our Hospl while under the influence of Chloroform he raved like a crazy man   "Oh what a horrid flag That secesh rag   God forgive me for ever fighting against the good old Flag   What can my father think of me But God knows I could not help it &c &c"   His father was from Penna   He was born south & attending school when the war broke out. His teacher raised a Co. & told him he would have to go anyhow & so he went with his schoolmates. This is not an isolated case   I believe there are thousands in the Rebel Army who would rejoice to see the old flag once more restored & waving triumphantly over their Chastened homes   God only knows how soon that day will come   But I cannot think it will be long delayed.   The strifes of the past have developed a profound respect among the southern people for their formerly despised brethren of the north   Sunday I was interrupted yesterday to sign for Lt Schultz's property. I had no trouble   But I spent a good portion of the afternoon & evening in assisting another officier in settling his accounts to go home

Today I am Regt Officer of the day   I will send you another of Stayley's letters in this letter or my next   I enclose a small picture of my Co. I have some views that I shall send soon   There is strong talk about our going to South Carolina. I don't credit it

I am very happy about the election   Nearly every State has asserted its Manhood   A few more blows now & all will be well. It is so cold today that I can hardly write & I have considerable to attend to. So I know you will excuse me for not filling my sheet

With much love I remain

Yours ever
James A. Barrett

Cant you steal one of lucy's pictures for Stayley   Nell must not be getting fickle

(a)

FORM 2—(b.)

Invoice of Ordnance and Ordnance Stores, *turned over by* Lieut Col Wm B Coan Com of 45th Regt Infty, N.Y.V. *to* Captain Jas A. Barrett, 45th N.Y.V. *at* Chaffins Farm, Va *on the* 14th *day of* November, 1864

(See notes on outside.)

in obedience to

NO. OF BOXES.	MARKS.	CONTENTS.	WEIGHT.	VALUE, per piece or lb.
2	Two	Bayonet Scabbards		
1	One	Cap Pouch		
1	One	Cartridge Box		
6	Six	Cartridge Box Plates		
4	Four	Cartridge Box Belts		
3	Three	Gun Slings		
18	Eighteen	Cartridge Box Belt Plates		
1	One	Waist Belt		
	1500	Rounds Elongated Ball Cartridges. Cal .577.		

The value of all Stores issued from an Arsenal, Armory, or Ordnance Depot, must, if possible, be stated.

I certify, *That the above is a correct Invoice of Ordnance and Ordnance Stores turned over by* me *this* 14th *day of* November, 1864, *to* Captain James A. Barrett

Wm B Coan
Lieut Col Comd 45th N.Y.Vol.

(IN DUPLICATE.)
(B. 22, 12. (3, 200.)

Form 2(b) Invoice of ordnance and ordnance stores
(Barrett Collection)

Thurs Nov 17 1864

Officer of the day   Not much to do   Officers' lesson in evening

Fri Nov 18 1864

Rebuilding our house. Drilling recruits two hours in afternoon   Pretty tired
Commenced raining   House not finished. Firing on our left. Turned out
N.C.O. School in A Co. interrupted in H. Co. to fall in.

Sun Nov 20 1864

Very stormy   Our house not very comfortable   The stove draws well Will
try to finish tomorrow   Received des list of Eugene Michon endorsed—
transferred to duty Aug. 1864.

[*Letter]
Hd Qrts Co H. 48th N.Y. Vols
In the Field Va Nov 20 1864
My Dear Jennie   Yours of 13th came to hand this A.M.   I had been looking for it for several days. I suppose you are now enjoying your short Vacation   Last Wednesday must have been a busy day with you   I want to hear about Em's wedding   I <u>know</u> you come off with flying colors from your School. You always did. Thank you for your description of the Bridal outfit. Of <u>course</u> I can understand & <u>see</u> the <u>whole</u> <u>thing</u>   I suppose Em is fairly settled down now & as much at home as if she had lived there always. I am no longer on the sick list   But I have it understood that I shall not go on Brigade Officer of the day   I drilled the Recruits 2 hours on Friday   It made me pretty tired   But I got through with It   The Rebs have attacked our line several times a little to our left lately   But as yet they have not thought fit to molest us. We frequently have alarms   But they only result in our turning out in a little less time than you can count 3 & manning the Fort. Our Regt is stationary here for the present. Our neighbors have harder duty. Lt Lacoppidan & I took down our house Friday to move it @ little & make it larger   It began to rain soon after & we rebuilt under difficulties   But we are getting settled again now & I have just nailed up a Cracker box for a table to write on. My wound has all healed up & I am getting strong every day   It is raining hard today & I have to keep our stove stuffed full all the time to make it comfortable   Our house is about 12 feet by 7 & the sides about 5 feet high. It is made of logs & the cracks are filled with mud.

Emma Jane's sketch of a log cabin
(Barrett Collection)

Our chimney is not finished   It is built of logs also plastered thick on the inside with mud. We hang papers around the sides to keep the pitch off. I had a letter from Charly today   It seems he did not go to the wedding   I hardly thought he would.   They have engaged a Mr Chadwick to preach for them   He is to be settled soon   I judge he is of the Longfellow style   Dr Farley says that if He was going to live his life over again He would ignore the little Church.   It is just like the Rev Dr   Very conservative & very jealous of his old opinions   Capts Carleton & Taylor & Lt Acker & Schultz have been mustered out & gone home   We hear that 3 or 400 Recruits are coming to us But they dont come   There is no news to write   I think with you that those journals are rather "one sided."   Please give the enclosed to Rebecca   I find I am getting ragged

There is a report that Banks (Nathaniel Prentice) is to be called to the Cabinet (Chief justice) & Butler Sect^{ry} of War.   If the latter is true   Things will have to move   Butler is an industrious man   But I have no confidence in him as a man   We are all very anxious to hear from Sherman.   He will turn up somewhere soon with a heavy blow to Rebellion.   There was a rumor that a large body of Rebels came over lately at Bermuda hundred & gave themselves up   It is not confirmed & we are waiting for the papers to tell us about it

I feel it in my bones that this Rebellion is tottering & about to fall.   Every State But New Jersey Delaware & Kentucky have joined hands for <u>Freedom</u> & thus embraced the "Tide in the Affairs" of Nations which leads to humor & Self Respect

History will record these passing events & in future years there will be <u>some</u> who will be forced to read in her pages a record which they would gladly erase.   How many votes for McClellan were there in Concord. I hope not many   I pity the Children of a Copperhead as much as much as I would of a Murderer

They ought to <u>Disinherit</u> their Parents & then change their name & sail with clean hands

Stayley is still with Sheridan & having pretty rough times   He says "it is" very cold there But that it seems good to always drive the enemy before him   The 48th are pretty good fighters But have never yet won a decided victory   It is true we have had much hard service   But never won many laurels   I shall expect another letter from you tomorrow   Until then Adieu with much love from Jimmy

Mon Nov 21 1864
Dropped as deserters
Michon not reported per Des list
Jonanin not reported from furlough Sept. 18
Burr not reported from furlough Nov. 12
Rainy day

[*Letter]

Hd Qtrs Co H 48th NYSVols
Near Richmond Va Nov 23 1864

Yours of 17th was recd
My Dear Jennie
Yesterday we were busy building a chimney all day & today it is awful cold. our fireplace dont warm the house yet But as soon as we get plastered up we will be very comfortable I have to sit with my overcoat on today & my hands are so stiff that I take the liberty of writing with a pencil. You will excuse it wont you? For I want to send this off today. Tomorrow is Thanksgiving Our Officers messes have obtained Chickens &c & intend to have a good Dinner   I have had one Invitation to dine out But declined. Our men will get up something probably on their own a/c Last year I got them up a <u>good</u> <u>Dinner</u>   But the Co Fund is low now   I have seen in the papers that a Thanksgiving Dinner had been sent to the Soldiers   But I dont see it. It is hardly possible to do it Some would get plenty & others none thus causing more dissatisfaction than benefit. The idea of sending relief to the Soldiers is very commendable   They deserve all that can be done for their comfort   But one half of Charity is in the proper expenditure of the peoples Bounty I have been reading today about Sherman's last movement   I am curious to hear where he will turn up   We think Savannah is to be the place

I should not wonder if he should manage by one of his master strokes to liberate our prisoners who have been suffering so long the nameless horrors of a Rebel prison. I pity our poor fellows who have to stand on picket these cold nights   It is very hard I assure you. I cannot forget them although I do not have to share their hardships. Our Regt is very lucky to be stationed at this Fort. We have the best quarters of any Regt about. I am getting stronger all the time now & I think when I come home again if nothing further happens to me I shall be as sound as ever. I have just cast off my coat   our house is finished & very comfortable

Yesterday I recd the School Report you sent me last <u>April</u>   I cant imagine where it has been   Capt Lacoppidan says when he goes home he is going to Concord to School in the Factory Village[172]   He spied your name in the Report   Of <u>course</u> you "<u>did</u> <u>not</u> <u>deserve</u>" the credit you got You need not take the trouble to tell <u>me</u> that   For you know I <u>pretend</u> to know you pretty well   But now I want to teach you a lesson (<u>presumptuous</u> <u>aint</u> <u>I</u>)

---

[172] In the mid-1800's, West Concord was called Factory Village.

Always take all the praise the world is willing to grant you   Ten to one you will come out about right at last. Did you enjoy the wedding? Somehow I imagine such parties are usually rather stupid & your letter makes me think that your enjoyment consisted in seeing others enjoy themselves

Why didnt Em have some one stand up with her. Wasnnt Uncle Barrett's family there   I should have expected Rockwood   Mr Swain always has to be peculiar   What did he mean by saying his father & mother were there   How happened Orville Fay & wife to be invited. I don't expect to go home again until the war is over & that will not be for 6 mos yet Very little can be done this cold weather. It would not surprise me to hear of the rebs suing for peace   I dont understand this new peace proposition that the papers talk about   Butler referred to it in his NY speech   I am expecting much from Sherman   His blows always seem to hurt

I cant say the same of ours. As Stayley says of our Regt   The 48th are good fighters   But they never yet won a decided victory. Stayley says he has very hard times with Sheridan   But it seems good to always see the Johnies run instead of attempting a retrograde movement [173] himself. We are studying the tactics now   Officers school Tuesday & Thursday night & Non Comd Officers school Wednesday & Friday nights

Now I have 2 Cos I spend one hour each on those nights   We make it quite interesting & hope to make it instructive & beneficial

I enclose you a piece of Army Telegraph wire such as is put up for temporary use. Now Jennie you must excuse this hurried scrawl   I know I am imposing on your good nature   But I cant help it this time

I have to slight some of my letters now that I have 2 companies   I have more interruptions Good bye   believe me with much love

Ever yours
JasA Barrett
Capt 48th NYSVol

---

[173] An orderly retreat usually designed to move away from an enemy. Weeks, Richard. Shotgun's Home of the American Civil War. Definitions of Civil War Terms. (2012). Retrieved December 15, 2015, from http://civilwarhome.com/terms.html

Chapter 20

Thanksgiving, 1864

> November 24, 1864-December 26, 1864--Provisions don't arrive--
> Description of Thanksgiving dinner--Newspaper article concerning
> incompetence of field hospital doctors --Witnesses execution of
> deserter--Sherman victorious--Observance of Christmas

[*Note that all the following transcriptions have been faithfully copied from the original document, as written by James, except where noted.]

[*James' diary entry]
Thurs Nov 24 1864
*Thanksgiving   Some companies pretty drunk. "H" sober. Officers drunk
as anyone   Writing nearly all day   Turkeys dont come. Received one Bbl
apples in evening.*

[*Letters]

Camp 48th Regt NYSVols
In the Field Va Nov 24 1864

My Dear Jennie

I did not get my letter into the mail last night after all & after I had gone to bed Miller brought me yours of 20th & one from Mother & Lizzie

You say "unless I come home" Now you havent been thinking that I was coming home this fall have you? There is not the slightest danger of my attempting to do more than I am able. My organ (I came near saying bump) of Caution is very large. I am not on the sick list now & I do all the duty there is to do. & have 2 Cos to attend to. Our Regt gives 2 Capt for Brig Officer of the day to take their regular turn with those of the other Regts. These 2 are supposed to be the Senior ones But as I am not proud of my rank I have not yet claimed the privileges of going on instead of the one now doing that duty. Capt Hutchinson is very happy to do it as it brings him into notice But the duty is rather severe & I dont like to try riding horseback so far. Capt Hilliard is the Senior Capt He has a ball in his hip & has been on light duty But it cut him to go on Camp Officer of the day & have to report to his juniors & so he claimed his rank. The officers think he is not so lame as he pretends. I don't think they think so of me. But still we don't always know who our friends are. If Lucy will give you a picture & you think it will do I will send it to Stayley

I don't like to appear in the light of a matchmaker   But I would like to please Stayley by sending it if I could get hold of an extra one   I thought Ellen B was going to spend the winter Becky will be lonesome wont she   I do wish They were nicely settled in the village where Becky would be more independent & Father would not be bothered with cattle running away &c & Mother would have less care. You must run in & take a rest on your way to & from school & cheer them up accasionally. Em started in style it seems   She did not follow the lesson you & Annie gave on a former accasion

So Abbie is promoted   Good for her   I think she will do herself honor there   She is a good Girl & a fine teacher. Why dont she ever write to me? Do you think Ned objects? I wrote last & she did not answer & so I concluded that she probably had her reasons. I hope she will have as good success as she has heretofore I think it will be pleasant for her in the village even if it is harder.

Nell's letter has not arrived yet. Of course she will tell me all about the various letters she has recd My first question will be   Has he been a Soldier? If not. Why not? There is an old "saying" "Beware of Vidders"[174] (I refer to those whose other halfs have departed) I dont know whether this applies to the "What is sauce for the Goose is sauce for the Gander". (This quotation is supposed to be either from Shakespear or Mother Goose) But it is always well to take all these things into consideration. You ask "Do I have any troubles?" Certainly I do It is rather hard to get up these cold mornings at 5 A.M. & then when it rains the water will come in to the tent & the mud wash off of the logs & the chimney takes much more heat up than it sends out & Lacoppidan complains if I put my over coat on & then But I guess that will do for once But I cant much now Our house is very comfortable I have no real discomforts here I wont complain as long as we have it so nice One would not have to be very patriotic to "fight it out on this line" even if it takes all winter I shall think of you much today & as I think I wonder where another Thanksgiving will find us I hope it will not find our Country still at war. Something seems to tell me "Hope on hope ever" "The darkest day Lives till tomorrow will have passed away" I have been away from home 4 Thanksgivings now But I hope I have not yet forgotten how to be thankful. It is over a year now since we were engaged I told you then that I did not believe in long engagements I did not then expect that the Army would hold me so long

But I have no regrets The year has been a checkered & eventful one for me But it has been a happy one. Your letters but above all your presence has helped me much to strive to prove myself worthy of your Confidence & your Love. As to some things you said They were but natural I admired your candor & appreciated the motives which prompted you I can truly say that I love you all the better for having spoken so frankly. You will remember I told you that I overcame all my doubts long ago Do you doubt it?

They are all buried beyond a chance of resurrection. My only doubt & fear is When shall I be able to offer you a Home? Home! It is a blessed word How doubly blessed it will seem to us after these years of strife. But we are all watched over & cared for by an Infinite one.

I will try & be submissive to his will knowing that "All will be well" at last. Our cook is making arrangements to give us a good dinner He cant have much variety But there will be very many who will fare worse. I understand that there are a quantity of Turkeys somewhere for the Soldiers But with all the cullings they will get before they reach the men I fear the rank & file will get little good from them. I found our Commissary Dep^t in a sad state here & many were the complaints I heard I have been trying to get it corrected & flatter myself that I have partially succeeded.

My Nigger (Colored boy) washed my shirt yesterday & when he hung it up it froze He supposed it was because he used cold water & washed it over in warm water made him show the white of his eyes to see it freeze after using warm water

Last Thanksgiving I was with Co A at Pope's Plantation H. Head They often speak to me of the good times they had there. I wish they could get some good cheer today But I suppose

---

[174] Reference to a Charles Dickens' character from *Pickwick Papers*. Tony Weller advises his son to "Beware of Vidders (Widows)." Widows were looked upon with suspicion. They were thought to be wily, worldly and calculating.

there are many north who will fare no better. There must be a wide field for Charity this winter   I hope it will not be a severe one. You must not feel anxious if you dont hear from Ned

He will get along   I think he has a good deal of tact   I think it depends a good deal upon the person how he fares

Some will always be disliked & others liked & favored. Always <u>hope</u> for the <u>best</u> & <u>submit</u> to the <u>worst</u> when you have to

Hoping that you may enjoy your Thanksgiving & that the next one pray find us no longer separated I remain

Yours very affectionately

Jas.A.Barrett

Nell Wood writes that she is living away from home in hopes of attending <u>another</u> wedding in Concord at some future time   I enclose you a sample of some of my <u>Literary</u> <u>Correspondents</u>   It has been in my pocket a good while

Emma Jane's sketch of a soldier
seeking warmth (Barrett Collection)

Hd Qtrs Co H. 48th Reg^tN.Y.S.Vols

Army of the James in the Field Va.

Thanksgiving evening Novr 24 1864

My Dear Mother

Another Thanksgiving day is over This is the 4th I have been away from our family circle on that joyous anniversary

It has been a very quiet day with me   I have been writing most of the day   As usual whiskey has been King of this as of all holidays in the Army   Thank God my company are sober One Serg^t of Co A is a little <u>sprung</u> But not troublesome.   I must talk to him when opportunity offers. Several Co^s got drunk and quarrelsome   They all had a half ration whiskey given them today   But many of our officers make fools of themselves   I had one sensible talk with our Chaplain this evening   He took tea with us (I guess his staff mess were too noisy for him) & then called in to my house for a little while. My chum is a very good fellow & dont get drunk But I dont sympathize with him much. I have thought of you all at home many times today. I trust another year will find us at Peace again & we returned to our quiet pursuits I think the time is drawing near I glory in the emphatic expression of honest Patriotic Manhood that our people so nobly made on Novr 8th I looked forward to the issue of that Campaign with more than ordinary interest.

The result more than meets my most sanguine expectations Truly this should be a day of thanksgiving indeed We none of us can begin to appreciate how important the events that are now transpiring are

We can all look back over our lives & see where we planted the "mile stones" which marked the Eras in our lives. The re-election of A Lincoln is an Era in our National life Its importance we none of us can measure now But it out shines all our Victories Our great Ship of State is rocking on Volcanic waves We have drifted into unknown & untried Seas It was beyond the power of human pilots to save us from the breakers which threatened to wreck our national life But an Infinite hand has all along guided the helm & is only waiting His own good time to say "Peace be still" Many there are of feble faith who have foundered in the waters To these the rebuke of the Master comes "Oh Ye of little faith" & the still small voice whispers "strive on strive ever" Stand fearlessly to your posts & quit yourselves like men An Almighty Power will give us Peace when we prove ourselves worthy of the Trust Until then we shall continue to be disciplined by the Nettle of Danger until we can boldly pluck the Flower of Safety. Thank God the sky is brightening Victory after Victory has crowned our banners The Voice of a mighty nation has declared it fixed & determined purpose. Our army like a huge Lion shaking its mane for a new encounter is in the best of spirits & firmly resolved to go on conquering & to conquer until Rebellion shall hide its infamous head forever. Our Navy is the admiration of the world & is today King of the Ocean.

Foreign Nations are looking with wonder and amazement But with jealous eyes upon the tenacity with which our govern^t clings to life They cannot understand the magic bonds that bind these States together in spite of Civil strife & foreign frowns. Gladly would they see these mysterious Cables parted & our young Republic swallowed up A sacrifice upon the Altar of Despotism. But meantime our Noble ship moves on Rebellion is fast crumbling beneath the vigorous blows of Grant Sherman Thomas & Faragut & others who so nobly battling for our countries cause. Yes we have much cause to be thankful Let us send up such a shout of joy & praise as shall send the blood throbbing through our veins with renewed life & inspire fresh courage & faith into the hearts of our countries brave defenders

Yours of 17th rec^d last night filled as usual with matter of interest The wedding must have been a rather grand affair. You must feel lonesome this winter without her. How nice it would be if you could be nicely & comfortably settled in the Village where your Father would have so much less care to weigh you down

I think you have done enough hard work to entitle you to take some comfort from your earnings & there is too much care & hard work on the farm

I think your visitors made a very short stay Don't you worry in the event of Becky popping off You will be cared for The same One who notices the sparrow will not furget you

I feel anxious about George Why don't you write to the PostMaster I think you had better do so at once.   We had a pretty good Dinner for Soldiers Roast Beef Roast & Boiled Mutton Fricksseed Chicken Oyster Pie 2 kinds of Potatoes Onions Apple Pie & Apple Dumplings. We hear that Turkeys are sent to the men But they don't come I expect that the commissaries are drunk or some Think of that kind & neglect it I have some idea of trying to get detailed in the Commissary Dep[t] I think I might be of perhaps more service there than here. I wrote to Rebecca about getting some cloth & boiling it & getting 2 shirts made for me I said she could send by mail But I have sold my overcoat that I left at home & I wish you would do it up & Express it to me as soon as convenient You can put the shirts in to the same bundle if you can get them made soon enough Adams[175] would forward it It can be done up in strong brown paper

                              Mark
                    Capt. James A. Barrett
                    48th Reg[t] N.Y.S.Vols.
                    2nd Brig 2nd Div 10th Army Corps,
                    Virginia
                              Yours Aff[ly]
                              Jas. A Barrett

[*James' diary entries]

Fri Nov 25 1864
Very muddy   Ground freezes by night & thaws by day   Chimney fixed to throw out heat   Deserter from Lesingdan's battery shot in front of our fort I had a good view of it   Twelve shots—nine took effect—he fell backwards without @ struggle at 3.20P.M.

Sat Nov 26 1864
Officer of the day   Wound rather sore today   Muddy as usual. I think my wound will break out again

Sun Nov 27 1864
Had my wound opened   It discharges freely   Rather stiffy. We are to commence company drills tomorrow—each wing in one company   An order read tonight that men arresting or shooting @ deserter can have twenty days' furlough recommended

---

[175] Adams Express was a shipping and delivery service and later became Railway Express Agency.

Mon Nov 28 1864

Co. drill commenced   Each wing in one company   Our regiment to do picket & fatigue duty in future.

Wed Nov 30 1864

Wound very sore—discharges considerably   Weather mild—Sent off Co. A. returns. Co. H. ready But waiting for Inpⁿ reports. Rebels heard cheering. Gen. Lee & wife rode along the lines, so deserters say   Maj. Elfwing paid me luck

Thurs Dec 1 1864

Winter comes in mild   Inspection this P.M. by Col. Coan   News of another victory by Gen. Schofield in Columbia Ala. Hood's army whipped

Fri Dec 2 1864

Letter from home   George is safe   Ned paroled   Em happy   Weather looking stormy

Sat Dec 3 1864

Mason Grover arrested Nov 27\64 & held Col. John Ely A.A. P. Marshall, Trenton, N.J. Supt. Rect service N.J. Storm brewing   Col. Barton returned last night. I think he will be mustered out.

Sun Dec 4 1864

Col. Barton was mustered out yesterday & left this A.M. at 4 o.c. Wound better   Signs of @ move

Wed Dec 7 1864

Most of our division left for Bermuda Hundred to embark about 4 P.M. Col. Granger 9ᵗʰ Me Vols Is in command of our division left here   I am in command of 2ⁿᵈ Provˡ Brig., 2ⁿᵈ Provˡ Div. 24ᵗʰ A.C. "nearly 1000 men & 12 officers."

Thurs Dec 8 1864

Some delay in getting in the field returns from the various detachments. Getting things into shape   203ʳᵈ short of rations I have to finish picket tomorrow I put my brigade into the trenches this morning to mark their position.   Our division known as provisional brigade of 3ʳᵈ Div. 24ᵗʰ A. C.   My command 47ᵗʰ & 48ᵗʰ N.Y., 76ᵗʰ, 97ᵗʰ, & 203ʳᵈ P.A. Vols. To be termed 1ˢᵗ Batallion Prov. Brigade 3ʳᵈ Div. 24ᵗʰ A.C. Formed my regiment into two companies   Sergᵗ Garaghan my right hand man

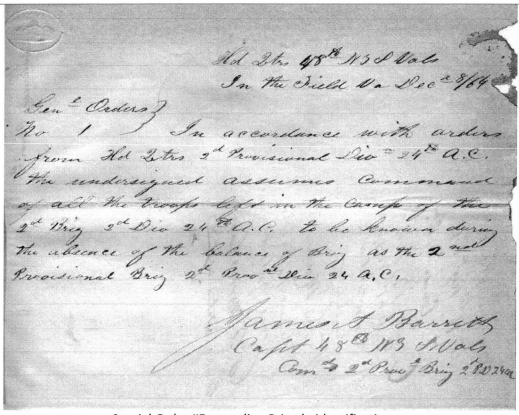

Special Order #5 regarding Brigade identification
(Barrett Collection)

Transcription of Special Order #5:

Hd Qtrs 48th NYS Vols
In the Field Va Decr 8/64

Genl Orders}
No 1   In accordance with orders
From Hd Qtrs 2d Provisional Divn 24th A.C.
The undersigned assumes command
Of all the troops left in the camp of the
2d Brig 2d Div 24th A.C. to be known during
This absence of the balance of Brig as the 2nd
Provisional Brig 2d Provnl Div 24 A.C.
James A Barrett
Capt 48th NY S. Vols
Comd 2d Provl Brig 2d P.V 2d A.C.

Fri Dec 9 1864

An officer wanted for picket I can't get excused I send an acting one My officers not fit for picket Serg^t Rumsey Co. E. returned I make him Acting Serg^t Major. Sent Corp^l Clark to Washington yesterday with Purcell of Co. K. to report to Adj. Gen.

Sat Dec 10 1864

Lawson of my co A. time out Firing heard in our front & right Kept under arms all day I feel pretty tired It snowed last night & it is cold under foot Butler of A returned to duty Soon sent for by the provost as a deserter

Sun Dec 11 1864

Ground white with snow Gen. D. a great excitement Was going to order us all under arrest for not having the men in the works at reveille They had stacked arms in co. streets I am still on duty. No one else here to run the machine Very muddy day & getting very cold at night. Orders come in fast Pretty busy reading them all

Mon Dec 12 1864

Very cold High wind all night Everything quiet

[*Letter]

Hd Qtrs 1st Bat^n Prov^l Brig 3^d Div 24th A.C.
In the Field Va Decr 12 1864
My Dear Jennie I have not rec^d your letters for the past week nearly. I supposed the mail has been intercepted by the Reg^t at Ft Monroe. I am reduced when I wrote last I was Brigadier[176] But my com^d is now termed a Battalion[177] I have over 900 men in the command & there is no end to the orders. I get all hours day & night I am liable to interruption

We had quite an excitement here on the 10th The Enemy appeared in our front & we manned our works all day The Genl seemed considerably excited But the Johnies did not trouble us They skirmished with our Pickets each side of us & charged the negroes on our left I believe the Nigs captured a number of the Rebs I have been pretty busy organizing my command & getting things settled. Col Granger gave me quite a compliment He said "If I had got a sore back my head was clear" & He was very much pleased with the way I managed affairs". Did^nt I stretch up my head at that though! But it took me down a little when my com^d was reduced from a Brig to

---

[176] A commissioned rank that is above a colonel and below a major general. Usually in command of a brigade. brigadier general. (n.d.) *AMERICAN HERITAGE DICTIONARY OF THE ENGLISH LANGUAGE, FIFTH EDITION*. (2011). Retrieved December 4, 2015, from http://www.thefreedictionary.com/brigadier+general
[177] A subdivision of a regiment.

a Battalion   The command is the same So "What's in a name?" Yesterday morning Genl Devins 3^d Div^n came round here & made a great fuss because our men were not in the works   I had their arms stacked in the rear of the works   Col Granger came round & said that Gen^L D ordered that the com^d officer be put in arrest

I said All right Col who will issue those orders & run this machine? He said "Oh go on Capt I have not ordered you in arrest yet" & "I will explain the thing to the Genl" A little while after he was more excited than before & said the Genl had been cursing him & threatening him with arrest & disgracing him generally. I keep on in the even tenor of my way & try to do my duty & not get frightened. Col G tries to do his best But don't always know how & says so (honest) We have considerable fun over some of his orders. Garaghan is here (my acting adj) He was not well & so did not go with the Reg^t He is a great help I give him com^d of the 48th Reg^t & have him for Adj Genl Aid &c. Col G offered to detail a Capt or Lt to serve as my Aid But I told him I could get along with Garaghan as I have a good clerk, Our Dr is with me we occupy the Col^s quarters Col G wanted me to go to Brig Hd Qtrs But I preferred to remain here I don't like to put on too many airs. I don't know where our Reg^t have gone   We heard from them off Ft Monroe & it is said today that they have landed at Norfolk I think they are going to N.C. or else coming back here I hope they wont be away from us long I am ready to turn over my honors & retire to the Com^d of my Co. I pity the poor fellows   They took nothing but Overcoats & Rubber Blankets & it is very cold

Dr & I get along like 2 brothers   I sent one man home rejoicing yesterday

Our mustering officer would not muster him out & I went to the next Div where they had a mustering officer who was a gentleman. Why cant people be accommodating   It is very easy to be courteous & makes one very popular I have often wondered at the scarcity of it in society We see the mask torn off from the superficial politeness of Society & the Boor stands out in his deformity

I have found the Chaplain of the next reg^t (203^d Pa Vols) hungry & taken him in to our mess for the present   I like him pretty well   But like most Chaplains I meet in the Army   He seems rather effeminate & seems like a mouse in a strange garret   Supper waits. So good bye with much love from yours affectionately

James A. Barrett
Capt 48th N.Y.S. Vols
Com^d 1st Bat^n Prov^l Brig 3^d Div 24th A.C.

*[*James' diary entries]*
Tues Dec 13 1864
Paddock relieved. Q.M. & Com. Appointed by Gen. Devins 3rd Div. for our Prov. Brigade. Troubles brewing in Q.M. Department. I have to draw rations in bulk for my battalion   Stoney acting Commanding Serg^t   Orton pretty lively   Rations drawn to 19th except 1 day coffee, 4 candles, 3 bread & 2 soap. 203rd to 17th

Wed Dec 14 1864

Cloudy   I find I am really junior to all the Captains in my command   I don't know how I happened to be put in command   I don't know but that I ought to give up to Capt. Bachman of the 203rd Pa   Lt. Orton ordered to report to me for duty   I send him back.

Thurs Dec 15 1864

Inspection tomorrow   Making arrangements settling up rations etc.   Some pickets firing heard.   We keep equipments on all the forenoon

Fri Dec 16 1864

Inspection today   It passed off very well better than I had expected

Sat Dec 17 1864

Had quite @ dispute with Col. Granger about Quartermasters   I get quite excited about it   I hope we will join our brigade soon   Dress parade in the 203rd Garaghan does very well

Mon Dec 19 1864

Quartermaster getting excited   Paddock goes to see Col. Granger   Capt. Lamb is going to see Gen. Terry   I guess we can run our machine   A deserter says Jeff Davis is dead.   Rumor of an early attack on Wilmington expected.   Last night we had good news from all sources.   Turned the men out of bed to cheer   Savannah probably taken   Sherman victorious   Hood badly whipped   Canada getting uneasy   "Everything seems lively"

[*Letter]

>Hd Qtrs 1st Batn Provl Brig
>3d Divn 24th Army Corps
>Camp 48th Regt In the Field Va
>Dec 19 1864

My Dear Jennie

Yours of 13th postmarked <u>Lincoln</u> was recd last night It was a fat mail for me one from you mother Lockwood & a Corpl of the regt Also a Paper containing lots of good news. Hood badly whipped Savannah taken   Canada anxious to restore good feeling & maintain order in her border & other items too numerous to mention

We turned our command out of <u>bed</u> to give some hearty cheers.   which they did in real good earnest making the camps all around echo & reecho with their rejoicings

Our pickets sang out to the Johnnies & asked them why they did not cheer. I will not repeat their reply.   But It was more profane than elegant

I am still in command of the remnant of the Brigade left here.   I get along very well so far I make others do the running for me. My health is good & my wound closed up again. I think I can truly say that my position has not puffed me up   I have not as yet "taken Wr-w-wr--wings & flown But am still "of the earth earthy" The same humble old sixpence as ever. I suppose it is proper that I should confess that I did have another of my <u>tantrums</u> the other day (you know I had one last summer)

The Colonel who commands what is left here of our Div was over here attempting to instruct me   I thought I knew as much (or more) as he   Well we had it some time I kept <u>cool</u> with him & talked <u>plainly</u> & of course obeyed his (written) orders or appeared to do so But when he was gone   I had to let off some of my suppressed wrath But I am <u>not</u> in <u>arrest</u> yet & what is more I do not fear it. I don't think <u>He</u> dares to take such a step

I endeavor to look after the men in my charge & report to Col _____ [178] But I care nothing for his <u>dignity</u> & ask no favors of him. <u>We</u> <u>can</u> <u>run</u> <u>our</u> <u>own</u> <u>machine</u>. "If we know ourselves & we think we do". Our Dr & I occupy the Col's quarters & get along like brothers   We have a good deal of fun over some of the orders that come here   But that answers for spice to flavor the monotony of our life. I would like to hear Curtis's lecture   I can readily imagine how interesting it will be.   I noticed what you say of Beecher[179]   People often say there is no use in trying to do their duty as they get no thanks for it or else perhaps some one else reaps all the benefit. A good action is never lost   The Economy of Nature does not allow waste & if this is true in material things   it is true in a greater degree in spiritual things We develop our natures both moral & physical   just in proportion as we conform to these great Laws As to the Promotion   I do not expect any.   I am not fit for it & if I get detailed out of the Reg^t I shall not be eligible   My name has been proposed for the Q.M. Dep^t This move has suspended action on it for a time   But when they come back or we join them   I presume there will be a demand for me again.   I shall be glad to rejoin our regular organization again for there are always many little things to annoy one situated as I am now. We are sort of hitched on to the 3rd Div^n & have to put up with some things not altogether agreeable My Shirts have not come yet I am anxiously looking for them as the ones I have are not exactly <u>becoming to an Officer</u>.

I have been amusing myself lately in trying to expose fraud & I saw one of my letters in the Herald the other day. I enclose it not that it is of any value   But just let you see how my name looks in print. I believe this is my first that has ever seen the light. They always get my middle name either H. S. or J.   I had to report a man as a Deserter yesterday from one of my Detachments   named <u>James Barrett</u> He came down with a batch of Recruits to the 47th N.Y. Vols. & was claimed by the 3^d N.H. Vols. I felt rather ashamed to report him. Now if you see this name reported   You may feel warranted in saying that it is not me. But I must close I am glad to see that Sherman's men are to have a Christmas Dinner They deserve it.

I think you will soon hear from our Div^n in some thrilling movement. Now with a Merry Christmas & Happy New Year to you   I remain with much love Yours very affectionately
Jas.A.Barrett

<u>Direct</u> as usual
except the No of Corps <u>24</u>th A.C.

---

[178] Referring to Colonel Granger
[179] Beecher, Henry Ward (1813-1887), U.S. preacher and writer.

Complaints Against Mustering-in Officers and Examining Surgeons.

INDIGNANT LETTER OF CAPTAIN BARRETT.

There evidently must be more care and caution exercised by the United States officers in the interior districts in reference to passing men as volunteers or substitutes, or our army will become merely a receptacle for imbeciles, vagrants and incapables. Examining surgeons and mustering-in officers hold most responsible positions. Upon their acts depend in a great measure the efficiency of the army. If negligent and pass or receive men wholly unfitted, or are influenced to this through personal solicitation or for pay, they are not only inflicting a great wrong, but are committing a great crime.

There are no points about which Mr. Blunt, chairman of our County Volunteer Committee, is more cautious and guarded than on this of paying bounty to bad men. Fortunately there are on duty at his office, as Acting Assistant Examining Surgeon, W. F. Brown, and Mustering in Officer, Captain R. O. Parker, United States Army—gentlemen who not only thoroughly understand their duties, but perform them fearlessly and impartially swayed by no influence whatever other than that of the public good.

There are therefore none who get through this popular and important county establishment for the army unless they are perfectly fitted, constitutionally and otherwise, for the duties of a soldier; but there are many turned away from those headquarters as totally unfitted who unfortunately resort to other places, and are accepted by the officers in charge. We give below a letter received by the chairman of the committee from a gallant captain in the army, protesting vigorously and justly against the reception into the army of the bad class of men referred to. We give this with the hope that the attention of government officers will be directed to it and will act accordingly.

> HEADQUARTERS, COMPANY H,
> FORTY-EIGHTH NEW YORK VOLUNTEERS,
> IN THE FIELD, Va., Dec. 6, 1864.

SIR—I have the honor to inquire whether you can inform me who is responsible for enlisting the following (worse than useless) men of my company, viz:—
————, of Company H, substitute for his son-in-law, October 20, 1863, at Tarrytown, New York, Tenth Congressional district. He has never done a day's duty, is thoroughly diseased throughout his whole system, lately dropped as a deserter while on furlough from hospital. ———— ————, substitute (smuggled in with whiskey), demented and nearly blind, enlisted October 20, 1863, at Tarrytown; never has done any duty; is now in hospital; when in the company I had to detail a good man to take care of him and lead him around at night. ————, volunteer recruit, mustered in by Captain Gregory, Brooklyn, New York, Dec. 19, 1863; he was recently dropped as a deserter, and I hear he has been arrested in New York while being smuggled into the service the second time. I understand you saw him, and wondered at his having ever belonged to this regiment. Some one is to blame for swindling the government by obtaining such men as these. There is a good deal of this work done, and I consider those men who will do it more enemies to our country than armed rebels in the field, and it would afford me great pleasure if I could be instrumental in bringing them to justice. I have often heard you spoken of as one who felt a great interest in public affairs, and I thought perhaps you could inform me who the parties were who passed these men. It certainly would be a libel to call them surgeons. I am, very respectfully, your obedient servant, JAS. J. BARRETT,
Captain Companies A and H, Forty-eighth New York Volunteers.

To ORISON BLUNT, Esq., New York city.

We can only add that the government officers or officers of the United States Army who would pass such men as are here referred to should have their straps pulled off, dismissed the service and punished by imprisonment in State prison.

New York Herald article dated December 6, 1864
(Barrett Collection)

[*James' diary entries]

Wed Dec 21 1864 *Stormy day   <u>Five</u> men shot as deserters   Sent to Hatchers for burial   Received an order to furnish clothing for prisoners   Went to see Maj. Reed about it   Returned the order to be forwarded for decision. A private of Co. E. 188th Pa. Vols has an order for muster out to accept @ Com^n in our regiment. H.E. Anderson. He has gone on furlough on the strength of it   Can't come in here, I guess   Dykeman died on steamer "Geo. Leary,"   Dec. 2, 1864 of pneumonia—buried at Hilton Head S.C.*

Sat Dec 24 1864 *A man tried to break in to the Sutler's last night   Bill fired twice at him   I think we will find him   Sent Butler to the provost yesterday   I get into another dispute with Granger about the <u>form</u> of @ charge   I finally go to Gen. Devins & then to his office & leave it   Put a guard on the Sutler's tent. Received @ ruler from Grover*

Sun Dec 25 1864 *Quiet day Report that 100 Rebels came over last night bringing Officer of day with them   We heard heavy firing   Cheers*

Mon Dec 26 1864 *Today observed as Christmas   Grapes & cranberries issued   Rainy day   Savannah taken, 150 guns, lots of ammunition, 25000 bales cotton. Cheers   Another muss with _____ [Col. Granger] I think I get the best of it   My temper suffering*

One of Emma Jane's embellishments
(Barrett Collection)

Chapter 21

Relieved from Command

December 27, 1864-January 15, 1865--Relates suffering and torture
of prisoners--Executions of deserters continue--General Butler
relieved of duty--Assumes command of the balance of brigade at
Chapin's Farm

[*Note that all the following transcriptions have been faithfully copied from the original
document, as written by James, except where noted.]

Tues Dec 27 1864   *The Rebs have heard something to cheer about to-night   I got an order relieving me from command   Lt. Col. Johnson 115th N.Y.V takes command tomorrow Gen. Devins decides that I must issue clothing to prisoners   I don't see it   I must turn it over to Col. J.   I receive my coat & shirts*

[The Cousins found the following in one of the scrapbooks in the Barrett Collection]

[This is Emma Jane's transcription of a letter written by James.]

Hd Qrts 1st Batn Provl Brig 3d Div 24 A.C.
In the Field Va   Dec 27 1864

My Dear Jennie

Yours of 11th and 18th were received yesterday. I received one of 13th before. I am ashamed to say that I have not read the message yet and can not therefore speak of its merits except that I have faith that it is all right. I suppose we have never had a President who has had so many earnest blessings invoked for him as Lincoln. His position is a proud one. His name will live in "Story and in song" as well as in the pedigree of families. How different is the case of the Southern chief. Curses will fill his winding sheet and the very weeds will droop in pity or in shame over his grave. Deserters say he is dead. I can not believe the Evil one can spare him from this world yet.

What makes your Aunt Wood depressed? I am sure she has done good enough in her life to make her last days happy. She has reared a large and honorable family and although they are scattered, they are all prosperous & well.

I hope "Benjy" will go to the lectures this winter. I would be glad to give him a ticket But perhaps it would not be exactly proper. How can you go if he doesn't? I have not seen the story you speak of about the little boy who gave his pet chicken which was all he had; but that single act stamps him a hero. If he lives, he will be an addition to society.

You must have been glad to see Ned He was very lucky in getting away from confinement so soon. I suppose he was not prisoner long enough to be much reduced. I should think it pretty hard to have ears of corn issued to me to live on. I have seen the cobs where the Rebels had stripped them, out on the picket. It is often strange to see what we can get used to. One of our men tells awful stories of hunger and suffering while a prisoner. He says there was a sick man one day who could not keep his beans on his stomach and he saw another man eat the beans that had been vomited. It is disgusting to think of, but the facts come glaring forth from many sources. Some one must answer for all this. The law of compensation is not annulled. Retribution will find its victims. Our poor soldiers have suffered untold physical torture, but from my heart I pity the guilty wretches for the mental agony that is sure to overtake them at last.

Did I write about a cross general? I have had no words with any general. It was Col. Granger of the 9th Me. That I got mad with. I got mad again the other day. An order came that made me fairly jump out of my chair. I indignantly sent it back requesting that it be sent to Corps Headquarters for decision. Our quarrel was in writing and not in words this time. But I still live and am not in arrest yet. I get the best of him every time. The order was for me to furnish clothing for some prisoners in the provost. He is getting now not to trouble me much. His airs, he finds, do not pass as currency at these Headquarters.

I saw another execution a few days since. Five deserters were shot in front of the fort. Fifteen more remain to suffer the same fate. These bounty jumpers will learn a lesson after a while.

Last night we were startled by hearing two shots in camp.   We rushed out and found that some one was trying to cut through the Sutler's tent & steal some bread.   The clerk heard and fired at him twice But he escaped.   He may turn up wounded yet.

P.M. I have had another muss.   Pretty mad.   I shall spoil my temper if I keep this way.   I wish we could get settled with our own brigade again.   He sent one of my returns back marked up just as if I were a school boy and he my teacher & the return and composition. I felt insulted and stood on my <u>dignity</u>.

We heard a great deal of firing in our front last night as if the rebs were fighting in their rear.   I hope it may be insurrection in their camps.   But good bye. With much love, I remain yours constantly

JamesA.Barrett

[*James' diary entries]
Wed Dec 28 1864
Turned over the command   Firing heard   We man the works   All quiet & we dismiss   I let Col. Johnson have Garaghan for Acting Adjutant. Col. Johnson messes with us   Sheridan helps him start   I feel quite relieved Commence on my pay rolls

Fri Dec 30 1864
Expedition back stormy, lousy, hungry & disgusted.

Sat Dec 31 1864
Mustered   Rolls can't be completed until Adjutant's desk comes up this P.M.

Sun Jan 1 1865
Busy on rolls   Cold & stormy

Mon Jan 2 1865
Regiment off again   Pay rolls left for me to finish   Maj. Dyer 9th Me Vols. in command   Busy. Capt. Hutchinson left here sick
Wed Jan 4 1865
Troops bivouacked last night at Bermuda   Some froze their feet

Thurs Jan 5 1865
Pay rolls sent off today—also A. & H. Q.M. and A.O.R.D. returns Regt. embarked this morning

Fri Jan 6 1865
Mild   Rainy

Sat Jan 7 1865

Still stormy   Two men[180] shot today in our front. Myrtha, formerly of Co. D. one of them. Calls himself Collins[181] & belongs to 8th Conn Have to be strict about men going through the works   An artillery Lt. gets indignant

Sun Jan 8 1865

Sutler returned & says Butler is ordered to Washington. Horses put on one half rations

Mon Jan 9 1865

Team gone to be shod   The sutler sends his team to help draw logs for a stable   Our mail stopped by Genl. Ames   I guess we will leave here before long   9 P.M. Picket firing heard   We turn out   Firing ceases & we dismiss It commences to rain hard

Tues Jan 10 1865

Stormy   Can't get our fire to burn. We make @ fire board & put up @ stove   Uncomfortable day   Roof leaks.

Wed Jan 11 1865

Pleasant day   Mud drying up   Commenced our stable   Stove works well Butler gone to Lowell

[This is Emma Jane's transcription of a letter written by James.]

Camp 48th Regt N.Y.S. Vols
In the Field Va   Jany 12 1865

My Dear Jennie

   Last Saturday two more men were shot out in our front—for desertion One of them used to be a drummer in this regiment. He was discharged in Sept. & enlisted again in the 8th Conn. If you look at that little picture of Co. D, you will see him—the drummer on the right

---

[180] James Myrtha (aka Murther/Marther/Collins) and William Dix. John A. Riggs. (n.d.). Union Soldiers Executions. Retrieved April 20, 2016 from genealogytrails.com/main/military/cwexecutions_union.html

[181] James Collins (aka Myrtha, Murther, Marther) enlisted at age 17 at Brooklyn, to serve three years, and mustered in as musician, Co. K, August 16, 1861; transferred to Co. D, no date; wounded in action, July 1, 1864, near Petersburg, VA; discharged for his wounds, no date. Report of the Adjutant General New York (1057). Retrieved April 20, 2016 from https://dmna.ny.gov/historic/reghist/civil/rosters/infantry/48th_Infantry_CW_Roster.pdf . He later reenlisted in the 8th Connecticut.

I dreamed the other night of meeting Fanny Norton and Charley.   It seemed as if they were engaged again.   I wish it would come true.   Maj. Dyer of the 9th Me. who is in command of the remainder of our brigade here knows Fanny very well.   I was speaking to him last night. I did not have a chance to say much about her then.

We turned out the other night pretty quickly.   Considerable firing was heard on the picket line, but nothing came of it. I guess some of the Rebs were trying to desert.   We are all feeling anxious about our expedition. Genl. Terry is in command this time and I think they will succeed in taking Wilmington—the Rebs' last port.   We are <u>all</u> <u>rejoiced</u> to hear that Genl. Butler has been ordered to <u>Lowell</u>, <u>Mass</u>. It is said he is ordered to report to <u>Mrs</u>. <u>B</u>. <u>F</u>. <u>Butler</u>. We hope he will stay there. We don't want him here.   He makes a great bluster, but I don't know what he ever accomplished yet.   We hardly dare to believe the <u>news</u> yet, but it looks very much like being shelved.

Our principal care here is to keep warm.   I have a team at work all the time drawing wood. The other day it rained so hard that water came right down the chimney and we could not make the fire burn.   I put up a stove but have to "work my passage" to keep it burning bright enough to warm the house. The Col's quarters are awfully cold—I would rather live in my little hut, but it is rather <u>more</u> <u>dignified</u> to be at Headquarters.   There is where the commanding officer is expected to be found. Capt. Hutchinson is left here. He is on the sick list. I don't think he is very sick.   I get rather disgusted with him.   He is very conceited & very unpopular. One of his men came to me & wanted me to keep a draft for him until he came back. I told him Capt. H. would stay here But he said he would rather I would keep it. I should hate to lose the confidence of <u>my</u> men so.

I understand fully what you mean by time seeming long. I can look back and in one light can hardly realize the lapse of time. But viewing it in another light, recalling the various incidents, circumstances and experiences of the past two years that dot the interval like so many milestones in life's passage, it seems to me as if I had lived a lifetime in that short period.

I send you a paper with Mr Chadwick's ordination in it and charge by Longfellow. <u>Good</u>!
With much love I remain

Yours
JamesA.Barrett

[*James' diary entries]
Sat Jan 14 1865
Deserters come in   Say Ft. Fisher is taken & Richmond being evacuated
Clothing received & issued   Giverney returned

Sun Jan 15 1865
General inspection   Our detachment looks very well   Received notice
yesterday of Burr's promotion   Wrote Adj. Gen. of N.Y. about it today

[This is Emma Jane's transcription of a letter written by James.]
Camp 48th Regt NYS Vols
In the Field Va Jan 15 1865
Dear Sister Rebecca

        Yours of 10th inst. is this day received. You did not tell me after all what the express was on my bundle. I sold the coat to a Lt. here—he is to pay the express, so you see I want to know the amount paid.

        You did not rightly understand me—my being relieved. I meant that some one had taken command over me. I don't undertake to much. It is understood that I am not able to do it. You need not flatter yourself that I shall rise any higher in office   There is not the slightest prospect of it. I have now got to the top of my ladder.   Any attempt to climb higher might and probably would result in a fall.   My Mother speaks about "my persecutions." I think she has outweighed them. I can't say that I have been persecuted. I was rather amused on the whole by what happened between me & _____ [Col. Granger].   It was not worth troubling myself about. It was only one of the little vexations of life that annoy and at the same time strengthen and educate us.

        I suppose you are all much surprised at the removal of Butler.   We think it a worthy New Year's gift to follow Sherman's Christmas. He is ordered to report to Mrs. Butler. It is hoped that under her instructions, he may learn a few salutary lessons about "how to be a gentleman," although when we remember the old proverb about "teaching old dogs new tricks", we cannot repress an inward fear that this closed book will always be numbered among the "lost arts" with him. Courts of Middlesex, welcome back your petty fogger[182]! Criminals, give vent to your joy, saying, "We have an advocate amongst us!" I think many people were infatuated with the principle of "Set a thief to catch a thief." I never had any confidence in B.F. Butler as a man and I believe we need manly traits in a soldier and a Genl. as well as in a citizen.

        I am in command here of what is left of our small reg—about 120 men.   We have not heard from the reg since they left. Deserters say that Ft. Fisher is taken and that Richmond is being evacuated. If the expedition is successful, we expect to follow & join them. If not, they will return here. Deserters come in daily and they all tell the same story. The soldiers are tired of fighting and desert whenever they get a chance.   I don't see them often as they don't come in much in our immediate front.   The swamp is too thick.

        Good night, with much love to all, I remain Very truly
                    Your Brother
                    James

[*Narrative]
        While at Chapin's farms on Jan'y 1865   Our Divn (the picked men of it) were ordered on the 1st expedition to Fort Fisher under Genl Butler.   I was left in command of the balance of our Brigade about 1000 men to look out for the camps & hold the line of works

---

[182] An inferior legal practitioner, especially one who deals with petty cases or employs dubious practices. pettifogger. (n.d.). *Oxford Dictionaries*. Retrieved December 4, 2015, from http://oxforddictionaries.com/definition/english/pettifogger

I did not feel that I had a very competent force to repel an attack, but we could do our best. A small force behind strong works can check quite an army if they stand up to their work   We had several alarms but no attack. Our Div^n returned in about a week with empty laurels, but were soon ordered on a 2nd and more successful expedition under Genl Terry.

Chapter 22

Capture of Fort Fisher

January 18, 1865-February 10, 1865--Fort Fisher captured--Account of officers' casualties--Rumors run wild about Richmond--Relates humorous stories of camp life--Importance of Fort Fisher's capture explained--Notes that looting of personal possessions of dead soldiers common--Boards "Sedgwick" to rejoin the regiment

[Note that all the following transcriptions have been faithfully copied from the original document, as written by James, except where noted.]

[*James' diary entries]
Wed Jan 18 1865
Two inspections @ week—the cleanest man to be recommended for furlough   Ft. Fisher captured on the 15th—1000 prisoners, 40 guns. Our loss 500. Gen. Curtis slightly wounded   Cols. Pennypacker & Bell dangerously wounded

Thurs Jan 19 1865
Pass granted   Fielder for 48 hrs. by Genl. Gibbon to go to 14th N.Y. Regt near Petersburg

Fri Jan 20 1865
I played Whist with Maj. Dyer & Dr. last night until 12 o'clock   We beat every game but one

Sat Jan 21 1865
Manned the works all day   Heavy firing at Dutch Gap   Rebel iron clad sunk 21 aground. Deserters come in. Baggage & some teams to be sent to Ft. Fisher[183]. Reveille   daylight

[*Letters]
Camp 48th Regt NYS Vols
In the Field Va Jan 23 1865

My Dear Jennie

Yours of the 15th was recd yesterday   I guess I won't scold you this time For if scolding affects you as it does me I should not get another letter for a fortnight   I don't think I can complain   You are real good about writing

I have seen a letter from Col. Coan   He was wounded in the scalp before the Charge Capt Lippincott was wounded again & Capt. Dunn killed. Sergt Pope of my Co. was killed & one other man in our Regt killed & about ten wounded   Our Regt came off lucky   Col Pennypacker comd our brigade is dead from his wounds. Col Bell comd 3rd Brig also died of his   It was an awful fight. But a Glorious Victory. Our whole Divn behaved splendidly. Deserters say that Wilmington is taken with lots of Cotton.   We are daily expecting orders to join them Col Coan writes that he

---

[183] Fort Fisher was a Confederate fort. It protected the vital trading routes at Wilmington, North Carolina, from 1861 until its capture by the Union in 1865. Fort Fisher. (October 21, 2015). *Wikipedia, The Free Encyclopedia*. Retrieved December 5, 2015, from https://en.wikipedia.org/w/index.php?title=FortFisher&oldid=686880880

will rejoin us soon He will be in com^d of the Brig. Our <u>Ex</u> <u>Gen</u>^l is <u>supposed</u> to be suffering from <u>dyspepsia</u>[184]

Terry stock is up now Vice Butler "Farewell Farewell" But pumpkins are not intended to hang on Trees But must be content to creep where nature designed them to grow. When we have no wings it is folly to fly. Emerson is right Men like water seek their level & find it too.

You thought right about Lt. Col Johnson He did relieve me 2 or 3 days before the return of the troops & when they went off again in3 days after He went with his Reg^t & got wounded. Maj Dyer 9th Me. is in Com^d since. We get along nicely My Dept^mt stands A No. 1 in the Battalion

It is raining. We have had much stormy weather lately & it is awfully muddy This Virginia soil is clayey & sticks. If we go to N.C. we will be in a Sandy Country & the Climate is milder. Peace Rumors are flying about very thick. I hope there will be no weak kneed compromise now.

I do not expect it Richmond papers are making ridiculous attempts at reconciling themselves to their various Defeats. They had Sherman just where they wanted him at Atlanta. We're going to crush him before he reached the coast & They inform us that Atlanta Savannah &c, are of no consequence to them & that our capture of Ft Fisher is "A Blessing in disguise."

I expect they will soon find it an undisguised Blessing to abandon their boasted Bogus Confederacy & give their allegiance again to the good Old Union. I heard the other day by a returned Prisoner of war that one of my Corp^ls is living whom I had reported killed. I can hardly credit it. But sincerely hope it may be true It will be good news to his friends

I think your Lecturers are getting personal I presume they touch lightly on the faults & dwell on the Virtues. I doubt the policy of such Lectures. It is well to "see ourselves as others see us" But I question the efficacy of such methods. I am getting pretty strong again now & think strongly of attempting full duty again when I rejoin my Reg^t I can but fail anyhow & it would be some satisfaction to have tried it. I fear our Officers are very poorly off at Ft Fisher

The men took their knapsacks and tents But The Officers left Baggage behind & some did not take their blankets even. It is surprising to see what men can get used to endure. Jennie You may expect me home by The 4th of <u>July</u> I don't think we will get this confederacy settled before that time. We have got considerable Cotton to confiscate yet. Don't try to coax me home sooner. All will be <u>right</u> in the end Good bye with much love from yours affectionately

James A Barrett

Direct as before
It will probably reach me in another state

Camp 48th Reg^t N Y S Vols   Jan^ry 24 1865
My Dear Jennie

It is a week since I wrote you   I have waited expecting every day to get a letter But we cant depend on the mails these days. We have Glorious news in the Capture of Ft. Fisher

---

[184] Dyspepsia is a condition of impaired digestion. dyspepsia. (n.d.). *Webster's New World College Dictionary*. Retrieved December 4, 2015, from http://www.yourdictionary.com/dyspepsia

It is the most substantial Victory our Div^n has ever had   2500 Prisoners 72 Guns & an effectual blockade of the Rebels last Port

The Pirates Tallehasse & Chickamauga are also cornered in Cape fear River & can not escape

They must necessarily soon fall into our hands.   Whether Wilmington will soon be attacked remains to be seen   Genl Grant's main object is gained by the possession of the Defences near the mouth of the River

He will not needlessly sacrifice life by pushing on if he can gain his object without. Genl Terry's success has completely clinched Butler's discomfiture. I think it will require all of Mrs Butler's winning powers to restore amiability to her Crestfallen Lord   I am waiting with nervous anxiety to hear the details of the Battle. It was a desperate engagement & our men are highly spoken of Our 3 Brig Commanders are all wounded. We have no further news   I fear that many of my comrades who so recently left us in all vigor of manly life have fallen in the bloody struggle I hear that our loss in Officers was heavy. If I had been there Very likely I would have been wounded if not killed   When I think of the past I am always reminded how kindly Providence has dealt with me & I try to be sufficiently thankful. We have a new Corp Commander Genl Gibbon He has ordered 2 Inspections a week when the Cleanest men are selected one from each Co & sent to Div^n Hd Qtrs & the cleanest of all gets a furlough. The best & neatest Reg^{ts} are excused from Fatigue &c. My Deth^{mt} will beat the others   But our number is so small that we don't count much. Do you ever see the papers   I will send you one occasionally if you like Altho it would be old before you would get it. One of my Deserters has been sent back to duty with \$10^{00} a month loss of pay. I gave him a little wholesome advice & gave him quarters   He looked very much ashamed.

I heard a good joke about a Chaplain the other day   He had been in Hosp^l where he made himself rather obnoxious to the other officers   Finally he announced his intention of going to the front stopping on the way for his baggage &c at the Pontoons. The Officers told the Negro driver that he was crazy & might try to get out to drown himself. When he got to the bridge   Mr Chaplain asked to stop   But Cuffy only put whip to his horses & said "Cant com dat" & carried him to his Reg^t A certain Capt had a man of his co die & made requisition on the Q.M. for 25 ^{lbs} Candles for the occasion. His claim being disputed   he indignantly referred to the Regulations where it stated that 25 ^{lbs} candles were allowed for Corps Hd Qtrs & he wanted them for Corpse Hd Qtrs. I rec^d notice a few days since that Burr of my Co was commissioned 1st Lt. in this Reg^t. I wrote at once protesting against it stating that he was not fit   I have heard nothing since. There is a greeny in a Penn Reg^t who has a com^n as 1st Lt also

He keeps coming over   But I wont have any thing to do with him & give him to understand that he cant be mustered. It is provoking to have Governors commission outsiders in Vet^n Reg^{ts} when we have good Serg^{ts} of our own who have earned promotion. If this last fellow ever gets mustered in our Reg^t He has got to be smart that's all. He will have to go before a military board first & be examined

I expect we will soon be ordered to join our Reg^t or else they will come back

I think you will soon hear of the Capture of Augusta & Charleston & the Evacuation of Richmond I enclose a specimen of New Jersey literature It came to Capt Strickland & I took it as his successor. Miller is waiting for the mail & I must close with much love

I remain yours affectionately

JamesA.Barrett

Capt 48th N.Y.SVols

[*James' diary entry]

Wed Jan 25 1865

 Reconnoissance talked of Rumor of evacuation of Richmond Our detachment will remain to man the redoubt if the others go out. Teams & officers' baggage ordered to Bermuda 100. We expect to join our regiment soon Borrowed $50.00 of Sutler on draft on N.Y.

[This is Emma Jane's transcription of a letter written by James.]

Awaiting Transportation

In the Field Va Jany 30 1865

My Dear Jennie

We have left our camp at last. Saturday morning we broke camp and marched down here about one half mile and now occupy an old deserted camp until we can get transportation to Ft. Fisher. A brigade of the 8th Corps took our place on the line of works and our quarters are now occupied by the 12th Va Reg^t

I intend to take the field again We are again attached to the department of the south and belong to Sherman's army. Garaghan is mustered 1st Lt and is Act. Adj.

I took a walk today along the line in front of the 25th Corps. I could see the Rebel pickets very plainly only about 200 yds. Away. It is a curious sight—two opposing armies quietly walking their beats within a stone's throw of each other. But they are very friendly. It would be pretty hot there if it were not so.

One of our Captains has returned from Ft. Fisher He represents the struggle there, as of the most desperate character. Our officers and men fought hand to hand. The importance of the victory can hardly be calculated. Five blockaders have already been taken and many others will probably run blindly into the snare set for them. There was a fearful system of torpedoes all set ready to be touched off by a magnetic wire, but the wires were cut by our shells and the connection destroyed. No doubt many lives were thus saved. A full chart showing where the torpedoes were and the manner of touching them off, was found in the fort. Our loss was astonishingly small considering the strength of the works and the large number of the garrison. About 200 of our casualties were caused by the carelessness of our men. There is always a strong desire for plunder when a hostile camp is captured. In this case, they were reckless enough to carry a lighted candle into the ruins of the magazine. The result was horrible in the extreme I can look with comparative calmness upon the suffering and death caused in legitimate warfare, but it seems clothed with double terror when caused by the recklessness and carelessness of our own men.

We expect to go on board transports tomorrow.   I don't know how I shall send this—probably by the Christian Commission. With much love, I remain as ever

Yours   JamesA.Barrett

[*Narrative]
Shortly after I rec^d some 200 recruits for our Reg^t & was ordered to proceed with them & what men I had to my Reg^t near Fort Fisher where we arrived about Feb'y 1st. These recruits were all Substitutes & very desperate set of men Stabbing affrays & fights & robberies were common & I had my hands full, but succeeded in getting them all along but about 3 or 4 who were missing. About this time I then took com^d of my co & went on full duty

*[*James' diary entry]*
Wed Feb 1 1865
~~John Murphy $271.00~~ Austin Williams—one pistol 243718 Marched down yesterday five miles & bivouacked near Bermuda 100. Received about 200 recruits last evening   They are scattered about   We are collecting them in today   Weather mild   Plenty of wood—very comfortable   Put up @ flag today   Report says Vice Pres. Stevens is in consultation with Gen. Grant to secure peace

Emma Jane's drawing of the American flag
(Barrett Collection)

Thurs Feb 2 1865
Two rations whiskey issued   Men in some regiments getting drunk Mine quiet   New men quarrel some.   Burr is troubled about his commission

[*Letter]

In the Swamp near Ft. Fisher
Feb 2, 1865

My Dear Jennie

Yours of the 1st 18th 25th 28th in Jan & 1st Feb'y greeted my arrival at the 48th Camp 7th inst I have been too busy to write before Yesterday we left camp in heavy marching order & advanced slowly through the <u>impenetrable</u> Swamps about 4 miles We are bivouacked here & are putting up marks. Several were wounded yesterday & some killed There was one report that I was killed & another that I was wounded But I am all right Several shots came near me & there is one Gun throwing shells over among us once in a while We left all our unarmed Recruits in Camp with Capt. Hutchinson who is not well I concluded to take my chances with the Reg^t again & I stand it very well. I waded through water above my knees & often had to cut my way through the swamps with my sword many places were too thick to get through I think we shall establish another line of works here & move the old camp My Co are in good spirits I fancy it makes inspires them afresh to see me with them again I never lack for a blanket or a cup of coffee or food as long as Co H has any The weather is fine here There is considerably firing on the Picket line & the Rebel works can be plainly seen. Schoffield's 23^d Corps are nearly all here I looked for Ned[185] But conclude his Div is not here I believe he is going to land at Masonboro Inlet 7 miles from Wilmington & take Johny in the rear, then we would have Hook between us deserters say. Richmond is taken by Sheridan. We do not believe it. Deserters like to tell good news thinking it will insure them better treatment. We expect some hard campaigning this month But Wilimington will pay for it. I suppose Ned Farmer's[186] Vessel is near here But I have no means of looking him up. The wood here is so pitchy that the smoke blacks us all up I don't know as you would know me Altho as you knew George I presume you are pretty good at recognizing folks. Your Remarks about New Years & its proper marks were excellent. I was too busy this year to think about good Resolutions I am aware that I need to make them. I played cards considerable on the way down here Garaghan & I are very lucky in Euchre & whist Is George much of a lady's man? I think Story should be confidential & own up his attentions are certainly suggestions of something more than common acquaintance Poor Aunty It seems she has gone to Hosp^l again I think she will spend her days there now I did not think she seemed herself last summer But she is always happy at the Hosp^l I sometimes think she is happier there than anywhere else. You need not send those Gloves at present. I see you trust yourself to drive alone. Have you improved I found a letter here from Stayley. It gladdened my heart for I had heard he was killed. I will enclose it. I think his letters worth reading. I will also enclose another letter from my N.J. correspondent I have not <u>answered</u> this last. Her son has been tried & is expected back daily to his Co with loss of Pay Thank you for the slippers make them long enough I don't think George will entice me to the Gold Regions at present While this war lasts. I belong to my country & if my health & strength is spared I intend to devote my energies to the benefit of my country. If I should be persuaded to go & you desired it I certainly would take you along. So Henry is not

---

[185] Edwin Farmer (Jennie's brother)
[186] Edward Farmer (Jennie's cousin)

cured of his western fever! How does Mary fancy going west I don't think Lizzie would fancy it much. If Rena writes to me I shall certainly answer it But I don't know her address in Washington I don't think I should consider it worth copying to send to you   I also found a letter here from Nell Please tell her she must not expect me to answer promptly now. She may keep writing whether I answer or not & knowing that I answer when convenient   Take the will for the deed. I am living now on coffee (Soldiers' Staff of life) Hardtack & raw Ham. It goes very well in the field   I hope I will never get worse fare. Did I promise to send you a hardtack? I think I promised someone   But I forget Garaghan & I rough it together   Our Companies are next each other   Mine is the Color Co   Garaghan is a good fellow & will make a fine Officer   He depends on me for a good deal of information on various subjects. He says he intends to come to my wedding   I have 19 Recruits in my Co   They are working in well   I have 2 of them with me. They have been drilled before. I took a disabled man along with me to carry a Haversack of food & a blanket for me So I get along nicely. One of his hands is useless so he will probably be transferred soon   My nigger was left at Bermuda   I am looking for a large one now   But they are scarce We will find plenty of them in Wilmington

One of my Sarg^{ts} was killed at Ft. Fisher & when found soon after was robbed of watch purse & even his shoes   The men in Their eagerness for spoils robbed friend & foe alike   Does^{nt} it seem horrid. I have no presentiments of serious soil this time   We consider the removal of Butler a great Victory for this Dept 2^{d} only to the capture of Fisher   He makes a very smooth defense But then He will lie   you cant believe him. We are confident of continued Victory & mean to bring this war to a speedy end. This Spring will be an eventful one & long to be remembered. Wilmington Charleston Augusta Richmond. If you have tears prepare to shed them now. Or rather clap your hands for the day of your deliverance is near. Our Brig Com^{dr} Col. Pennypacker (Breveted Brig^{r}) is going to get well. His lady love is at Ft Monroe nursing him   He is a noble fellow I hope he may be spared   Col Coan is north But expected back soon   Capt Miller was com^{d} Maj$^{r.}$ But is now discharged for disability. I suppose Hilliard will now be Maj^{r} & I Com next to him. Do you think I am ambitious? Dunbar is Senior Capt   But is detached from the reg^{t} & will never be prom^{d} Garaghan will be Cpt^{n} soon. His name has gone on. Tell Nell that her invitation to her examination did not reach me until the 8th of Feb'y I shall have to conclude she did not want me there. I have but one Envelope with me So I will enclose a note to George—Our mails here are very irregular. I presume you are enjoying the day at Church   It is a beautiful day & very little firing   There seems to be a truce all along the lines & we are having a very quiet Sunday. Our Pioneers are at work putting up works.

As we marched out yesterday I shook hands with a Capt. Scott of Pennypacker's Staff. He was killed before noon   I can hardly believe it. Our brave men are going fast   But a good time is coming & that soon. Let us work & pray for it & meantime I remain

Yours affectionately

JamesA. Barrett

Capt 48th N.Y. Vols

Fri Feb 3 1865

Nicholas Liginthaler $140.00. Roused at 12 o'clock last night—gave out four days' rations & marched to Bermuda 100. Embarked on board "Gen. Sedgwick." My detachment, 76th Pa, 4th N.H & some detailed men 600 in all. I gave the command to Capt. Hilliard. Sailed at 6 A.M. Ten days' rations on board Some of our cooks left Had to abandon ten boxes crackers. Arrived at Ft. Monroe 2 P.M. Went ashore—met Lippincott At anchor all night

Sat Feb 4 1865

Sailed at 6 A.M. Seasick Can't eat today Garaghan & I room together Quiet passage Men orderly Michaels very efficient

Sun Feb 5 1865

Passed Hatteras 10 last night I feel better this morning but very weak Eat a little breakfast with some difficulty Arrived off Ft. Fisher 2 P.M.

Mon Feb 6 1865

Crossed the bar 3 P.M. Issued two days' rations Can't get boats. Expect to go ashore in morning with small boats

Tues Feb 7 1865

Stormy night—too rough to land in small boats

[*Letter]

Steamer Genl Sedgwick Off Ft Fisher
Feb 7 1865

My Dear Jennie

I will just write a line I expect to land soon we have been waiting 2 days to land & must now land in small boats we have 200 Recruits on board Rough fellows many of them But I have them in pretty good controll This is a very strong place No Troops but ours could ever take it Batteries bristle up on every side Our Regt are 3 miles away We land today. The Storm is clearing up

Good bye with lots of love from yours affectionately
JamesA.Barrett
Direct as usual 2d Brig 2d Div 24 Corps

[*James' diary entries]
Wed Feb 8 1865
Landed about noon in @ tug & joined the Reg^t. about 3 miles up

Thurs Feb 9 1865
Changed camp—good place—pitched tents

Fri Feb 10 1865
Commenced drilling recruits   Orders to move in morning. 3 days' rations

Chapter 23

10,000 Union Prisoners

> February 21-March 07, 1865--Two skirmishes--Takes Wilmington--
> Rebels give up 10,000 prisoners--Many look like walking skeletons--
> New commission as a Major--Hoke falls back--Details of returning
> prisoner's health conditions--Sherman's battle at Mud River loses
> 2,000 men--Sherman sends 30,000 refugees to Wilmington--Country
> is sacked--Richmond falls--Petersburg victory--Lee surrenders at
> Appomattox

[Note that all the following transcriptions have been faithfully copied from the original document, as written by James, except where noted.]

[*Narrative]
We were constantly marching & remarching, flanking the enemy out of one position after another. Had quite a sharp skirmish on the 21st & marched triumphantly into Wilmington on the 22d Feb'y   It was a strange sight to witness the welcome from the blacks   They were very demonstrative   But we were not to tarry long here. The retreating enemy were burdened with about 10000 prisoners   To recapture these we made a forced march all day & towards evening skirmished with the rear of their column at N. E. station where they crossed the river & burned the bridge after them   But by a flag of truce they consented to give up their prisoners & we halted & went into camp here to receive, feed, nurse & clothe these famished creatures.

They were a happy set in spite of their condition which was wretched in the extreme. Ragged, filthy, & half starved they looked like living skeletons Nothing but their new found liberty could inspire them with sufficient strength to walk to Wilmington as they did most of them   But many were too far gone to help themselves at all   A large portion soon died   The rest were sent north.

We soon returned to Wilmington & afterwards marched to Cox's bridge where a part of the column did a little skirmishing & kept up our march with some few delays until we arrived at Raleigh   In the battle before Wilmington Feb 21st our Maj. lost a leg & I was appointed acting field officer & our Lt Col soon receiving a com^n as Col & the Maj Lt Col I was commissioned Major but was never mustered in because the former Maj'r being in Hosp^l & not able to return to be mustered in his advanced grade kept the vacancy locked against me

[*James' diary entries]
Sat Feb 11 1865
All armed men left camp at 7 ¼ A.M.   Heavy orders—3 days' rations
Officers' baggage sent to B'g.H'd.Q't'rs   Hard getting through the swamps
203rd on skirmish line   Capt. Scott killed   Several wounded in the 203rd
One of our men got @ bullet in his boot   Heavy skirmishing   We advance
about 3 miles and bivouacked   Put up works

Sun Feb 12 1865
Pleasant day   Slept well—relieved in afternoon by Paines' Div. & marched
to the rear   Issued 3 days' rations   Surf too high to march up the beach
Bivouacked in the woods Smoky I was reported killed

Mon Feb 13 1865
Cold night   Garaghan appointed Aid B'g.H'd. Q't'rs   Maj. Harding 203rd Pa
Vols.—commanding Col. mustered   Capt. Cook—Major   Essington feels
rather sore

Tues Feb 14 1865
Orders to move at sundown   Marched up the beach 8 or 10 miles
Pontoons late   Our movement discovered & we return   Arrive in camp at 4
A.M. tired, wet & hungry   Rainy night

Wed Feb 15 1865
Slept well @ few hours   Blankets wet   Clearing off   Feel stupid but stood
the march well

[*Letter]

In the Woods 4 Miles from Ft. Fisher N.C.
February 15 1865

My Dear Jennie   Last time I wrote we were under orders   But the surf was too high that night &
we bivouacked in the woods. Last night we started at Sundown & marched 6 miles up the beach
intending to cross a pontoon & flank the Enemy   But there was a delay in getting the Pontoons up
& the Enemy discovered our design   So we returned again & bivouacked arriving here at 4 A.M.
tired wet & hungry It cleared off today & we are nearly dried again. We did not take Wilmington
this time   But will soon. I stand it very well. The march was heavy & many strong men fell out.
Yours with much love   JamesA. Barrett
Excuse this scribble we have to be economical with paper. Our baggage is at the rear

[*James' diary entries]
Thurs Feb 16 1865
Moved camp & pitched tents   Received some clothing   Sherman taken
Branchville   23rd Corps crossed the river

Fri Feb 17 1865
Marched down to the point & crossed to Smithville   Bivouacked

Sat Feb 18 1865
Took up our march at 3 P.M. Marched six miles & bivouacked for the night
in the woods

Sun Feb 19 1865
Marched at 11 A.M. to Ft. Anderson. Rebs evacuated early this morning
as we were in their rear   They expected us up along the river   If we had
been @ little earlier we would have bagged 2500   Four brigades of 23rd
Corps follow them up   We cross the river & bivouack & reconnoiter   Genl.
Terry two miles in front   Johnny on the run

Mon Feb 20 1865

Fine day   Marched slowly toward Wilmington   Skirmishing in front   Bivouacked & threw up works   The enemy strong in our front

Emma Jane's pen and ink drawing
"Marching to Wilmington" (Barrett Collection)

Tues Feb 21 1865

Rations short & scarce   Rumors of rebels still falling back   We expect to charge today   Move to the left   Surprised & fired into from rebel works   48th deployed as skirmishers & advance under heavy fire. I am in command of reserve   Maj. Elfwing wounded-- lost @ leg   Reserve all deployed   Short of ammunition. Pretty hot   Gunboats open   We fall back in the evening & form @ new line. Works thrown up in our rear   Our brigade ordered to leave   We march back to the right where we were this morning   Our regiment behaved nobly today   Hilliard in command of the Reg^t. He is very plucky & does well

Wed Feb 22 1865

Slept 3 hours—roused about 7 A.M. & marched to Wilmington, which was taken this morning   Washington's birthday well celebrated   Our men very tired but in good spirits   Plenty of tobacco in Wilmington   I secured 300 lbs. for the 48th. We start on @ rapid march after the Johnnies who are on the run with 8000 of our prisoners with them   Marched 10 miles & captured

*the pontoons over N.E. river   Rebels stand on the other side   We secure
some prisoners & some of our prisoners.   Our advance skirmish with the
enemy   Myrick's battery engaged   Our brigade halt in the evening &
bivouack for the night   Very tired   Many of our prisoners secreted in the
woods*

Thurs Feb 23 1865
Went in to camp.

[*Letter]

10 Miles beyond Wilmington N.C.
Feb 23 1865

My Dear Jennie

I have just got inside a tent again & will snatch a few moments to drop you a line.   I have been very busy the past 10 days Marching and Countermarching continually flanking the Enemy until we have driven him from Wilmington & He is still on the run. The 17th we crossed from Ft Fisher to Smithsville On the 18th we marched round to the rear of Ft Anderson on Cape fear River 19th marched into the ft which had been evacuated during the night.   The Rebs were terrified when they found that the Yanks were in their rear We immediately embarked & crossed the river Next morning marched slowly towards Wilmington.   Our advance encountered the Enemy in a few Miles & drove them inside their works we threw up breast works that evening within range of their artillery & leaving the Negroes to hold the line Marched to the left   next morning the 21st & soon encountered the Johnnies

When our Regt were ordered out as skirmishers. 5 Cos were at once deployed & I took Comd of the reserve of 5 Cos. The 48th advanced in gallant style under heavy fire & drove the Rebs inside their works when we were ordered to halt Line Maj Elfwing lost a leg & 17 men were killed & wounded I was soon obliged to deploy all my reserve to strengthen the skirmish line. Thank God I escaped unhurt & many were the congratulations I received on account of it. Capt. Hilliard is now in Comd of the regt & behaved himself finely.   We fell back in the evening & marched back to the right bivouacked a few hours & yesterday morning marched in triumph through Wilmington to this place The Rebs flying before us.   They destroyed the bridge across the N.E. River & made a stand.   They have about 8000 of our prisoners with them & we hoped to catch & liberate them before they reached the river There was some skirmishing in our front all the afternoon yesterday   But our Brigade were not engaged. I believe some pontoons have been taken and expect we will advance soon

We are now in camp until we can get some rations up Our march yesterday was very rapid & our men very much exhausted.   Every one's feet are sore   I have stood it very well although I feel tired & stiff. Our Regt recd much praise for the manner in which they fought. I was proud of them. They behave nobly.

The fortifications about the city are very strong   But were not proof against the flanking propensities of the Yanks The people in the city white & black greeted us with hearty welcome It is a proud thing for a Victorious Army to march through a Conquered City The tattered Flag of the

48th waved proudly on the left of Co. H. & excited considerable attention. A good many of our Prisoners have escaped & come in to us & we hope to secure the most of them yet. I know very little that is going on that I am not immediately engaged in. Our Gen^{ls} keep their own secrets & I am glad they do. The papers will give you more news than I can   This year has be freighted wih Victory thus far. Mobile Savannah, Charleston, Wilmington evacuated. I expect the Confederacy will evacuate soon & leave us in Freedom & peace again Col Coan is back again. He is in com^d of Ft. Fisher. He will probably leave our Brigade Capt He will permanently Com^d the Reg^t

Now Good bye with much love from

Yours Affectionately

Jas A. Barrett

[*James' diary entries]

Fri Feb 24 1865

Rebs want to exchange our prisoners   Terry declines & they are to be paroled   Stormy

Sat Feb 25 1865

Rebs short of food   Preparing to receive our prisoners   Still stormy. Brigade officer of the day

Sun Feb 26 1865

2000 prisoners received today   All the doctors busy

Mon Feb 27 1865

Saw 2000 of our paroled prisoners pass   They look very sick   The sickest are coming last   God help them   Dick & cart arrived.   Mess started

[*Letter]

Camp 48th Reg^t N.Y.S. Vols

N.E. Station N.C.   Feb 27 1865

My Dear Jennie   Yours of 12th is rec^d   I am glad you are over your blues   We are still here in camp I sleep with my Serg^{ts} My Valisse is expected today when I shall have a tent   I managed to borrow a Shirt today while I had mine washed   It is nearly 3 weeks since I have had a change Luckily I have kept clear of Vermin   I hired a Darky at Wilmington But he failed to come along   My little boy is not strong enough. I am going to get another   There are plenty at Wilmington I live with the Co Pork hard tack & coffee   I think we shall be here a week   The Rebs burned the RR bridge here & cut the Pontoons But we brought our Guns to bear on The Pontoons & They are now ours   Our Pickets are now on the other side of the River. Hoke found himself short of food & transportation & wanted to exchange those 10000 Union Prisoners   Terry would not exchange & so He paroled them & we are now receiving them 2000 a day commenced yesterday   The well ones come first & the sick ones last   I saw the 1st installment pass here this morning   It was a pitiable sight. If these are the well squad God help the sick ones. It is said that the woods are filled with Deserters from the Rebel Army on the other side of the River, & that Hoke himself is falling back to fortify & make another stand   I fear that He is using these prisoners as a catspaw to effect his escape   But Humanity compels us to halt & care for these poor creatures   Believing that we can flank him out of his new positions as we have from his old ones

Besides I think he will find <u>obstructions</u> in his path   We are 10 miles from Wilmington & hold the famous Weldon R.R.   It is about 150 miles to Weldon   It is said that the Rebs are out of rations & do not know where to look for new supplies

My health is very good   It is a great satisfaction to be successful   I have never known before the enthusiasm one feels in belonging to a victorious Army. Our Div$^{\underline{n}}$ is now reaping its reward for hard & faithful service. We are so far out of the world that it takes a long time for us to get the news   We heard of the fall of Charleston & these prisoners say Petersburg is evacuated   I expect Richmond will follow in a few days. I hear Capt Buttrick has gone home. What was it for?

I expect we shall soon advance again & exchange compliments with Hoke   We hope to finish him up soon & put a speedy end to the Rebellion

I hope to be home by the 4th of July   Everything looks bright now

The tale of Rebellion is universally hopeless whether told by the lips of the Inhabitants Deserters prisoners or the pen of Richmond Correspondents

The very air whispers Peace   My Dreams are full of Home. I feel as confident of it as of any unrealized truth. I suppose you closed your School on Saturday & are now enjoying your Vacation   I am glad to hear of your dissipations as you term them

Please accept every opportunity of enjoying yourself that may offer itself & be sure I am glad of it

Capt Hilliard is in Com^d of the Reg^t He talks some of resigning   Maj Elfwing is doing well. He will probably go into the Invalid Corps. Tomorrow is Muster day & I have the Rolls[xxi] to make out   I have lots to do the coming week & you must excuse me if I do not write much   With much love to all friends   I remain

Yours very affectionately
James A. Barrett
Direct 2^d Brig 2^d Div$^{\underline{n}}$
~~Fort Fisher~~ N.C.
Wilmington

[*James' diary entries]
Tues Feb 28 1865
Mustered   Baggage arrived   Garaghan A.A. Ins. General. Commence on pay rolls

Wed Mar 1 1865
Stormy   Very busy on rolls   Turned over property Co. A.

Thurs Mar 2 1865

*Move camp down near Wilmington   Good place   Brig. officer of day
Horse to ride   Establish picket line   Rosin & turpentine [187] found in large
quantities   Report the fact   Drink of milk*

Fri Mar 3 1865

Commence my rolls in earnest today   I have @ good house to work in

Sat Mar 4 1865

Finish rolls today   Owen very good clerk   Grover returned

Mon Mar 6 1865

Q.M. returns sent off today for Jan. & Feb. Cos. A. & H.

Tues Mar 7 1865

Visited Wilmington   Low place & very dirty   Prisoners dying fast

[This is Emma Jane's transcription of a letter written by James.]

Near Wilmington N.C.   Mch 7 1865

My Dear Jennie

We are now in camp about two miles from the city   The 23rd Corps have moved out with ten days' rations towards Newbern. We are expecting orders every day.

It is supposed that Lee has evacuated Richmond & is concentrating his forces in or near "that last ditch." I think there is to be one more big battle. It will be short   But decisive. The confederate soldiers do not stand up and fight as they used to.   Constant defeat has unnerved and discouraged them. The name of Sherman is a terror to the whole rebel army. I believe our 2nd division is getting to be pretty well known to them also and our approach is considered a pretty good excuse for them to leave.

Our prisoners are now about all over. I believe we have received about 1000 officers and 8 or 10000 men. Such sights as they are, I don't want to see again! It fairly makes one's blood turn cold and many were the vows of revenge uttered by our men when occasion should offer   It is not possible to exaggerate the sufferings our poor men have endured. Hungry, emaciated, ragged, dirty and lousy! May God forgive their cruel tormentors for they surely knew not what they were doing. Their was skin fairly black with dirt. In many cases, soap would hardly have any effect. The dirt had fairly become encrusted in the skin. It would seem as if men might keep washed but you must remember that they had no soap and in many cases, even the water was filthy.

---

[187] It is used chiefly as a solvent and drying agent in paints and varnishes. turpentine. (n.d.).
Columbia Electronic Encyclopedia, 6th edition. Retrieved December 16, 2015, from
http://www.infoplease.com/ce6/sci/A0849766.html

Most of these men have gone north but many of the sick ones are still in Wilmington. They are dying off very fast. The city is a very filthy place. I fear there will be much sickness there unless strict measures are taken to have it thoroughly cleansed.

A great many of our prisoners have enlisted in the rebel army   Poor fellows! They were tortured into it. Several told me about a Sergeant and a Corporal of mine who went out and enlisted to get clear of the prison pen.

I was brigade officer of the day [188] the first day we came here in camp and when I established the picket line,   I found a large quantity of turpentine and rosin secreted. I reported the fact and presume it will be secured.

We are living pretty comfortably here. We get plenty of shad and other fish   but there is not much in the provision line except what we bring. The country seems to have been pretty well exhausted. Our men found some pork buried   but not much of a quantity.   There are no sweet potatoes. I got a good drink of fresh milk outside the picket line the other day and enjoyed it much.

Our recruits have joined us again and we have armed them   We are now drilling them & getting ready for the next move. A number of them have given us the slip and I expect have got off among the paroled prisoners. We have to watch our recruits pretty sharply at first until we get them broken in and disciplined.

The provost marshal is the busiest man in town. The citizens are flocking to take the oath. There is crowd there all day. The negroes are being gathered up for the soldiers. I have seen a great many go by here to join the colored regiments.

Burr got his commission on a forged recommendation. He says some one else did it. I don't know what will be done to him but he will not be mustered. Col. Coan is trying hard to get our regiment filled up so as to muster in @ full corps of officers. Our reg. has lost heavier in officers during this campaign than any other about here. It is said @ 48th officer is sure to get hit in every mess we have.

Please remember me to all friends. I cant write to all in these times. Good bye with much love from

Yours affectionately   JamesA.Barrett

[*James' diary entries]
Wed Mar 8 1865
Co. drills commenced every P.M. My recruits get along finely

Mon Mar 13 1865
Orders to move at 1 P.M. in heavy marching orders   Marched through
Wilmington & crossed the river   Marched three miles & bivouacked
Anderson followed with cart & mess kit   Left sick men & guard in camp.

---

[188] An officer (in the armed forces, police, etc) on duty at a particular time. duty officer. (n.d.). *Collins English Dictionary*. Retrieved December 16, 2015, from
http://www.collinsdictionary.com/dictionary/english/duty-officer

Tues Mar 14 1865

*Fine day   Marched seven miles & received orders to return to camp
Found 83 recruits there   Took up our march at 4 P.M. to N.E. Station
arriving about 8 P.M. in hard rain   My nigger is not along   Overcoat &
blanket lost   Lacoppidan's darky is along with tent   I sleep with my rubber
over me   Wet night   Anderson & mess cart don't come up   Nigger lost
with overcoat & blanket*

Wed Mar 15 1865

*No breakfast   Brig. officer of the day   Horse to ride   Weather cleared off
Marched at 7 A.M. Bivouacked at night   Rainy night   Roads poor   Good
supper at headquarters   On the staff for the march as provost to keep up
the rear   Col. Coan is in command of the brigade   Mustered yesterday*

Thurs Mar 16 1865

*Marched at 7 A.M. about seven miles & halted for rations   Pleasant camp
Busy with guard   No coffee issued   We live well   I am getting to like my
horse*

Sat Mar 18 1865

*Fine morning   Slept well in a house   Nice people   I have bought some
coffee for my co. & guard*

Sun Mar 19 1865

*Slow march in rear of division   Rapid march in evening to catch up
Bivouacked in evening*

Mon Mar 20 1865

*Our brigade passed Duplin Court House   In advance today Sherman
cavalry near   Hard march all day   Men have sore feet   Bivouacked at 5
P.M.*

Tues Mar 21 1865

*Fine day   Fighting going on near by   Rebels supposed to be making a
stand at Smithville   We forage plenty of meat & fowls   Sherman had a big
fight day before yesterday near Mud River   Lost 2000 men   Rebs charged
seven times   We had them hemmed in against the river, But they have
crossed & burned the bridge   We go into camp & wait for pontoons   Rainy
night*

Wed Mar 22 1865

Took charge of a foraging party of 75 men   Crossed Mud River & went
about five miles   Got two loads pork—2000 lbs   Returned in evening
Camp in Waynes Co. near Cox's bridge

[This is Emma Jane's transcription of a letter written by James]

Camp 2d Brig 2d Div 24 A C
Mch 22 1865

My Dear Jennie

On the 13th our regiment crossed the river at Wilmington to accompany the pontoons some 20 miles and get some cavalry across. On the 14th we were ordered back. Found some 80 recruits in camp.   This enabled Col. Coan to be mustered & he took command of the brigade. We started that P.M. and marched to N.E. Station and have been on the march ever since making from 10 to 23 miles a day. On the 15th I was brigade officer of the day & had charge of the rear guard. My duty was to prevent straggling and keep the men closed up.   That night Col. Coan asked me if I would like the job for the whole march as he saw that I kept them up pretty well. At first I declined   but on second thought accepted as I have a horse to ride. Luck! It is @ thankless job   But saves me much fatigue. It is too much like driving cattle.
Mch 24 1865

I had to stop & go out foraging with two wagons and 75 men   We crossed the river and went four or five miles   Found about 2000 lbs. pork & got pretty near to the Johnnies. Some of the 1st brigade were gobbled yesterday two miles this side of where I went. We took pork, bacon, chickens and pigs and got back all safe. Today there is some fighting going on the other side of the river. We expect to rest a while now & get up supplies.

I stand the campaign very well. I started intending to do my duty as far as I was able trusting to Providence for the necessary strength and I have thus far been sustained. I have faith to believe that I will get along as well in the future as in the past.

We have met Sherman's forces at this point. They are rough fellows and leave little behind them. I don't see how Sherman ever gets them into a fight.

This country is very much run over. Everything is taken. I pity the poor people.

Emma Jane's illustration
of a poor family **(Barrett Collection)**

I don't know how they will live. Sherman has sent 30,000 refugees to Wilmington. We get no mails here. We expect the railroad to be opened soon to a station ten miles away. Our men have had no coffee or sugar since we left Wilmington. Nothing But pork & hard tack. We have to forage our pork now. I got enough for our brigade for one day when I went out. Can you picture me as a highway robber?

I gave my overcoat & blanket to my nigger to carry when I started and I have not seen him since. I had my rubber with me. But I have fared well on the staff. I mess with the Col. and live well. We have a mule and cart go along and I have picked up some blankets which I carry on the horse.

In case of a fight, I am to form my rear guard & take charge of the unarmed recruits. We are drilling them now & I shall arm them soon.

The trees are in blossom & remind me of home--Nearly all the people we find claim to be Union. If they have friends in the army, they were "forced in." We cant trust them much. We have the task before us of restoring confidence. The changing masters is difficult sometimes. We thought that Johnson was nearly bagged But he escaped across the river. I think he has commenced another "masterly retreat" like the one before Atlanta. Sherman's men are very sanguine & brag @ good deal. We tell them they have not campaigned in Virginia yet.
Mch 26 1865

We marched down here yesterday & are now in camp near the R.R. Facin's Station—63 miles from Wilmington. The cars are running to Goldsboro I dismissed my rear guard today & have returned to my regiment for duty. I have an idea that I shall stay here two or three weeks & get supplies. When the Virginia roads get good so that Grant can move, we shall be on again.

Good night with much love from

Yours affectionately

JasA.Barrett

*[*James' diary entries]*
Thurs Mar 23 1865
Started with another foraging party But gave it up as a corps was crossing the river First brigade was driven in & some men captured I went two miles farther than they yesterday Lucky escape Changed horses Have @ good one now

Fri Mar 24 1865
Wagons sent away last night Reports that Wheeler's Cav^ly was on this side of the river It turned out to be Wilson Recruits assigned yesterday I got two Gave Wertz a receipt for $230.00 Sent it by express to Gerrish Took @ ride today Country sacked People in want Rations will soon come up Three days' coffee

Sat Mar 25 1865
Marched 16 miles to Facins Station near R.R. & went into camp

Sun Mar 26 1865

Dismissed my rear guard & returned to my regiment   Col. Coan well satisfied with the way I have done the duty

Wed Mar 29 1865

Brigade officer of the day   Hilliard thrown from horse & hurt   About 90 recruits received yesterday

Thurs Mar 30 1865

Sent out @ party under Lt. Dawson to forage for officers mess   Wrote to Alton Mil Prison, Ill. about Parilla of my Co. captured Olustee, Fla. Windy & cold

[This is Emma Jane's transcription of a letter written by James to an unknown recipient.]

Our Troops are to keep the road open from Wilmington to Goldsboro & Schoffield from Newbern to furnish supplies to Sherman.   We are getting our regular rations now and expect a supply of clothing soon   Our men need shoes sadly. Many of them are barefooted.

We have papers to the 24th. Gold down to 150 ½   Rumor says that Jeff Davis has given up to Lee to settle with Grant. I would rejoice to see further bloodshed avoided,   but I am jealous of any further attempt at compromise.   Let the rebels lay down their arms or we will argue the case with them by a little more grape and canister.

One of our officers has a servant nearly white, who was a slave in Columbia. He says he was always contented and supposed slavery to be the right and natural condition of his people. Numbers of churches told him that it was scripture doctrine and he "accepted it on faith." Is it strange? I have known people north believe things just as blindly. He says he did not suppose they were capable of taking care of themselves and did not know what liberty was   But he has tasted it now & nothing would tempt him to be a slave again.

I have poor luck with servants. I gave up my little nigger that came from Fla. With me, to Lacoppidan at Wilmington and hired a big one. He took my overcoat, blanket and tent and left. I then hired another strapping fellow but let him go to see his brother yesterday and he hasn't come back. They are tasting freedom, I suppose and I must not complain. It is not to be expected that they are all honest, although the little fellows I have had before have been very faithful.

Capt. Hilliard was riding out with some friend last evening & got a little merry & was thrown from his horse and hurt considerably. He seems to be in a stupor today and is rather feverish. I can't have much sympathy for him. If he will drink, he must pay the penalty.

I am temporarily in command of the reg. It is filled up to nearly 900 men. After we have drilled a little more, we can make quite a show. I am trying to scare Lt. Anderson into sending in his resignation. I think I may succeed. He is a clever fellow enough, but not fit for an officer. He was a private in the 188th Pa. Vols and had only been out a few months. His friends got Seymour to commission him and we could not prevent him from being mustered and he is assigned to my company. I gave him a plain talking and told him he must study if he expected to hold his position, for the Sergeants now knew more than he. He was thankful to me for my advice & borrowed my

Tactics next day. We are now talking about an inspection of officers as likely soon to take place. He swallows it all & looks anxious. I guess he will resign. It may seem a little wicked, but I really think it is a kindness to him.

*[*James' diary entries]*
Tues Apr 4 1865
Drilled battalion two hours   Warm   Hilliard pretty sick   We glory in the name of 10th Corps again

Wed Apr 5 1865
Hilliard gone to hospital   I am division officer of the day—Lacoppidan drills battalion today   Col. Latelle takes command of brigade   Col. Coan returns

Thurs Apr 6 1865
Richmond fallen   Petersburg ours   Good news   I am to be Acting field officer   Lippincott's resignation received   Hilliard won't come back Stayley at Morehead City   2nd Brigade in our corps   Visited picket line The negroes do duty well

Fri Apr 7 1865
Brigade officer of the day   Capt. Ferguson returned   I help him fix papers Property condemned in my name   Order from Grant to followup Johnson (Johnston)   Lee hard pressed   Losing men by desertion   Anderson's resignation accepted   I am appointed acting field officer   Arms received for recruits

Sun Apr 9 1865
Four days' rations issued   Orders to move tomorrow   Packing up   I have hired @ servant

Mon Apr 10 1865
Marched about 15 miles escorting the train   Halted a little before dark 203rd went to Cox's Bridge to meet supply train—to meet us at Bentonville

Tues Apr 11 1865
Brigade officer of the day   Marched at 6 A.M.   Marks of hard fighting Halted at 10 ¼ to build @ bridge   Marched at 2 ½ & went into camp at 5 P.M.

Wed Apr 12 1865

We take the rear today 12.45 News received of Lee having surrendered his army at Appomattox CH [Court House] on the 9th Great cheering March at 5 P.M. until midnight Hard march

Thurs Apr 13 1865

Cloudy morning Two miles from Smithfield & 20 from Raleigh Our regiment escort @ train of 50 wagons loaded with provisions March about ten miles, stopping to feed at @ planter's house

Fri Apr 14 1865

March at 7 A.M. The people very poor & suffering from want & our men give them their hardtack. Halt at 12 at night Train safe About three miles from Raleigh we rested to feed at about 2 P.M. & killed some cattle. The men had no meat issued for several days Rumor of Johnson [Johnston's] surrender He dont like to surrender to Sherman

Sat Apr 15 1865

Very stormy All wet Church steeple in plain sight Orders to move at 9 A.M. countermanded with the probability that we shall not march any further in this direction Moved @ short distance & went into camp in @ pleasant place in the woods Clearing off in the afternoon I occupy @ wall tent with the Dr

Sun Apr 16 1865

Pleasant morning Dress parade in afternoon Orders received in the night to be ready to move in the morning

Chapter 24

News of Lincoln

April 17, 1865-June 3, 1865--Rumors of Lincoln's assassination--
Announcement of Lincoln's death--Great sorrow--A view of life in
Raleigh after war's end

[Note that all the following transcriptions have been faithfully copied from the original
document, as written by James, except where noted.]

[*James' diary entries]

Mon Apr 17 1865
*No move yet   Rode into the city of Raleigh   Pretty place & nice gardens
Rumor that Lincoln has been assassinated   No news of Johnson's
surrender yet   Forage party sent out.   I try @ gray horse that Mercier
picked up—like him very well   Think of buying   Short of rations   Men
getting hungry.   Cars are running   Lt. Morton deserted.   Mail expected*

Tues Apr 18 1865
Regiment inspection by Lt. Smith   Look bad   Moved camp

Wed Apr 19 1865
*Drills commenced   Johnson surrendered all troops this side of Mississippi
Lincoln's death confirmed   Mail arrived   My name sent on for @
commission*

Carte de visite of President
Lincoln, circa 1865

Emma Jane's sketch
of flag at half-staff
(Barrett Collection)

Carte de visite of entire Lincoln
family including dead son

Thurs Apr 20 1865
*Reviewed by Gen!. Sherman   Our corps march past his quarters in column
by platoon   He looks worn   Camp near the city not @ good place*

Fri Apr 21 1865
Drills resumed—fixing camp   Officers getting mustered   Showery   I am on
@ board of appraisal for captured horses   All extra animals to be turned in

Sat Apr 22 1865
Board met & appraised five horses   Garaghan's is $20.00   I am Division
Officer of the day at 4 P.M.   Boil under my arm very sore

[This is Emma Jane's transcription of a letter written by James.]

Camp 48th N.YS Vols
Raleigh N.C. Apr 22, 1865

My Dear Jennie

Thank God the war is over at last! "A few more days" the General says & he hopes to conduct us to our homes. It only remains to arrange the formal terms of peace. We are now in camp making ourselves as comfortable as possible.

We were reviewed by Gen. Sherman a few days ago. Johnson has surrendered all troops this side of the Mississippi. Gen. Terry occupied Raleigh on the 14th driving Johnson out. Since then the terms of peace have been made and only remain to be ratified formally. I suppose I am telling you no news. Such news flies fast & has doubtless reached the remotest point ere this.

Lincoln's death casts a universal gloom over the army. It is the only check to our exuberant joy. His record is crowned with glory. He was one of Nature's noblemen, "He has finished his work" and the world is better for his having lived in it. It seems sad to lose our President at such a time as this   but "the judgments of the Lord are true & righteous altogether." God knows what is best for us! Let us accept & be thankful alike for our joys and our sorrows, knowing that they are all intended for our good.

I don't know how soon we shall be sent home   but we confidently hope it will be soon. I feel pretty sure that I shall spend the 4th of July at home. If I do, I have a presentiment that a certain school will have an injunction put upon it.

I am still Acting Field Officer. Hilliard is at Wilmington on court martial duty. I don't think he will come back to the reg after he finds that I <u>outrank</u> him in favor. Col. Coan asked me the other day about promotion. I stand next in seniority to Hilliard but Col. Coan doesn't like him. He asked me if I considered H. a good commanding officer. I said I thought he did as well as he could, but did not think he succeeded very well. I did not wish to influence him but if he chose to recommend me, I should do my best. I believe he sent my name on, but when I get the commission, I don't expect I can be mustered until Maj. Elfwing is discharged. Poor man! He has had a second amputation performed. I don't think he will survive it.

Dr. Throop & I have a wall tent together and are very comfortable. I have just had a captured horse apprised and intend to buy him to take home with me. My servant proves well. He is about as white as I am. I expect to take him north with me and get him a situation.

Good bye. Hoping to see you soon, I remain

Yours affectionately
JamesA.Barrett

Sun Apr 23 1865

Visited my guards & picket   Pleasant day   Churches open but I can't well attend today   Horse is better today than ever   Sent Owen to copy reports of the Board of Appraisal on horses

Mon Apr 24 1865

Inspection by one of the inspectors of the colored division   Walling returned—looks well   Letter asking about Belois (Belaise)   answered Commenced on pay rolls.   I am on sick list   Boil under arm very sore

Tues Apr 25 1865

Got the horse at last

Wed Apr 26 1865

Nine Lts. mustered today.   Halstead 1st Lt. Co. H.   St. John 2nd Lt.   Great rejoicing last night over Johnson's surrender   Rockets fired etc.   I had to drill the reg. yesterday   Today Col. corps officer of day

[*Letters]
Camp 48th Regt NYSVols
Raleigh N.C.   May 2 1865
My Dear Jennie

Yours of the 16th ult is recd   I must plead guilty of remissness in writing of late   But I have had a good deal to attend to   We have now finished our Pay Rolls & Returns & in a few days are to have a grand review when that is over we are to have only 2 drills per day & will get more leisure   Our Officers are mostly young & need some assistance   I as executive Officer have to keep these wheels from clogging, & look after the general good.   I think we shall remain here now until Civil authority is restored & then I hope we will go home.   It may take 6 months   But our duty is light & we have a very pleasant place near the R.R.   It seems like civilization to see the cars running regularly again   We see a good many of returned soldiers from Lee & Johnson's Army They flock in here to take the Oath & get horses & mules to put in their crops   They all seem glad to be out of the army.   Now the war is over we expect to see Dunbar & Hutchinson back   They wont get much respect when they come   Hilliard will probably get his back up & resign when he finds me ahead of him   Do you think I had better come home now or wait until I can muster again & come home with the Regt?   You know I always <u>listen</u> to advice & like to <u>know</u> my <u>friends</u> <u>wishes</u>. Furloughs are being given now   But I dont want one until I go for good.   We have all sent for crape to trim our Flag & never on our Arms in respect to our beloved President   All hearts are sad at his loss & many are the maledictions spoken against the foul assassin   But I doubt not it is all for the best   Nothing else would have so firmly united our People to the support of the Gvomt   I little thought when I beheld Victory dawning so brightly upon us that we were yet to cast upon the Altar already so heavy with sacrifice Our Country's brightest treasure.   He has gone   But not dead   He really lives more now than ever   His life was full of good deeds   His death has infused the spirit of those deeds into the Nations Heart

He bore the cross meekly humbly & patiently & finally died upon it. Johnson is coming up to his duty like a great man & will I hope prove himself equal to the task. His task will be @ difficult one. Reconstruction is no Childs play

These people will try & keep their slaves & in some localities may succeed for some time to come   Things are not going to settle down permanently this year or next   it will take time to make a country like this thrive like the North

I am glad that treason is losing its tongue at home   What do Copperheads do with themselves. I should think they would burst. My health is good   My wound has not troubled me I begin to think it will be fall before I get home. I cant get Stamps here & being out have to send all letters without   Good bye with much love from
Yours JasA.Barrett
Capt 48th NYSVols

Camp 48th Regt N.Y.S.Vols
Raleigh N.C. May 4 1865

My Dear Jennie

Your Sudbury letter of 30th Mch was recd yesterday   It must have been <u>marching</u>. I am sorry that my folks feel neglected   think I ought to come in & grumble some for I am sure I have written more letters home than I have recd

I may be mistaken I may have missed some during the late Campaign   Work of more importance has taken up my attention   But I generally do answer all my letters. We are having beautiful weather now & everything Is looking fresh & Spring like   I was Divn Officer of the Day the other day & rode round considerable & had all Offal[189] & Dead animals buried that I could find   I like this country much better than any I have seen

The people are getting legal again & anxious to restore Civil law

Other Corps have moved out & now we are getting supplied with stores We have been rather short   But can get Flour & potatoes now & manage to live very well   Our Regt has been heavily reinforced with Officers of lots 9 Sergts were mustered last week as 1st & 2d Lieuts. Maj Elfwing is better   He did not have a second amputation after all   He expects to come back & muster as Lt Col

I wrote to George the other day & shall write home soon not waiting for a letter   What is he doing & what are his expectations. He said something about coming down to see me if I was in a Garrison   I expect to stay here until I go home & should be very happy to see any of my friends here   If he wants to see the Country & a little of Military life perhaps he would enjoy a trip down here. When is Henry going West. I must invoice an extra quantity-of grey hair now in honor to my new Niece   Please express to the young lady my kind regards. & tell her she may call me Uncle

---

[189] Dead or decomposing organic matter. offal. (n.d.). *Collins English Dictionary*. Retrieved December 16, 2015, from http://www.collinsdictionary.com/dictionary/english/offal

as long as she will behave herself   You can use kisses or pinches as a medium of introduction whichever you may think best suited to the health of the young lady

When she gets a little older I will try to introduce myself without an interpreter   I guess Ned will be mustered out soon   I understand some of those western Reg^{ts} have started home   I hope our turn will come soon   But we have got lots of Recruits   I don't know how it will be managed   I see the Northern papers are inclined to blame Sherman for the course he took with Johnson   I think it is pretty <u>cheeky</u> for any of those fellows north who never heard a bullet sing to attack our Veteran Chief

He has done enough to ensure him lasting respect & honor & I think it would be good taste for some of these fellows to cultivate the Virtue of Humility & to be very cautious how they criticize Men who are so far superior to themselves that they are unable to appreciate their actions. We are going to Commence our Schools again for Officers & N.C. Officers. We drill 5 hours @ day & are trying to set the men up   But we have not got the material in the Reg^t in decent shape to go home with. I find it rather pleasanter to drill on horseback than on foot

Good bye with much love

From yours affectionately
JasA.Barrett
Capt 48th N.YS Vols

*[*James' diary entries]*
Sat May 20 1865
Moved at 8 A.M. to relieve the 76th Pa Vols. in the city   They steal the stores given them to guard   Pleasant camp row about tent

Sun May 21 1865
Lt. Fletcher's discharge received   The vacancy not to be filled   Strange my commission dont come

Capt. James A. Barrett,

48th Regt. N. Y. V.   Official letterhead (Barrett Collection)

[*Letter]

Camp 48th Regt NYS Vols
Raleigh N.C. May 24 1865

My Dear Jennie   Yours of Apr 30th & May 15th were recd yesterday   Our mails are coming more regular now as Rail Communication is complete to Washington   Our Wilmington letters were delayed a long time   I was about to write a letter of inquiry about Charles Gerrish   I have not heard from him in a month or more

Thank you for the advice   No doubt it fell on good ground   My health is good now   My wound has been entirely well for a long time My duty is not hard & I propose to ride a horse home with the Regt if nothing happens to prevent

I think about August will find me on my homeward way. We moved camp on Saturday 20th. We are now in the city doing guard duty over commissary stores   Trains on the R.R. &c The Regt that was here stole so that they had to be relieved   We are getting along nicely thus far altho our men come on guard duty pretty often   Our camp is in a beautiful place & the location is airy & healthy   Col Coan is still on Court Martial duty & I am in Comd of the Regt   I have no drills except Dress Parade & Inspections

The parties that we sent out to establish Local Police have been very successful   They manage to find arms enough to arm a company

We are daily expecting our Capt Garaghan back with 40 men from his expedition   There are still some wandering Guerillas scattered about the country robbing whoever they may find But things are settling down pretty fast now   Vance has gone to Washington to feel the Hemp Market Prest Johnsons vigorous effort will soon bring others to justice & this State will soon have a Government of its own   Things always work for the best Altho it is hard sometimes to see it in that light   I mourn Lincolns death as much as any one & shall rejoice to see the guilty ones brought to justice

It was a foul plot against as noble & just a Man as ever ruled a Nation

His death has now Crowned his work as "Finished" & Oh how Eloquently.
Could his life if spared have done as much? I think not. He "has finished his work." & Another has taken up the Sceptre to perform a different But perhaps an equally difficult work.

It may prove that the active impulsive energy of Andy Johnson is more appropriate for the times than the quiet conservative & forgiving spirit of our late Chief

These Rebellious states require a firm hand to rule them & bring them back to loyalty There seems to be a disposition like Pharaoh of old & harden the heart & not to let the Children go.

I am sorry to hear such news about our little Church in Brooklyn   They launched out too expensively at first & did not count the cost. Where does Lizzie live now   It must be a relief to her to get the children into the Country   She has @ difficult task to perform   But she has done it thus far faithfully. Thank you for your "Magnanimity"[190] Please return my Love to "Molly" (with interest of course) & I hope your memory will always serve you as well

I have got to go down town to help Inspect some Reg^{ts}   I will write @ letter home tonight or tomorrow   Good bye from

Yours affectionately
JamesABarrett

[*James' diary entries]
Mon May 29 1865
Dunbar coming back   Going to see it out

Tues May 30 1865
Reenforced by three officers & 190 men

[*Letter]
Camp 48th Reg^t NYSVols
Raleigh N.C.   May 31 1865

My Dear Jennie
Yours of 22^d is rec^d   Our mails come very regular now   I have no news to write   The Officers of our Reg^t are to be examined Friday   I expect all sorts of questions will be asked. Of course I expect to get stuck on some   A number of Reg^{ts} in our Divⁿ whose term expires next fall are to be mustered out soon   I suppose their recruits will come to us

Charlie writes that he is about to buy little place in Concord & hire housekeeper & Servant & settle his mother down   I fear he will find it difficult to get just the right sort of person.

I have not decided yet what I shall do when I come home   Very likely I may go back to Swain's again   Story is still anxious to go in to business & thinks we could do well in the dry goods business   I think I could sell goods very well. But I cant decide until I come home   Something will invite me   I am confident   I always was lucky & my good fortune ought not to forsake me now. Burr was tried by Court Martial   But before his sentence was published he with some 20 others broke jail & escaped to parts unknown

---

[190] The fact or condition of being magnanimous; generosity. magnanimity. (n.d.). *Oxford Dictionaries*. Retrieved December 4, 2015, from http://oxforddictionaries.com/definition/english/magnanimity

My horse is getting gay now that we get full rations I like her very much. Capt Dunbar writes me that he is coming back   He means to <u>see</u> it <u>through.</u>   I wonder if he expects a welcome Or if he thinks he will take com^d of the Reg^t   It may take him down little to have to go into the line & com^d his Co

He is Senior to me But I don't think he will get com^d over me

My commission has been issued & is expected daily. I cant be mustered   But I hear that they do muster Officers holding commissions when they muster them out of service so that they can wear their rank home. We like our location here very much

The duty was hard on our Men & we have got a detail of 180 more men to help. 2 of our young Officers are under arrest for Drunkenness & 1 for neglect of duty   The latter will get clear the others probably will be dismissed

It often happens that they feel sure about something & put the first one they pitch on under arrest.

I took a nice ride out into the country the other day to get some cherries & fresh milk   It is a very pleasant country & with good company there are some very pleasant rides

I see by the papers that Johnson is hunting up the rebel leaders pretty sharp   I want to hear of their being hung & then I will be satisfied

I think they will hang Lee for allowing the barbarities on our poor prisoners. As for the Rebel Turner who commanded at Libby I can not imagine a punishment bad enough for him. We can hang him But God alone can <u>really</u> punish him

There are several rich families right round our Camp   They are culturally civil But it is plain to see they do not love the union too well   They don't want to see Davis hung. The poor people do want him hung. Breakfast waits & I have got to go away inspecting

So good bye with much love

JasABarrett

[*James' diary entry]
Sat June 3 1865
Finished Rumsey's case today   Made my plea in court & cleared him
Examined before the board   I don't wish to stay in the army   Div. officer of
the day

Chapter 25

Commission Comes Through

June 3, 1865-June 30, 1865--Mother writes letter--Commission is
sent to Washington by mistake--Commission to Major finally arrives

[Note that all the following transcriptions have been faithfully copied from the original
document, as written by James, except where noted.]

[letter from James' Mother]

Concord, June 3rd, 1865

My Dear Son

Yours of 19th came to hand last night and I hasten to answer it as it takes so long to reach you there may be a chance of your not getting it before you start for home for I don't think you are in duty bound to do all the work and have none of the honor after all you have done for in the last six months and no notice being taken of it I would resign at once and come home for I don't see as you are bound to stay longer, and I think your health requires it   not but what you can be useful there, by precept and example but have you not taxed your Brain and muscles long enough for others, in office without compensation. to decline doing it longer. I feel that you have. and advise you to leave at once, and come home where you will be appreciated, without exposing yourself so much,   we all feel that you deserve promotion but let promotion go   and leave all such disappointments as not worth thinking of in comparison to health

I suppose if you had not thought you would wait for promotion you would have come before G H [George Henry] went away   he has not gorn yet went to New York last Saturday and came home Thursday night has gorn to Boston today and expects to go down monday and tuesday is engaged to take tea at Mr James Woods--have not heard him say when he thinks he shall go back to Colorado but thinks he may not go for a week or two if so you may get   home before he starts   I was very much gratified to have him receive letters from you   the last arrived while he was gorn last Wednesday Election Day your Father Aunt Dorcas Mary & Baby and myself went over and spent the day with Emily had a very pleasant day and I did not get sick only very tired the next day we attended the Union services in the Orthodox Church which was decorated with flowers and evergreen surrounding mottos   heard a very interesting Sermon from Mr Reynolds   the other services except the singing (which was very good) I could not hear your Aunt Dorcas has been boarding at the Middlesex a few weeks is not very well and Charles has been on twice since she has been there he finds its not the place for her there and concluded to start off with her to Brooklyn yesterday he came Thursday morn   she could not sleep nights well and I dont wonder   I dont think I could   it was a great mistake to have her come out of the Hospital untill a proper place could be procured for her   Charles intends to buy a house in Concord and furnish it and get some Lady to superintend and a Girl to do the Work and have a home for the Gerrish family thinks they have been from pillow to post about as long as is best.   he says if his Mother dont stay only a few weeks before she has to return to Somerville he intends to make the experiment and then there will be a home ready for her when she gets better.   I think he will find it a very difficult matter to find a Housekeeper that will suit your Aunt one she will feel is prudent and pleasant &c   no one but a Wife can fill that place satisfactorily in my view.   But we kept silent on the subject and did not allude to his getting a Wife   I expected your Father would certainly allude to it but he did not.   Charles thinks his business is somewhat changed so that he expects to come to Boston as often as once a month through the year and he can slip up to Concord and spend the Sabbath &c   Story has commenced to come up and board at the Middlesex this week to be with his Mother her going off so sudden I think will be quite a disappointment to him unless he found she was getting bad and in that case it will be a great relief to him.   Charles is strong in faith that he knows how to manage her and shall succeed in raising her spirits   he said he did not know how it would affect him a long while but he was going to make the trial he thinks he knows more about her wants than I think with our experience he does Perhaps its well for him to make the trial she has not been up here only to call, since she came from Somerville   at first Mary and the Baby and Georgy were here and we did not feel that it would be quiet enough for her and she woul after they went home say when I asked her to come up and make us a visit that she wanted to get so she could sleep well first we did not urge it hard. for we had a young Girl fresh from Ireland who knew very little about work which, made it hard for us to get along without Company especially to entertain one who was not well   I fear that the Boys thinks it strange that we did not urge her more to come up here and stay instead of going to the Tavern.   If I was well I should reproach myself but as I am not I feel it would not be a good place for her up here   she needs more cheerfull looks than my sad face, and, deaf ears to contend with. Sarah Barnes is in Town for a few days   has been quite sick has had a bad cough for two months and has raised some blood   she is going back next week and takes her little boy with her   has left the hospital for good and is going to live with her husband.   Anna hurt her Ankle last fall and has been lame ever since   her eyes trouble her very much so that she seems Dubbly afflicted   poor Girl I feel for her.   weak eyes is indeed a great affliction what I have been familiar with the most of my long life and now Old Age makes them worse.   we have enjoyed seeing George but it dont seem as if we saw much of him   he is going to Boston so often and one place and another that the time flies rapidly and I cannot bear to think of his going back there again but I don't know as anything would tempt him to stay in Concord.   he thinks there is nothing going on here and appears delighted with Colorado   thinks its so heathy there that if Mr Thompson would go there his eyes would get well and renewed health as well as wealth   that money can be made there   in most any way   I should think he would be discouraged with thinking he could ever persuade one of his connections to think so   He talked with Henry (Warren) about it but could not succeed. Henry writes in fine spirits   thinks he can support his family much easier there than he can here. intends building a house amediately as the rents are so high that he could pay for the house in five years. I think he has a hard row to hoe to support two establishments Mr Belden would be willing to board Mr & Mrs Warren for three dollars a week apiece and then they could rent the farm so that would help pay but Mr Warren don't like to live in the city Mrs M [Warren] would be delighted with it. Oh how we shall miss them I don't like to think of it feel as if I should never see them again.   how trying it is to have families so separated. If you come home I suppose you wont feel easy until you go off to N York and then we only see you once a year for a day or two at a time. Charles Gerrish says he thinks with your knowledge you would do well to be married and settle down on this farm the next week is June Court and Mr Thompson has a case and he and Emily are comeing over and spend the week with us in the month of May We had three swarms of bees come out and got them nicely hived. all last Summer your Father thought that he should have to put off old Kate and now he is looking out for a horse to match

Fanny we can not bear to think of his parting with Old Kate but I think he will   there has been a number of applications to buy her Mary says she wishes her Husband would sell theirs as Mr Warren is rather afraid of him and would not be afraid of Kate and she meant to write to Henry about it   she thinks they could any of them drive Kate and should enjoy it their horse does pretty well and Lizzie is not afraid to drive him but he rears up sometimes so that Mr W (Warren) don't like to have much to do with him. I flatter myself this will be the <u>last</u> letter that I shall write you in your military life from your affectionate Mother who feels greatful that you have been spared thus far and can now hope that your hardships and exposures are almost over and soon you will be with us.

EB.   [Elizabeth Prescott Barrett]

[*James diary entry]
Mon June 5 1865
Sent off returns for May

[*Letter]

Hd Qtrs 48th Regt NYSVols
Raleigh   N.C. June 7 1865

My Dear Jennie
        Yours of 29th ult is recd   I am glad you are getting along so nicely & that you have so pleasant a boarding place. Next time you go to Bedford you must take fair weather. We are having fine weather here now But it is pretty warm
        Blackberries & other berries are getting plenty & New Apples begin to come in
        I like my horse very much   She rides as easy as a cradle   But she has a wound that troubles her some yet
        It is very pleasant to ride out into the country with good company. We have a new Governor now   The rich folks about here don't like him & From what I hear I think he is like Bennett of the Herald. I wrote you that one of our New Officers was under arrest for neglect of duty. His case was tried before Court Martial Friday & Saturday
        He engaged me as his Council & I conducted my first <u>Suit</u>. I succeeded in proving his entire innocence & in my Defence censored severely the party who thus endeavored to shield himself by seeking another victim. Saturday the Board of examination met at these Hd Qtrs to examine our Officers

I was examined first as I had got to go on Div<u>n</u> Officer of the day. It was not a very hard ordeal   They asked me some questions in Battalion & Brigade movement   But did not deem it <u>necessary</u> to go into details as we were <u>acquainted</u>   I told them I did not wish to remain in the service   But wished to go home as soon as I could consistently

We are discharging all our men whose time expires before Sept 30<u>th</u> & expect to be filled up with remnants of disbanded Reg<u>ts</u>   I begin to think that our Reg^t will be retained at least another year. When we get well settled & are filled up & get enough Officers I think I shall resign   The War is over now & Altho the Board tried to persuade me that the Interests of the service would be served by my remaining (<u>Soft</u> <u>Soap</u>[191]) I think my friends have more claims on me than my Country has now.   My Commission was sent to Washington as they thought we were enroute for that place   It has been sent for & is expected daily

Elfwing is not doing well   But still hopes to be well enough to muster   I want to be mustered before I go home   I presume I can muster with a silver leaf if I wait a few months longer

I cant muster at all until Elfwing decides one thing or another. Hutchinson is discharged for Physical disability & Absence without leave   He failed to send the regular required Certificates

Capt Dunbar (<u>Beat</u>) writes me that he is coming back   It is just what we expected now that all danger is over   He wrote me in quite a patronizing way   He is senior to me by old Commission   But I shall rank him now & offers to present me with a Corps Badge   I answered his letter <u>officially</u> But said <u>nothing</u> about his <u>kind</u> <u>offers</u>

My Boy <u>John</u> noticed me this Morning that he wished to leave & go into the Country & get a Home. I consented of course & wished him luck. He is the best servant I ever had   But I have a very bright small boy who will answer my purpose very well as long as we are in Camp. He has the best manners for a small boy that I have everseen in anyone. I am teaching him his letters & think of taking him north with me if he proves well. You need not expect me before Augt or Sept^r   I might perhaps get home sooner by resigning

But I want (for my Friends sake) to wear home as many honors as I can   If I do not have to wait too long. Miller will be mustered out now soon. Burr was sentenced to 10 months hard labour

But he broke jail & has gone to parts unknown. There is a good bit of of talk about Texas & Mexico   I think an Army could easily be raised for service there   I for one do not propose to go. I am anxious to get settled in life   I have drifted & tossed on the waves of life long enough to make me long to anchor in some quiet harbor of Peace. Hoping before long to be able to talk it all over with you   I remain yours very affectionately

JasA.Barrett

Capt 48th NYSVols

---

[191] Use of persuasive talk; to cajole, flatter. soft soap. (n.d.). *American Heritage Dictionary of the English Language, 4th edition*. Retrieved December 4, 2015, from http://www.yourdictionary.com/soft-soap

Sat June 10 1865
Received four officers & 340 men from 117th N.Y.V.

[*Letter]

Camp 48th Reg^t N.Y.S. Vols
Raleigh N.C. June 10 1865

My Dear Jennie

Yours of 3^d inst is rec^d What makes you think I am feeling miserably or that my wound discharges

I am strong & well & my wound has been entirely healed for a long time   If I do get a little bilious once in a while I know just what to do to nip it in the bud. My Commission was sent to Washington by mistake

The Col has sent for it. The Col is now in Com^d of the Brig & I of the Reg^t We are getting about 300 new men today from the 117th N.Y. Vols which has gone home. This will fill us up full again. I think our Reg^t will be retained until Congress meets & makes provision for a regular Army If I find that they will go home in the fall I shall probably stay to go with them

I was allowed to look at the Roll of honor the other day (Confidentially of course) as made up by the Board of Examination for Officers   Perhaps you would like to know how I stand. Well perhaps I will tell you some time if_____ Enough to say I am not put down below 1st class. That is not egotistic is it? We are to have 4 Officers from the 117th   I believe one of the Capt^{ns} is senior to me   But I expect to be breveted so as to keep Com^d of the Reg^t as I cant be mustered at present.

So Sallie Barnes is going to live with her husband is she? I am glad of it   What a pity they are not more congenial. But hers is not a solitary case & it is not to be wondered at either considering the way matches are too often made

There are very few people in the world who seem to really appreciate what constitutes a "good match"

A few paltry thousands will with most people weigh more than any other consideration. Better far to be content with poverty with peace of mind than to roll in riches midst unpleasant associations & connections. Am I beginning to preach? I will not follow this any longer   You dont exactly understand about the Veterans   They first enlisted for 3 years or during the war   They then reenlisted for 3 years unless sooner discharged & rec^d a large bounty   But I contend that they have richly earned the bounty & should be discharged as soon as any. But Gov^{mt} seems inclined to retain them because they have given them a big bounty   The Substitutes have not rec^d any bounty from Gov^{mt} But have rec^d a very large bounty from private sources This the Gov^{mt} do not seem to consider   I don't know whether I shall remain in Com^d of the reg^t or not   Col Coan wants me for A.A.A. Genl & I believe they have got my name at Corps Hd Qtrs for some outside duty   Perhaps Superintendent of Freedmen[192]   I am drifting on the tide of Fortune & intend to make the best of what this fickle mistress (***Note: There is a dark stain in the margin of the paper with a notation...Sorry but cant help it Inkstand tipped <u>over</u>) may have in store for me. J.B. Brown is in a new business. Settling discharged officers & soldiers Claims   There is a good deal of competition in that business. N.Y. has an agent to settle the accounts of N.Y. Officers gratuitously

Is Ned going to remain in the service. We have 2 Officers in arrest for drunkenness & disorderly conduct

They have been tried & will probably be dismissed   We have had to put them under guard some of the time

We all feel very much ashamed of having anything of the kind in camp   I am really sorry that I cant hope to see Geo Henry   But I don't think it will be possible

I have not called on a single family yet since I have been in this City   There are several apparently very nice families near our camp

But I imagine they are pretty strong secesh & I don't incline to seek an acquaintance which might be terminated unpleasantly by my plain speaking   For I have got somewhat in the habit of speaking what I mean in plain Anglo Saxon

With much love I remain yours very affectionately
James A. Barrett
Capt 48th N.Y.S.Vols

[*James' diary entries]
Mon June 12 1865
Received my commission as Major Hilliard returned to the regiment & is
allowed to loaf awhile.

Tues June 13 1865
Capt. Downer left for twenty days

Wed June 14 1865
Chaplain's resignation received & approved

Sat June 17 1865
Five men on furlough   Rumsey released from arrest   Received Sergt.
Toole & Corpls. Seavely & Stevens to the ranks   Officers rather undignified

---

[192] An agency of the War Department set up in 1865 to assist freed slaves in obtaining relief, land, jobs, fair treatment, and education. Freedmen's Bureau. (n.d.). *Random House Unabridged Dictionary*. Retrieved December 7, 2015, from http://dictionary.infoplease.com/freedmens-bureau

Mon June 19 1865
Hilliard's detail arrived   He dont like it

Tues June 20 1865
Forwarded @ complaint about rations. Wrote for Des lists of some men of 117th N.Y.Vols

Wed June 21 1865
Inspection today   I inspected one company in 97th & two in 76th Pa Vols. Our regt. inspected at 6 P.M.—best of all. Issue of meat falls short   I make a complaint Massett is rather huffy   I give him fits

Thurs June 22 1865
Lt. Seaward objects to anyone being mustered in existing vacancies   I can't be partial

Fri June 23 1865
Escorted 203rd Pa Vols. to depot   Regiment looks well

Sat June 24 1865
Detachments to be mustered out

[*Letter]

Hd Qtrs 48th NYSVols
Raleigh N.C.   June 29 1865

My Dear Jennie

Yours of 17th was received Yesterday   I must plead guilty in setting the time of my returning farther off   But it is the developing circumstances that causes it & not any disposition on my part to deceive you. It is impossible to say when I shall be able to get home But I firmly intend to the coming Fall

Many think that our Regt will be discharged in the Fall. If it is It would be greatly to my advantage as well as my satisfaction to go home with my Regt   If I find that there is no prospect of being discharged I intend to resign in Augt or Septr   I expect to be mustered in a week or two & then <u>again</u> as soon as I can hear from Albany after that. I hope the Varioloid[193] will not prove serious   You must not be afraid of catching it & I don't think it will trouble you   I think you have got tired of Factory Village   What is it that provokes you now. Have you recd another letter? As you do not mention the Cause I cannot advise. If there is any flogging to be done that you are not equal to just say so & I will try & come home for a few weeks & settle the party or parties at once

---

[193] A mild form of smallpox occurring in persons who have been vaccinated or who have had smallpox. varioloid. (n.d.). *Random House Unabridged Dictionary*. Retrieved December 4, 2015, from http://dictionary.infoplease.com/varioloid

I think your arrangement of dining at Mrs Danwa's is a very good one   They are very pleasant people & good Company   How does Mr Thompson succeed in the Law. You say he is going to be over to Court again.

Next time you must remember & "go in when it rains" I think I remember a proverb about that. So Becky got her pluck up at last. Why did'nt she have all her teeth out & done with it   I shall expect to see a new set when I come home again.

I cant say yet what I shall conclude to do   I would like to see a little quiet life when I get out of the Army   But I sometimes think I am made for an active position somewhere   For somehow I am always obliged to be busy wherever I am. I don't wish for Idleness But I do thirst for quiet social life   I am getting heartily tired of this responsibility over men   I do not like to have to punish men for offences they ought to know better than to commit   I am getting along finely   I think the discipline of the Reg^t is improving   When I do punish I punish severely. & try to make an example

It is perfectly safe about here now   I do not ride out without company But there is no danger in riding anywhere now. The Country is completely subdued

There is the problem yet to solve as to the exact status of the black man. The southern people dont fancy his having the right to vote   I say if they are intelligent enough let them vote.They are the best union people here   We have a good many applications for Safe guards to live at houses all about within 5 miles of here   So that our men are pretty well scattered   It is going to take a long time to get things settled here so that all will be regularly employed

The Negroes many of them do not yet understand exactly how to go to work. Another year they will have learned something about their necessities & will also learn how to go to work to get a living. The Provost Marshal[194] is the busiest man I know   I went in the other day to see him a little while & all sort of cases were brought before him for settlements. I think this Country will need a good many Justices of the Peace. I frequently have complaints made by Negroes about not getting their dues &

Please send me those 2 gloves for the right hand I have 2 left handed ones here   Also please send me a few lumps of Gum Arrabic[195]   I want it to dissolve & use in the office.

Tomorrow is Muster day & I am to Inspect & Muster this Reg^t for Pay. We shall be very busy until about the 5th of July   I dont know what will be done to Celebrate the 4th But expect the most prominent Celebration I shall witness will be Caused by Drunkenness. I do not enjoy Holidays at all   On the Contrary I am always glad when they are over   Those 2 Lieuts are Dismissed the service & went home this morning   My Orderly "Laxy" is recommended to take the

---

[194] The Provost Marshal is the officer in the armed forces who is in charge of the military police (sometimes called the provost). A Provost Marshal may also be in charge of the execution of punishments. Provost Marshal. (n.d.). *Wikipedia, The Free Encyclopedia*. Retrieved December 4, 2015, from http://en.wikipedia.org/wiki/ProvostMarshal

[195] Gum Arabic or gum Acacia is a tree gum exudate and has been an important article of commerce since ancient times. It can be used as one of the ingredients to make candy, soft drinks, cosmetics, cough syrup, glue or ink. gum arabic. (n.d.). *Random House Unabridged Dictionary*. Retrieved December 4, 2015, from http://dictionary.infoplease.com/gum-arabic

place of one of them   Our Officers are all Homesick & do not seem to take the interest they ought. Some want to resign   But I cant approve them now as we have so few officers   I intend soon to approve a few that I want to get rid of. We have just got all our baggage from Norfolk that has been stored there for the past year & Dress Coats are budding out again   Several Officers in the Brig are having their wives come down here to live   It is very pleasant no doubt

But I think it spoils an Officer as a <u>Soldier</u> to have his wife in Camp

He is always neglecting some duty to go about with her. How should you like to come down here? I think I see you color up & say a pretty question to ask after the Above   But don't get angry   I meant <u>nothing</u> you may expect me home by September if <u>nothing</u> happens to prevent &c

Good bye with much love from yours affectionately

JamesABarrett

Capt Com^{dg} 48th NYSV

Hilliard is detailed as Ord^{ce} Officer at Greensboro, N.C. He don't seem to like it

Received at _Raleigh N.C._ this _30th_ day of _June_, 1865.
of _Capt James A Barrett 45 N.C._ the following Ordnance and Ordnance Stores
as per invoice dated the _30th_ day of _June_, 1865.

36	Springfield Rifled Muskets Cal 58
13	Enfield Rifled Muskets Cal 577
3	N.C. Officers Swards
2	Musicians Swards
45	Bayonet Scabbards
48	Cap Pouches
49	Cartridge Boxes
55	Cartridge Box Belts
52	Gun Slings
3	N.C.O Waist Belts & Plates
48	Waist Belts (Privates)
50	Waist Belt Plates
2	Ball Screws
60	Screw Drivers
1	Spring Vice
3	Band Spring Punches
27	Tompions
60	Wipers
1	Instructions for making Ordce Returns
950	Rounds Elongated Ball Cartridges Cal 577

Form 3 (A)—For Issues or Transfers of Ordnance Stores
(Barrett Collection)

Chapter 26

Post Provost Marshal of Raleigh

July 4, 1865-August 21, 1865--War officially over--Provost Marshall
duties in Raleigh--Letters to Jennie details what being Provost
Marshall entails--Concerns about Negroes' reactions
to being made "free"

[Note that all the following transcriptions have been faithfully copied from the original
document, as written by James, except where noted.]

[*Narrative]
At Raleigh it was announced that our work was probably done & we were ordered to make ourselves as comfortable as possible, but were soon surprised with an order to draw 3 days rations & be ready to march against Johnson at a moment's notice.

Our men were in excellent heart & furious over the recent news of Lincoln's assassination. Our order to march was countermanded & lucky for Johnson & his rebel horde that they made terms when they did for our men would have carried death & destruction with them if they had again been put on the war path.

The war was now really over & we settled down to Provost duty at Raleigh   Our Col was called to the Com^d of the Brig & I had Com^d of the reg^t until after July 4th When I was appointed Post Provost Marshal with my office in the Supreme Court room in the Capitol   My duty was to keep order in the city restrain the sale of liquor, prevent & punish outrages by soldiers, Administer the Oath of Allegiance settle petty disputes among the citizens & freedmen & give advice to all who asked for it. I had charge of all the prisoners in the several places of confinement

I had a Lieut for assistant & 3 picked companies with their officers to do the patroling & other duty.

Emma Jane's drawing of arms at rest
(Barrett Collection)

State Capitol Building, Raleigh, NC. The northwest suite on the first floor served as the Supreme Court chambers from 1843-1888 (Courtesy of Library of Congress Prints and Photographs Division Washington, D.C. 20540 USA http://hdl.loc.gov/loc.pnp/pp.print)

Tues July 4 1865

Did not put on camp guard & the men are very quiet   I stay in camp all day

Wed July 5 1865

Rumors of being mustered out   Reports sent for   Ordnance returns sent off

Thurs July 6 1865

Sent off M. & Pay rolls   P.R. to Major Binney, Norfolk, Va

Fri July 7 1865

Sent off returns of C.C. & G. E. & finished turning over my property to Lt. Halstead   I expect to be appointed Post Pvo Marshal.-Vice Maj. Dyer, Maj. Butts nor Martin won't do

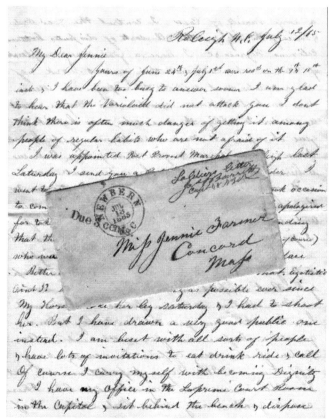

Photocopy of an original letter dated July 12, 1865 and envelope.
(Barrett Collection) The transcription continues on the next page.

Raleigh N.C. July 12 1865[xxii]

My Dear Jennie

Yours of June 24th & July 1st were rec[d] on the 9th & 10th inst & I have been too busy to answer sooner I am glad to hear that the Varioloid did not attack you I don't think there is often much danger of getting it among people of regular habits who are not afraid of it

I was appointed Post Provost Marshal of Raleigh last Saturday   I send you a Paper with my 1st Order I went to see Gen[l] Ames for instructions & He took occasion to compliment me some (Soft Soap of course) He apologized for taking me from the Com[d] of my Reg[t] by pretending that there was no one else (among Capt[ns] & Majors of course) who was really competent or suitable for the place

Better believe I held my head up after that. Egotistic Aint I? Well I have been busy as possible ever since My Horse broke her leg saturday & I had to shoot her. But I have drawn a very good public one instead. I am beset with all sorts of people & have lots of invitations to eat drink ride & call   Of course I carry myself with becoming Dignity

I have my offices in the Supreme Court Room in the Capitol & sit behind the bench & dispose a large variety of Cases   I control the good order & Police of the City & settle all sorts of disputes between Citizens Negroes &c I have a good many complaints of Citizens who cant make their servants work & of servants who cant collect their pay   One man has lost his Horse another his wagon & wants an order to oblige the one who now has it to give it up. A man or a woman gets knocked down & came to me to give them justice   A Circus is here now & I of course have free entrance with my friends & guards. I am a terror to Rum holes[196] & Ruffians generally & give my men orders to keep order without regard to Life I just as lieve[197] kill a thief or blackly[198] as not

Every body wants to keep on the right side of the Provost Marshal. I live in Camp yet But expect to board in town soon

Men & women came in for 30 Miles around here to ask some question or to lay some question before me for settlement. An order from my office is usually very effective. The Negro population are not as industrious as they should be   There are a good many who had rather loaf or steal than work. I pick up some of these Idlers & make them work on the streets for their living Civil Authority is getting established   But I do not allow them to interfere with me   The Mayor &c are rather jealous & seem anxious to have control. I have to keep them in check some. I am

---

[196] Rum holes another term used to identify a saloon Wright, John D. *The Language of the Civil War*, Rumhole (n.d.), from https://books.google.com/books?isbn=1573561355

[197] "Lieve" or "lief" archaic terms that mean gladly lief. (n.d.). *Random House Unabridged Dictionary*. Retrieved December 4, 2015, from http://dictionary.infoplease.com/lief

[198] "Blackly" an archaic term that means menacing or sinister blackly. (n.d.). *Webster's New World College Dictionary*. Retrieved December 4, 2015, from http://www.yourdictionary.com/blackly

thinking of issuing an order prohibiting the wearing of Rebel uniforms & insignia of rank by returned soldiers from Johnson's or Lee's Army.

You must excuse the want of Stamps on my letters I cant get any here You need not address me as Major until I sign myself as such. I am waiting patiently to hear of Elfwing's discharge But it don't come I think it will come sometime this month. So you cant leave Factory Village after all. I don't know But the facination of the place will cause you to induce me to settle there. Perhaps I could go into business with young Damon Who knows Wouldnt that be a good plan

I recd a letter from Nell last night & will answer soon I must close now & go to the office Goodbye with much love from yours affectionately

James A Barrett
Capt 48th NY Vols
& Provost Marshal

Camp 48th Regt NYSV.
Raleigh N.C. July 22 1865

My Dear Jennie

Yours of 9th Inst was recd 2 days since But I have been to busy to answer it I also recd the Glove & Gum Thank you fer them I don't think you will leave Factory Village. What is it that makes you dissatisfied there I never have heard any real reason yet. Poor Annie seems to be very unfortunate. She has had a great deal to bear. It almost seems more than her share   But He knows best. I am a firm believer in the Doctrine that "all is for the best" & try to accept everything accordingly   It is sometimes hard to reconcile it   But the clear eye of Faith does not shrink nor doubt. Give my love to Annie & Abbie &c. You speak of the way in which Mr. Clark takes his Wife's death. I never know how to understand such cases. If he has any belief in a Higher Power   Why cant he trust Him To be sure it is sad very sad to lose or part with friends. But after all if we have any faith at all We would not wish them back again. It is decidedly wrong to wish for death. Life was given Wisely for some Purpose & will be taken when the proper time comes & It only remains for us to make the most of it.   I was pleased with the speedy termination of the Conspirators[199].

I hope Davis & his crew will soon follow   But I fear not Delay is dangerous & I am afraid some scheme will be formed to save him. You don't mean that you are going to NH to live do you. That would be a great way out of the world & perhaps My Regt will be mustered out this fall. Capt Dawner is in Comd of the Regt now & I think does fully as well as I could myself. I am getting along nicely in the Provost's Dept. Several Regts have been mustered out & sent away & during the preparations were rather demoralized

But I shut up all the Rum shops & confiscated a good deal of liquor & kept Patrols constantly out & have succeeded in keeping things very orderly I have all sorts of characters to deal with & all sorts of crimes. Men & Women alike are brought before me. I wish I could give you a true photograph of my office at 9 A.M.

---

[199] Referring to the conspirators that planned Lincoln's assassination.

Men & Women come to take the Oath A white man complains of a Negro & a Negro of a white man One man has lost his mule another his wife One has had his watch stolen Another his head broken &c &c &c I judge them all as fairly as I can. There is a terrible lack of Morals in this Country & I fear & know that our soldiers & even Officers do not as a general thing either by precept or example tend to improve the state of things It makes me provoked to hear Men & Officers speak about the Ladies who come south to teach the Negroes The highest motive that any of them will give them credit for is to seek a Husband & they very often ascribe to them a very much worse motive There are several Mass Girls here teaching They find some trouble in getting board There is a good deal of prejudice against them. They have a hard row to hoe & get no credit for it except the satisfaction of doing their duty A Mr. Leland from Boston is in Charge of them. I took occasion the other day to tell him how things are here & to Caution him to advise his wards not to trust all who appear respectable The Negro question is <u>the</u> question here now. There are some cases of abuse But Cuffy is lazy & shiftless & considerably inflated with the idea of being <u>free</u> He has yet to learn the responsibility of freedom & educate himself into an industrious self supporting Citizen I think Agitators error insisting on the right of the Negroes to Vote They don't understand them The Negro is no more fit to vote now than the emigrants at Castle Garden I would like to give them a chance to elevate themselves & when they are competent give them the right to vote. Much harm is done by some would be philanthropists who fill the negroes heads with all sorts of foolish ideas of hostility to their late masters All this is wrong The Negro is free. No one disputes it He is now dependent for labor & support upon his late Master or some one else & it is Clearly for his interest to cultivate a kindly feeling with the people. A feeling of antagonism between employer & employed is always injurious to the laboring class, & Reformers can better employ their time than in cultivating a quarrelsome spirit.

The Freedmen's Bureau can do a great deal of good or a great deal of harm according as they allow unprejudiced wisdom to govern them

But there will be more or less corrupt men employed & they need strict watching. There is a wide field open before them Let them purchase plantations & settle unemployed   Men & Women upon them with a live Yankee to teach them how to get along I will close now

With much love from

Yours affectionately

JamesABarrett

Capt 48th NYS Vols

I must frank again as I cant get stamps Please excuse

Camp 48th Reg^t NYSVols

Raleigh NC   July 27 1865

My Dear Jennie

Yours of 19th is rec^d You have really quite a family gathering What is Ned going to do If he will come down here I think I could put him in the way of making a good thing   These people don't understand the free labor system & want to get hold of energetic Yankees to run their Machines for them

How would you like to live here a few years? How does Ned²⁰⁰ bear himself stripped of Military authority   I wonder how it seems   It is so long since I have tried it I can hardly imagine Abbie's Ned[xxiii] [Jennie's cousin, Edward Farmer] is fortunate in being assigned to duty so near home

When will they be married   I must get home if only for a few days if I can to be present on that occasion

Jennie's cousin, Edward "Ned" Farmer and Abbie [Abby] Buttrick Farmer
(Barrett Collection)

You ask if I felt calm at losing my horse   Why not   It is only one of the incidents of life You know the proverb about spilt milk &c   I have learned it & generally practice on it   I am going to get a drawing of my Office   Capt Lang of our Reg⁴ is doing it for me   I will send it to you when it is done.

I do a variety of duty   I act as a general Judge for all sorts of cases. I suppose the Mayor would do a portion of what I do   But I have lots of cases come in from 30 or 40 Miles from the city I have got things pretty quiet now & am beginning to take it easy. We hear rumors of more troops to be mustered out   I should not wonder if all were mustered out but one Reg⁴   Very likely ours would be the one to stay   It would if the people here had the say about it   I believe our Reg⁴ is the best here   But I am not much proud of it after all   Those last <u>Subs</u> were a hard sett & most of them never were in a fight to make them sober & steady.   We have to watch them very close They cant be trusted or depended on. Thieves and Cutthroats often make good fighting men & after

---

²⁰⁰ Edwin Farmer (Jennie's brother). Edwin had enlisted in Company C, Ohio 102ⁿᵈ Infantry Regiment on 6 September 1862 at the age of 19. He was promoted to Full Sergeant in October, 1862. Edwin became a 2ⁿᵈ Lieutenant in February, 1863. Promoted to 1ˢᵗ Lieutenant in October, 1864 and finally attained the rank of Full Quartermaster in February, 1865. He was mustered out on 30 June 1865 at Nashville, Tennessee. U.S. National Park Service. *Civil War. Search for Soldiers*. (n.d.). Retrieved December 15, 2015, from http:www.nps.gov/civilwar/search-soldiers-detail.htm?soldierid=E6C9CD9B-DC7A-DF11-BF36-B8AC6F5D926A

being <u>purified</u> by <u>fire</u> make good Soldiers   But common Camp Discipline cant expel the evil spirits that possess them   I hope those men who are thus represented take much pleasure in thinking they have done their duty   I am getting acquainted here some now & learning something of southern sentiment   The people are completely whipped & subdued & I believe willing to accept what the Gov^{mt} demands But they were not convinced that they were wrong   They went into the Rebellion for their independence & they still think that they would be better off by themselves   I would not have them do otherwise   I do not believe in instant Conversions & If they believed in secession at first They cant have lost their faith so soon Although they may have found it impracticable

They are more resigned to the loss of their slaves than I expected they would be   But have no faith in the capacity of the Negro to support himself & find it difficult to accommodate themselves to free labor. They dont understand how to get along under the paid system

The Negro is idle & rather suspicious & disposed to think that he can go & come when he choses without regard to the wishes of the one who hires them   It will take some time to settle these things & for both parties to learn what obligations belong to them respectively   But time will do it & If the Freedmen's Bureau are wise & discreet they can help along the good work a good deal   I have shut up all the liquor shops in the City & am getting along first rate   Good bye with with much Love from yours affectionately

JamesABarrett
Capt 48 NYSVols

Camp 48th Reg^t NYSVols
Raleigh N.C. Aug 3 1865

My Dear Jennie

Yours of 26th ult is rec^d I presume you have had a fine time at the beach I would like to have been one of the party   I wonder if you are having as warm weather as we are here

The sweat fairly runs off of me in streams some days. But I am very healthy & enjoy myself very much   I never knew time fly faster than with me now   I am so very busy at my office that a day seems as nothing

But I have got so now that I take it easier than I did at first   My office hours are from 9 to 12 & 2 to 5   But I don't feel obliged to be there myself all the time   My assistant is very useful & I trust him a good deal & when I want to go for a ride or a visit I don't hesitate to leave. We get lots of Peaches & Melons now   I almost live on them   Why dont Abbie & Ned get married?   I suppose Ned will be stationed at some post when he gets to be Chief Engineer. I think your Brother Ned can make more money South than West if he only strikes the right place

I think I could make money in North Carolina if I should try   What do you think of it,   One of my neighbors made a very liberal proposition to me the other day

How about your School   If you don't like it give it up & take a little recreation. One of our Officers is engaged to a girl out in the country here   He goes out most every night & sometimes stays 2 days at a time   The Officers blackguard him a good deal But he dont seem to mind it. I dont see what he finds to fancy about her   We all think he will get over his infatuations when he goes North & sees Northern girls

Quite a number of our soldiers are married   Some of them have their wives in Camp   It is the last place I should wish to take a wife to   I have made the acquaintance of several very pleasant families here who are loyal now altho they were secesh   I find them very pleasant

Perhaps not exactly congenial   But they are courteous & Polite. They feel somewhat bitter still I cannot wonder at it considering how they have suffered   They are perfectly submissive now   The Negro question is all that troubles them   They are very much opposed to universal suffrage & I must say I dont blame them   The Masses of the Negroes are by no means fit to vote   Besides the Northern states don't give him that privilege & it don't look charitable to force such a measure upon them when even the North are not prepared for it. I don't know what is going to become of all the swarms of children & feeble ones among the slaves. Their late masters are many of them ruined & cant support them & the able bodied men are selfish & dont feel inclined to even support their families   They seem to think they ought to get paid full wages no matter how large their family is or how helpless. This labor question is at present a knotty one & they need some live Yankees here to solve it for them   The Negro is suspicious & unused to the habits of freedom   He has got some lessons to learn & some of them will learn them by hard & dear experience   The black Children are dieing off like sheep   Their habits of herding together are not calculated to promote health & now Doctors are scarce & their former masters have lost their interest in them & they are often left to suffer & die unattended by any medical aid   This seems hard But it is unavoidable   I sometimes think it is providential that they do die off so fast. I doubt not but they are better off than living   For I don't see what is to become of so many non producers when even the producers are hard pressed just now to make both ends meet

You may think by what I write that I have changed my views on the Negro question since coming south. But I say what I see. & I think that many good philanthropists at the North talk & act blindly & would accomplish much more good if they would look calmly & dispassionately at the actual state of things as they exist   One at such @ distance can hardly judge of the wants & necessities of a class of people among whom they have never associated & much harm may result in jumping at unwise or unsound conclusions

With much love to all I remain
Yours very affectionately

JamesA.Barrett
Capt & Pro Marshal

[*Narrative]
I generally found my office thronged every morning with all classes of men & women who had come to take the oath, ask advice, or get information or redress of wrongs   Some often came 70 miles. I gave the Oath to a Cousin of our recreant President (Johnson) who could not write & had to make his mark.

[*Letter]

Camp 48th Regt NYSV
Raleigh NC   Aug 21 1865

My Dear Jennie

     Yours of 8th inst is recᵈ   I am glad to see you enjoying yourself so well   I hope to be with you soon   I was relieved as Pro Marshal last Friday   Our Regᵗ has orders to Muster out at last & we are commencing on our Rolls   We hope to get mustered out by the last of the Month & get to N.Y. by Sept 5ᵗʰ or 10ᵗʰ. It will take us about a week there to have our Rolls examined & get Paid off. I hope to get home by Oct 1/65   You need not write me again at this place. You may write to N.Y. if you like unless you choose to <u>go</u> in <u>person</u>
     I shall be happy to meet you there   I presume we shall Rendevous at Hart Island unless we manage to get permission to stop in Brooklyn   Every day seems a week now. But it will soon pass away. I propose to loaf until Thanksgiving or until I can get a good chance to go into business. I dont know whether I shall be able to get Mustered as Major or not   Elfwing don't come & I don't know whether he will   If he comes & gets mustered   It will give me a chance   I suppose we will be recᵈ by several Regᵗˢ at N.Y.   I was partially in joke about living in Raleigh & partly in earnest   There is a good chance here for me   But I think I have exiled myself about long enough already to entitle me to spend the rest of my days in civilized life   Our Col is in business at Lawrence Mass & has hinted several times something about business as if he would like me to go in with him I am going to take my time & wait for something to turn up. No doubt some opening will present itself   There always did   Our Military rules are pretty strict here. Officers must have a pass to go to the City   I believe a good many go without a pass after all   I am going to Roanoke Island in a day or two on Regimental business   Col Coan is back with the Regᵗ now as Divⁿ & Brig Hd Qtrs have been given up at this place   Now we are about going home we are all building Castles for the future   I need not say that these pictures all have silver linings I can hardly realize that I am really going home to be a free man again   But it is really so I believe   As to that silver lining that remains for me to find   But I have a theory that any one can find one who really looks for it in earnest
     We have No Band now   But we have a very good Glee Club who sing well & play pretty good on a Banjo &c,   They afford us a good deal of entertainment   I have concluded not to take my Nigger home   I should not know what to do with him
     Please remember me kindly to all friends & tell them they may expect me about Oct 1/65 & believe me with much love

Yours very affectionately
James A Barrett
Brevᵗ ²⁰¹ Citazen State of Mass

---

[201] An honorary promotion in rank, usually for merit. Officers did not usually function at or receive pay for their brevet rank. brevet (n.d.) *Glossary of Civil War Terms*. Retrieved December 4, 2015, from http://www.civilwar.org/education/history/glossary/glossary.html#B

[*Narrative]

About Sept 1st I rejoined my reg^t & prepared for our discharge.

We were all delighted at the prospect of soon going home & set about the necessary work with a will & were discharged at Hart Island[202] N. Y. Harbor about the middle of Sept.

---

[202] Hart Island, sometimes referred to as Hart's Island, is a small island in New York City at the western end of Long Island Sound. The island has been used as a Union Civil War prison camp, a lunatic asylum, a tuberculosis sanatorium, potter's field, and a boy's reformatory. Hart Island, New York. (December 3, 2015). *Wikipedia, The Free Encyclopedia.* Retrieved December 5, 2015, from https://en.wikipedia.org/w/index.php?title=HartIsland,NewYork&oldid=693616942

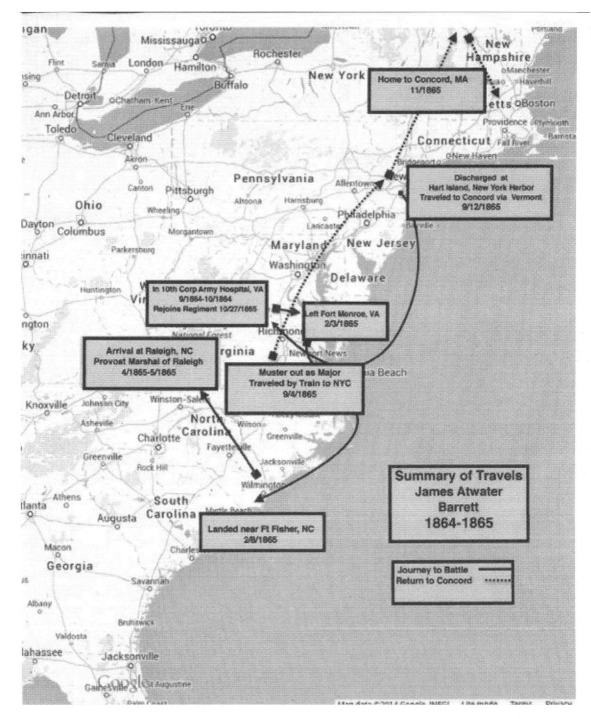

Summary of James' travels, 1864-1865
(Courtesy of Google INFGI, 2014)

It is assumed that the following article appeared in a New York newspaper [September, 1865]. It was found glued to one of the pages of Emma Jane's scrapbooks. Unfortunately, the name of the newspaper in which it appeared and the date had been cut off. [The Cousins have included a written transcript of the article on the next page.]

ARRIVAL OF THE FORTY-EIGHTH.

The Gallant Veterans are Ignored by the City Authorities.

Brooklyn Honored by Her Soldiers and Disgraced by Her Politicians.

A Citizen and His Lady Form the Escort and a One-armed Veteran Welcomes the Soldiers Home.

Four years ago the organization of the Forty-eighth Regiment New York Volunteers was begun and successfully ended in Brooklyn, by Rev. Mr. Perry of Fleet Street Methodist Church and Mr. Luther B. Wyman, a well-known citizen.

Mr. Perry, who was a graduate of the West Point Academy, led the regiment to the field himself, but died of apoplexy eighteen months after entering the service. Throughout the war the regiment has been kept well up in the front; and has had no respite so long as the fury of the contest raged.

The following is a list of battles in which it has participated:
Hilton Head, November 7, 1861.
Port Royal Ferry, January 1, 1862.
Siege of Fort Pulaski, from February 4 to April 11.
Pocotaligo, S.C., October 2.
Bluffton, June 10, 1863.
Morris Island, July 10.
Fort Wagner, July 18.
Siege of Fort Wagner, from July 10 to September 7.
Olustee, Fla., February 20, 1864.
Chester Heights, Va., May 7.
Drury's Bluff, May 14 to 16.
Bermuda Hundred, May 18.
Cold Harbor, June 1 to 14.
Petersburg, June 30.
Cemetery Hill, July 30.
Deep Bottom, August 14.
Strawberry Plains, August 16.
Siege of Petersburg, Aug. 28 to Sept. 28.
Laurel Hill, September 29.
Fort Gillmore, September 29.

Chapin's Farm, October 7.

Darbytown Road, October 17.

Williamsburg Road, October 27.

Federal Point, N.C., December 25.

Fort Fisher, January 15, 1865.

Fort Anderson, February 17.

Wilmington, February 21.

Northeast Station, February 22.

Cox's Bridge, March 21.

Bentonville, March 22.

Raleigh, May 16.

With the above honorable record the regiment found itself at the close of its labors, when the Rebellion crumbled before its final blows, and it was no more than reasonable to suppose that the citizens of Brooklyn would be eager to accord them the honors due such good and faithful service.

On the 2d inst. the regiment left Raleigh, N.C., on its way homeward to be mustered out, and notice was sent to our city authorities that they were coming; but there seems to have been no notice taken of their telegrams, for yesterday Mr. Luther B. Wyman, finding no preparations were going forward for their reception, engaged Dodworth's Band, and with his lady met the returning veterans at the Battery Barracks, New York, where they arrived at 3 o'clock yesterday afternoon.

Headed by Mr. Wyman, the regiment marched to Fulton Ferry and came over to Brooklyn. Here, to the eternal shame of our officials, not the slightest token of recognition awaited them. At the City Hall Park the gallant veterans halted for a few minutes, but not a single official was on hand to extend them the courtesy which was their due. The only reviewing parties present were the Mayor's Messenger, Lieut. Charles Schurig, a one-armed veteran of the Fourteenth Regiment, and two reporters.

After wearily waiting for some minutes for an official recognition, the brave fellows marched back to New York, indignant at the insult to which they were subjected. But with the glorious battle record they bear, the Forty-eighth can well afford to pass it by in contemptuous silence. With the citizens of Brooklyn, however, it is different. This willful neglect of our country's champions has branded us forever with indelible disgrace.

If the difference between the furore of departure in 1861 and the coldness of yesterday's reception of gallant men be the criterion by which we may judge the gratitude of Americans, then indeed are republics ungrateful. When the howl of rebel legions was fairly in our ears and resounding at our firesides, which the thunders of the enemy were heard on the Pennsylvania border and penetrated to the very doors of our National Capitol, we avowed ourselves the friends of the soldiers who were doing battle for us, and whose blood was drenching a soil far from their homes. In that hour of general gloom and distress, assurances both official and private were not lacking of the eternal gratitude of the citizens of this city to her gallant sons and defenders; and conscious of the justice of their cause; and reassured by the words of comfort whispered from behind, they recklessly plunged into the very jaws of death, and plucked forth the victory, honor, and peace that we now enjoy. And now when their work is over and they return maimed, depleted—a remnant of the gallant thousand that we urged forth to stand between us and death and national disgrace—it is to find our hearts are dead to sentiments of gratitude; that, having used them for our purposes, we cast off and ignore them when they are needed no longer, and no dark cloud in the immediate future shakes our souls with apprehensions. If the disgrace of yesterday be indorsed by the people of Brooklyn, it is a brand of cowardice put upon them—it is a proof of their treachery in sending forth men to suffer and die for them under incentives and representations of honor and glory that they are the first to ignore on the completion of the work.

But this is not the act of our people; it is not the act of Brooklyn, whose loyal and gallant acts—whose wealth, magnanimity, and sturdiness—have been all devoted from the first to the maintenance of the Union and the welfare of its soldiers. With such antecedents, she is not the one to forget brave men and gallant actions. Though on the bright record of her past there rests a stain, an indelible disgrace, it is not by her act it has been done.

The wretched political worms who at present sway the destinies of our city, and who by a single act have it in their power to disgrace us forever, are alone culpable for yesterday's shameful remissness. Fattened with plunder and the prospects of future spoil, our city officials—who during the war were abject worshippers and fulsome adulators of the soldiers, and canted loudly of their devotion to their interests—now cannot find the time to grasp the returned veteran by the hand, nor give him any official recognition. Weary, and mayhap hungry and athirst, the gallant soldiers with their tattered flags called for them and found them wanting. More hungry and weary still, the brave fellows returned to New York, to find among strangers the generosity that was their due here at their proper home.

But the people of Brooklyn, we hold, will not tamely submit to this disgrace. All concerned in this shameful insult may learn in the future, to their cost, that the City of Churches is not willing to cast away thus the brightest jewels in her crown—the cherished heroism and the glorious deeds of her sons.

Excuse on the part of these unfaithful public servants is worse than useless. Nothing can palliate the irremediable shame of yesterday's coldness but the punishment an outraged public knows so well how to administer at the proper time.

The flags of the Forty-eighth fluttered proudly and indignantly from our inhospitable wharves yesterday, bearing off with them the honor they would have conferred upon us. Let our people see to it that they avenge themselves on the guilty officials for their loss.

Luther B. Wyman, "Father of the 48th"
(Barrett Collection)

To Mr. Wyman belongs the only credit due Brooklyn or any of her citizens. Out of his own pocket he paid for the band that struck the rejoicing notes on the arrival of the veterans; and he himself, determined on doing his duty as a citizen, if the officials and people did not, accompanied the gallant boys on the march, and was the only Brooklynite who took an interest in them to bear out his professions of 1861. All honor to this public spirited Brooklynite! Let his name be remembered!

The regiment, after its melancholy march through our deserted streets, found a rest and rations in the Battery Barracks. The following officers return with it:

Field and Staff.—Colonel, Wm. B. Coan; Lieutenant Colonel, Nere A. Elfwing; Major, James A. Barnett[203]; Surgeon, Chas. A. Devendorf; Assistant Surgeon, J. Mott Throop; Quartermaster, Z. Paddock, Jr.; Adjutant, B. Seward.

---

[203] This is a typographical error. It should read James A. Barrett.

Line Officers.—Co. A.—First Lieutenant, G. Dawson; Second Lieutenant, B. B. Rumsey. Co. B.—Second Lieutenant, John Laxcey. Co. C.—Captain, A. H. Ferguson; Second Lieutenant, E. J. Barney. Co. D.—Captain, H. Lang; First Lieutenant, Wm. E. Tuttle; Second Lieutenant, James Haney. Co. E.—Captain, H. T. Garrigan. Co. F.—Captain, A. Lacoppiden; First Lieutenant, E. J. Readman. Co. G.—First Lieutenant Geo. W. Fagans; Second Lieutenant, R. B. Root. Co.H.—Captain, Jas. A. Barrett; First Lieutenant John Halstead; Second Lieutenant, Miles St. John. Co. I.—First Lieutenant, John Giles. Co. K.—Captain, C. B. Umblebee; First Lieutenant, Peter Smyth; Second Lieutenant, Louis Holmes.

Non-Commissioned Officers.—Sergeant Major, Luke Snyder; Quartermaster Sergeant, Joseph Stoney; Commissary Sergeant, G. W. Shannon; Hospital Steward, P. B. Monell; Drum-Major, John Stevenson; Fife- Major, Edward Hastings.

Colonel Elfwing accompanied the regiment in a carriage, having lost a leg at the assault on Fort Fisher, and therefore being unable to do duty mounted.

The appearance of the forty-eighth was soldierly and respectable, and would have done honor to any city. The boys will be paid off and mustered out in a few days, and it is to be presumed that they will not forget the politicians who have treated them so shabbily.

OUR RETURNING BRAVES.

The Arrival and Reception of the Forty-Eighth Regiment.

The Forty-Eighth Regiment, (veterans,) raised in Brooklyn four years ago, by the Rev. Mr. Perry, at that time pastor of the Pacific Street Methodist Church, arrived here last evening about dusk. They came over the Fulton ferry, and marching up Fulton street to the music of Dodworth's band and their own drum corps, passed by the residence of Mr. Luther B. Wyman, and were appropriately saluted.

Mr. Wyman and some other gentlemen, whose names we cannot now recall, aided in raising this regiment, which was originally called the Continental Guard.

Our citizens generally will recollect that the Guards encamped in the vicinity of Fort Hamilton, where, on one occasion before their departure, they gave an entertainment, which was attended by many thousands of people. We recollect very well how nicely their camp was fitted up, and how beautifully and artistically the streets and little yards in front of the tents were arranged and decorated. The fete champetre passed off to the satisfaction of every one, and in a short time thereafter the regiment embarked on two steamers at Fort Hamilton, and proceeded to their destination.

Col. Perry, who originally commanded them, was a graduate of West Point, and in his early days aided, very materially in wresting the state of Texas from the Mexicans — the same Texas which since turned on its defvers, but is now back again under the folds of the Starry Flag, and, it is hoped, will cut up no more didos. Colonel Perry participated in several of the principal battles fought by General Sam. Houston, on the side of Texas, and General Antonio Lopez Santa Anna, one of the most conspicuous military chieftains of his time. The engagement at San Jacinto finished his career on this side of the Neures river and Texas became an Independent State.

The regiment, since their departure from Fort Hamilton, have made an excellent record, as the following battles and sieges in which they participated will show:

Port Royal Ferry, S. C., Jan. 1, 1862; siege of Fort Pulaski, Ga., 1862; Cooswatchie, S. C., Oct. 22, 1863; Morris Island, S. C., July 10, 1863; Fort Wagner, S. C., July 18, 1863; Olustee, Fla., Feb. 20, 1864; Chester Heights, Va., May 7; Drury's Bluff, Va., May 16; Cold Harbor, Va., June 1; siege of Petersburg, va., July and August; Cemetery Hill, Va., July 30; Deep Bottom, Va., August 14; Strawberry Plains, Va., August 16; Chapin's Farm and Fort Gilmore, Va., Sept. 29; New Market Road, Va., Oct. 7; Fort Fisher, N. C., Jan 15, 1865; Wilmington, N. C., Feb. 21; Wilmington to Raleigh, N. C., March 15 to April 15.

Their reception in Brooklyn was not at all flattering. In fact it was shabby. They marched through the City Hall Park, headed by a band hired and paid for by Mr. L. F. Wyman. Nobody, bearing an official character, was there to receive them. Lieutenant Charles Schurig, who passed through all the great battles in which the 14th Regiment participated, commencing at Bull Run the first, and ending in the Wilderness, stood on the City Hall steps, and with his one remaining arm, gave an official welcome to his brother veterans. Lieutenant Schurig occupies the position of Mayor's Messenger. Supervisor Booth was also present, but had no authority to do anything on the part of the City in the way of receiving this fine regiment of heroes.

The 48th, now commanded by Colonel Wm. B. Doan, after reviewing the Mayor's Messenger, Supervisor Booth and the City Hall marched through several streets, and finding no resting place returned to New York and put up at the Grand Hotel on the Battery, where it is believed they were provided with the usual soldier's fare.

They are around town to-day, and as nearly all the members belong to Long Island and Staton Island, they are engaged in visiting their friends.

RETURN OF THE FORTY-EIGHTH REGIMENT.— The 48th Regiment returned last evening quite unexpectedly, and our citizens and authorities who would have delighted to have done them honor, had no opportunity of doing so. We regret this very much, but we cannot see where the blame belongs. The only person in Brooklyn who appears to have had any foreknowledge of the regiment's return was Mr. Luther B. Wyman, and he kept the knowledge to himself until the last moment, that he might have all the glory of singly and alone representing the people of Brooklyn. Mr. Wyman attained his object, and is no doubt gratified by the report of the proceedings in the morning papers, which places the whole affair in a most ludicrous light. The report reads as follows:

"The Forty-eighth veteran regiment, which was raised in Brooklyn four years ago by the Rev. Mr. Perry, of the Fleet Street Methodist Church, assisted by Mr. Luther B. Wyman, a distinguished citizen of this city, arrived home yesterday. Mr. Wyman and his lady received them on the part of the citizens, and when the regiment passed through the City Hall Park they were reviewed by Lieutenant Charles Schurig and two reporters. The Lieutenant was a member of the Fourteenth Regiment Militia and served three years, during which time he lost his arm. He now occupies the position of Mayor's Messenger, and as such represents the city. Supervisor Samuel Booth was also present, and that ends the list of either city or county officials."

The Veterans must have felt flattered by this reception. Whether Mayor Wood deputised his messenger to review the regiment, or whether that gentleman volunteered as a military aid to Mr. Tryman "on the part of the citizens," the act was equally creditable to Lieut. Schurig. The reporter evidently came near missing Supervisor Booth which would have been a great injustice to the Supervisor, who, being a candidate for Mayor, must make all the points he can. For fear that a suspicion might cross the mind of the reader that some other important functionary had been overlooked, the reporter explicitly states that Booth "ends the list of city or county officials. It was a sorry affair, and the report we have quoted from makes it appear ridiculous. For the credit of the city an explanation is needed. No regiment that Brooklyn sent to the war, has deserved more honor than the 48th; our citizens are justly proud of them, and would have given them a hearty welcome home, and we doubt not the Mayor and Common Council would have done their part, had they been apprised of the movements of the regiment. The Veterans took the city by surprise, and to that they must attribute the coldness of their reception. There is yet time to make some suitable recognition of the services of the regiment, and we trust that steps to that end will be at once taken.

BROOKLYN NEWS.

THE FORTY-EIGHTH VETERAN REGIMENT VOLUN-TEERS—THEIR COOL RECEPTION IN BROOKLYN.—The Forty-eighth Veteran Regiment which was raised in Brooklyn, four years ago, by Rev. Mr. PERRY, of the Fleet-street Methodist Church, assisted by Mr. LUTHER B. WYMAN, a distinguished citizen of this city, arrived home yesterday. Mr. WYMAN and his lady received them on the part of the citizens, and when the regiment passed through the City Hall Park they were reviewed by Lieut. CHARLES SCHURIG and two reporters. The Lieutenant was a member of the Fourteenth Regiment Militia, and served three years, during which time he lost his arm. He now occupies the position of Mayor's messenger, and as such represented the city. Supervisor SAMUEL BOOTH was also present, and that ends the list of either city or county officials. The regiment departed from Brooklyn about 1,100 strong, and after being recruited on several occasions to make up for losses in battle and by disease, comes back 800 strong, and as fine a looking set of men as ever shouldered a musket. They participated in the battles of Pocotaligo, Morris Island, the siege of Fort Wagner, Pulaski, Olustee, Chester Heights, in Virginia, Drewry's Bluff, Coal Harbor, Petersburgh, Deep Bottom, Strawberry Plains, Explosion of the Mine at Petersburgh, Cemetery Hill, Chapin's Farm, Fort Gilmore, New-Market Road, Fort Fisher and Wilmington. The regiment left Raleigh, N. C., on the 2d of September, and arrived here yesterday. Dodworth's Band, hired at the expense of Mr. L. B. WYMAN, furnished the music in their march through the streets of the city, and they were provided with lodgings for the night in the Armory of the Fifty-sixth Regiment, Raymond-street. They doubtless had their own rations, as nothing was provided for them.

Brooklyn newspaper article describes the homecoming of the 48th
(This media is in the public domain in the United States, 2016)

Copy of military discharge
(This media is in the public domain in the United States, 2016)

SPECIAL ORDERS,
No. 298.

HEADQUARTERS OF THE ARMY,
ADJUTANT GENERAL'S OFFICE,
Washington, December 29, 1885.

Extract.

*   *   *   *   *

2. By direction of the Secretary of War, under the act approved June 3, 1884, and to complete his record, the muster into service of 1st Lieutenant *James A. Barrett*, Company H, 48th New York Volunteers, November 10, 1863, is amended to take effect August 28, 1863; his muster into service as captain, same company and regiment, September 12, 1864, is amended to date June 25, 1864; his discharge as captain, September 1, 1865, is amended to date May 16, 1865; he is mustered into service as major, same regiment, to date May 17, 1865; mustered out and honorably discharged as major to date September 1, 1865; and he is mustered for pay in said grades during the periods embraced between the aforesaid dates.

*   *   *   *   *

BY COMMAND OF LIEUTENANT GENERAL SHERIDAN:

R. C. DRUM,
Adjutant General.

OFFICIAL:

Copy of amended military rank of Major
(This media is in the public domain in the United States, 2016)

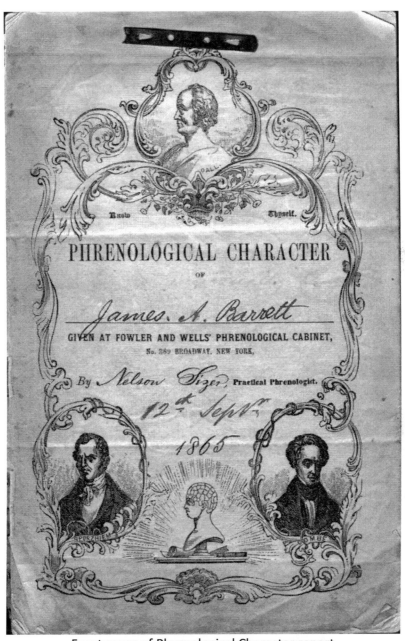

Front cover of Phrenological Character report
(Barrett Collection)

On September 12, 1865 James visited the Fowler and Wells' Phrenological[204] Cabinet at 389 Broadway, New York. The examination and written report was completed by Nelson Sizer, Practical Phrenologist.

James A. Barrett

Your head measuring 23 ½ inches is unusually large. Fortunately for you however you have a good substantial body and a weight of 160 lbs is pretty well adapted to give support to a large brain. If you could make 10 or 15 lbs weight you would be less likely to become nervous or dyspeptical. Your large brain if much used will absorb and use up vitality quite as fast as your body is able to supply it. You have a large pair of lungs, a source of power and health. The digestive system is not quite so amply developed. You should guard against everything that tends to impair the digestive power and break down the system. Tobacco would be injurious; coffee would also injure you; pepper and mustard and other condiments of the table should be laid aside. They do nobody any good but if a man has but little brain and a large body he has a good deal of surplus steam to work off somewhere and it can be employed in repelling enemies to health as easily as to be employed in physical labour. You have a natural desire to think and know to reach out into the realm of the Unseen and Unknown and find out the truth. You are not satisfied with a surface view, with superficial knowledge you want fundamental knowledge philosophical truth absolute ideas. You have a large Secretiveness and if you were educated in Engineering you would excel. Your perceptive organs are not quite so large as the reasoning and reflective organs consequently you frequently are at a loss for facts though rarely if ever at a loss for reasons with which to explain facts.

---

[204] Phrenology, which was made popular by Fowler and Wells, was thought to be a science through which the mind could be studied. "The Mind is the Man." It was a psychological theory or analytical method based on the belief that certain mental faculties and character traits are indicated by the configurations of the skull. phrenology. (n.d.). *Random House Unabridged Dictionary*. Retrieved December 4, 2015, from http://dictionary.infoplease.com/phrenology

You appreciate mirth and amusement. You would appreciate music. You are naturally cheerful merry fond of sport fond of society and capable of making your mark in society. You are not a great talker but you generally say something that hits the mark. When you speak, it means something. Your large Constructiveness might be used in manual skill but you are more adapted to planning contriving superintending, than you are to bring your mechanical judgement to a practical issue. You can think for a dozen pair of hands. You have strong kindliness of disposition for those who are in trouble which makes you useful to the poor and the afflicted. Your Reverence is not strong. If you had a little more tendency to worship more disposition to exercise devotional feeling it would be an improvement to your character. Your Hope is fairly but not excessively developed. Your Spirituality gives you faith in that which is unseen and supernal. You have a fervid imagination. With your reasoning intellect with your Ideality and Imagination you are well qualified to write or speak or to appreciate writing or speaking which deals with the speculative and the theoretical the beautiful and that which has a margin that sweeps into the other life. You have force of character, coming from your Combativeness and Destructiveness; power of punishing wrongdoers and ability to protect and defind yourself your rights and interests and to command respect. You are not to be trifled with are capable of being quite severe when aroused. You enjoy the good things of the table well enough and with your generosity and friendship your alimentiveness leads you to be hospitable to give others an opportunity to share with you in that which is good. You have very strong social feelings; there is hardly an end to your friendship. When your affections are awakened your whole life and energy and intellect and property are mortgaged to your friends. They have a claim on all that is yours. Your interest in children is uncommonly strong. As a father you would be loving and towards pets you would show yourself very tender. You love home you love Woman. You are adapted to awaken affection towards yourself and to feed it and keep it. You are more cautious in action than you are prudent in speech. You are apt to tell your purposes and make confidants of your friends. You cling to life would rise above sickness and wounding and recuperate when the average of men of your constitution would give up because they have less of the clinging fondness of life tha you and that keeps you up. Your desire for property being strong would enable you to manage business with economy. You would do well in some large business you would not be satisfied with that which is small and unimportant You have a broad nature especially in your affections and intellect and sympathy and that broadness will take hold on persons and would lead you to do something more than ordinarily important. If you had an education, the law would perhaps be the best avocation for you. If you have not an education something which requires commercial or mechanical talent would suit you. Carry on a large store or factory you could plan for either well. You would want practical persons to help you work out your ideas to make them practical and useful but you would know how to select and control persons. You are self reliant proud spirited persevering watchful affectionate high tempered when aroused, ingenious financial and philosophical.

Chapter 27

Home to Concord

November 15, 1865-November 20, 1865--Waits to be discharged--
Letters to Jennie--Visits Rutland, Vermont--Comes home to Concord,
Massachusetts

[Note that all the following transcriptions have been faithfully copied from the original document, as written by James, except where noted.]

New York Nov 15 1865
My Dear Jennie

Yours of 11th is just rec^d I arrived here from Con this morn Sold my wood lot for 1250.00 Am to have the money Decr 1st I walked all over the lot & walked back to the Hotel on Monday. Was pretty tired but it did not hurt me I am getting strong again I expect to be in Concord by Saturday unless I conclude to go home through Rutland I bought a $5.00 sewing Machine for Becky the other day. & have it in my valise I have had first rate luck so far & got through with my business much easier & quicker than I expected I have some notion now of going up into Vt after some Cattle to take down & sell. But I may conclude to wait & write first All my friends here are inquiring when I am to be married I expect to have quite a delegation of them on to spend the Holidays I will close now as I want to run round considerable today.
With much love to all I remain
                    Yours very affectionately
                    JamesA.Barrett

Rutland Vt Nov 20 1865
My Dear Jennie

Here I am in Rutland I met Rockwood in N.Y. Friday & came home with him next day. He escorted a Mrs Hathaway who wanted to come to Rutland She was very good company & we had a very pleasant trip via H,R,R,R arriving at Uncles at 9 P.M. Found the folks all well Minnie & Mr Dunton live with Uncle Minnie looks as young as ever Her maternal cares do not seem to wear upon her at all. Mr D is very considerate & tends the baby a great deal. I went to church all day yesterday in a hard snowstorm & heard two excellent sermons from Mr Seaver A young man lately settled here He is very smart & interesting & preaches without notes. Today is mild & pleasant but very muddy I have ridden round with Uncle to see the place which has doubled in size since I was here before. I am going off with Rockwood this P.M. to Southerland falls

I don't know when I shall go home They seem very glad to see me here & will press me to stay several days I expect to get home by the last of the week unless I find something that will pay me to stay a little longer I have some notion of buying a car load of Cattle to take down if I can find them Cheap I talked with William Wood about business But did not decide on anything definite

He said he would like to secure my services & wanted no references & If he could shape things to that end He would try & do so He is to consider it & write me in a week So I presume I shall find a letter awaiting me when I get home

I was very sorry to hear that Aunt G was worse I think she will have to go to Somerville & spend the remainder of her days Indeed I think it is the best thing for her. It is a great disappointment to the boys But Charlie seems resigned to it. He says he intends to keep up his Home in Concord just the same

I improved the opportunity to vote while in Brooklyn Mr Leete has sold out his interest in the banking business & is now out of employment George is in the same store with Hersey

Brown. Millie was going to start for Concord Saturday with Joe Gleason   So I suppose she is with you now

       Lizzie is well. Mattie is in hopes that we shall live in Brooklyn

       With much love to all I remain yours very truly

           JamesA. Barrett

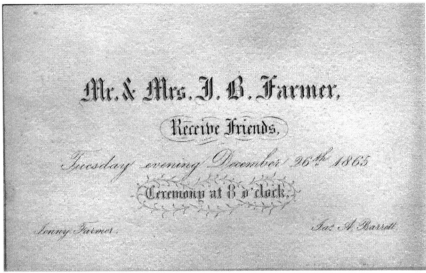

Wedding card
(Barrett Collection)

Epilogue

[James' narrative account]

My Story is a simple one just what thousands of others might write. I entered the service from sense of duty. I tried to do my duty in my plain & simple way. I had no lofty ambitious schemes to satisfy, No natural military talent to develop, & there was nothing which savored of the Hero in my record. I felt the responsibility which belonged or should belong to positions of trust & always did what I could for the comfort & health of my men. When in camp I used to send to N. Y. for numerous articles of Clothing or luxury which were called for & for which the sutlers charged such extravagant prices & furnished them at a small advance on N. Y. prices. This I began in a small way as an accommodation to meet a pressing want, but it proved a stroke of policy in giving a certain degree of popularity which if not altogether deserved was of considerable service to me. The first 2 years of our service Or I should say 18 mos were somewhat monotonous   14 mos in Ft Pulaski   our time came to hang heavy. Several of us formed a Dramatic Club, fitted up a Theatre, painted scenes, procured costumes & drove dull care away 3 evenings each week One of our lady "Stars" (a Soldier dressed) was said to be the prettiest lady in the department. These fixtures were afterwards moved to St Augustine Fla where the 48th Theater was a great attraction. We afterwards built a building 100 by 40 at Hilton Head where we finished a very nice one, But were ordered away into active work before we had used it much, & sold out just in time to cover our outlay. There is a good deal of satisfaction in looking back over the scenes of the past & thinking of the exposures dangers & trials that were endured   I never would have believed it possible But there was one watching over us to Whom "all things are possible" & Man's necessity becomes God's opportunity   I came out from the war with better health than I entered it. My wounds acted as Counter Irritants & carried off some old chronic complaints. I have never been troubled from my wounds except once soon after my discharge I was laid up a month from one wound breaking out & several pieces of bone coming out   God grant that we may never have another war   But gathering wisdom from the past May we recognize the great vital principles involved & cast the weight of our influence in the scale of Eternal justice & Equal rights to all, male & female black & white alike   Then will prosperity dawn upon us & we shall be in truth & in fact   The land of the friendless & the home of the free.

James A. Barrett
70 Graham Ave
Brooklyn, L.I.

Index

A

Acting Adjutant Colonels
  Johnson, 292
Actonites, 68
Adams
  Nehemiah, 205
Adams Express, 280
Adjutants
  Maylow, 249
Anderson
  H.E., 288
Annapolis, 15, 92, 246
Appomattox, 321
Artillery, 209, 212, 215, 225
Atlanta, 241, 299, 318

B

Bacon
  Mr., 157
  Mrs., 157
Banks
  Nathaniel Prentice, 272
Barlow
  Frank, 234
Barnes
  Sallie, 250, 340
  Sarah, 336
Barrett
  A., 229
  Clara Hosmer, iii
  Elizabeth Prescott, 115, 338
  Ellen, 82, 181, 182
  Emily Augusta (Em), 11, 96, 243, 260, 271, 274, 276, 335, 337

Emma, 83
Emma Jane, ii
George (George Henry), 19, 36, 47, 116, 124, 196, 247, 280, 281, 303, 334, 336, 341
George Farmer, iii
George Minot, 71, 102, 334
Ned, 17, 122
Nellie Prescott, iii
Rebecca (Becky), 13, 35, 71, 87, 96, 276, 279
Samuel, 103
Sherman, 157
Barton
  Miss Clara, 254, 255
  Mrs., 46, 141, 149, 174
Barton Dramatic Association
  B.D.A., 37, 129, 141, 188, 192, 194, 196, 197
Barton's Brigade, 173
Barton's Flying Brigade, 216
Barton's Foot Cavalry, 216
Base ball, 36
Bates
  Mr. (George H.), 153, 158, 228, 229, 258
  Mr. and Mrs., 11
  Mrs. (Mary C.), 13, 19, 31, 97, 143, 154, 181, 234, 242, 258
Batteries
  Brayton, 99
  Myrick's, 311
  Taylor, 98, 99, 107, 121
Battles
  Bull Run, 14
  Chapin's Farm, 258
  Chester Hill, 204
  Cold Harbor, 222, 223
  Drury's Bluff, 210
  Fort Wagner, 58, 61
  Gettysburg, 67, 102

Moore

Emma, 157

Morehead City, 320

Munroe

Alonzo, 117

Musicians

Dickson, Robert, 247

Myrtha (Collins), 293

N

N.Y. & Lawrence Riots, 93

Nayes

Mrs., 10

Negro Shouts, 114

New Years

1863, 45, 134

1864, 134

New York, 376

New York Harbor, 14

New York Riot, 68

Newspapers and Magazines

Atlantic, 51, 168

Cavalier, 256

Fowler & Wells Monthly, 261

Frank Leslie's Illustrated Newspaper, 49

Herald Times Tribune, 191

New South, 141

Palmetto Herald, 180

The Herald, 141

Times, 234

Nine Acre Corners, 68

North East Station, 308, 316, 317

Norton

Miss, 180

O

Olustee, 319

Ordnance and Weaponry

20 lb Parrotts, 50

Casement guns, 50

Columbiads, 49

Grape & Canister, 215, 319

Howitzers, 50

James Rifle pieces, 49

Parrott guns, 49

Rockets, 122, 326

Shells, 215

Telescopic Rifles, 59

Torpedoes, 187, 301

P

Paines' Division, 308

Palmer, D.D.

Abraham J., v

Parilla, 319

Petersburg, 245, 250, 320

Pickets, 59, 120, 177, 184, 192, 215, 265, 285, 301

Pike's Peak, 12, 20

Pilatka (Palatka), 172, 191, 192, 194, 195, 196, 198, 203

Plays

Box & Cox, 48

Family Jars, 48

Othello, 48, 174

Richard the Third, 48

The Idiot Witness, 48

Pocotaligo, 33, 134

Point of Rocks, 218, 248

Pontoon Bridge, 218

Pontoons, 309, 312, 316

Popes Plantation, 75, 111, 113, 121, 135, 277

Port Royal, 25

Port Royal Ferry, 26, 134

Post Provost Marshal, 348

Prescott

George, 67

George (Colonel George Lincoln), 26

Nell, 158

Prescott, M.D.

William, i

Prescott's Regt., 67

Presidents

Johnson, Andrew, 329, 331

Lincoln, Abraham, 127, 163, 242, 258, 264, 267, 279, 291, 324, 325, 329, 348

Prisoners, 265, 310, 311, 312, 314, 315

Women, 222

Prisons

Alton Military, 319

Andersonville, 242

Privates

Belaise, Abraham, 326

Burr, Louis W., 84, 273, 315

Butler, James, 283, 288

Clark, David, 209

Dykeman (Dikeman), John P., 214, 247

Eckel, Charles R., 247

Edwards, James L., 147, 148, 149

Englehardt, Frank, 204

Erfurth, August, 247

Freeman, James, 189

Giverney, James M., 294

Grover, Mason, 281

Hallsted, Samuel, 247, 248

Hanselman, Jacob, 204

Jonannin, Adrian, 273

Lawson, Edward M., 209, 283

Liming, Charles, 209

Mackey, Frederick, 191

Maier, Michael, 204

Mercier, George A., 324

Michon, Eugene, 273

Miller, Francis, 205

Newhart, Christian, 225

Owen, Samuel V., 209

Pearsall, John H., 189, 245

Pedro, Joseph H., 147

Purcell, Thomas, 283

Ryan, Michael, 227, 228

Q

Quartermasters

Paddock, Zachariah Jr., 177, 284, 285

Quartermaster-Sergeants

Stoney, Joseph, 256

R

Raleigh, 321, 324, 325, 350

Supreme Court Room, 350

Rebel Cavalry, 184

Rebels

Capt. Dickson's (Dickison's) Cavalry, 177, 184

Morgan, John, 242

Turner, 331

Reconstruction, 327

Regiments

9th Maine Vols., 281

Connecticut 7th Infantry, 27, 33, 214

Connecticut 8th Infantry, 293

Indiana 13th Infantry, 162, 214

Maine 9th Infantry, 291, 292, 294, 299

Maryland 9th Infantry, 58

Massachusetts 24th Infantry, 249

Massachusetts 54th Infantry, 61

Massachusetts 55th Infantry, 185

Massachusetts 5th Infantry, 17

New Hampshire 4th Infantry, 305

W

Wakeman

  Miss, 141

Warren

  Deacon, 118

  Lizzie (Lizzy, Mary Elizabeth), 35, 83, 97, 196, 304

  Mrs. Mary, 70, 88, 118, 163, 250, 304, 334, 336, 338

  Nathan Henry (Henry), 153, 172, 173, 191, 247, 303, 327, 337

Washington D.C., 20

Weldon, 313

Weldon R.R., 313

West Point, 46

Wheeler

  E., 228

  Henry, 107

Whiskey, 142, 210, 211, 212, 278, 302

White Feather, 195

White House Landing, 218, 219, 224, 225, 227

Williams

  Austin, 302

Wilmington, 285, 294, 298, 303, 308, *309*, 310, 312, 314, 315, 317, 318, 319, 325, 329

Wood

  Ellen, 17

  James, 89, 182, 334

  Mary, 156, 244

  Mr., 155

  Mrs., 237

  Nell, 181, 278

  William, 153, 374

Index of Illustrations and Photographs

Appendix

James' Timeline During The Civil War Years

July 27, 1861	Enlisted in the 48th Regt. N.Y.S.Vols. under Col. James Perry's command
Aug. 16, 1861	Mustered as 1st Sergeant at Camp Wyman, near Fort Hamilton, NY
Sept. to Oct., 1861	Camp Sherman, DC- Fort Monroe, VA
Oct., 1861-62	Hilton Head, SC- Port Royal, SC- Port Royal Ferry, SC- Seabrook, SC- Daufuski Island, SC
Apr. 10, 1862	Witnessed Fort Pulaski, GA bombardment
June to July, 1862	Ill for six weeks (bilious fever) at Daufuski Island, SC- then Fort Pulaski, GA
July, 1862 to June, 1863	Fort Pulaski, GA- Promoted to 2nd Lieutenant (Dec. 29, 1862)
June, 1863	Sailed to St. Helena Island, SC- Folly Island, SC- Morris Island, SC
July 18, 1863	Battle of Fort Wagner, SC
July 18, 1863	Wounded at Battle of Fort Wagner, SC– Sent to N Y City hospital
Aug., 1863	**Home to Concord, MA**- Leave of Absence for recuperation
Aug. 28, 1863	Promoted to 1st Lieutenant
Oct., 1863	Rejoined Regiment at Beaufort, SC- Moved to Seabrook Island on Hilton Head, SC
Oct. to Nov., 1863	Beaufort, SC

Nov. to Dec., 1863	Pope's Plantation on Hilton Head Island, SC
Jan., 1864	Fort Mitchell on Hilton Head Island, SC
Jan. to Mar., 1864	**Home to Concord, MA**
Mar., 1864	Returns to Fort Schuyler, NY- Sails to Hilton Head Island, SC- Jacksonville, FL
Mar., 1864	Sails to Palatka, FL- Rejoins regiment at Camp Palatka
Apr., 1864	Evacuation of Palatka, FL- Sails to Jacksonville, FL
Apr., 1864	Sails from Jacksonville, FL- Hilton Head, SC
Apr., 1864	Hilton Head, SC- Fort Monroe, VA- White House Landing, VA
May, 1864	Battle of Bermuda Hundred, VA
June 1, 1864	Battle of Cold Harbor, VA
June 2, 1864	Wounded at Cold Harbor, VA
June 10, 1864	Douglas Hospital, Washington, DC
June 17, 1864	**Home to Concord, MA** for recuperation
June 25, 1864	Promoted to Captain
Sept. to Oct.,1864	Sails from NY- Rejoins regiment near Richmond, VA- Sent to 10th Army Corp Base Hospital
Oct., 1864	Rejoins Regiment near Richmond, VA
Jan., 1865	Capture of Fort Fisher, NC- James left in command of Brigade
Feb., 1865	Left Fort Monroe, VA- Landed near Fort Fisher, NC

Feb. to Mar., 1865	Skirmishes on the way to Raleigh, NC
Apr., 1865	Arrived in the city of Raleigh, NC
May 17, 1865	Promoted to Major
July to Aug., 1865	Post Provost Marshal of Raleigh, NC
Sept.1, 1865	Mustered out as Major
Sept., 1865	Traveled from Raleigh to Baltimore and then onto Hart Island, NYC
Oct., 1865	Traveled to Vermont
Nov., 1865	**Home to Concord, MA**

James' Accounts and Records
Expense Account 1863-1865

1863

Item:	Cost:	Item:	Cost:
Enfield rifle	$18.00	(Oct. 16) Sundries	$2.00
Bag scabbard	.45	(Oct. 19) Book	1.00
Cup pouch	.45	Sundries	1.00
Gun sling	.25	(Oct. 21) Stamps	1.00
Cartridge box	1.02	Chair	1.50
Cartridge plate	.07	(Oct. 22) Candle	.50
Cartridge belt	.55	Trunk	5.00
Waist belt	.32	Steel collar	1.00
Waist belt plate	.07	Washing	.75
Screw drivers	.23	Picture	2.00
Wipers	.20	(Oct 22) Tassel and straps	2.75
----belt	.35	(Oct 26) Caps	2.00
----belt plate	.25	Books	2.50
Spring vice	.30	Sundries	1.50
Ball screw	.13	(Oct 31) Board to date	11.45
Tompion	.02	(Oct 31) Board in advance	3.75
Military blouse	14.50	(Nov 13) Board and washing	10.00
Pants	7.50	Cot	1.50
Vest	4.00	Sundries	1.00
Cap	5.00	(Nov 25) Board on a/c	16.80
Shoes	1.50	Present M & J	70.00
Surgeon	16.50	Thanksgiving prize	10.00
Uniform coat	20.00	Book	1.20
Straps	7.00	Sundries	2.50
Sundries	15.00	(Dec 12) Board and washing	10.00
Ring	11.00	Postage	2.00
(May 7) Stamps and washing	1.50	Sundries	2.00
(Oct.) Port Royal	8.00	Socks	3.00
(Oct. 10) Board and sundries	10.00	Lemonade	5.00
(Dec 12) Photographs	$7.00	(Dec 20) Board to date	$5.00

Item	Cost	Item	Cost
Balance % in Co A	5.50	(Dec 25) Shirts and present	15.00
(Dec 18) Sundries	4.00	(Dec 31) Stove	6.00
(Dec 19) Board to date	5.00		
Blanket	3.25		
Stove	25.00		
Pants	3.50		
Candles and collars	4.50		

1864

Item:	Cost:	Item:	Cost
(Jan 3) Tobacco for horses	$1.50	Bronxville	$2.00
Board to date	15.00	(Mar 4) Fair	2.00
Sundries	4.00	Central Park	2.50
(Jan 20) Pants	3.55	Fare to Florida	15.00
Washing	.75	(Mar 20) Shoes	2.10
(Jan 29) Sundries	3.00	Board	2.00
(Jan 31) Board to date	10.00	(Apr) Servant and washing	4.00
(Feb 3) Fare to N.Y.	3.00	(Apr 10) Sundries	5.00
Sundries	4.00	(Apr 19) Fare to H. Head	8.00
Overcoat, cap and boots	54.00	Bal. board to date	4.30
Lecture	2.00		$758.20
Photo	3.00	(Sept 5) Fare to New York	8.60 (2)
(Feb 9) Fare to Concord	8.00	(Sept 6) Haversack	4.50
(Mar) Watches and chain	121.00	(Sept 12) To Petersburg	6.00

Item	Cost	Item	Cost
Fare to N.Y.	20.00	Overcoat, rubber blanket, etc	14.25
Photo	1.50	(Sept 14) Servant	1.00

Item	Cost	Item	Cost
(Sept 17) Tobacco	$2.50	(Nov 7) Board to date	10.00
(Sept 20) Clothing %	6.50	Sundries	5.00
Messes	6.00	(Nov 23) Board to date	10.00
Servant	5.00	(Nov 25) Cap	3.50
Gold Pen	2.00	Sundries	10.00
(Oct 7) Henry Miller	20.00	(Nov 30) Board to date	6.00
(Oct 26) Board	31.00	(Dec 21) Board to date	15.00

1865

Item:	Cost:	Item:	Cost:
(Jan 4) Board to date	$10.00	May 11 Mess broken up	
(Jan 11) Stove etc	10.00	(May 22) Paid cash	
Board to date	5.00	(May 24) Paid cash	
(Feb 8) Board to date	20.00	Mess	$20.00
(Mar 13) Board to date	10.00	(May 16) Difference in horses	80.00
(Mar 26) Board to date	11.00	(May 24) Paid cash mess	50.00
(Apr 15) Board to date	15.00	(June 1) Paid cash mess	10.00
(Apr 25) Horse	20.00	(June 4) Paid cash mess	20.00
(Apr 28)	15.00	(June 8) Paid	10.00

Saddle		cash mess	
Bridle	6.00	(June 26) Paid cash mess	10.00
(Apr 29) Board to date	10.00	(June 28) Paid cash mess	5.00
Board to date	15.00		

Servants' Account

Hired Andrew	April 4, 1864
Apr. 8	Coat 1.50
Sept. 13	Cash 1.00
Sept. 20	Cash 3.00
Oct. 20	Cash 1.00
Nov. 1	Cash .50
Nov. 25	Cash .50
Dec. 15	Cash 1.00
Jan. 4	Cash 1.00
Jan. 31	Cash 1.00
Mar. 9	Cash 2.00
Mar. 9/65	Hired Charles at $10.00 per month
Mar. 14	Deserted
Apr. 9/65	Hired John Alexander at $10.00 per month
May 25	Cash 6.00
June 7	Cash 14.00
June 7 John left me	

Known Record of Letters That Were Received and Written to Various Recipients

Indicates that original letter is in the family's personal collection
**Emma Jane's transcription of original letter, now missing*

1861 Letters received	**1861 Letters written**	
	Apr. 21	*Father
	May 25	*Father
	July 28	*Friends, *Father
	Sept. 30	*Friends At Home

1862 Letters received	**1862 Letters written**	
	Apr. 2	*Charley

1863 Letters received	**1863 Letters written**	
	Jan. 10	*Lizzie
	Jan. 20	*Jennie

	Feb. 14	*Father

	Mar. 1	*Mother
	March 8	*Jennie

	April 21	Father

July 21	*Jennie

	October 2	**Jennie
	October 4	**Jennie
	October 7	**Jennie
	October 9	*Friends at home
	October 10	*Lizzie
	October 16	**Jennie
October 23	*Jennie, *Rebecca	

November 1	Jennie, Nell F	November 1	**Jennie
November 2	Mother, Jennie, Lizzie	November 2	Nell, *Mother, Lizzie, **Jennie
November 6	Taft, Jennie, Rebecca, Abbie	November 6	Taft, Rebecca, *Jennie, Abbie
November 7	*Father	November 7	Mrs Bates
		November 16	Jennie

November 18	Jennie, Father, Howland, Sparks, Mrs. Bartley	November 18	Howland, Mrs Bartley
		November 19	*Jennie, Father
		November 22	Jennie, J.M. Prescott
November 24	Mary, Lizzie, Sallie, Annie, Jennie, Gerrish, Mrs Bates	November 24	Gerrish, Mary, Lizzie, Mrs Bates
		November 26	*Jennie
November 27	*Father		

December 3	Mrs McCann, Jennie	December 3	*Jennie
December 10	Jennie, Mother, Nell F., Charley, Corp¹ Vredenberg		
		December 11	*Mother
December 20	Jennie, Lizzie, Henry		
December 25	Lizzie Oct 18th, Jennie	December 25	**Jennie
December 27	Jennie, Mrs. Bates, Charley G		

1864 Letters Received   1864 Letters Written

January 4	Charley G	January 1	*Unitarian Sunday School Students Brooklyn
January 5	Jennie, Mother		
January 6	Henry W		
January 9	Henry W, Sallie Barnes		
January 11	Jennie, Nell F., Lizzie	January 11	**Jennie
January 12	**Charles P. Gerrish		
January 20	Jennie, Rebecca, Charley G., Howland	January 20	**Jennie
January 29	Jennie, Gerrish, Mrs. Scanlan		

		March 9	**Jennie
		March 11	*Jennie
		March 13	**Jennie
		March 14	**Jennie
		March 15	*Jennie
March 16	Jennie, Nell F., Mother, George, Sallie		
		March 18	*Jennie
		March 20	*Jennie
		March 23	**Jennie
March 28	Jennie, Ord Dept	March 28	**Jennie
March 31	**Jennie		

		April 1	*Jennie

		April 4	*Jennie*
April 5	Mother, Jennie	April 5	*Jennie*
		April 10	*Jennie*
April 12	Jennie	April 12	*Jennie*
April 13	Henry, Charley		
		April 14	*Jennie*
		April 16	**Jennie
April 20	Jennie, Do, Rebecca, Mr Lockwood, J.B. Brown, Dr Webster Treas' N.Y. I.		
		April 22	*Jennie*
		April 26	*Jennie*

		May 5	**Jennie
		May 8	**Jennie
May 15	Charley		
		May 17	**Jennie
May 19	Jennie		
May 20	Jennie, Nell, Annie, Charlie, Kate Stockpole		
May 23	Charley		
May 25	Mrs. Bates		
		May 26	*Jennie*
		May (Undated)	*Jennie*

		June 2	*Jennie, *Mother*
		June 10	*Friends at Home*

July 8	*Charles P Gerrish*		

		September 6	*Jennie*
		September 10	Jennie, Mother, Charlie
		September 11	**Jennie
September 12	Jennie		
September 13	**Jennie	September 13	Jennie, Mother
September 15	Charlie		
September 16	Jennie		
		September 17	**Jennie
September 20	Jennie	September 20	*Jennie*
September 26	Jennie, Mother, F. Miller	September 24	Stayley, Charlie, **Jennie
		September 27	*Mother*
		September 30	**Jennie

October 3	Jennie, Gerrish	October 3	Charlie

		October 4	Jennie
		October 6	Nell F., Annie
		October 7	H. Miller
		October 9	**Friends
October 11	Jennie		
October 14	Rebecca, Jennie, Miller		
October 15	*Charles P Gerrish		
October 16	Jennie		
		October 11	Jennie, Garaghan
		October 15	Jennie, Rebecca, Gerrish, H.P. Moore
		October 16	Nell Wood
		October 17	Jennie
		October 19	Pro Marshall, N.Y., Pro Marshall, Balt.
		October 20	Dr. Trion Jr., **Jennie
October 21	Gerrish, Jennie, Annie, Cornell, Stayley	October 21	**Jennie, Gerrish, Cornell, Annie
		October 23	Stayley
October 24	Jennie	October 24	**(Unknown Recipient) Jennie, Gerrish, J.S. Fowler
October 26	Jennie		
		October 27	Jennie, P.M., S.N.Y. P.M., 3rd Div.
October 28	Nell		
October 29	Jennie, Rebecca, Charlie		
		October 30	*Jennie

		November 1	Q.M. Gen., Miller & Co., Gerrish, Nell F., Rebecca
November 3	Jennie		
		November 4	Jennie, Sallie B.
November 5	Jennie	November 5	*Jennie, Nell Wood
November 6	Charlie	November 6	Laxy, Rogers
		November 7	**Charlie
November 8	Story	November 8	P.M. Gen. N.Y.
		November 9	**Story
November 12	Jennie 2, Howland, P.M., N.Y.S., Emmie	November 12	*Jennie
November 13	Stayley, Laxy, Moore, Sallie B.	November 13	Laxy, Stayley, Moore H.P., Sallie B.
		November 14	Emmie
		November 15	Howland

Date	Received	Date	Written
November 16	Nell W.		
		November 17	Nell W.
November 20	Jennie, Gerrish, P.M. 3rd Dist.	November 20	Gerrish, *Jennie
November 22	Jennie		
November 23	Jennie, Mother, Lizzie	November 23	*Jennie
November 24	Nell F.	November 24	*Jennie, Lizzie, *Mother
November 26	Jennie	November 26	Nell F.
		November 27	Jennie

Date	Received	Date	Written
December 2	Jennie	December 2	Mrs. McCormick, E.R. Groves, Jennie
December 3	Jennie, P.M., N.J.		
		December 4	Jennie
December 8	Jennie	December 8	Jennie
		December 12	*Jennie
December 17	Nell, Britton	December 17	Jennie
December 18	Jennie, Mother, Lockwood, Corp., Clark	December 18	C. Blant
		December 19	*Jennie
		December 20	Mother, Stayley,**Jennie
		December 21	Lizzie W., Lockwood
		December 22	Cuyler Hosp.
December 24	Jennie, M.D. Romson	December 24	Jennie, O. Blunt
		December 26	L.B. Wyman, E. R. Groves
December 27	Jennie	December 27	**Jennie
December 28	Jennie	December 28	*Jennie

1865 Letters received   **1865 Letters written**

Date	Received	Date	Written
January 5	Jennie, Nell	January 5	Jennie, Nell
January 11	Jennie	January 12	**Jennie, Charlie
January 12	Jennie, Charlie	January 15	**Rebecca
January 15	Rebecca	January 20	Mrs. Bates
January 19	Mrs. Bates	January 23	*Jennie
January 22	Jennie	January 24	*Jennie
January 23	L.B. Wyman	January 30	**Jennie
January 28	Charlie		

Date	Received	Date	Written
		February 2	Dr. Strickland,*Jennie
		February 7	Mrs. Sears, * Jennie, Charlie
February 8	Jennie, Nell, Mother		
February 10	Jennie, Mrs. Groves, Long Ordinance	February 10	Adj. General Pope's, Brother, Pat. Rogers

February 16	Jennie, Lippincott	February 12	**Jennie, George
		February 15	*Jennie
		February 17	*Jennie
February 20	Jennie		
		February 23	*Jennie
February 26	J.B. Brown, Jennie		
		February 27	J.B. Brown, *Jennie

1865 Letters received   1865 Letters written

March 5	Jennie		
March 7		March 7	**Jennie
		March 8	Charles
		March 9	Lippincott
March 12	George	March 12	Mr. Wyman, Gerrish, Nell F.
		March 13	Mr. Swain
March 15	Jennie		
		March 22	**Jennie
		March 26	*Jennie
March 27	Jennie		
March 29	Mr. Wyman	March 29	Gerrish
		March 30	Mr. Wyman, **Jennie

April 6	Jennie, Mr. Swain		
April 9	Jennie	April 9	Jennie, Gerrish
		April 22	**Jennie
April 28	J.B. Brown		

		May 2	*Jennie
		May 4	*Jennie
		May 19	*Jennie, George
		May 24	*Jennie, Mother
May 25	Jennie, Mother		
May 28	Howland		
May 29	Charlie	May 29	Howland, Charlie
May 30	Jennie, Dunbar		
		May 31	*Jennie

June 3	*Mother		
June 6	Jennie		
June 7	Nell	June 7	*Jennie, Nell
June 10	Jennie	June 10	*Jennie, Nell
		June 12	Gerrish
June 16	Mother, Jennie		

		June 17	Lippincott
		June 18	Jennie
		June 21	Mother
June 28	Jennie		
		June 29	*Jennie

July 1	Charlie, W. Wood	July 1	Charlie, Wm. Wood
		July 12	*Jennie
		July 22	*Jennie
		July 27	*Jennie

		August 3	*Jennie
		August 9	**Jennie
		August 21	*Jennie

| | | November 15 | *Jennie |
| | | November 20 | *Jennie |

Barrett residence
25 Lewis Ave. Brooklyn, N.Y.
(Barrett Collection)

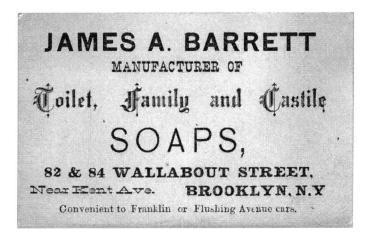

Business card (Barrett Collection)

James is photographed sitting in the doorway (lower left) at
the soap works (Barrett Collection)

James (center, wearing dark hat) sitting with workers

Brooklyn, N. Y., February 8th, 1889.

Comrade:

An effort is being made to erect a monument over the grave of our late Col. JAMES H. PERRY, at Cypress Hills Cemetery. His grave has been sadly neglected, and no stone marks the spot.

It is now proposed to erect this monument before Decoration Day, under the auspices of the Church over which he ministered, the Veteran Regiment he commanded, and the Grand Army Post which bears his name.

Last June, in response to an appeal from a Committee of James H. Perry Post, the Rev. J. O. PECK, of Hanson Place Church, delivered a very earnest and eloquent memorial sermon on Col. Perry (which was printed by the Post, and a copy of which will be sent you if desired), to a crowded house. Several G. A. R. and Veteran Associations were present, and at the close a very liberal collection was taken.

We still need about $400.00 to obtain the kind of Granite Monument we want to get, and we are anxious to secure this amount as soon as possible. I have been requested to inform such comrades of the 48th Regiment as would be likely to wish to give something, of the steps we are taking, so that the 48th Regiment may be duly represented in this last token of respect to our late commander.

Any amount you may wish to give will be duly credited if sent to,

Yours in F. C. & L.,

JAS. A. BARRETT,

PRESIDENT 48TH REG'T VET. ASS'ON & CHAIRMAN J. H. PERRY MONUMENT COM.,

25 Lewis Avenue, Brooklyn.

Monument to Colonel Perry
(*48th N.Y. S. Vols.,* A.J. Palmer, D.D., 1885)

Remarks at Colonel James H. Perry's Grave
[The following was found in one of the many scrapbooks in the Barrett collection.]

Remarks at Colonel James H. Perry's[205] Grave
Major James A. Barrett
(Chairman of the Monument Committee)
May 30, 1883

Comrades, twenty years ago last June, Col. Jas. H. Perry, 48th Regt. N.Y.S. Vols., died. He was the first prominent man from the city of Brooklyn who lost his life in the War of the Rebellion.

For twenty years, that silent, unmarked grave has been sending up its mute appeal for honor and recognition. But God giveth his beloved, rest.

He gives them justice too, for

"Justice conquers evermore"
And he who battles on her side
God, though he were ten times slain,
Crowns him victor glorified,
"Victor over death and pain, forever."

And so it came about four years ago, it was put into the hearts of a few veteran soldiers to organize a G.A.R. [206] Post and from the names of our local heroes, they chose that of Col. Jas.H. Perry for their title and when they sought this spot to decorate his grave with fragrant flowers, that eloquent plea was heard and was not heard in vain.

Comrades, there is a tender cord of sympathy in every soldier's heart for every other soldier who had the arm to strike and the soul to dare in defense of the flag of his country. That G.A.R. Post felt then and there that they had a mission to fulfill. The question of a monument was agitated. The Methodist Conference was appealed to as he had for many years, been an earnest and faithful minister in that church, and for a time there was some promise of success. But several years passed and nothing was done.

Last year the Jas. H. Perry Post appointed a monument committee to go earnestly to work, determined to leave no stone unturned until this reproach of twenty years had been redeemed. But in that time, a generation had passed away and another had taken its place. During that twenty years, most of those who knew and loved him here, had gone to meet him on that far off shore. Few, very few remained who intimately knew him in life.

But that few were sought out and they were found loyal and true, and their interest was awakened, and they in turn, aroused an interest in others which grew and blossomed and bore its fruit, and here is the result!

Comrades, who was this whose memory we seek to honor today? I had the honor and privilege to serve in his regiment and knew something of the mettle that was in him, and now as I

---

[205] James H. Perry was the first Colonel of the 48th, New York State Volunteers.

[206] Great Army of the Republic was a fraternal organization of veterans of the Civil War.

look back over that vista of years, I can see his tall, commanding figure standing straight as an arrow, six feet two inches in height, with broad shoulders and a massive, well shaped frame which easily carried 250 pounds in weight. His snow white hair formed a fitting crown for that magnificent head which took a 7 ¾ cap to fit it. He had a courage that knew no fear, a cool self possession that never forsook him, a dignity of manner and air of command that stamped him at once and always, as a leader of men.

Comrades, do you wonder that his regiment loved and honored their Colonel? Can you wonder that that June day was a sad day for the 48th Regt., "When we steadfastly gazed on the face of the dead and bitterly thought of the morrow."

Time will not allow me to give you his record in detail. It is very well given in a memorial sermon by Dr. Peck which can be had at Post Headquarters. I will simply say, he was educated at West Point, resigned in three years to enter the Texan War for Independence, with rank of Col. He won honor and distinction. Towards the close of that war, something occurred to give his mind a serious turn and he left the army and spent twenty three years as a minister of the Gospel in the Methodist Church. He was a pastor of four churches in the city of Brooklyn. But when Sumpter's gun fired the northern heart, it fired the slumbering patriotism in his breast, and he resigned his Pastorate, buckled on his sword, and offered his life to his country. He became Colonel of the 48th Regt., N.Y.S.Vols., and bent all his energies to make it a model regiment.

Under his drill and discipline, that regiment soon enjoyed a reputation in the department of the south similar to that which the 7th N.Y. held in N.Y. In less than a year, we were called to mourn his loss, but the 48th never forgot the discipline they received at his hands, and the proud record they afterwards won, was largely due to that discipline.

Comrades, I believe that from that upper Heaven, he was permitted to witness with pride that glorious record. In over four years' service, they never faltered, but faced death and met it too, on many hard fought field as their casualty list of nealy 1000 killed and wounded will clearly prove.

"Brave Soldier rest, thy work well done,
And while with loving hands, we bring
These tributes for our offering,
May we, like thee, for Right press on!"

Comrades, it was no light responsibility you assumed when you adopted the name of Col. Jas. H. Perry for your standard. Guard it with jealous care and let it be an incentive to nobler action and a more heroic Patriotism.

"Lives of great men all remind us
We can make our lives sublime,
And departing, leave behind us
Footprints on the sands of time."
"Let us then be up and doing
With a heart for any fate;
Still achieving, still pursuing,
Learn to labor and to wait.'

FORT WAGNER & REBEL PRISONS.

VET. ASS'N
48th
REGIMENT.

⇥✳ Rev. A. J. PALMER, ✳⇤
Pastor of St. James' M. E. Church, Kingston, N. Y.

WILL DELIVER A LECTURE

under the auspices of the

VETERAN ASSOCIATION

OF THE

48th Regiment, N. Y. S. Volunteers,

AT THE

HANSON PLACE M. E. CHURCH,

Wednesday, Feb. 22, 1882, at 8 P. M.,

On his recollections as a member of this Regiment, of the storming of Fort Wagner, S. C. and his nine months' experience in five rebel prisons.

The 48th was a Brooklyn Regiment, commanded by the late Col. JAMES H. PERRY, former Pastor of Hanson Place and other Methodist Churches in this city.

Those who have heard this lecture can testify that it is an eloquent and soul-stirring account of that terrible charge in which two-thirds of the men and seven-eighths of the officers of the storming party of the 48th Reg't proved their courage and patriotism by shedding their blood.

The proceeds of this Lecture are to be used as a nucleus of a fund for compiling and printing a history of the Regiment.

Admission, 25 Cents.

Tickets to be had at the door, or of either member of the Committee.

HENRY ACKER, 343 *Hudson Ave.*   A. ELMENDORF, 475 *Washington Av.*
GEO. B. STAYLEY, 353 *Adams Street.*   E. J. BARNEY, 691 *President St.*
GEO. W. BRUSH, M.D., 144 *Lawrence.*   JAMES A. BARRETT, 25 *Lewis Ave.*
DAVID B. FLETCHER, "Du Bois," 826 *Fulton Street.*

(Barrett Collection)

New York Feby. 16th 1882

Jas. A. Barrett Esq,
    25 Lewis Ave.
        Brooklyn

Dear Sir:

    Your letter of Feby. 15th inviting me to attend a lecture by Rev. A. J. Palmer on Fort Wagner, on Feby. 22d, is at hand. While thanking you for the kind invitation I regret that owing to other and previous engagements for that day, I will not be able to accept.

        Truly Yours,

        U. S. Grant

The letter above was written by U.S. Grant in response to an invitation extended by James to attend Rev. A. J. Palmer's lecture given on February 22, 1882. This letter was found in the Barrett Collection.

War Department
Washington City
August 2nd, 1883

29 53 / B.

Sir:—

I have the honor to acknowledge the receipt of your letter of the 20th ultimo, enclosing, and commending to favorable consideration, one of the 19th ultimo from Mr. James A. Barrett of No. 25 Lewis Avenue, Brooklyn, New York, requesting permission to have copies made of certain rolls of the 48th New York Volunteers.

The

James was actively participating in collecting accurate and detailed information as part of a collaborative effort to write about the history of the 48th New York State Vounteers. The letter above was written by Abraham Lincoln's eldest son, Robert Lincoln, Secretary of War in response to his request. It was found in the Barrett Collection.

In reply I beg to state that the rule of the Department, long since adopted, and founded upon considerations of public policy, is to decline any and all requests for copies of muster rolls, &c., from the official files, as such rolls are necessary for purposes of verification in claims growing out of personal services, &c., during the War and in protecting the government against the perpetration of fraud in connection with such claims

claims.

In view of the regulation referred to, I am constrained to decline the request made in behalf
of Mr. Barrett.

It is proper to add, that the
previous request of Mr. Barrett
to which you refer as having
been granted by the Department
was not for copies of muster-
rolls, but was simply for a
list of casualties of the above
named regiment.

Very

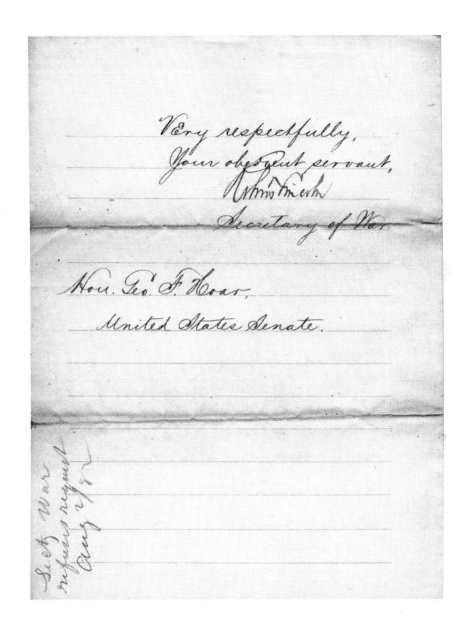

Very respectfully,
Your obedient servant,
Wm. Mecdn
Secretary of War

Hon. Geo. F. Hoar,
United States Senate.

(Barrett Collection)

These obituaries were found glued inside the back cover of one of the Barrett copies of the *48th N.Y. S. Vols.* by A.J. Palmer.

In Brooklyn, N.Y., 14th inst., James A. Barrett, 53 yrs. Capt. Barrett, as he was generally called, although he had attained to the rank of Major in the Forty-eighth Regiment of New York Volunteers, was born in Concord, Mass., and in his veins ran the heroic blood of the embattled farmer-folk of 1775. He enlisted in 1861, and was with the regiment from its organization till it was mustered out at the end of the war. From the rank of Sergeant, he rose to that of Second and then First Lieutenant, became the Captain of his company in 1864, and Major of the regiment in the following year. The Forty-eighth was one of the regiments that shared with the colored Fifty-fourth of Massachusetts the fortunes of the terrible assault upon Fort Wagner, when of its sixteen officers fifteen were killed or wounded, and of the five hundred men who went into battle only eighty-five answered the roll-call the next day. Lieut. Barrett was among the wounded, and his story of the day's events and the unspeakable horrors of the night was more affecting to the writer of this tribute to his memory than any other story of the war which he has ever heard or read. His service as an Orderly Sergeant was more precious in his recollection than any of his later honors. No man was ever prouder of his regiment than he was of the Forty-eighth. During the last years of his life, his principal and arduous avocation has been the collecting of material for a history of the regiment and money for its publication. A task that never would have been accomplished without his enthusiasm and his patience was so near to its completion when he died that the finished volume, which he never saw, might have been laid upon his lifeless breast. To "endure hardness as a good soldier" was the invariable habit of his life. And there was not a little hardness in his lot. His refuge from it all was in the happiness of his domestic circle. His bluff and hearty manliness was an inspiration and delight to all his friends. He was a man of positive convictions, and he spoke them out in simple, downright fashion. He was no carpet knight, but a man of somewhat rude exterior semblance, which could not conceal the warmth of his affections nor his kindly will. He was a friend for evil days, and every way so manly and sincere that the place where Emerson is buried is not so honorable but that it will be made yet more so by his dust.

J. W. C.

Obituary from an unidentified N.Y. newspaper.

James A. Barrett, late Major Forty-eighth Regiment New York Volunteers, a much-loved and respected comrade of George C. Strong Post, died last Monday. Comrade Barrett enlisted as First Sergeant in Co. H, Forty-eighth Regiment New York Volunteers, Colonel James H. Perry commanding, in July, 1861. He was First Lieutenant at the capture of Morris Island, S. C., July 10, 1863, was seriously wounded and became perfectly helpless for some months. He rejoined the regiment in Florida in time to take part in the unfortunate battle of Olustee, Florida, February 20, 1864. He also participated in the engagements at Drury's Bluff and Cold Harbor, Va., where he was wounded in the right shoulder slightly, and also in the right hip, the ball passing completely through him, coming out at the left hip. The wound being serious he was sent home to Concord, Mass., for three months, and rejoined the regiment just previous to the attack on Fort Fisher, in which he took part as Captain of his company, having been promoted. Soon after he was commissioned Major, and was in command of the regiment until July 4, 1865, when he was appointed Provost Marshal of Raleigh, N. C. On September 1, 1865, the regiment was ordered North to be mustered out of service, and Major Barrett went home wearing honorable scars and an enviable reputation as a soldier and an officer. Comrade Barrett has been an active member of the Grand Army since July 20, 1881, joining James H. Perry Post at that date, and was at one time its Senior Vice Commander. In January, 1885, he assisted in organizing George C. Strong Post, and since the muster-in of that Post he has been the Chairman of its Board of Trustees, and no member of the Post has worked harder for its advancement than has Comrade Barrett. He has left a vacancy that cannot well be filled. He was an honest man, a kind friend and a true soldier and comrade. His funeral took place last Thursday, and was attended by the Post in a body and by many comrades from other posts.

Obituary from *N.Y. Times*

[207] His "knighthood" was not bestowed as an honorary title in a formal ceremony. This is in reference to his bravery and valor earned on the field of battle.

Emma Jane's illustration of cap and sword at peace
(Barrett Collection)

In Memoriam
A life so loving, always deep and true
Its march serene, as planets set and rise
Taking each good that came as flowers drink dew
Living for others, but without self-sacrifice,
Because thyself was served in helping all.
Not slight of duty at life's sternest call
In patient cheer when tides had ebbed and gone,
And hero still, and victor, passed thou on!
In closer sympathy with Heavenly ruling,
Thou wast my sunshine on perplexing themes.
My God, make clear my vision, schooling
My lagging purpose to its highest dreams.
Oh, let me live the truest that I know
And trust Thee till the darkness fades and
Morn shall glow.

-Jane Farmer Barrett-
Feb. 1887

Cincinnati, Dec 17th 1885

Mr. George F. Barrett

My dear sir:

Your letter conveying the sad intelligence of your father's death just at hand. It is only a few days ago that I received a letter from him in reference to the publication of the history with which he had been so intimately connected; and now he is no more.

He was my dear friend, tried and true, and since the death of Lieut. Lockwood, my old school mate friend and comrade, I have had no attachment among the members of the old 48th so close to my heart as his. I know of no one in the regiment whom my father more delighted in speaking of. He knew his sterling worth, and kindly sympathizing heart as did all who came in close contact with him, and often have we extolled his many virtues. He was an universal favorite during the period of his service, and regret now at his loss will be felt by all.

To lose a father in the prime of life is a sad misfortune, and one it is difficult to become reconciled with. Yet you have the happy consolation of knowing that he was a good and true man and will have his reward in a better world.

You and yours have my deepest sympathy, and a friendship which will be ever ready for you as it was for him in his life time.

With kind regards,

Yours sincerely,

D.W. Strickland

Law office of
Strickland & Lehmer
Rooms 23, 24 & 25 Sinton Bldg.

D.W. Strickland
Charles Lehmer

East Bloomfield, Dec. 20, 1885

My dear sister Jennie,

With what a blow the sad news of James' death came upon us—we had not heard of his sickness at that time.

O my dear sister, what can mortal life say, or pen write, to assuage such grief as yours—A dear, good, true man, faithful and earnest—almost in the prime of his life cut down by your side. I know how you will miss him every where—you alone can tell of the aching void—words cannot fill it—but you have our tenderest sympathy in your great sorrow—be brave and look upward—Religion only can console us in these dark hours, we feel and know that there is a higher Power that "Doest all things well." It is well with <u>him</u>—you have a little longer to wait and toil—let your children be your comfort and consolation. How the little girls will miss their father.

George is getting to be a young man, how much he can help you, he will be your stay. We have thoughts and talked of you so much during the past few days and wished we were a little nearer—wished we could come to you. I have waited before writing because I did not know where a letter might find you. I am so glad that Nellie can be with you for a little while, glad you can have her for counsel and advice.

We received Georges' letter Wed. morning and one from Mrs. Heald Wed. evening saying that Millie was sick—it completely upset Lizzie, she has been sick all the week—she was out to dinner today—They have heard from Millie again, she is better.

I suppose George will go back to Neb. as he is established there, Will he not? We shall all be so interested and anxious to know what you are going to do—we feel that it will be very lonely for you in Brooklyn. If George goes back I hope he will stop in Bloomfield. Don't you think he can?

Write us about James' sickness. Had he been ailing long? I do not think he has been well in a long time. I think if there ever was a good man, he was one—thoroughly good and unselfish. I cannot realize that I never more am to meet him in this life. My dear sister, how much more than I can tell you do I feel for you. May God be your help and your strength. With very much love and sympathy from us all believe me

Your loving sister
M. F. Leete [Mattie Farmer Leete]

Chas. G. Curtis, Commander,
     833 DeKalb Avenue.

Edward S. Earle, Adjutant,   Brooklyn, N.Y. January 18th
1886.

     551 ½ Lafayette Ave.

R.B. Keeler, Quarter-Master,
     305 Schermerhorn St.

Mrs. James A Barrett.
     Dear Madam-

At a regular Encampment held Jany 11th the Committee appointed in behalf of the Post. Presented the following letter, which was read and adopted by a vote of the Post.

We recognise Gods hand in the great bereavement, in which you are bereft of a devoted, faithful, and loving, Husband; and the Comrades of the Post of one of our most earnest and faithful workers. As a Comrade we knew your husband to be one who could never do enough for the "Old Soldier", his Widow, or Orphan. This love made him a staunch supporter of the principles of our Order.

We can readily understand how such a spirit breathed in the home, must have endeared him to the loved ones there.

The history of his soldier life, how bravely he led, how patiently he suffered from wounds, is one which we treasure with pride-

As a comrade, he not only bound us to himself, but to each other in a way not to be forgotten. Our loss is very great, but how insignificant when compared with yours.

We desire to emulate his spirit towards those he has left behind. Believe us, we are ready to stand by you and yours. May the Blessed Master, the great Comforter, sustain you, and give you peace-

                           Moses G. Young.
                           John J. Arnaud.   }   Committee
                           H.A. Morse

Chas. G. Curtis,   Edw. S. Earle,
     Adjutant   Commander

(Form 21.)

Treasury Department,

SECOND AUDITOR'S OFFICE,

Washington, D. C., Dec 29, 1886.

By Treasury Certificate No. 67416, the Accounting Officers of the Treasury have admitted a balance of $99.39 in favor of *yourself* as *widow* of *James A Barrett*, late *Major* Co., 118 Regiment of *N.Y. Vols*, and when an appropriation for its payment shall have been made by Congress, said certificate will be transmitted to the Paymaster General, U. S. A., at Washington, D. C., who will forward to *you* a check for the amount, less $_____ attorney's fees, payable to *his* order. This settlement is for _____ from the _____ of _____, 18__, when to the _____ of _____, 18__, the time

Pay & allowances Dec 14-31/62 amounting to $ 8.40

Bounty allowed by Act of Short paid Dec 31/64 $ 5.17

Diff. between pay 1st Lt. Aug 28/63 to Nov 9/63 12.00

" " " 1st Lt & Capt. June 28/64 & Sept 11/64 25.66

" " " Capt & Maj July 1/65 to Sept 12/65 24.80

Short paid June 30/65 3.54

Pay as Capt Sept 12/65 5.23

Balance 3 mo's Pay Proper 300

Less balance due in clothing 830 114.04

" Pay & clo. as Lt Dec 14 & 30 4.56

" Tax 4.77 14.63

One Discharge & S.O. #798 enclosed $99.39

He was enrolled subsequent to July 2/61 and discharged prior to a service of two years for promotion, hence not entitled to bounty Commissioned officers are not entitled to bounty. The pay & allowances are received as Capt from May 17/65 to June 30/65, equal amount due in Major for same period.

Your attention is invited to the following extract from an Act of Congress approved July 7, 1884:

"That the Secretary of the Treasury shall at the commencement of each session of Congress report the amount due each claimant whose claim has been allowed in whole or in part to the Speaker of the House of Representatives and the presiding officer of the Senate, who shall lay the same before their respective Houses for consideration."

Under this provision of law the above-named settlement will be reported to Congress.

Respectfully,

Wm H. Day

Auditor.

By S

James H Barrett
#25 Lewis Ave
Brooklyn N.Y.

(Ed. 2-24-'85—10,000.)

Form 21 Final Settlement (Barrett Collection)
Monetary equivalence in 2016 is $2550.00

Emma Jane's Scrapbook Treasures

(A letter from Jane Farmer Barrett to her daughter, Emma Jane's husband, Frederick Lothrop)

Dear Fred.

   I've had a mind for some time to inflict an epistle upon you and as Em, is in the writing business   Here goes—I'm not a very enterprising person at present but hope to do better presently.

Your blessed sister traveled away over here from town the other night and brought me a pretty posy and a loaf of fine Federal bread.

Mrs. Arden came yesterday to visit me (I found because she thought me ill) and I looked better than she for she was completely fatigued with a bit pot of primrose and a large tumbler of jam. I could have shaken her but one does not <u>shake</u> <u>saints</u>. I wonder sometimes if she ever thinks of doing things for <u>her</u> <u>own</u> comfort.

I told her yesterday that we were not told to love our neighbor <u>better</u> than ourselves. She <u>does</u> enjoy reading and well improves her opportunities.

It seems that John Haynes Holmes is coming from an $8000. salary at the Church of the Messiah N.Y. City where he is a young able divine, to be minister of Lincoln Centre at $6000. He likes the Institutional work which Mr. Jones had so effectively planned. He was his strong friend and spoke at the Memorial services which Wm. Kent (member of Congress from Cal.) presided.

Mr. & Mrs. Kent when they lived here in Chicago helped along Lincoln Centre very much with their money and influence. We trust it will not be long ere you can turn your face homeward. Is it not glorious that the war is really over. **My *husband (but we were not married then) was obliged to stay several months at Raleigh as provost marshal before he could return. He said he had some funny times settling marital disagreements among the colored people &c. He always took so much interest in his men and many called him Uncle Jim altho' he was only about thirty. He was wounded twice very badly and the Dr. said if he had been in the habit of using liquor, he could not have recovered as he did. He was such a dear, good man; the best ever,**

Thanksgiving was grey and wet and cold. We three ate chicken, onions, cranberry sauce, mince and squash pie, which your better half made and it was all right. We had invited company but were obliged to withdraw the invitations.

I think I'm not writing news: With much love and all good wishes
         Yours affectionately
         Mother Barrett

*Referring to James A. Barrett

Photo of an older Jane "Jennie" Farmer Barrett
(Barrett Collection)

The following was also found in one of Emma Jane's scrapbooks. A copy was given to Jenkin Lloyd Jones.
Mrs. Jane Farmer Barrett
(written about mother to give to the minister for her funeral remarks)

Born Feb. 14, 1836 in Concord, Mass. she was surrounded wih an atmosphere of poetic and historic interest. Born on the old farm, in a house surrounded by tall elms, she attended school in the little old country school house, and on Sundays, attended double service in the old meeting house.

Emerson, Thoreau and the Alcotts were neighbors, of whom her interesting recollections were a delight to all. Often would friends get her to tell stories of how the grandfathers helped to drive the British back at Concord Bridge.

She taught school up to the time of her marriage to James Atwater Barrett in 1865 after his return from the Civil War where he attained the rank of Major. Their life in Brooklyn, N.Y., was a happy one, and there the family was reared.

At Mr. Barrett's death in 1885, the family sought the home town of Concord for shelter and companionship.

Later in 1890, the family moved to Chicago to make a home for the son who had located there. Here she found religious help and inspiration under the teaching and leadership of Jenkyn Lloyd Jones.

And here she enjoyed the wide freedom and progressive spirit of a western city, remembering the home town for its poetic inspiration and its glorious memories.

Mrs. Barrett has left friends who will never forget her gentle, retiring manner, her beautiful presence, her fine sense of duty and justice and her strong and ever helpful example of what an unselfish life may be. She left a devoted family in February within a few days of her 84th birthday.

An inspiration, precious, bright
To guide our faltering steps aright.
Once more through sun and shower we've fared,
No longer o'er the field we roam;
The day is done, we linger still
Beside the pasture bars.
-By Mother.

Emma Jane kept many magazine and newspaper articles of interest in multiple scrapbooks. The cousins have perused these many times through the years. Turning the pages usually produced new discoveries and the significance wasn't obvious at first. One of them was just the first page of an article entitled, "From Concord to Chicago." Upon closer examination, it was discovered that it was an article eulogizing Jane Barrett. It incorporated Emma Jane's brief summarization of her mother's life. We were uncertain as to the location and date of the publication. After some detective work it was discovered that the article, in its entirety, may be found in the magazine entitled "Unity", Volume 82 on pages 320 and 321. It was published on Thursday, February 20, 1919. The senior editor was Jenkin Lloyd Jones.

From Concord to Chicago

"Ah, did you once see Shelley plain,
And did he stop and speak to you
And did you speak to him again?
How strange it seems and new!"

In the passing hence of Mrs. Jane Barrett on February 1, another link to the past is broken. She was born in Concord, Massachusetts, February 14, 1836, into an atmosphere of poetic and historic interest. Her home was on an old farm, the house surrounded by tall elms. Like many another New England child, she went to school in the little country school-house and on Sundays drove to town to attend the double service in the old meeting house. But it was her great privilege to be born into perhaps the richest spiritual environment which America has ever had to offer any child. Emerson, Thoreau, and the Alcotts were her neighbors, and her recollections of them in her youth were a keen delight to the friends of after years. She remembered Thoreau's long walks—often interrupted by a chat with her father—who was also a lover of nature. There were many pleasant stories to relate of the Alcott family. She would tell of the various things Mrs. Alcott would do herself rather than call her husband "down from the Seventh Heaven" to help.

All through life, Emerson was Mrs. Barrett's great teacher. In the few weeks before the end came, she greatly enjoyed listening to the last two volumes of his Journals, and to his sketch of Thoreau. The scenes and the people mentioned in them were all familiar to her. The everyday saying and doings of these true New England democrats were public possessions and as heirlooms handed down to the next generation. Her grandfathers[208] helped to drive the British back at Concord Bridge, and she often repeated the story, to the great delight of those who heard her,--of the Redcoats who sought in vain for the ammunition cleverly secreted in the old farm house[209].

As a child, Mrs. Barrett was greatly interested in books and a treasured compliment came from her old school master when he said "she read with a tone." Life's experiences of joy and sorrow came to this New England maiden of the long ago. First a school teacher, and then in 1865 her marriage to James A. Barrett, after his return from the Civil War where he attained the rank of Major. He too hailed from Concord and his ancestors were hers also. Their life in Brooklyn, New York, was a happy one, and there the children, one son and three daughters, were reared. After Mr. Barrett's untimely death in 1885, the family sought the home town of Concord for shelter and companionship, and later, in 1890, moved to Chicago where the son was located.

In Brooklyn, John Chadwick was their friend and minister and his poetic and uplifting spirit was ever a comfort and help. With such an inheritance and environment, it was natural that Mrs. Barrett would find religious help and inspiration under the teaching and leadership of Jenkin Lloyd Jones, and just as natural that he should draw help and inspiration from such a parishioner.

He glorified in what he called her "fine New England conscience" and rested in the thought of her anchored faith. Her life was indeed rooted in the fundamental verities. She "believed in soul, was very sure of God." She knew the needs of the spirit,--hymn, prayer, and ritual fed her soul and helped her as they helped him. She lived very close to the heart of the Eternal. Her life was nurtured by hidden springs; hence the poise and peace which radiated from her presence. It was strength, comfort, and encouragement to minister to such a life as Mrs. Barrett's Sunday after Sunday through so many years. How faithful she was to the Sunday services and study classes! How loyal and generous in her support of all that All Souls Church as tried to do! But after all, she herself was the greatest contribution that could be made to the life of any church—alert to every new question of the day, but gentle, quiet, unobtrusive, like the "meadow streamless" that Whittier sings of, where "fresher green reveals alone the noiseless ways they go."

Mrs. Barrett's son, daughters and three grandchildren (James Barrett Peterson, William Hosmer Peterson and Dorothea Peterson) survive her. Her beautiful presence, her fine sense of

---

[208] This is in reference to Lieut. Joseph Hosmer (1735-1821) and Col. James Barrett (1710-1779).
[209] Referring to the farm house owned by Col. James Barrett. It has been restored by the Save Our Heritage Foundation. In 2014, it was acquired by the National Park Service and formally identified as being part of the Minute Man National Historical Park in Concord, MA..

duty and justice and her strong and helpful example of what an unselfish life may be will abide as precious memories to them and to her many friends.

It was a privilege to have entered into this fellowship and inheritance.
"Thanks be to God that such have been,
Though they are here no more."
E.LL.J.

Photo of headstones at Sleepy Hollow Cemetery, Concord, MA
(Barrett Collection)

48th New York State Volunteers Infantry Regiment

Time-line
General Statistics
Battles and Skirmishes
Deceased Soldiers
Battles and Casualties
Lou Evans' Tribute

Timeline for the 48th N.Y.S. Vols. Infantry Regt.

Hawks, S. (2016). *Civil War in the East*. Retrieved February, 2016
from civilwarintheeast.com/us-regiments-batteries/new-york-infantry/48th-new-york/

1861

September 10	Organized at Brooklyn, N.Y. under Colonel James H. Perry, Lieutenant Colonel William B. Barton and Major Oliver Beard
September 17	Left State for Annapolis, Md. Attached to Viele's 1st Brigade, Sherman's So. Carolina Expeditionary Corps
October 21-November 7	Expedition to Port Royal, S.C.
November 7	Capture of Forts Walker and Beauregard, Port Royal Harbor, S.C.
November 7-8	Hilton Head, S.C.

1862

January 1	Port Royal Ferry, Coosaw River, S.C.
January 28–April 11	Siege operations against Fort Pulaski, G.A.
April 10–11	Bombardment and capture Fort Pulaski
April	Garrison duty at Fort Pulaski, 10th Army Corps. Dept. of the South
June 18	Colonel Perry died at Fort Pulaski, Georgia. Lt. Colonel Barton promoted to colonel, Major Beard to lieutenant colonel, and Captain James Green of Company F to major
August 5	Tybee Island
September 24	Skull Creek
September 30 – October 13	Reconnaissance on May and Savannah Rivers
October 18	Kirk's Bluff, Coosawhatchie River
October 22–23	Expedition from Hilton Head to Pocotaligo
October 22	Pocotaligo, Coosawhatchie
November 7	Expedition on U.S. Steamers Potomski and Darlington up Sapelo River, and destruction of salt works
December 24	Lt. Colonel Beard discharged

1863

January 1	Major Green promoted to lieutenant colonel and Captain Dudley Strickland of Company H to major
May	Moved to Hilton Head, S.C., then to St. Helena Island, S.C. attached to 10th Army Cos. G and I remained at Hilton Head
June	Moved to Folly Island, S.C. attached to 2nd Brigade
July	Attached to 2nd Brigade, 2nd Division, Morris Island, S.C.

July 10	**Attack on Morris Island, S.C.** Captain Louis Lent and 5 enlisted men were killed and 18 enlisted men wounded
July 11 and 18	**Assaults on Fort Wagner, Morris Island** Lt. Colonel Green, Captains James Farrell, Frederick Hurst and James Panson and 79 enlisted men were killed or mortally wounded, Captains Nere Elfwing and William Lockwood, Lieutenants James Barrett, Albert Miller and Joseph Taylor and 87 enlisted men wounded, and 1 officer and 63 enlisted men wounded, and 1 officer and 63 men missing or captured
July 18- August	Siege of Forts Wagner and Gregg, Morris Island
August – October	At St. Augustine, Fla. Companies G and I at Fort Pulaski
September 21	Major Strickland promoted to lieutenant colonel
October	Duty at Hilton Head and Beaufort, S.C. attached to District of Hilton Head, S.C.
November 9	Captain William B. Coan of Company E promoted to major

1864

January	Attached to Barton's Brigade, District of Hilton Head, S.C.
February 5–7	Expedition to Jacksonville, Fla. Attached to Barton's Brigade, District of Florida
February 8–22	Expedition into Central Florida attached to Barton's Brigade, Ames' Division, District of Florida
February 20	**Battle of Olustee** The regiment lost 1 officer and 498 enlisted men killed or mortally wounded, 1 officer and 498 enlisted men killed or mortally wounded. 2 officers and 143 enlisted men wounded and 22 enlisted men captured or missing
March 10	Occupation of Palatka
April 22–28	Moved to Gloucester Point, Va. Attached to 2nd Brigade, 2nd Division, 10th Army Corps, Army of the James, Dept. of Virginia and North Carolina
May 4–28	Butler's operations on south side of the James and against Petersburg and Richmond attached to 1st Brigade, 3rd Division, 18th Army Corps
May 7	Port Walthall, Chester Station
May 12–16	Operations against Fort Darling
May 14–16	**Battle of Drury's Bluffs** Captain Samuel Moser and 23 enlisted men were killed or mortally wounded and Lieutenant Van Rensselear Hilliard, 3 other officers and 79 enlisted men wounded
May 16–28	Bermuda Hundred
June 1–12	Moved to White House Landing, then to Cold Harbor. Attached to 2nd Brigade, 2nd Division, 10th Army Corps
June 1–12	**Battles about Cold Harbor** The regiment lost 1 officer and 13 enlisted men killed or mortally wounded, Colonel Barton, Captain Albert Miller, Lieutenants Barrett and Aden Lippencott and 58 enlisted men wounded, and 14 enlisted men missing or captured
June 7	Lt. Colonel Strickland discharged
June 15–18	**Assault on Petersburg** The regiment lost 4 enlisted men killed or mortally wounded and 1 officer and 12 enlisted men wounded
June 15	Siege operations against Petersburg and Richmond begin

June 20	Captain John Fee of Company A mortally wounded near Petersburg, dying of his wounds on July 18 at Fort Monroe, Virginia
June 25	Bermuda Hundred
July 2	Major Coan promoted to lieutenant colonel
July 19	Captain Samuel Swartout promoted to major
July 30	**Mine Explosion, Petersburg** Major Swartout, 2 other officers and 6 enlisted men killed or mortally wounded, 20 enlisted men wounded, and 2 enlisted men missing
August 13–20	**Demonstration on north side of the James**

August 14–18	**Strawberry Plains, Deep Bottom** The regiment lost Captains William D'Arcy and John Tantum, 1 other officer and 14 enlisted men killed or mortally wounded, Captain Joseph Taylor, 1 other officer and 28 enlisted men wounded, and 11 men missing
August 24–25	Bermuda Hundred
September 28-30	**Chaffin's Farm, New Market Heights** The regiment lost 2 officers and 1 enlisted man wounded and 2 men missing
October 27–28	Fair Oaks
December 3	Colonel Barton mustered out
December 5	Captain Nere Elfwing of Company B promoted to major
December 7-25	Expedition to Fort Fisher, N.C. Attached to 2nd Brigade, 2nd Division, 24th Army Corps

1865

January 3–15	2nd Expedition to Fort Fisher, N.C. attached to 2nd Brigade, 2nd Division, Terry's Provisional Corps, Dept. of North Carolina
January 15	**Assault and capture of Fort Fisher** Captain James Dunn of Company E and 2 enlisted men were killed and 3 officers and 11 enlisted men wounded
February 11-12	Cape Fear Entrenchments
February 11	Sugar Loaf Battery
February 18-20	Fort Anderson
February 21	Fort Strong
February 22	**Capture of Wilmington** The regiment lost 5 enlisted men killed or mortally wounded and 1 officer and 9 enlisted men wounded
March 1– April 26	Campaign of the Carolinas attached to 2nd Brigade, 2nd Division, 10th Army Corps, Dept. of North Carolina
March 6–21	Advance on Kinston and Goldsboro
March 14	Lt. Colonel Coan promoted to colonel, Major Elfwing to lieutenant colonel and Captain James Barrett of Company H as major
April 9–14	Advance on Raleigh
April 26	Bennett's House, Surrender of Johnston and his army
May–August	Duty at Raleigh and in the Dept. of North Carolina
August 16	Mustered out at Raleigh under Colonel Coan, Lieutenant Colonel Elfwing and Major Barrett

General Statistics
(*48th Regt. N.Y.S. Vols.*, A. J. Palmer, D.D., 1885)

Number of enlistments:

1861	167
1862	190
1863	220
1864	224
1865	581
Year Unknown	9
Transfers from N.Y. Independent Battalion and 117th N.Y. Vols.	300

Total: 2191

Casualties in engagements with enemy were 947 or 43%. Deducting the recruits of 1865, none of whom were in more than one action (Wilmington), and with only three wounded, the loss increased to nearly 59%. Including deaths from disease, the percentage of losses in action to the whole number is nearly one half, and without the 1865 recruits, two thirds.

Killed or died of wounds received in action	236
Wounded	623
Taken as prisoners	88
Died of disease	87
Died at Andersonville, Richmond and other Confederate prisons	40
Commissioned officers were killed or died of wounds	17
Commissioned officers wounded	28
Enlisted men became commissioned officers in the regiment	58
Enlisted men became commissioned officers in other commands	17
Number of men that re-enlisted and became "Veterans"	331
Number of "Veterans" that were mustered-out Sept. 1, 1865	186

Battles and Skirmishes

Location:	Date:
Port Royal, SC	November 7, 1861
Port Royal Ferry, SC	January 1, 1862
Savannah River, SC	April 1862
Fort Pulaski, GA	April 1862
Coosawhatchie, SC	October 22, 1862
Pocataligo, GA	
Morris Island Batteries, SC	July 10, 1863
Fort Wagner, SC	July 18, 1863
Olustee, FL	February 20, 1864
Chester Heights, VA	May 7, 1864
Drury's Bluff, VA	May 16, 1864
Cold Harbor, VA	June 1st to14th, 1864
Chester Hill, VA	June 18, 1864
Cemetery Hill, VA	July 30, 1864
Deep Bottom, VA	August 14, 1864
Strawberry Plains, VA	August 16, 1864
Siege of Petersburg, VA	June, July, August and September, 1864
Chapin's Farm, VA	September 29, 1864
Fort Fisher, NC	January 15, 1865
Federal Point to Wilmington, NC	
Wilmington, NC	February 21, 1865

**Battles and Skirmishes that the 48th were engaged in during the Civil War as recorded in James' journal. According to other sources; some of the names and or dates may have been incorrectly listed. This may have been another example of Emma Jane's editing

List of Deceased Soldiers

The following list are soldiers from the 48th who died at Andersonville, GA from Gold Soldier Stars 1864. This is a handwritten list found on letterhead glued inside the back page of Palmer's book in the Barrett Collection.

Name:	Company:	Date:	Cause of Death:
C. Cadmus	Co A	June 19	Ana
E. F. Doughty	Co A	Oct 16	Div
A. Melich	Co A	Oct 26	Scs
Fred Hoffman	Co B	Aug 8	Scs
A Peterson	Co B	Sept 18	Dia
E Knabe	Co C	June 8	Dia' c
John Clark	Co D	June 18	Dia' a
B Graft	Co D	July 21	Dia
S. G. Douglass	Co D	Aug 20	Is. p
G Degarmo	Co E	Aug 6	Scs
J Dolan	Co E	June 14	Dia'a
J Halse	Co E	Oct 30	Scs
H Holstenstein	Co E	May 31	Dia'c
John C Smith	Co E	Sept 3	Dys
Pat Boyle	Co F	Sept 16	Dia'c
F Slater	Co F	July 5	De
F Smith	Co F	June 10	De
C.Z. Emery	Co G	Sept 8	Scs
J S De Witt	Co H	Sept 20	Scs
S Maa	Co H	Aug 24	Scs
B Wilson	Co H	June 5	Dys
J Alliger	Co I	Oct 26	Wds
W Tuttle	Co K	July 4	Is.p

48th Regiment Battles and Casualties

PLACE.	Date.	Killed.		Wounded.				Missing.		Aggregate.
				Died.		Recov'd.				
		Officers.	Enlisted men.	Officers.	Enlisted men.	Officers.	Enlisted men	Officers.	Enlisted men.	
	1862.									
Port Royal Ferry, S. C.	Jan. 1	....	....		....	....	3	....	....	3
Commodore Tatnall's Flotilla, S. C.	28	....	....		....	....		....	....	....
Battery Vulcan, S. C.	Feb. 4							....	....	....
Fort Pulaski, Ga.	April 10–11							....	....	....
Tybee Island, Ga.	Aug. 5									....
Skull Creek, S. C.	Sept. 24									....
Bluffton and Crowell's Plantation, S. C.	30	....	....		....		1			1
Elba Island, S. C.	Oct. 1	....	....		....			....	....	....
Kirk's Bluff, S. C.	18	....	....	1	....			....	....	1
Coosawhatchie River, S. C.	22	....	....		....			....	....	....
	1863.									
Bluffton, S. C.	June 4	....	....		....					....
Morris Island, S. C.	July 10	1	5	....	....	....	19	....	....	25
Morris Island, S. C.	14		1	....	1	....	1	....	2	5
Battery Wagner, S. C.	18	3	61	3	18	4	87	3	63	242
	1864.									
Sanderson, Fla.	Feb. 12		1							1
Olustee, Fla.	20	1	38	....	10	1	143	....	22	215
Near Palatka, Fla.	March 17									....
Near Palatka, Fla.	21	....	....							....
Near Palatka, Fla.	29	....	....							....
Near Palatka, Fla.	31	....	....							....
Operations against Petersburg and Richmond, Va	May 5–30	....	....							
Port Walthall	6–7	....	6		1					
Proctor's Creek	12	....	....	1						
Drewry's Bluff	14–16	1	8	....	15	4	79	....	....	115
Bermuda Hundred	18–26									
Cold Harbor, Va.	June 1–12	....	1	....	4		4			
First assault	1	1	10	....	3	4	56	....	14	93
Before Petersburg and Richmond, Va.	June 15–Dec. 20	....	5	1	3	....	14	....	....	23
Assault of Petersburg, Va.	June 15–19	....	3	....	1	1	12	....	....	17
Mine Explosion, Va.	July 30	3	5	....	1		20	....	2	31
Strawberry Plains, Va.	Aug. 14–18	3	12	....	2	2	28	....	11	58
Chaffin's Farm, Va.	Sept. 29–Oct. 2	....	....			2	1	....	2	5
Fort Fisher, N. C.	Dec. 25									
	1865.									
Fort Fisher, N. C.	Jan. 15	1	2	....		3	11	....	....	17
Cape Fear Intrenchments, N. C.	Feb. 11–12	....	....					....	....	....
Smithfield, N. C.	15	....	....							....
Fort Anderson, N. C.	18–20	....	....							....
Near Wilmington, N. C.	21–22	....	2	....	3	1	9	....	....	15
Campaign of the Carolinas	Mar. 1–April 26	....	....							
Bennett House, N. C.	April 26	....	....	....						
On picket, Feb. 24, 1864		....	....	....	1	....	....	....	....	1
Total loss		14	160	4	65	22	484	3	116	868

48th N.Y. Infantry Regiment-battles and casualties during the Civil War-
(Courtesy of N.Y. Military Museum and Veteran's Research Center)

Luis Evans' Tribute

Luis Evans concludes his book about the Forty-Eighth Regiment with the following:

Our Colonel called for "Home, Sweet Home" from the
Band; and with memories of the dear ones far away, and the
Unbidden tears stealing to our eyes as we thought of our Northern homes,
We lifted our swords, presented our arms, and vowed that flag
Should never be dishonored.[1]

> Captain Daniel C. Knowles, 48th New York
> *The History of the Forty-Eighth Regiment New York*
> *State Volunteers, In the War for the Union, 1861-1865*

To the officers and men of the 48th New York, the war through July 1863 must have seemed a strange mixture of both boredom and sheer horror. Up to the time of the assaults on Morris Island and Fort Wagner, there had been little occasion for the unit to fight as a regiment. Yet, in a period of just nine days, the regiment had been reduced to a battalion—half its original size. The survivors of the attacks on Morris Island and Fort Wagner now had to struggle with the issues of reassembling their command, as well as its morale.

Two months of rest and refit in St. Augustine proved helpful to the regiment, and its subsequent postings to low threat camps and details around Beaufort, South Carolina, also aided in the unit's recovery. In November of 1863, Companies G and I, from Fort Pulaski and Tybee Island respectively, rejoined the regiment. Many of the wounded officers and men from Fort Wagner also rejoined the regiment in earnest about this time. Additionally, 156 new conscripts, sent from the North, and 150 men transferred from "Les Enfants Perdu," the New York Independent Battalion, joined the regiment. The addition of these men greatly strengthened the unit's number.[1]

In December of 1863, reenlistment of the regiment's veterans began. Despite having faced many tragedies and deprivations, nearly 300 men of the 48th took an oath to continue to fight for the Union cause. Still, the regiment would never be as formidable in size, nor as effective a fighting force, as it had been before the fights for Fort Wagner and Morris Island. The regiment would go on to fight for two more years, serving in many of the war's others campaigns—Olustee, Bermuda Hundred, Drewry's Bluff, Strawberry Plains, Chaffin's Farm, Cold Harbor, Petersburg, Fort Fisher and Wilmington.[1]

But despite serving with valor in these campaigns, the 48th's reputation would be inextricably linked to the failure of Fort Wagner. Yet, they had not failed in their duty. Although they were unwitting participants in a poorly led effort, they, nonetheless, accomplished everything they were tasked to do. They had borne the

Confederate defenders' withering fire, breached Fort Wagner's defenses, and held a segment of the fort until reinforcements came up. Only one other regiment, the 6th Connecticut, could make that claim...

The officers and men of the 48th New York were among the finest soldiers who served the Union during the Civil War. Their heroic deeds during the campaign for Charleston in the summer of 1863 rank among the noblest of the war and, despite their absence at more publicized campaigns, such as Gettysburg, Vicksburg, Chancellorsville and Chickamauga, they showed no less courage and gave no less effort than soldiers who fought at there. At Morris Island and Fort Wagner, the officers and men of "Perry's Saints" proved, by their valor and actions, that they were truly "men of glory."[1]

[1] Palmer, Abraham J. *The History of the Forty-Eighth Regiment New York State Volunteers, In the War for the Union, 1861-1865* (Brooklyn: Veteran Association of the Regiment, 1885), 234.
[1] Palmer, 128-130; and James M. Nichols, *Perry's Saints or The Fighting Parson's Regiment in the War of the Rebellion* (Boston: D. Lothrop and Company, 1886), 188-189.
[1] Palmer, 130; and Frederick Phisterer, *New York in the War of the Rebellion, 1861-1865* (Albany, New York: J.B. Lyon Company, 1912), 2357-2358.
[1] Nichols, 174-175; and Palmer, 104.
[1] Evans, Luis M. *So Rudely Sepulchered: The 48th New York Volunteer Infantry Regiment During the Campaign for Charleston, July 1863* (Fort Leavenworth, Kansas: U.S. Army Command and General Staff College, 2000), 94-96.

Linda is deciphering an entry in James' diary

Meliscent [Penny] and Patricia [Patty] are reading letters
while Linda listens and types.

The Cousins visiting the recently restored Col. Barrett's Farmhouse at the Minuteman National Historic Park, Concord, MA. (left to right) Penny, Patty, Linda and Les

This project was one of discovery, toil and conundrums. It has taken the Cousins close to five years to complete this endeavor. There were old family photos to identify and the challenges of deciphering handwriting from over 150 years ago. Our work has led to discussions of stories that had been told and retold over weekly lunches. The long hours of research led to new discoveries, adventures and new found friends and acquaintances. This book has been a team effort and has strengthened our family bonds with a common purpose.

Leslie [Les] is proofreading.

Taken in front of the demilune at Fort Pulaski, GA

This photo was taken while on one of our family adventures at Andersonville, GA.
This was a research trip in preparation for our next book.
(Left to right) Linda, Meliscent [Penny] and Patricia [Patty]

Our ancestors left us with a legacy of treasures that
will lead us on our journey to complete our next book.

Endnotes

[i] *"Upon the news of the battle of Bull Run, and the call of the president immediately after for the 75,000 additional troops, Mr. Barrett at once resolved to come to the rescue, and in July, 1861, enlisted as first sergeant in company H, Capt. D.W. Strickland, 48th Regiment New York Volunteer Infantry, James H. Perry, Colonel. The regiment was ordered south in the expedition to Hilton Head, S.C., where they arrived after a perilous and dangerous passage, being closely crowded, in an unsafe steamer. Witnessed the magnificient display of our navy in the capture of the fortifications at Hilton Head, and the glorious and triumphant victory it there achieved, on the 8th of November, 1861.*

In the spring of 1863 went in the expedition against Charleston, S.C., by the way of Folly Island, having spent the previous year at Hilton Head, and in the reduction and capture of Fort Pulaski, Ga., a most fatiguing process and unhealthy situation.

The regiment participated in the capture of Morris Island, Charleston, S.C., on the 10th of July, 1863, and in the unadvised, ill-timed and unsuccessful assault upon Fort Wagner, which proved so destructive to hundreds of brave volunteers of the union army. Sergeant Barrett had been promoted to second, and then a first lieutenant. The assault on Fort Wagner was made, (and injudiciously, as our best military officers say,) in the night, which was the principal cause of the failure. The men went into the conflict with determined courage and enthusiasm. They waded the moat and scaled the parapet. While about half way up the parapet, Lieut. Barrett, as he was leading and encouraging his men, received a wound by a fragment of shell passing through his right thigh, but as it did not hit the bone or lacerate any of the large blood vessels, he was able to stand, and soon expecting to gain a decided victory, his enthusiasm impelled him onward, and he gained the summit, leaped into the bastion amid total darkness. The men soon became confused, and the union men fired upon each other. A retreat was soon ordered, but there were but few, but what were killed or wounded. Lieut. Barrett crawled out over heaps of dead and wounded, and by the help of his sword for a cane he eventually succeeded in reaching camp, successfully eluding the vigilance of the rebel parole there were pacing the beach. Upon reaching camp and having his wound dressed, the excitement over, he became perfectly helpless and exhausted. His company of 500 came out with but 200 men. After the wound was partially healed, and he was able to ride, but not yet walk, he was placed in charge of an

447

outpost as a commander of company A, and soon after removed to Pope's plantation on Hilton Head, to perform picket duty. Here were about 500 negroes, and Lieut. Barrett embraced the opportunity to learn their habits and opinions, which were favorable if honestly dealt by, but in their illiterate and uncultivated state were liable to be imposed upon by wicked, designing men. They made good soldiers. They had a grand thanksgiving dinner, and a good time, soon after which Lieut. Barrett was restored to his own company, and in December, 1863, the company re-enlisted, with few exceptions. It had been recruited up to 300. This entitled them to thirty days furlough, and to receive the honorable title of veterans. After the furlough the company proceeded south and joined the regiment in Florida soon after I had fought the unfortunate battle of Olustee, February 20, under the command of Gen. Seymour, who planned the unsuccessful assault on Fort Wagner. The army having lost all confidence in him as a commanding officer, he was relieved, to the joy of all. The regiment was soon ordered north to join the army on James River, Va., under Gen. Butler. Landed at Glouscester Point, where they prepared for field service, and sailed for Bermuda Hundred, thence by a tedious march to the vicinity of Drury's Bluff. On the 15th of May the army advanced on the works of Drury's Bluff, and captured two lines of works. The next morning, May 16th, by reason of a dense fog, of which the rebels took advantage, the union army was suddenly assailed on right, left, and centre, and forced to retire and abandon the capture of Richmond for the present.

From here the regiment was soon sent to the White House, where upon landing they drew three days' rations, but were ordered to march before they were issued, but secured coffee and sugar, which Lieut. Barrett designates as the soldier's "staff of life." After marching all night and the next forenoon, the regiment arrived at Cold Harbor, about 2 o'clock, P.M., and were ordered immediately to charge the works, without giving them time even to relieve themselves of their knapsacks. The men made a gallant charge, captured one line of works and 500 prisoners. While rallying some stragglers lurking behind, Lieut. Barrett received a slight wound in the right shoulder, but not sufficiently severe to disable him from duty. Among the prisoners captured on this occasion was the captain of one of the artillery companies, who was a female, and it is said that the burial party found several females among the rebel slain. It was 10 o'clock, P.M., before the regiment was relieved and allowed a little rest. The next morning, June 2, the regiment advanced to the support of the attacking party, under a galling fire, and soon after arriving at the scene and taking their position, a ball from a sharp-shooter struck Lieut. Barrett behind or back of the right hip, passed completely through him and came out at the left hip, a distance of eleven inches from the place of entrance, beside passing through twenty thicknesses of his rubber blanket, and shattering the lower end of the spine. Two soldiers conveyed him to the rear, where 8000 wounded men lay waiting for transportation to the White House. Lieut. Barrett lay on the ground here for two days before his turn arrived to be conveyed to the White House. After a few days he was put on board a steamer for Washington, and placed in a hospital, and shortly returned to his father's house in Concord, Mass., where, by good nursing, under the assiduous attention and skilful treatment of the family physician, Dr. Bartlett, he recovered. After remaining home for three months he returned to his regiment, but was placed upon light duty for five months longer, before he was able to take the field. But in the meantime his regiment had been active, and fought many severe battles, and was now ordered in the expedition against Fort Fisher. Upon the arrival of 200 recruits for his regiment, Lieut. Barrett was ordered to take them to the regiment at Fort Fisher. Many of them were substitutes, and proved refractory and treacherous, but he succeeded in getting them to the place of destination, with three or four exceptions. He here took command of his company, having been promoted to a captain, and performed full duty, being constantly marching, and counter marching, flanking the enemy, first at one point and then at another, and on Feb. 21, 1865, had a severe skirmish with the enemy, and the next day, Feb. 22, marched triumphantly into Wilmington, N.C., amid the hearty welcome and joyful demonstration of the colored population. From here our army made forced marches, in hope of recapturing the 10,000 union prisoners then in the hands of the enemy, but by their crossing the river and burning the bridge after them, they failed to accomplish it. In a few days, however, the rebels consented to parole them. They were poor, filthy, famished creatures, mere walking skeletons. Some were able to walk to Wilmington, where they were well cared for, but very many of them were so far gone by starvation and cruel treatment by the rebels that they died. The residue were sent north. About this time, the Major having lost a leg in the battle before Wilmington, Capt. Barrett was commissioned Major. The regiment soon moved towards Raleigh, N.C., where it arrived, and where the whole army became highly exasperated at the news of the assassination of President Lincoln.

They were soon ordered to draw three days' rations, and be ready at a moment's warning to attack Johnson's army. But news soon arriving that Johnson had surrendered, the order was countermanded, which virtually closed the most wicked and uncalled for rebellion on record.

Major Barrett had command of the regiment until the 4th of July, when he was appointed Post Provost Marshal of Raleigh, where the people thronged to his office to take the oath of allegiance to the United States, some coming from 70 miles distant for that purpose. Major Barrett administered the oath to a cousin of President Andrew Johnson, who could not write, and was obliged to *make his mark. On September 1, the regiment was ordered to prepare to return home and be discharged, which took place at Hart Island, in New York harbor, about the middle of September, and Major Barrett went to his home, wearing honorable scars and an enviable reputation as a soldier and an officer."*

Prescott, William, M. *The Prescott Memorial: 1500-1870 Or A Genealogical Memoir of the Prescott Families in America. In Two Parts.* Boston: Henry W. Dutton & Son, 1870. (Pages 129-131)

[ii] ***About The Regiment*** *– Colonel James H. Perry received authority from the War Department, July 24,1861, to recruit a regiment of infantry at Brooklyn. This regiment was recognized and numbered by the State authorities September 14, 1861. It was mustered in the service at the United States for three years, between August 16 and September 16, 1861. The regiment received by transfer, January 30, 1864, a portion of the Enfants Perdus(a French term, meaning lost children: soldiers sent to a dangerous post.). At the expiration of its term of service, the men entitled thereto were sent to New York city, September 17, 1864, and there discharged September 20, 1864, and the regiment continued in service. June 9, 1865, the officers and enlisted men of the 117th Infantry, not mustered out with their regiment, joined this by transfer. The companies were recruited principally: A,C, G and I at Brooklyn; B at Brookly and Peekskill; D—Jersey Company and Die-no-mores—in New Jersey; E at Brooklyn and New York city, and in New Jersey, Massachusetts and Connecticut; F at Brooklyn and New York city; H at Brooklyn, and in Monmouth county, N.J.; K at Brooklyn and Galesville.*

48th Infantry New York State Volunteers. +cNew York State Military Museum and Veterans Research Center. Retrieved 02/03/2014 from
https://dmna.ny.gov/historic/reghist/civil/infantry/48thinf/Main.html

[iii] The 1860 United States Federal Census of the 3rd District 11th Ward Brooklyn, Kings County, New York (Page 103) lists the following persons living in the same household: George M. Bates (Age 41, Occupation- Merchant), Mary Bates (Age 40), Martha C. Bates (Age 12), George S. Bates (Age 9), James A. Barrett (Age 28, Occupation- Clerk), Charles P. Gerrish (Age 27, Occupation- Clerk), Ellen Sweeney (Age 45, Occupation- Servant) and Annie Gibbon (Age 16, Occupation-Servant). The address of the home, as listed in the New York City Directory was 237 Cumberland St. Brooklyn, New York.

SCHEDULE 1.—Free Inhabitants in _2ᵈ Divis¹¹ Wᵈ Benas_ in the County of _Kings_ State of _New York_ enumerated by me, on the _16ᵗʰ_ day of _June_ 1860. _Thoˢ P. Norris_ Asˢᵗ Marshal.

Post Office _Brooklyn_.

		The name of every person whose usual place of abode on the first day of June, 1860, was in this family	Age	Sex	Color	Profession, Occupation, or Trade of each person, male and female, over 15 years of age	Value of Real Estate	Value of Personal Estate	Place of Birth, Naming the State, Territory, or Country				Whether deaf and dumb, blind, insane, idiotic, pauper, or convict		
1	2	3	4	5	6	7	8	9	10	11	12	13	14		
20	582	George M. Bates	41	M		Merchant		500	Mass							20
21		Mary "	40	f				400	" "							21
22	" "	Martha C.	12	f					" "		1					22
23	" "	George S.	1	M					" "							23
24	"	James A. Barret	28	M		Clerk		200	"							24
25	"	Charles H. Guerith	21	M		"		200	"							25
26	"	Ellen Sweeney	45	f		Servant			Ireland							26
27	"	Annie Griffin	14	f		"			Ireland							27
28	486	[blank]														28

No. white males, 14.   No. colored males, ___ No. foreign born, ___ No. blind, ___ 13500   2780   No. idiots, ___
No. white females, 25.   No. colored females, ___ No. deaf and dumb, ___ No. insane, ___ 27800 / 41300   No. paupers, ___   No. convicts, ___

Census, U.B. *1860 United States Federal Census, Brooklyn, New York*. Washington, D.C.: National Archives and Records Administration (Courtesy of Ancestry.com)

[iv] James Atwater Barrett worked for James P. (Prescott) Swain & Co. Swain was the son of Meliscent Barrett and Joseph Swain. Established as a New York City merchant, James Prescott Swain purchased the old Underhill mill in Bronxville, New York. He established a water-powered stone factory making screws and axles and grinding grist. He built a mansion near the river and bought swathes of land on both sides of the train tracks where he pastured a herd of cattle.

James Prescott Swain was married to Catherine Eliza Prescott. Catherine Prescott was the daughter of James Minot Prescott and Lucy Atwater Tyler. **James Minot Prescott** was the **brother** of **James A. Barrett's mother**, Elizabeth Prescott Barrett.

> *By the earnest solicitation of a black man, a slave of Hon. Freeman Walker, Mr. Prescott (James Minot Prescott) consented to purchase his wife with one child, for a house servant. The number of children rapidly increased, and, upon the death of Mr. Walker his black man was exposed to sale at auction by his executors. Mr. Prescott, moved by sympathy for him and his family, bid him off. "Finding himself more and more entangled in our country's curse," to use his own strong language," he resolved to clear himself from this deep stain and to remove his family from its polluting influence....*
>
> *Consequently, with a becoming and commendable spirit, Mr. Prescott, in 1831, took his family to New Haven, Ct., when he returned to Augusta (Ga.), he made arrangements with the Colonization Society for sending his eight slaves to Liberia.*

By becoming a surety for others (outside of his own business) he became embarrassed, and thereby detained in Georgia until he was relieved by taking the advantage of the bankrupt law.

After his release, Mr. Prescott went into the commission business in the city of New York, and in 1844 became a partner in business with his son-in-law, James P. Swain, under the firm of J.P.Swain & Co. He resides at Bronxville, New York.

Prescott, William M. *The Prescott Memorial: 1500-1870 Or a Genealogical Memoir of the Prescott Families In America. In Two Parts.* Boston: Henry W. Dutton & Son, 1870. (Page 93). *Photo History of Bronxville.* Retrieved September 14, 2016 from www.villageofbronxville.com/.../files/a-photo-history-of-bronxville.

[v] The Civil War broke into open warfare in April, and on April 15, 1861, Lincoln called for 75,000 troops to put down rebellion. Ellsworth helped recruit these soldiers. He raised the 11th New York Volunteer Infantry Regiment (the "Fire Zouaves") from New York City's volunteer firefighting companies, and returned to Washington as their colonel. Ellsworth died shortly after returning to Washington. On May 24, 1861 (the day after Virginia's secession was ratified by referendum). President Lincoln looked out from the White House across the Potomac River, and saw a large Confederate flag prominently displayed over the town of Alexandria, Virginia. Ellsworth immediately offered to retrieve the flag for Lincoln. He led the 11th New York across the Potomac and into the streets of Alexandria uncontested. He detached some men to take the railroad station, while he led others to secure the telegraph office and get the Confederate flag, which was flying above the Marshall House Inn. Ellsworth and four men went upstairs and cut down the flag. As Ellsworth came downstairs with the flag, the owner, James W. Jackson, killed him with a shotgun blast to the chest. Corporal Frances E. Brownell, of Troy, New York, immediately killed Jackson. Brownell was later awarded the Medal of Honor for his actions.

[vi] There were several recipes that were used to make this medicinal elixir. Stabler-Leadbeater Apothecary Shop in Alexandria, Virginia produced a popular cough expectorant that included in its ingredients, paprika and alcohol. Other recipes used cayenne pepper, finely ground myrrh and brandy. Hot Drops were touted to settle queasy stomachs, nausea and diarrhea due to the excitement of battle or panic. The elixir was also used to treat colic, cholera morbus, dysentery, palsy, pleurisy, wounds, sprains, etc.

Cavileer, Sharon. *Virginia Curiosities, 3rd: Quirky Characters, Roadside Oddities & Other Offbeat Stuff*: Rowman & Littlefield, 2013. (Pgs. 7-9)

[vii] The Cousins found this newspaper article glued to scrapbook page. Unfortunately, the name of the newspaper and date is missing. One of the Cousins did more research

and it was found that in 1879 did own the Blue Wing lode (hard rock) mine that was located in Clear Creek County in Colorado. It should be noted that the article below states "…This indicates a working yield of over $3,000 coin value per ton." In 2016, $3000 would be equivalent to $66,528.66.

A few days since, Mr. Geo. H. Barrett showed us a fine button of silver, weighing 13½ ounces, taken from eleven pounds of ore from the Federal lode, on Saxon Mountain. This indicates a working yield of over $3,000 coin value per ton. He also showed us, at the same time, some beautiful, large specimens of genuine silver glance, the best that we have ever seen from any lode in the territory. This lode is being worked regularly, and we are informed that they have a good vein of rich sulphuret ore.

viii *Nathan Henry Warren was born in Concord, Mass., on December 9, 1827, and attended the public schools of that vicinity until thirteen years of age, when he went to the Concord Academy, then kept by John and Henry Thoreau, the latter of whom afterward became well known as a naturalist, lecturer and writer. He remained at school until he was eighteen years of age, and then took charge of a farm which his father had purchased near the center of town, and selected as a special branch of business the breeding of Ayrshire stock, then coming into notice as superior for dairy purposes. After the passage of the fugitive slave law by Congress, in 1850, the section of the law which imposed a fine of $1,000 upon any person who should harbor, assist, or, when called upon, refuse to recapture in Massachusetts, and Mr. Warren, with others, organized societies to assist fugitives. Until the War of the Rebellion, it was his duty, as conductor upon the Underground Railroad, to take to a secure place upon his premises, and keep until a party could be made up, such persons "fleeing from service" as arrived in Boston. These persons were forwarded from station to station until they reached Canada. In 1860, while serving in a "Wide Awake Club," Mr. Warren contracted so severe a cold that a bronchial affection was the result, and for several years the question whether he could live on the coast of New England remained unsettled. In the winter of 1863, he went to Hilton Head, S.C., bought one of the abandoned plantations, which were being sold by the Government for non-payment of taxes, and tried the experiment of raising a crop of cotton. With regular weekly wages as the incentive, instead of the lash, the experiment was a success, and he sold the plantation in the summer of 1864, with a fine crop of cotton nearly ready to gather, and came to Arlington,*

Ill., where his brothers and present partners were then doing a grain and lumber business. It was decided to open a grain commission house in Chicago, which was done in April, 1865, under the firm name of N.H. Warren & Co., composed of N.H. Warren, Cyrus T. Warren and Charles C. Warren. There has been no change in the firm since that time. They commenced building grain elevators, are about six millions of bushels a year. Mr. Warren has been twice married; first to **Mary Prescott Barrett (James A. Barrett's sister)**, *in Concord, Mass., on April 26, 1849, and had the following children: Mary Elizabeth, Ella, George Henry, Alice and Charles. He was again married in July, 1879, to Mrs. Minerva T. O'Hara, and they have one child--Paul Livingston.*

Andreas, A. *History of Chicago from the Earliest Period to the Present Time in three volumes.* Chicago: A.T. Andreas, 1884. (Volume 2)

[ix] Corporal George Durand died of wounds received near Bluffton, Virginia.

Palmer, A.J. *The History of the Forty-Eighth Regiment New York State Volunteers.* Brooklyn 1885: Veteran Association of the Regiment (Page 256)

[x] "...many amusing things occurred at Fort Pulaski, like the adventure of Lieutenant Edwards of Company C (an excellent officer but strict disciplinarian), who had announced to his company that while upon drill, under no circumstances whatever should there be any **talking in the ranks**, and threatened to punish the first man who should speak a word. Then he proceeded with the drill of his company, giving his orders, "forward," "guide right," "left wheel," and so on until the company was facing the stairway that leads to the parapet of the fort, in front of which was an old well, without any covering, and half-full of water, towards which the lieutenant was walking backwards, saying "left," "left," "left," until suddenly he reached the well and went into it. When he succeeded in pulling himself out, thoroughly wet and mad, he upbraided the company for not warning him of his danger, and was reminded of his order **not to speak under any circumstance**. He joined heartily in the joke after he had changed his clothing." Palmer (Pages 59-60)

[xi] *"General Hunter again assumed command of the Department after the lamented death of General Mitchel, and life at Fort Pulaski resumed with us its monotony. Our routines were all routine. Many sports, however, we're engaged in to while away the time, and all will recall the fishing for sheep's head, the duck-shooting in Calabogue Sound, the rowing, base-ball, and other sports. Our baseball nine was a success. In games with picked nines from other regiments it generally won the laurels. In a game with the nine of the Forty-*

seventh New York, played at Fort Pulaski, January 3, 1863, it won by a score of twenty to seven. But the great source of amusement **was the theatre**. It may be doubted if anything (in that line) was as fine in the war as the three theatres which were erected respectively at Fort Pulaski, Ga., at St. Augustine, Fla., and at Hilton Head, S.C., by the Forty-eighth Regiment, where entertainments of a not unpretentious class were given by the actors and actresses of the "Barton Dramatic Association." It so happened that there were in the Forty-eighth several professional actors, and especially one scenic artist. Major Barrett, who was its president, has furnished from memory a list of the members of the Association, and a sketch of its career:

James A. Barrett, *President*.

Robert Dixon, *Stage Manager and Tragedy*.

James White, *Heavy Tragedy*.

C.L. Harrison, *Scenic Artist and Costumer*.

A.J. DeHaven, *Property Man and Comedian*.

Wiliam H. Owen, James Barnes, Joseph Murphy,

John Dupree, *Comedy and Song*.

E.J. Barney, Thomas B. Wood, James S. Wyckoff,

J.L. Michaels, *Walking Gentlemen*.

Lewis W. Burr, Abraham J. Palmer, *Leading Ladies*.

Vitruvious Witcomb, *Old Lady*.

N.W. Pease, John Stewart, *Chambermaids*

The Regimental Band, *Orchestra*.

Colonel Barton gave us permission to use an out-building, 25 x 70, for the purpose, and detailed all the mechanics that were needed to do the work; and in a very short time, considering their facilities, they had erected a very well-equipped and attractive little theatre near the north dock, with a stage at one end, private boxes, orchestra, side-scenes (parlor, kitchen and street), and a drop-curtain on which was painted the bombardment of the fort. They sent to New York for canvas, paint, costumes, lamps, a printing-press, and books of plays, and improvised a chandelier and foot-lights out of old tin-cans. The theatre seated about one hundred persons. On the opening night an address was delivered by Corporal Michaels, followed by the farce "Family Jars;" that by the "The Flea" by Owens of Company H; then an exhibition of light balancing by De Haven; then the first act of the tragedy of Richard III.; a song by Dickson; and the whole concluded with a tableau of Washington's grave. It was a fine success. At first we played simple comedy, such as "Box and Cox," "The Secret, or a Hole in the Wall," "rough Diamond," and the like; but the dramatic element soon asserted itself and ventured upon three act of "Othello," against the judgment of most of the officers, who said that they did not care to hear such a piece "murdered." The company felt that their reputation was at stake, but *with White as Othello, Dickson as Iago, Burr as Desdemona, and Palmer as Emilia, the play was pronounced a great success by the few officers who had consented to witness it, and a loud call was made for the production of the whole play in five acts. This was done and received with great applause. From that time our reputation was established, and the fame of the "Barton Dramatic Association" soon spread throughout the Department. Major Barrett writes, "Our two leading ladies were said to be the handsomest women in the Department." The regular play-nights were Mondays, Wednesdays, and Fridays; but the fort soon became a popular resort for visitors, and we were often called on to give special entertainments for the benefit of guests. On the night before the expedition started for Bluffton, the writer played Trudgeon in the "Ghost on the Wall," and captivating the heart of the captain of the transport on which we embarked that night, shared his hospitality during the expedition. In this way incidental benefits came to the actors.*

In June, 1863, we closed our little theatre, and in the real tragedy in which we participated on Morris Island, the tragedies we played were soon forgotten. Subsequently the fixtures of the theatre were transferred to St. Augustine, Fla., when the remnant of the regiment was stationed there after the fatal losses of Fort Wagner. At a later period they built another theatre 40 x 100, at Hilton Head, where they played to crowded houses of citizens and soldiers, until marching orders sent them once more to the front. The "Barton Dramatic Association" has long been a story of the past, but its memories are pleasant still to all who participated in its pleasures." Palmer (57-61)

The New South Newspaper. (November 28, 1863). Vol. 2 no. 12. Retrieved December 4, 2015 from http://www/sc/edu/library/digital/collections/newsouth.html

"Our theater (located in St. Augustine, FL) is an institution of which its projectors may well be proud. It was organized by the members of the 48th New York Regiment, while quartered here last summer, and was transferred to the 24th Massachusetts upon their arrival a few weeks ago. The building appropriated by the company is a long, low edifice, near the barracks, and in olden time was used as a hospital. In one end of the room, which will seat comfortably an audience of six or seven hundred, a capacious stage has been erected, with scenery and appointments which are really handsome. The last performance was on Monday evening, in honor of Brig.-Gens. SEYMOURE and SPRAGUE, before whom two farces of "My wife's Second Floor," and "Number One Around the Corner," were performed in a very credible manner. The Stevenson Glee Club lent its attraction to the occasion, and an orchestra of ten or twelve performers furnished very agreeable music. These entertainments are very popular with the townspeople and the theatre promises a fund of amusement of the entire winter. To the soldiers themselves belongs the credit of maintaining the establishment."

xii John Charles Fremont (January 21, 1813-July 13, 1890) was an American military officer, explorer, and politician who became the first presidential candidate of the anti-slavery Republican Party. He was extolled as "The Pathfinder" by the penny press in the 1840's and is often referred to "The Great Pathfinder" by historians. During the American Civil War, President Abraham Lincoln gave him command of the Department of the West. He had limited success in his brief tenure; but he was noted for running his department autocratically, and made hasty decisions without consulting Washington D.C. or President Lincoln. After Fremont's emancipation edict that freed slaves in his district, he was summarily relieved of his command for insubordination.

Retrieved November 30, 2015 from Shotgun's Home of the American Civil War
http://www.civilwarhome.com First Published: January 7,1997 Webmaster: Dick Week
John C. Frémont. (2015, November 23). In *Wikipedia, The Free Encyclopedia*. Retrieved
November 29, 2015, from
https://en.wikipedia.org/w/index.php?title=John_C._Fr%C3%A9mont&oldid=691926654

xiii Bloom, Nicholas. June 4, 2015. Brooklyn Past & Present: "All the World's a Stage-Even the
Confederacy-for Brooklyn Soldiers Fighting in Civil War". Retrieved April 25, 2016 from
Brooklyn Historical Society website http://www.brooklyn history.org/blog/2015/06/04/all-
the-worlds-a-stage-even-the-confederacy-for-brooklyn-soldiers-fighting-in-civil-war/

"On the back wall of Brooklyn Historical Society's critically acclaimed Personal Correspondents exhibition, under the heading "Facing Death," resides a grim and tragic quotation from the letters of James Beith, a private in the 48th regiment, New York Infantry.

"There is nothing thought of the poor soldier when he gets killed, only for to dig a hole and throw him into it, then sometimes hardly cover him with enough of dirt."

The quotation is from a letter which Beith wrote to his brother in May of 1864, while his regiment marched north through the brutal and desperate final months of the Civil War in Virginia, angling towards the Confederate capital in Richmond. Certainly the most gripping of Beith's letters, his words here touch on the useless horrors of war, and specifically the way "poor soldiers"--privates, infantrymen, usually those from the most modest means—were pawned and dehumanized, bearing a disproportionate brunt of the war's tragedy. But research on Beith's earlier years in the war reveal another, very different reality *for the "poor soldiers" of the 48th NY: frustrating inaction, boredom, and a spectacular ability to create diversions and entertainment for themselves. And how do a bunch of city boys from Brooklyn entertain themselves? The theater, of course!*

For the first three years of the Civil War, James Beith's regiment was stationed on the coastal islands and swamps of the Deep South, rotating between Hilton Head, SC, Fort Pulaski, GA, and San Augustine, FL, waiting for the Union Army in Virginia to make its way southward. Unfortunately, the Union Army in Virginia was doing no such thing, instead finding itself stalemated and pushed back up into Pennsylvania, leaving Beith and the rest of the 48th NY stranded for years, fighting in minor skirmishes to hold their position. To keep their soldiers happy and diverted, officers allowed for a variety of games and contests, including an "Olympic Games," animal hunts, military skills competitions, and a company band (of which Beith was a part). Besides these more traditional military-style diversions, several soldiers in the 48th NY also asked to build a stage and to start a theater company. Their officers consented, and The Barton Dramatic Association was born in June of 1862 at Fort Pulaski, GA."

Bloom includes a citation from Palmer's book describing the preparations for the theater. He then continues…

"As it turns out, the Barton Dramatic Association was a wild popular success, first among the soldiers of the 48th NY, then among the other Union regiments stationed around the Deep South coastal islands, and finally even among the local inhabitants—theoretically their adversaries—who came to see their plays in throngs. The 48th uprooted its theater and took it with them when they re-stationed at St. Augustine and then at Hilton Head, establishing a popular following at each location, even as many of the major players lost their lives in between stations.

The officers first allowed the soldiers to put on only farces, comedies, and other "vulgar" plays because they did not consider the low-ranking actors and directors worthy of more substantive material. So when members of the Association asked to put on <u>Othello</u>, the officers initially refused—not due to the possibly transgressive or controversial racial politics of the play, which didn't occur to them, but rather because they didn't want to see a Shakespearean tragedy "murdered" by amateurs.

Contrary to the officers' assumptions, however, there were several professional actors and a director in the lower ranks. These theater professionals staged a few acts of Othello and convinced some of the officers to come watch the performance. The performance "was pronounced a great success" by these officers, and they consented to the theater putting on Othello in its entirety. This performance, according to Abraham Palmer, is what launched the Barton Dramatic Association into local fame...We are greatly indebted to Palmer for his singular "biography" of the 48th NY, an account that contains its share of tragedy and violence, but is most remarkable for how it continuously pivots between drudgery, levity, and brutality, much as the experience of the Civil War must have for soldiers like Beith and Palmer. One can only imagine the emotional heft of theater in the midst of these circumstances: performed by actors who literally in the process of risking their lives, who may have lost their best friends or fellow actors within days or hours of their performances, to audiences of civilians and soldiers whose physical and emotional foundations were undergoing violent revolution."

Kirsch, George B. October 24, 2012. "Hurry Up and Wait and Play Ball" Retrieved April 25, 2016 from http://mobile.nytimes.com/blogs/opinionator/2012/10/24/hurry-up-and-wait-and-play-ball/?referer=NYTimes

"As hundreds of thousands of Billy Yanks and Johnny Rebs enlisted in the Union and Confederate Armies during 1861 and 1862, military and civilian officials and journalists from both sides recognized that soldiers who trained for deadly combat would need relief from their endless drills and chores. Among other activities, people on both sides urged soldiers to take up the relatively new sport of baseball.

The United States Sanitary Commission, a voluntary relief organization that raised funds and supplies for the Union Army, recommended that "when practicable, amusements, sports, and gymnastic exercises should be favored amongst the men." It listed baseball among the approved pastimes. The New York Clipper, a weekly sporting newspaper, endorsed games in camps, noting the "beneficial effect they have on the spirits and health and how they tend to alleviate the monotony of camp life." It added, "They also lead to a wholesome rivalry between companies
and regiments, and augment the espirit de corps of the same, to an extent that to those who have not witnessed it, it would appear marvelous."

Southerners agreed. Dr. Julian Chisolm, an author of a manual of surgery for the Confederate Army, suggested that while in camp "temporary gymnasia might be established...He listed "manly play of ball" as part of a soldier's daily exercise schedule...

Though the men pursued all manner of activities, from boxing to an early version of football, during the first year of the war, baseball emerged as the soldiers' favorite team sport. Senior officers approved, and a few joined or watched the action...

...One of the more celebrated baseball matches among the Union soldiers (and one that remains shrouded in mystery) is a contest between nine men from the 165th New York Volunteer Infantry and a team picked from soldiers of the 47th and 48th New York Infantry Regiments, held at Hilton Head, S.C., on Christmas Day 1862. According to Abraham Mills, former president of the National League, a crowd of 40,000 spectators watched the game. A Christmas Day report of the
New South, a local Hilton Head newspaper, reported a baseball game that was probably this contest, describing it as a "ball match between the 'Van Brunt' and 'Frazier' base ball clubs, with the latter nine victorious (the score was not reported). The game probably wasn't as grand as Mills made it out to seem..."

[xiv] The Army used contrabands as laborers to support Union efforts and soon began to pay them wages. The former slaves set up camps near Union forces, and the Army helped support and educate both adults and children among the refugees. Thousands of men from these camps enlisted in the U.S. Colored Troops when recruitment started in 1863. At the war's end, more than 100 contraband camps existed in the South, including the Freedman's Colony of Roanoke Island, where 3500 former slaves worked to develop a self-sufficient community.

[xv] As to the origin of this word in the phrase "Three cheers and a tiger," the following explanation has been given. In 1822 the Boston Light Infantry, under Captain Mackintosh and Lieutenant Robert C. Winthrop, visited Salem, Massachusetts, and encamped in Washington Square. They loved rough-and-tumble sports, and one day a visitor exclaimed to one, who was more obstreperous than usual, "Oh, you tiger!" The phrase became a catch-word, a term of playful reproach. On the route to Boston some musical genius sang an impromptu line. "Oh, you tigers, don't you know," to the air of "Rob Roy McGregor, O!" The Tigers by name soon began to imitate the growl of their protonymic. At the end of three cheers a "tiger" was always called for. In 1826 the same organization visited New York, being the first volunteer corps from Boston to visit another State. At a public festival the Tigers astonished the Gothamites by giving the genuine growl. It pleased the fancy of the hosts, and gradually became adopted on all festive and joyous occasions.

Walsh, William S. *Handy Book of Literary Curiosities* (1909). Retrieved November 30, 2015, from https://archive.org/stream/handybooklitera04walsgoog#page/n1056/mode/2up

xvi Henry Ward Beecher was the son of Lyman Beecher and brother of Harriet Beecher Stow. He was a graduate of Amherst College and Lane Theological Seminary. From his pulpit at the Plymouth Church in Brooklyn, New York he advocated for liberal causes. These included "temperance, women's suffrage, abolitionism, evolutionism, and scientific biblical criticism." He was known for his passionate and persuasive oratory drawing as many as 2,500 people to his Sunday sermons. He was not afraid to take on the controversial issues of his day; such as, the Kansas-Nebraska Act and the Free-Soil Movement. Beecher raised money to support a volunteer Union regiment when the Civil War began. He toured England in 1863 to persuade audiences of the value and righteousness of the Northern cause.

xvii The 10% Reconstruction Plan decreed that a state could be reintegrated into the Union when 10% of the 1860 vote count from that state had taken an oath of allegiance to the U.S. and pledged to abide by emancipation. Voters could then elect delegates to draft revised state constitutions and establish new state governments. Lincoln guaranteed southerners that he would protect their private property with exception of slaves. All southerners would be granted pardon; except high-ranking Confederate army officers and government officials.

xviii The Sinking of "USS Housatonic" on 17 February 1864 during the American Civil War was an important turning point in naval warfare. The Confederate States Navy submarine, "H.L. Hunley" made her first and only attack on a Union Navy warship when she staged a clandestine night attack on the "USS Housatonic" in Charleston harbor. The Hunley approached just under the surface, avoiding detection until the last moments, then embedded and remotely detonated a spar torpedo that rapidly sank the 1260 ton sloop-of-war with the loss of five Union sailors. Although the victory was Pyrrhic and short-lived, since the Hunley herself was sunk during the attack with the loss of all eight Confederate crewmen, the "H.L. Hunley" became renowned as the first submarine to successfully sink an enemy vessel in combat and was the direct progenitor of what would eventually become international submarine warfare.

xix Prostitution experienced its largest growth during 1861–1865. Some historians have speculated that this growth can be attributed to a depression, and the need for women to support themselves and their families while their husbands were away at war. Other historians considered the growth of prostitution to be related to the women wanting to spread venereal disease to the opposing troops.The most notorious area for prostitution was in Tennessee. Before the outbreak of the war, Nashville recorded 207 prostitutes; however, in 1863 reports claimed to have at least 1500 prostitutes. The area where these prostitutes could be found was known as Smokey Row. In an infamous campaign to rid the city of the "public women", Lt. Col. George Spalding loaded the women on to the steamboat Idahoe. The women were sent to Louisville, where they were not allowed off the ship and sent further along to Cincinnati. Many of the women became sick due to lack of food and were forced to turn around and return to Nashville. Once they arrived back in Nashville, Lt. Col. Spaulding created a system of registration similar to European ones. He inadvertently created the first legal system of prostitution. This is the set of regulations he set up:

> That a license be issued to each prostitute, a record of which shall be kept at this office, together with the number and street of her residence.

> That one skillful surgeon be appointed as a Board of Examination whose duty it shall be to examine personally every week, each licensed prostitute, giving certificate soundness to those who are healthy and ordering those into hospital those who are in the slightest degree diseased.

> That a building suitable for a hospital for the invalids be taken for that purpose, and that a weekly tax of fifty cents be levied on each prostitute for the purpose of defraying the expense of said hospital.

> That all public women found plying their vocation without a license and certificate be at once arrested and incarcerated in the workhouse for a period of not less than thirty days.

Sex in the American Civil War. (April 5, 2016). In *Wikipedia, The Free Encyclopedia*. Retrieved April 11, 2016, from
https://en.wikipedia.org/w/index.php?title=Sex_in_the_American_Civil_War&oldid=713606338

[xx] In 1864, Grant was given overall command of all Union armies. He devised a coordinated strategy that would strike at the center of the Confederacy from multiple directions. General Butler was to attack Richmond from the South by landing on the James River below Richmond called Bermuda Hundred. Butler operated in such a tactical inept fashion that the attack aimed at Drewry's Bluff proved to be a failure. General Beauregard drove him back into a small peninsula enclosed by the James and Appomattox Rivers. Butler was 'bottled up' and was of no strategic value to the overall plan to defeat the South. Sherman's taking of Atlanta and eventually marching to the sea was another part of Grant's strategy. The plan for General Sigel to invade the Shenandoah Valley and destroy Lee's supply lines failed. Each of these strategic moves were designed to stretch southern army's resources to minimize its effectiveness. As General Meade and the Army of the Potomac began their Overland Campaign in May 1864; Jefferson Davis was unable to send reinforcements to General Lee. Both Lee and Grant borrowed troops from General Butler's bottled up sector, thereby extending the war for another year.

[xxi] James kept a plethora of accounts or rolls for his regiment. The Barrett Collection includes an original Register of Company "H" 48th New York State Vols.

The register measures approximately 12" x 7 ½" and contains a variety of information about inventories of individual soldiers, ordnance, equipage, casualties, desertions and deaths.
(Barrett Collection)

William H. Havens Sergt

19

Description

Age	Height		Complexion	Eyes	Hair	Occupation	Born	Enlisted	Mustered				Others	Relations		County	Remarks
	Feet	Inch	Florid	Blue	Black	Farmer	New Jersey	Dec 22 63					8 years		Bridgeton	Vet Vol
19	5	7½													210	190

Clothing Account

Date of time	Doll cts	Rank	Signature	Witness
Dec 22 64	40 89	Sergt		
April 65	10 78		William H Havens	
Aug 31/65	13 97			

John F. Lacey Sergt

17

Description

Age	Height		Complexion	Eyes	Hair	Occupation	Born	Enlisted	Mustered				Others	Relations		County	Remarks
			Florid	Blue	Brown	Farmer	Bohemia	Dec 22 63					3 years		Paid State	Vet Vol
									Dec 22 63						110	190

Clothing Account

Date of time	Doll cts	Rank	Signature	Witness
March 64	24 93	Sergt		
Aug 2 64	10 00		John F Lacey	
Oct 19 64	2 90			
Nov 16 64	11 60			
Dec 30 64	3 45			
Aug 18 65	8 75			
Dec 5	4 75			
	93			

216 Casualties in 48th Regt. ...
during the Campaign in Virginia

Names	Rank	Killed	Missing	Wounded		When	Where	Remarks
				Mortally	Slightly		1864	
Co. A					1	May 16	Drurys Bluff	
...					1	" 7	Chester ...	
...					1	" 12	...	
...					1	" 15		
...					1	" 15		
...				1		" 16	Drurys Bluff	
...					1	" 16		
...				1		" 16		
...			1			" 16		
...				1		" 19	Bermuda ...	
...					1	" 19		
...			1		1	June 1	Cold Harb	
...				1		" 2	"	
...					1	" 3	"	
...			1		1	" 5	"	
Corporal					1	" 30	Petersburg	
Co. B					1	May 7	Chester ...	
...					1	" 7		
...			1			" 12	...	
Corporal				1		" 16	Drurys Bluff	
...					1	" 16		
...					1	" 16		
...		1				June 1	Cold Harbor	
...		1				" 1		
Capt.				1	1	" 1		
Private			1	1		" 1		
...				1		" 1		
...				1		" 2		
...					1	" 5		
...					1	July 16	Petersburg	
Co. C								
Private				1		May 7	Chester ...	
...			1			" 16	Drurys Bluff	
Captain		1				" 16		
Private						" 16		
Corpl			1			" 16		
Sergeant		1				" 1	Cold Harbor	
Private					1	" 1		
Corpl					1	" 1		
Private					1	" 1		
...				1		" 1		
Sergt			1			" 1		
...					1	" 2		
Corpl Sergt					1	" 30	Petersburg	
Co. D								
Sergt		1				" 1	Cold Harbor	
...					1	" 2		
Sergt		1			1	May 16	Drurys Bluff	
Corpl					1	" 16	Drurys Bluff	
...					1	" 16	Drurys Bluff	

The original letter of July 12, 1865 to Jennie was recently returned to the family collection. The following story was related to the cousins over lunch in Redlands, California. The letter's journey has been amazing. Michael May lived in Nebraska in 1987 on a large farm. He spent his off-time exploring the surrounding countryside. Usually, the exploration was done by horseback enabling him to get to otherwise inaccessible areas. On one occasion Michael decided to try a different mode of transportation. He had just bought a bicycle from a second-hand store. Riding along the country roads proved to be a pleasurable experience.

As he related his story, he said that he remembered it being a very warm day. Looking for a shady spot to rest; he turned onto a side road. He found what he thought to be an abandoned farmhouse. There was also a very large tree a short distance away. After resting a little in the shade; Michael decided to explore the house.

He described the interior of the house as if the occupant had just left. It felt surreal. There was a heavy layer of dust on everything and papers scattered here and there on the floor. In the corner was an old trunk. Michael raised the lid and remembers seeing letters and a pair of spectacles. He picked up one letter, saw that the envelope was in pristine condition and noticed the date. He opened the envelope and read the letter.

He felt that the letter was very special and tucked it carefully into his pocket. Michael closed the lid of the trunk leaving everything else the way it had been. He rode his bike back to his farm and later that evening read the letter out loud. Several questions came to mind. Who were these two people? What happened to them? Did James survive the Civil War? How did the letter get to Nebraska? Was there a way to return the letter to the family? Michael carefully put the letter away for safekeeping.

In 1991, Michael moved to California. He began working for Loma Linda University Hospital. Over the years, he shared his experiences of living in Nebraska with his co-workers. He brought the letter that he had found in the abandoned farmhouse and shared its contents with Nancy Hernandez. There was some discussion as to how to find any family members that might have interest in the letter.

In 2012, Nancy started searching the Internet. She decided to search "James Barrett". She found an entry for Save Our Heritage Foundation in Concord, Massachusetts. The foundation had been raising money to save the Barrett Farmhouse. The farmhouse had been faithfully restored. There had been a 300th birthday celebration for Col. James Barrett and it was hoped that the Farmhouse would soon become part of the Minuteman National Park. Nancy read that the Project Coordinator was Jim Cunningham.

She contacted Jim and explained about the letter. Jim immediately guided her to contact Penny Gill. He explained that she was the great granddaughter of James A. Barrett and that the family was writing a book that included all the original correspondence that they had in their collection. He was sure that the family would indeed be interested in obtaining the letter. Nancy and Michael scanned the letter and included an explanation. Penny, in turn, contacted the rest of the cousins. Everyone was excited.

Working through various obstacles, finally after 1 ½ years, Nancy and Michael were able to meet with family members Penny Gill, Les and Linda Peterson. Michael presented the family with the original letter and envelope and in turn, copies of photos of James A. Barrett in full uniform and Jennie Farmer were presented to Michael. During the next three hours over lunch, Michael related his story about his discovery in Nebraska.

The family was able to answer the questions that he had always wanted to know. Both Michael and Nancy were relieved and happy to know that James survived the Civil War and that he and Jennie did marry. The abandoned farmhouse had actually been owned by the son [**George Farmer Barrett**] of James and Jennie.

George and his wife Lucy Virginia Stuckey did not have children. After George died, Lucy continued living on the farm. Lucy Stuckey Barrett moved into a town when she was elderly and passed away there. Why the trunk was left behind in the farmhouse is a mystery. Lucy had donated Barrett family antiques to a museum in Lincoln, Nebraska.

Since that luncheon meeting; an effort began to search for the old trunk and its contents. The cousins were hoping that more family letters and memorabilia could be recovered. Plans for a trip to Nebraska for some of the cousins had been proposed. Research of deeds and tax records uncovered the succession of owners of the property. Calls were made to the local town and historical society. The current owner was located and contacted. He related that the old barn was gone and the only reason the house still existed was due to its unusual cement roof. The owner had no knowledge of the old trunk or of its contents. He did say that that abandoned buildings in the area had become prime targets for people looking for anything of value. The whereabouts of the trunk is still a mystery.

xxiii *YEARS OF SERVICE ENDED. CHIEF ENGINEER EDWARD FARMER TO BE RETIRED TO-MORROW. HE HAS REACHED THE AGE LIMIT—HIS CAREER DURING AND SINCE THE CIVIL WAR—AN HONORABLE RECORD.*

*Another break is to be made in the ranks of men who are now chief engineers, but who saw service in the engine-rooms of the old-time warships, when the Nation was fighting for life, as juniors and assistants, and contributed in no small degree to the sea strength and efficiency of the Northern forces and the downfall of the Confederacy. **Edward Farmer**, who has been in charge of steam engineering department of the Navy yard since August 22, 1895, when he succeeded Chief Engineer S.L. P. Ayres, will be retired to-morrow, having reached the age limit of sixty-two years.*

Edward Farmer was born in Vermont, but when he was appointed third assistant engineer, on May 3, 1859, he was credited to Massachusetts, and that State has been his home ever since. He was attached to the home squadron for two years. In 1861 he was promoted to second assistant engineer and attached to the Mohican, of the South Atlantic Squadron. When the war demanded the services at home of all available engineers, he was attached to the gunboat Kanawha, of the West Gulf Blockading Squadron, and was on that steamer when she made her record-breaking stay under steam of nearly five months with Admiral Farragut's fleet.

On May 20, 1863, while on the Kanawha, he was promoted by Admiral Farragut to first assistant engineer, the promotion being confirmed later by the department. In the closing months of the war he was on the Alabama, of the North Atlantic Squadron, and in 1866 - '68 was on the Shenandoah, in the East Indian waters, returning to the Boston Navy Yard in the latter year for three years of shore duty. On March 4, 1871, he was made chief engineer, and was sent to sea for three years, in charge of the engines of the Ticonderoga, of the South Atlantic Squadron, returning to Boston at the end of the tour for another stretch of shore duty in charge of stores at the yard.

His next sea duty was on the Alert, of the Asiatic Squadron, and following this he was for seven years in charge of the class in steam engineering at the Naval Academy in Annapolis.

When the famous White Squadron began its "tour of evolution," Mr. Farmer was in charge of the engines of the Chicago. This ended his sea duty, and from December, 1891, to May, 1893 he was in charge of the shops at the Portsmouth or Kittery yard, going from there to the Boston yard, whence he was transferred to the larger field of the New-Work yard.

The chief, who is tall and spare of frame, has an attractive personality, and is one of the most courteous and affable men in the service. His eyes are as keen and watchful as ever, and he is a standing refutation of the idea that the usefulness of a man is over when he has passed the threescore mark. Conscientious in the discharge of his duties, he has set a standard in the machine shops of the yard which is entirely creditable to his administration. Since he assumed control nearly every ship of the North Atlantic Squadron has been in his hands, as well as some of those on foreign stations. One of the largest jobs whch have been handled in the shops in this term is the placing of new engines in the Chicago, in place of those run by him when the white cruiser was young in the service. The man has outlasted the engines, and is good for many more years of usefulness.

The only child of Mr. and Mrs. Farmer, is the wife of First Lieutenant Edward R. Lowndes, of the Marine Corps, who is now on duty at the Marine Barracks in Norfolk. The chief engineer and his wife will make their home in the Back Bay District of Boston after they leave Brooklyn, and will carry with them the best wishes of their associates at the yard and their many friends in civil and social life.

[This is a newspaper article about Edward Farmer (1836-1918) which is found in the family collection. Unfortunately, to fit a scrapbook page, someone cut off both the date and name of the newspaper. An approximate date of the article is March 1, 1898; when he would have celebrated his sixty-second birthday.]

Made in the USA
San Bernardino, CA
30 January 2020